Aesthetics and Ideology

A VOLUME IN A SERIES FROM
The Center for the Critical Analysis of Contemporary Culture

Aesthetics

and

Ideology

Edited by

GEORGE LEVINE

Rutgers University Press
New Brunswick, New Jersey

Library of Congress Cataloging in Publication Data

Aesthetics and ideology / edited by George Levine.

    p.   cm.

   Includes bibliographical references and index.

   ISBN 0-8135-2058-4 (cloth) — ISBN 0-8135-2059-2 (pbk.)

   1. Literature—Aesthetics.   2. Criticism.   3. Literature and

society.   4. Politics and literature.   I. Levine, George Lewis.

PN45.A25 1994

801′.93—dc20   93-31173

                                                    CIP

British Cataloging-in-Publication information available

Myra Jehlen's essay draws on her "Introduction: Beyond

Trancendence," in *Ideology and Classic American Literature,* ed.

Sacvan Bercovitch and Myra Jehlen (New York: Cambridge University

Press, 1986), pp. 4–14. Reprinted by permission

Arnold Rampersad's essay appeared in slightly different form in

Profession 91. Reprinted by permission of the Modern Language Association of America.

For Jennifer and Beryle
Coworkers and dear friends

■ CONTENTS ■

III. Form, Disinterest, and Ideology

IV. Liberatory Aesthetics

■ ACKNOWLEDGMENTS ■

THIS BOOK HAS by now a long history, and its existence depends on the generosity and good will of many colleagues and friends. I first discussed it with Carolyn Williams, whose ideas made a big difference, particularly in the choice of contributors. Her warm and generous personal and intellectual presence has mattered greatly to me and to this book as it has mattered to the growth and strength of the Rutgers Center for the Critical Analysis of Contemporary Culture since she joined me, as Associate Director, in 1989.

In addition, no editor I have ever worked with has been as supportive, as thoughtful, as intellectually important to a project as Leslie Mitchner. She encouraged me to turn my initial ideas into a book, and throughout she has been my sounding post. She has helped see each of the essays through revisions and improvements and has given me an extraordinary number of good ideas. I am deeply grateful for her hard and imaginative work and for her personal enthusiasm and generosity.

For four years, Jennifer Church has been an invaluable assistant and friend. Her work in the early months of this project was indispensable, and she has continued to help although she has moved to another university. I am, as ever, grateful for her assistance, and since her departure I have greatly missed her. Beryle Chandler, the guiding light of the Center for the Critical Analysis of Contemporary Culture, assumed the work of assistant on this project, and she has worked wonderfully to keep me and the contributors in order and to make the project possible after all. As coworker and friend, she has, as usual, been wonderful.

I have badgered all too many people with the intellectual and organizational problems that derived from work on this book. But I want to thank in particular the contributors, many of whom have waited too patiently for their essays finally to appear, many of whom have struggled through several revisions, all of whom have been wonderfully cooperative and helpful (if, in some instances, a little late). Their good spirit has made a difficult job ultimately a thoroughly satisfying one.

■ ix ■

Aesthetics and Ideology

■ GEORGE LEVINE ■

Introduction

Reclaiming the Aesthetic

I CONCEIVED THIS BOOK in response to the radical transformation of literary study that has taken place over the last decade, a transformation for which enormous claims have been made but whose full implications—especially in these times of constricting budgets and intense criticism of academia—critics have not been entirely ready to confront. That transformation is not simply a matter of a new emphasis on theory over what used to be called "primary texts" or a blurring of the distinction between the two. Nor has it to do with the welcome expansion of the curriculum, the admission into what is often too easily defined as the "canon"—as if that had ever been a stable set of texts resistant to the vagaries of time—of works by women, non-Europeans, African-Americans, Native Americans. The transformation I am talking about is, of course, partly related to these things. But it is most distinctly connected to a fundamental change in the conception of what constitutes the "literary," a change that might challenge the very existence of departments of literature in universities: Can, in fact, a category, literature, be meaningfully constituted? If so, once constituted, is it worth much attention? Is not, after all, the real subject of literary study ideology, the real purpose political transformation?

This change, in the hands of too many practitioners, has led to a reductive assimilation of literature to ideology or to a resistant sense that the literary and the political should have nothing to do with each other. While these reductivist views are far from universally accepted, they have grown out of or with several phenomena with which humanistic study has become recently comfortable, but which need to be challenged or heavily qualified: first, a shift in emphasis from interpretation to theory (which has, oddly, become a subject somehow independent of the literary texts it ostensibly works out of or against), from questions about what texts might "mean" to questions about the systems that contain them, about material conditions, hermeneutics, mediation, discourse, all of which tend to a new emphasis on self-reflexivity; second, a resistance to (or demystification of) the idea of literary value, particularly of literary greatness; third, an increasing emphasis on the necessity for interdisciplinary study; fourth, a virtually total rejection of, even contempt for, "formalism"; fifth, a determination that all things are political and hence that the function of literature and of literary study is primarily political; sixth, a view that the study of literature is not an adequately serious or important vocation—not only because literature divorced from its sociopolitical context serves in culture only as ornament or mystification, but because it is really indistinguishable from other forms of language (as against the dominant assumption of the now nefarious "New Criticism") and merely another part of the culture; and finally, the movement to replace literary study with cultural studies. Literature by itself has no special purchase on culture, no special authority as commentary or representation. An important critic is reported to have said that "the only relation literature as such has to culture as such is that it is part of it."[1] The job of the critic is not to study literature but to study culture—a disciplinary responsibility hitherto assigned to anthropology. With some very well known exceptions, most critics either deny that literature is a definable category of discourse or are inclined to believe that exclusive study of it is complicit with unattractive political and social positions.

While I am obviously not entirely enamored of the developments I have outlined, my objections are to reductivism and simplification, not to the broad tendencies. As with most of the colleagues I respect, my "anti's" are impeccable: I am anti-foundationalist, anti-essentialist, anti-universalist, and I do not believe in the possibility of that view from nowhere that gets one beyond contingency. I welcome the new historicism, in lower case, as well as the recognition that all literature needs to be understood in relation to the local and the time-bound; and I am as comfortable as one can be with the necessarily uncomfortable inevitability of diversity and undecidability, whose absence in criticism always leaves me a bit suspicious.

My uneasiness with the current critical scene is that whereas critics like Fredric Jameson, Edward Said, Stephen Greenblatt, and Eve Kosofsky Sedgwick (not to mention several of the contributors to this volume) have wonderfully enriched the possibilities of literary criticism, their sensitive and complex relation to texts and strong conviction that those texts have enormous cultural significance often, in their followers, reduce critical practice to exercises in political positioning. In the current critical scene, literature is all too often demeaned, the aesthetic experience denigrated or reduced to mystified ideology. Moreover, in discovering the complicity of texts with an ideology they never formally articulate, critics tend to assume that they are smarter and more honest than the writers, who either didn't know what they were doing, or, worse, thought they could get away with their devious moves. And what I am attempting in this book and this opening chapter is movement toward a climate of opinion that will not identify deference to the text and admiration of it with political complicity, will not assume that the text is a kind of enemy to be arrested, will not inevitably associate the "literary" with a reactionary right, or dismiss the aesthetic as a strategy of mystification of the status quo. More positively, I am trying to imagine the aesthetic as a mode engaged richly and complexly with moral and political issues, but a mode that operates differently from others and contributes in distinctive ways to the possibilities of human fulfillment and connection.

Much of the research that now wins tenure at major universities does not display a primary interest in literature; of the recent movements that have transformed the study of literature only American deconstruction—a strategy of reading now in deep political trouble not only with the right but with the left—has been primarily occupied with literary language and its idiosyncratic difficulties. The formalism of the New Criticism is, for many of my students and colleagues, merely a mistake, and has nothing to teach them. The notion of literary greatness has, for the most part, slipped away into the hands of academic conservatism or of brilliant critical eccentrics, like Richard Poirier or Harold Bloom. Otherwise, while the "classics" continue to be taught in university classrooms all over America with unflagging energy, only undergraduates are allowed aesthetic enthusiasm for, say, Shakespeare, Milton, Emerson.

Having learned from literature itself many of the ideas and attitudes that now dominate the critical scene, and having cared too much for its extravagant power to shape and reshape experience and feeling, I am concerned now to join in efforts to rescue it from its potential disappearance into culture and politics; I want to do this, however, not by assigning it some transcendental and universal value; not by denying the importance of cultural studies or the uses, as evidence, to which literature is regularly put; not, of course, by denying that literature and the aesthetic are historically bound to ideology. Rather, this book is designed to deny the reductivism implicit in some of the ideas I have sketched out at the start, and to rethink literature by rethinking the idea of the "aesthetic" and the possibility of "value" within the terms and assumptions characteristic of the best contemporary criticism and theory. The essays gathered here explore from many vantage points the relation between the aesthetic and the ideological, locating in the realms of historical particularity and contingency something of the specialness of literature, and moving toward an understanding of that specialness that will in no way undercut the remarkable critical and theoretical achievements of the last two decades. The roster of contributors should make clear, as their essays certainly will, that this is not a belletristic effort to ground art and criticism in the gorgeously mindless personal moments that often lie behind lifelong dedication to the study of literature, or to sentimentalize and remystify the experience of "art."

At the risk of reconstructing the polarity against which this essay is constructed, I begin at what for many was the beginning: most of the readers of this book probably starting early in their lives, will have had extraordinary moments reading a novel or a poem, listening to music, looking at a painting, gazing out at a landscape—moments when they have felt overwhelmed, perhaps on the verge of tears, the whole body thrillingly tensed. Such moments have led many to careers in the arts or in criticism, in which the almost mindless physicality of that engagement with what might be called the beautiful or the sublime has been displaced by professional strategies of unsentimental analysis, demystification and historical contextualization, and the discovery that the very "experience" was probably invented in the eighteenth century with the development of the idea of the aesthetic. But the initiating impulse for literary critics and analysts of culture was very often the feeling that those moments, and the "objects" that seemed to have produced them, were of such value that they merited the professional dedication of the rest of their lives.

In the discourse of literary and cultural criticism, even before the developments outlined in my first paragraphs, that value has been dismissed or minimized or sufficiently historicized that it has lost, for those whose careers have been shaped by it, precisely the power it had to initiate careers. But the social and historical location of art and its criticism, the recognition of literature's entanglement with the politics of its moment, does nothing to deny its peculiar power to move and engage, or the critic's responsibility to account for that power. Much of the most interesting criticism of our time might seem to "account for" it by demonstrating that a work of literature's ostensible position disguises very different and clandestinely attractive attitudes toward gender, politics, or race. Behind the surfaces of narrative and the verbal ingenuities of poetry lies the reigning ideology that literature ultimately furthers or confirms and that recent criticism has taken as its responsibility to expose. [2] The preoccupation with that ideology often seems to displace interest in anything else that might be going on in literature or attends to the literature only to show that it is, in fact, an ideological mystification. Yet my argument is that the ideology is so delicately and complexly entangled in the textures of literature itself that no discussion of the ideological without attention to the formal can have any but the most reductive relation to what texts are up to, how they get their work done.

In order to make clear what claims I am and am not making about aesthetic questions, I pause here to invoke briefly two strong examples of criticism whose concern is clearly with ideology despite their remarkable sensitivity to the way particular texts have worked, and which have helped set the critical agenda for the last decade. The first, Eve Kosofsky Sedgwick's brilliant work on "male homosocial desire"—one of the founding books in contemporary gender studies—wonderfully explains and exposes the complex patterning of gender relations, the continuities of "homosocial" with "homosexual" desire, the triangulation of males with women, and the implications for women of this kind of patterning. My point about it, however, is not to "disagree" with its arguments. It is a rich and illuminating criticism that makes literature more, not less interesting. Like much of the best criticism written today, it is, however, using literature primarily as a means to broad cultural conclusions. Sedgwick reads a series of texts, from Shakespeare's sonnets and William Wycherly's *Country Wife* through Tennyson and Whitman and several nineteenth-century novels and, in almost every case, opens new possibilities of reading. It is a remarkable and indispensable performance.

The problem is not so much that Sedgwick isn't "literary." When Matthew Arnold criticized Byron, he praised him as a "passionate and dauntless soldier of a forlorn hope, who . . . waged against the conservatism of the old impossible world so fiery battle," and found him important to middle-class readers who see about them "an aristocracy materialised and null, a middle class purblind and hideous, a lower class crude and brutal."[3] This is hardly "literary" in the sense espoused, say, by William Bennett or Lynne Cheney. The mutual implication of literature and ideology is part of the point of my argument. The problem is that in using literary texts to write history and to tease out of literature sociological evidence about the culture's attitudes and actions towards homosexuals and women, it is very difficult—as difficult as in Arnold's case—to take the "evidence" as authoritative.

Sedgwick's is a subtle and important project, but it does not seem to me to be fully alert to the question of the status of literature itself. Certainly, it is not concerned with or making judgments about the "value" of the works discussed or any of their possibly "redeeming" qualities; it is not seriously concerned with the formal properties of the works except as literary conventions confirm or shape the patternings in which she is interested. If literary criticism really is social criticism, then it needs to confront the question of what sort of authority it can have. Implicitly, it seems to me, there is a tension between Sedgwick's instinct to read literature imaginatively, and her decision to use her texts to make the cultural argument. While all of them have or had great cultural currency and thus might be taken as shedding light on what the culture as a whole felt, or didn't quite know or allow that it really felt, they make a rather weak argument for the broad cultural conclusions Sedgwick seems to be trying to reach. It is for this reason, I believe, that such invaluable criticism as hers can lead critics astray.

The power of Sedgwick's book, for me, is in what it can say of the literature. Insofar as Sedgwick reads these texts by opening up secrets that nobody until now has been willing or able to discuss, she does wonderful criticism, problematic cultural analysis. Literature here becomes a resource for a new way of talking about culture and society but is in a sense transparent in that its validity as evidence is not questioned. This is particularly ironic because so much of contemporary criticism is devoted to heightening consciousness about the nature of the medium itself. Yet by calling attention to the mediation of literary texts, such criticism often implies that analysis of its mediation will provide satisfactory evidence about the state of the culture.[4]

Indispensable as Sedgwick's book is, I believe that the assumptions that govern its entire enterprise need to be engaged directly and consistently. It may well be that the more "important" project is cultural, not literary, although I would want to argue that the two are, in the end, inseparable. It is a matter of whether the same criteria apply to the two objectives. If the study of literature ought in fact to be understood as a study of culture, parallel with (even using the methods of) anthropology, sociology, political science, the primary responsibility of critics is to be good historians and social scientists, to know how to use their materials. Learning to read correctly entails learning how to see the text in all its complicated interweavings with history and society.

I am in total sympathy with the notion that the margins of literature are indeed porous, and that the place where literature and literary criticism end and the social sciences begin cannot be comfortably defined. In any case, my remarks are not to question Sedgwick's analysis of homosocial desire, but to require attention to how the overall argument of the book (quietly assuming, as it does, that it is telling us something important about the way society thinks and behaves) implies very complicated arguments about the way literature works in culture, arguments that social sciences might want to query or challenge. Its implicit argument (perhaps one that Sedgwick has not thought about or would not agree with) is that literature has no special standing inside (or outside) culture, and that reading it in ways that nobody has been able to do before can tell a lot about how it has *really* operated inside its culture and about what the culture does and believes. The question of what sort of evidence about culture "literary" texts provide has by no means been resolved and the status of books like Sedgwick's—"cultural studies" texts, they might be called—is not to me self-evident.

Stephen Greenblatt, in what is perhaps the "founding text" of the new historicism, begins the enterprise with a more direct address to the problems with which I am concerned here, and he does so as a more overtly "literary" critic than Sedgwick (whose book appeared a year later). His opening statement about the grounds and assumptions of his project is so much to the point that I quote at length:

> I have attempted . . . to practice a more cultural or anthropological criticism. . . . A literary criticism that has affinities to this practice must be conscious of its own status as interpretation and intent upon understanding literature as part of the system of signs that constitute a given culture; its proper goal, however difficult to realize, is a *poetics of culture*. Such an approach is . . . necessarily impure: its central concerns prevent it from permanently sealing off one type of discourse from another or decisively separating works of art from the minds and lives of their creators and their audiences. I remain concerned, to be sure, with the implications of artistic representation as a distinct human activity . . . but the way to explore these implications lies neither in denying any relation between the play and social life nor in affirming that the latter is the "thing itself," free from interpretation. Social actions are themselves always embedded in systems of public signification, always grasped, even by their makers, in acts of interpretation, while the words that constitute the works of literature that we discuss here are by their very nature the manifest assurance of a similar embeddedness. Language, like other sign systems, is a collective construction; our interpretive task must be to grasp more sensitively the consequences of this fact by investigating both the social presence to the world of the literary text and the social presence of the world in the literary text. The literary text remains the central object of my attention in this study of self-fashioning in part because, as I hope these chapters will demonstrate, great art is an extraordinarily sensitive register of the complex struggles and harmonies of culture and in part because, by inclination and training, what interpretive powers I possess are released by the resonance of literature. I should add that if cultural poetics is conscious of its status as interpretation, this consciousness must extend to an acceptance of the impossibility of fully reconstructing and reentering the culture of the sixteenth century, of leaving behind one's own situation: it is everywhere evident in this book that the

> questions I ask of my material and indeed the very nature of this
> material are shaped by the questions I ask of myself.[5]

The self-conscious literariness of Greenblatt's project distinguishes it in
many respects from the work of others who have followed him as new historicists. His sensitivity to literary mediation keeps him alert to the questions of how exactly literature works—or does not work—as evidence and
how it comments on or reflects or influences culture. And he confronts directly the fact that in certain respects he is doing the work of anthropology;
moreover, he helpfully recognizes the oddness of his doing so with literary
texts. While he takes pleasure in the "impurity" of his project—literature as
participating in a culture-wide system of signs and thus always implicated
in other discourses—he retains a firm, if not entirely theorized, sense of literature as a "distinct" human activity. This sense is an indispensable aspect
of any engagement with the aesthetic, any avoidance of the sort of reductivism that comes to equate the aesthetic with ideology, or to subsume it under
ideology. (I would suggest that it is also indispensable to the developing
institutional battle over the humanities and research in the humanities because it will certainly be necessary in the next few years that students of literature be ready to define what it is they are doing to an unsympathetic
taxpaying world or concede that literature is no longer a subject or a discipline.) But Greenblatt only alludes to it. In justifying his use of literature to
do what might be thought of as anthropology, he claims that "great art is an
extraordinarily sensitive register of the complex struggles and harmonies of
culture."

But in the end, Greenblatt treats literature as a resource (an indispensable one because of the special virtues of "great art") for anthropology. The
objective is anthropological knowledge, however "impure" it might be,
rather than what Greenblatt in fact does so wonderfully—analysis of the
ways in which the literary and the ideological are implicated in the peculiar
textures of language. And Greenblatt's charming confession that he uses
literature because he is trained to interpret it in effect suggests that any other
resource might be used depending on one's disciplinary training.[6] Of
course literature is inevitably hybrid and impure, and the disciplinary
boundaries we have erected are hopelessly artificial. But it is important to
notice to how small a degree literature is the subject even of the most literary of critics, like Greenblatt. In addition, the notion of "great art" that
Greenblatt sustains and that infects all of his readings is not thought
through: it is a given of the anthropological work. Whatever might be distinctive about literature (except its cultural sensitivity, which is called into
question by other critics, like Michaels, who allow it no special cultural authority), that distinctiveness has no privileged place in the work of cultural

poetics. Despite Greenblatt's sophistication and despite the importance of *Renaissance Self-Fashioning,* he does not really address the problem—nor do many of his followers—of the relation between aesthetics and ideology.

Indeed, very little work has been done on the problem, looming for me larger with each developing critical movement. How can one reconcile aesthetically driven engagement in the experience of literature with an increasing tendency to see it as only one among equals within a cultural system of competing discourses, and as part of a study whose object is not literature but anthropology or sociology or history? Literature lives implicated in and in tension with all of these other discourses, none of which is "pure." Sedgwick and Greenblatt are good critics insofar as they are good historians, and good historians insofar as they are good critics. Literature cannot be imagined as somehow divorced, by way of the aesthetic, from the moral and political issues that engaged Samuel Johnson and Matthew Arnold as much as they engage Sedgwick and Greenblatt; yet no criticism that refuses distinctions between aesthetic and instrumental functions of language can do justice either to the aesthetic or the ideological.

The impurity of the discourses is often belied by the tendency of much criticism to focus so intently on the moral and the political that what counts is no longer the process, the complex movements of language, but the score: does the test come out for or against? Even the best of our critics can give the impression that that's what they are about. But why, then, should we read literature at all if what we want to know can be discovered through other materials? Even more difficult: why should critics read or encourage the reading of literature if their project is to expose its implicit cooperation with political, social, cultural forces that many critics who have loved literature have spent their lives resisting?

Why, for example, read Dickens, who, as Sedgwick puts it in her discussion of *Our Mutual Friend,* contributes "to the 'Gothic' project: the psychologization and political naturalization of homophobia about men."[7] Or why read the Victorian novel at all if, as D. A. Miller argues in an equally important book, equally sensitive to the movements of literary language, its point "is to confirm the novel-reader in his identity as 'liberal subject,' a term with which I allude not just to the subject whose private life, mental or domestic, is felt to provide constant inarguable evidence of his constitutive 'freedom,' but also to, broadly speaking, the political regime that sets store by this subject."[8] Miller's answer, as I understand it, is that it enables readers to see how this bourgeoisifying project is carried on in other, contemporary, forms. In effect, the point of reading literature sensitively is to warn readers against reading literature. If one objects to the idea of the "liberal subject" and to the political regimes that rely on it, why further propagate texts enlisted on the side of the enemy? Edward Said's argument in

Culture and Imperialism raises the question in a different way. "In the main," he says, "the nineteenth-century European novel is a cultural form consolidating but also refining and articulating the authority of the *status quo*."⁹

In the larger argument of his book Said in fact addresses, however marginally, the question I am raising here, and I will return to his argument and his cultural predicament shortly. But it is important to note first that the point I have quoted is consonant with Miller's and Sedgwick's (she argues interestingly about the relation between homophobia and imperialism). Said is everywhere concerned with how the imperial project is interwoven with literature, how the literature of the West is in certain respects incomprehensible out of the context of empire and the antiphonal texts written in the empire by its (former) subjects.

▪ ▪ ▪

I speak for none of the contributors to this volume, but I have the privilege, as editor and inviter, of speaking about them and, perhaps, even of forcing them into the unnatural perspective I am providing. I have worried about whether it is possible to recuperate a sense of the distinctive value of literature without losing the crucial insights provided by ideological criticism and contemporary theory. Arnold Rampersad, in his essay included here, puts the very point: "It seems to me," he says, "that it takes an absolutely superior mind and spirit to both pursue the so-called demystification of literature and continue to love books." For many, the idea of "absolutely superior mind and spirit" is itself troublesome because, among other things, it effaces the material bases of power from which the idea of superiority is expressed; but in addition, for many, as Rampersad seems to fear, there may be no need to "continue to love books." Part of the point of this volume, however, is that there is a need, and that the work is difficult. The essays gathered here seem to me to make an important contribution to exactly this sort of difficult recuperation.

For many of the contributors, the problem of the "aesthetic" in its engagement with or mystification of the ideological is not a problem. What might, for them, be discerned as a problem is the historical use to which the aesthetic has often been put, or the very need that people like me feel to continue to think of the aesthetic as something that cannot be completely subsumed under other larger categories, all of which must be seen as culturally and historically contingent. But however each writer negotiates the question, my sympathy with their struggles (several have confessed to me that the project was much more difficult than they had initially imagined it to be) is intensified, even as I try to write this opening chapter, by my own uneasiness and uncertainty. Part of the history of the aesthetic, especially in the nineteenth century, is a recognition of the way indulgence in it is a form of privilege (this recognition might be seen as part of what drove poor Ruskin mad), a way to separate oneself from those with "inferior taste." And the history of criticism in the last twenty or so years is in part a history of the developing recognition of the political embedding of all discourse in its material culture, and thus a history of the exposure of disguised complicities.

In any case, this book, and this introduction, have required that I face directly my own anxieties about what my passion for literature will seem like to the critical culture with which I want to claim alliance. Terry Eagleton has argued that the "aesthetic," in "asserting the claims of affective experience against a ruthlessly exclusivist reason is in principle progressive," but that in Britain at least it is "effectively captured by the political right."[10] When I decided to invoke that "affective experience" to begin this book, I realized that I risked enlisting myself in the tradition of Edmund Burke, Arnold, and T. S. Eliot and alienating all of those readers who, like me, find that tradition deeply suspect. But I decided to take the risk precisely because I have much admired writers like them and have found them wonderful and liberating as well as politically repulsive. As an adolescent I was shocked by Eliot's anti-Semitism and later came to loathe the form of his high Anglican turn; when I was in graduate school, I was depressed by Arnold's mystification of culture and even more by his location of that culture in the State. But I continued to read and admire them both and to value (and question, of course) their stunningly rich subversions of Enlightenment rationality, a rationality that was used to serve both bourgeois utilitarian capitalism and its radical antitheses. Beginning this book with the language of the affective, the sublime, the aesthetic, I hoped to rescue from the wreckage of the mystified ideal of the beautiful the qualities that allowed for such rich ambivalences. Eliot is anti-Semitic and worse. Arnold is both statist and snob. I wouldn't be without the writings of either of them. That, I recognize, puts me and this book under suspicion.

Does literature have any standing that might, even for a moment, exempt it from the practical and political critiques to which all other artifacts of culture are apparently subject? When art seems, directly or indirectly, intentionally or inadvertently, openly or surreptitiously, to sustain, create, justify, or forward politically or socially objectionable ends (from whose perspective?), are there any grounds for giving it the privilege disallowed to other enemies of the good, the true, and the just?

There have, of course, been plenty of strong arguments in the last decade against the idea of the specialness of literature. Many have relatively comfortably accepted Terry Eagleton's position:

> If it will not do to see literature as an "objective," descriptive category, neither will it do to say that literature is just what people whimsically choose to call literature. For there is nothing at all whimsical about such kinds of value-judgement: they have their roots in deeper structures of belief which are as apparently unshakeable as the Empire State Building. What we have uncovered so far, then, is not only that literature does not exist in the sense that insects do, and that the value-judgements by which it is constituted are historically variable, but that these value-judgements themselves have a close relation to social ideologies. They refer in the end not simply to private taste, but to the assumptions by which certain social groups exercise and maintain power over others.[11]

Literature, that is to say, is real enough, but only as it is constructed for purposes of domination by particular empowered groups. Again, this sort of analysis, transforming the aesthetic into a category of political dominance, transforms the kind of experience I invoked at the start of this essay into a manifestation of some systemic power of which the perceiver is unaware.

The aesthetic, when it is invoked as an aspect of human nature, links the ostensibly unique experiences of the individual to the species, allowing for the conception of "good taste"; it secretively imports all the hierarchies of society. It is only fair to say about Eagleton that when, in *The Ideology of the Aesthetic,* he addresses the issue of the aesthetic and its relation to ideology more fully, he attempts to do justice to the destabilizing power of the affective, validated against Enlightenment rationality, and allows for its capacity to disrupt the exercise of power by the "certain social groups" invoked here. That is, he allows for it but argues that historically this power has been appropriated by "those groups."

But the Eagletonian kind of appropriation of the aesthetic by politics is almost a given of much contemporary theory. Questions of literary value are for the most part beside the point of criticism, as are arguments for literature's distinctiveness, and when they occur they can be felt to be an embarrassment. The best known responses in recent years have been self-righteously moralistic, lamentations over the loss of clear standards of literary excellence. Indeed, those who have faced and answered the question of value—like Allan Bloom—look very much like those certain groups who are struggling to "maintain and exercise power over others." Many of those who have attempted to argue for literary value have clearly pandered to popular audiences through self-righteous and universalizing rhetoric that posits a generalized human nature and remains blind to its own provincialism. Critics have been reluctant to make themselves allies of this kind of critique. But whatever the reason for reluctance to engage the question of literary value, critics have not been able or willing to account, for example, for their own continuing preoccupation with the texts that are being exposed as imperialist, sexist, homophobic, racist, and in most respects ideologically pernicious, but that have long been "canonized."

The persistence of these "classics" is not to be explained simply as a consequence of the attempt to exercise and maintain power (obviously, much of the criticism that returns to them is designed to expose and reject that attempt). Nor can it be accounted for entirely by the inertia of traditional study of literature and the hardened (financially constrained) disciplinary structure of our universities, nor because these texts serve as sensitive registers (as Greenblatt argues) of the way the culture does its political work outside of the ostensible activities of politics. The category of the aesthetic needs to be reconsidered if only because it is so clear that the "classics" continue to be disruptive and difficult and pleasurable (of course, the question then becomes, to whom, under what conditions, with what exclusions?). For the most part, however, while there have been plenty of excellent arguments about the way "high art" serves political purposes and about why critics should not see it as superior to popular art, or about the way the category of the aesthetic was invented to serve particular politico-historical purposes, there have not been a lot of arguments about why—other than for the purposes of demystification or to learn what the culture itself takes seriously—*Moby Dick* or *Heart of Darkness* deserves and inspires attention and rereading.

In reflecting on the high stakes in these questions, and particularly on the price of taking stances associable with "liberal" ideological positions, I note the case of Said, one of the dominant figures in contemporary criticism. His work has consistently explored and exposed the deep implication of ostensibly literary discourse in the politics of Western imperialism and the suppression of "inferior" races and cultures. While *Culture and Imperialism* might serve as a kind of summa of a recent tradition of postcolonial critique, Said is sometimes criticized now as a mere "liberal humanist." His forthright valuing of the great (I use the word nervously, following his example) novels of English literature while he demonstrates their complicity with the imperialist project has got him in trouble with many whom he has taught. Interwoven in his powerful argument about the way the nineteenth-century novel served to reinforce the ideology of imperialism is a thread of continuing respect for the very literature he is exposing and for its capacity to resist the simplifications even of its own ideological commitments.

Said has risked arguing for distinctions that have, to say the least, fallen out of fashion. For him the point about literature is that it is "radically, quintessentially hybrid," and its separation, under the aegis often of the idea of the aesthetic, from "the worldly domain" is a failure of the moral and aesthetic imagination. But one reads the Western texts still, finding in them resistances to their own ideologies, as Said finds in Joseph Conrad formal devices that intimate what Conrad cannot himself support—as, for example, the recognition that the "darkness" "was in fact a non-European world resisting imperialism" (30).

Said clearly believes—despite his heavily political orientation—in a kind of intellectual free space that might be associated with the realm of the aesthetic. He speaks, at the start of *Culture and Imperialism,* of how, in writing the book, "I have availed myself of the utopian space still provided by the university, which I believe must remain a place where such vital issues are investigated, discussed, reflected on. For it to become a site where social and political issues are actually either imposed or resolved would be to remove the university's function and turn it into an adjunct to whatever political party is in power" (xxvi). It would be easy to mistake this for Allan Bloom's imagination of the university as a place to "maintain the permanent questions front and center," and to "protect reason from itself, by being the model of true openness."[12] But in his claims for literature and his claims for the "utopian space" of the university, Said is not talking about "permanent questions" and makes no claims for an ultimate Arnoldian disinterestedness. He is concerned—and annoyed—throughout his book with the possibility that literary study has, as he puts it, only "slender public consequences" (318), and determined to allow for a place in which "public consequences" are deferred.[13] He does share with Bloom and Arnold a sense that immediately interested and politically directed study is dangerous, but for him the danger is that where such study is explicitly sanctioned it will inevitably be repressed by or in the service of the powers that be.

There must be a distinction between aspiration to some impossible ideal disinterested stance, and the effort to resist, in certain situations, the political thrust of one's own interests in order—in those situations—to keep open to new knowledge of alternative possibilities and to avoid the consequences of simple partisanship. There is something utterly nihilistic, not to say counterproductive, about the extension of the truism that everything is political into a practical obliteration of all grades of interest in all circumstances. Even if the Arnoldian and Bloomian ideal of intellectual free space is merely utopian and ultimately a mystifying and disguise of actual power, the notion that the university is not or should not try to be fundamentally different from partisan political institutions is merely absurd.[14]

If *everything* is political, discriminations between, say, a classroom debate and a political debate, between a novel and a campaign speech, are

mere mystifications. A careless reader might hear in Said's effort to preserve a space to think through, for example, the difficult questions of imperialism, an echo of Bloom's romanticizing of a gentrified academe, and
guilt by association might well follow. But the "free space" of the university is, of course, constantly contested; part of its politics is the attempt to
resist simple partisanship, the attempt to resist forces that disallow what
they regard as political—which usually means what is opposed to their own
politics.

Said's kind of political engagement is criticized by political allies because it entails recognition of the complex value of texts he seems to be discrediting politically; and he talks as though it were possible both to value
and demystify at the same time. He sustains practical and subtle discriminations in order to recuperate values and ideas coopted historically by the
right but not inevitably "right." In this critical climate, at this difficult if
energizing moment, criticism threatens often to become not so much an
attempt to understand those visceral moments of aesthetic pleasure as an
essay in exposure of the way those moments—the sense of the aesthetic—
are in effect ideological constructions. There is no foundational experience
and no knowledge outside the discourses of culture; and surely, there is no
innocence. Said might be taken as one of those "superior minds" Rampersad invokes—one who continues to "love books" while he pursues the so-
called demystification of literature. The love is not sentimental or blinded.
It is, in the end, eminently practical because it resists the pure logic that
leads to arguments against academic freedom and against the First Amendment, arguments that, from whatever political perspectives they derive,
must lead to the closing down of spaces now occupied both by literature
and critiques of the kind that, for example, Said, Miller, and Sedgwick have
developed. [15]

My apparent swerve—in the discussion of Said's liberal position on academic questions—from the subject of the aesthetic and its relation to ideology, is no swerve at all. I am trying, first of all, to suggest how difficult it
is, in the contemporary critical climate, to resist or qualify in any way the
primacy of the ideological project of criticism, and thus how difficult it has
been for my contributors to confront head on the possibilities that the aesthetic and the ideological do not match. In particular, it is difficult to imagine the aesthetic as a space of freedom, disinterest, and "the rich, all-round
development of human capacities." [16] Yet, however thoroughly absorbed
into dominant ideological formations the aesthetic has been, it has always
served also as a potentially disruptive force, one that opens up possibilities
of value resistant to any dominant political power. (The danger of a relatively free art in totalitarian countries is the most obvious evidence for this.)

I want, secondly, to argue for a pragmatically understood "utopian space"—a space whose existence, ironically, is full of important political consequence because such a space inevitably encourages what is normally disallowed: a sense of the real complications of simplified and mystified issues and the voicing of unpopular and repressed ideas and values. The aesthetic has long been associated with this notion. In this volume, both Peter Brooks and Geoffrey Harpham invoke Friedrich von Schiller, who imagined an aesthetic state, a place of freedom. The aesthetic offers, distinctly, something like the space of the university implied by Said. But such a utopian space is, perhaps oxymoronically, a contested space, one that is never entirely free from the delusions of ideology or combats for control. It is never literally free, and all who occupy it are obliged to keep in mind its exclusions and contestations. The utopian space of the aesthetic is always situated within particular societies and political organizations. But if the possibility of this fragile freedom is denied, and the aesthetic is only more of the same, a disguised category of political assimilation or conscription, it becomes a subject for history or sociology, and will indeed ultimately be lost in the byways of cultural studies.

The indictment of literature by the people who write about it and teach it is so powerful that unless they (and I include myself among "them") can pause to rethink our relation to it, certain other kinds of rethinking must necessarily follow. For example, in the present circumstances the teaching of literature can only be justified as a way to divert young minds from the mistakes of several millennia of Western culture. The "monuments" of that culture begin to look like political landposts erected not by the people who wrote the texts but by the cultures that used them.

"Demystification" of literature is not enough, the transformation of literature into textual evidence for anthropological and sociological commentary is not enough, and a commitment to the value of literature and formal analysis of it is not prima facie a politically suspect activity. Literature remains a subject worth studying "in its own right" (however complicated that idea has become), and such study should exist both as a part of the anthropological, sociological, historical, and cultural studies that now dominate, and parallel to them. In fact, as I am arguing and as several of the contributors to this volume imply, cultural study *requires* the sorts of literary and formal analytical skills that have been associated with the New Criticism.

While this book is constructed out of deep sympathy with the current movements in cultural studies, a strong sense of the value of criticism that locates texts in new ways within the history, politics, and ideology of its culture, and a continuing and aching concern with the problems of race, gender, and class to which so much literary study is devoted these days, I want to emphasize here, in spite of all this—ultimately, I think, for the sake of all this—the central importance of the aesthetic. So what is to be said for the aesthetic aside from the goose bumps of intense personal encounters with literature and art?

While I speak here entirely for myself, and not for the contributors, I would argue, first, for that much contested utopian space. Although utopia is nowhere, and certainly not here, the space of critical work within the university and the space of the aesthetic are potentially very different from the spaces in which the battles of economics and politics, class and gender, get fought out instrumentally and daily. The space I argue for is fully consistent, I believe, with Bruce Robbins's anti-utopian argument. "In order," he says, "to take the true measure of the real but relative freedoms we have, we have to stop positing spaces of freedom which . . . inevitably mask someone's servitude. . . . Not disembodied freedom, but diverse embodiedness and incomplete servitudes have to become the common-sense view of intellectual work."[17] The aesthetic remains a rare if not unique place for almost free play, a place where the very real connections with the political and the ideological are at least partly short circuited. As Derek Attridge argues, "literature can act powerfully to hold the political and the ethical up for scrutiny by means of its power of suspension, momentarily dissociating them from their usual pressing context, performing the ethical decision and the political gesture." The aesthetic is not outside of politics (indeed, several of the essayists demonstrate that the aesthetic, far from serving the cause of the ideological status quo, has had historically revolutionary connections). But it makes its way by indirection and by infusing all questions with affect and value.

Second, the aesthetic is a realm where something like disinterest and impersonality are possible. Again, I make this claim without believing in any ultimate "disinterest" or in that disreputable objective view from nowhere—all knowledge is situated. There are degrees of interest, and, I would argue, the very political stances that so many of the works of cultural study espouse are possible only in that they are felt to emerge disinterestedly, from a clear-eyed view of the way things are. As the aesthetic provides a space where the immediate pressures of ethical and political decisions are deferred, so it allows sympathy for, and potential understanding of people, events, things otherwise threatening. Of course, the Arnoldian and Kantian ideal of a deep subjectivity that connects all with all is a dangerous conception—and one unnecessary for an idea of the aesthetic as I am arguing for it. It is simply the case that the aesthetic reception of literature and art allows, even if it only occasionally achieves, a vital sense of the other.

Indeed, I would argue that the by now conventional association of the dominant developments in literary criticism and theory with some form of political left is largely justified—to their credit, I would add. It seems at first odd that a predominantly white and middle class profession has such a disproportionate (to that of the society at large) number of members who are preoccupied with injustice to non-whites and non-professionals (and who are therefore regularly accused of bad faith and hypocrisy). And it can be explained in part by the way literature has operated on critics. This way is, of course, ostensibly counter to the Foucauldian one that we have seen operative in the work of D. A. Miller, Eve Sedgwick, and Edward Said; that is, it takes literature not as a disguised seduction into dominant bourgeois values, but as potentially the reverse. Again, I quote Attridge:

> Modernism's foregrounding of language and other discursive and generic codes through its formal strategies is not merely a self-reflexive diversion but a recognition (whatever its writers may have thought they were doing) that literature's distinctive power and potential ethical force resides in a testing and unsettling of deeply held assumptions of transparency, instrumentality, and direct referentiality, in part because this taking to the limits opens a space for the apprehension of the other which those assumptions had silently excluded.

The very notion that literature can do things other than what its writers thought they were doing, a long-standing commonplace of criticism, reinforces this notion of impersonality.[18] Not that the writers had no investments, but that they worked in a genre that could subvert personal intentions. The distinctiveness of literature, not only of modernism, lies in this condition.

But the aesthetic leads neither to the left nor to the right. It is politically unaffiliated, and can be put to use for any politics—as several of the essayists show and as Eagleton himself has argued. The idea of free space, for instance, has a strong connection with recent arguments from the right; but that idea is also essential to the protection of the left, which often needs a space that is minimally politicized in order to achieve any voice at all. Where else but in the realm of the aesthetic can things be taken to the limits in the way that Attridge describes?

I want to risk a third point about the value of the aesthetic, one that worries me a lot but that, in the present political climate, probably needs to be suggested. One of the dominant elements in contemporary criticism is the attack on literature for having been enlisted in the cause of developing and enforcing *internal* constraints so that the illusion of "freedom" can be maintained while the state is actually governing and so that civil society can operate with the least possible disruption. Regenia Gagnier puts the point this way: "The aesthetic has been a site of state power since the rise of modernity, whose social organization depends less upon external constraints and visible exercises of authority than upon an ideological model of self-regulating and self-determining subjectivity." This is arguably true of modern commercial and industrial democracies, although the place of the aesthetic in other societies—where it is often perceived as a threat and is thus subject to strong governmental control—is surely different.

But even in advanced capitalist countries like the United States, this is surely not invariably the case. It may be that "dissident" literature is ultimately coopted into the model of "self-regulating and self-determining subjectivity," but however contentious such writers may be, it is difficult to think of Richard Wright or, in another mode, Langston Hughes, or, now that we are learning to read her, Zora Neale Hurston, or Toni Morrison as confirming that cooperation with the state. I would argue that writers who have become canonical, like Melville and Whitman and Dickinson, similarly resist such absorption despite much interesting work pointing toward Gagnier's conclusion.[19] Literature works in complicated ways and may perhaps in the same sentence resist and affirm. It tests the limits.

My argument here, however, rests on the assumption that to a certain extent, the Foucauldian critique is correct, and much literature works as a means of acculturation or politicization, helping its readers to choose their society's values. But I want to ask, especially in the current geopolitical situation in which the fear is not so much the imposition of authoritarian power from above as the fragmented and genocidal activities of national and subnational groups, whether we can as yet begin to talk of the *value* of internal constraints. It has been a given of recent criticism that literature's participation in the work of its society is a bad thing. I want to question this assumption. In suggesting that it has always been one of the functions of art to help create community, to work within the possibilities of its historical moment and location, I am not suggesting that its indirect persuasions are always either "good" or "bad." I am suggesting that literature, even dissident literature, functions within a society to help create a desirable community. The focus on the way narrative within capitalist democracies helps to internalize the societies' values, and thus to serve as replacement for external policing functions, makes things sound a lot worse than they are, or at least might be. One alternative would be to make the governing assumptions of the society sufficiently unattractive that the policing would become literal and determined by bullets and bludgeons.

But I value literature, as whole cultures often do, because—in spite of its endless diversity and refusals to make things comfortable—it is one means to some larger sense of community, to an awareness of the necessity of personal compromise and social accommodation, civilization entailing always its discontents. Part of the value of the aesthetic is in the way it can provide spaces and strategies for exploring the possibility of conciliations between the idiosyncratic and the communal. The location of authority in subjectivity is not necessarily a hidden agenda of authority, but often a quite overt effort to create a subjectivity that is committed to the collective. George Eliot was, for example, quite explicit in her narratives in seeking to imagine a society in which private desires were totally harmonious with public good. Can one imagine a good society in which internal regulation is not a condition for adequate functioning? Is the project of developing a considered subjectivity (alert to the abuses of power) always to be considered a bad thing?

The aesthetic is part of a discourse of value: it is in this respect never dissociated from the personal, the social, and the political. But it allows the exploration of possibilities in ways no other modality does. Its very conventionality, manifestation in "novels" or "poems," for example, frames those explorations within a finite system of assumptions, codes, attitudes, feelings that help to construct a community. It may, indeed, exploit secret codes that deceive those who read into misperceptions of the degree of their own choices. But the aesthetic has no particular political commitments. It leaves itself open to endless and indeterminate interpretations. It offers, in the options society can create, the closest thing to "free choice," the least oppressive of its forms. While it has been salutary and illuminating to focus, as criticism has been doing since *Discipline and Punish,* on the degree to which institutional, ideological pressures are always operative, and thus to expose and "demystify" texts that have seemed, on the surface, to be liberatory, such focus has also done considerable damage to an area of human creativity and imagination that provides one of our last resources in this politically and commercially overdetermined civilization for precisely that internalization of value that makes any kind of civilization possible.

What I am talking about here is close to the position Raymond Williams, another cultural critic who took quite seriously the notion of "great literature," espoused in his later works. He is consistently concerned with a "knowable community." To take one example, in his discussion of sociology and literature, he tries to identify the "specific literary phenomenon," which he describes as "the dramatization of a process, the making of a fiction, in which the constituting elements, of real social life and beliefs, were simultaneously actualized and in an important way differently experienced, the difference residing in the imaginative act, the imaginative method, the specific and genuinely unprecedented imaginative organization."[20] The very specificity of literature, on which Peter Brooks, Susan Wolfson, and Derek Attridge focus in their essays here, are the conditions for an understanding of a society's "world-view." But yet more directly to my immediate point, Williams goes on to argue that the "creative acts" of "major individual talents" "compose, within a historical period, a specific community: a community visible in the structure of feeling and demonstrable, above all, in fundamental choices of form" (25). What great art does through its form is both compose and reflect community. This is altogether another take on the Foucauldian perspective that, in effectively denying "major individual talent," in finding all individual acts of imagination determined by larger constricting social systems, makes community simply oppressive, and makes imagination not liberatory but delusive. My emphasis in this volume (not always shared by its contributors) is on the imaginative and the liberatory.

This puts some very heavy pressure on the aesthetic. Engaging it is peculiarly difficult because it requires self-conscious disengagement from the immediate pressures of particular ideologies and particular political commitments. It requires the most rigorous coming to terms with those aspects of literature that resist precisely what our rituals of demystification are attempting to expose. Inevitably, there will be failures to notice; there will be blindnesses to the actual material and perspectival conditions that shape our readings and interpretations. The knowable community to which we aspire may be self-deluding and provincial. It's a risk worth taking. I am happy to see politics as an inescapable element of all human creation and to read every text into its political moment. But I ask, breathlessly and nervously, for the opportunity not, as I try to come to terms with the specific forms of literature, to use my understandings of these texts in a political program that turns them into instruments and destroys that very small breathing space of free play and disinterest left to those who risk finding value even in the literature that seems to despise them.

▪ ▪ ▪

In gathering the essays for this book, I sought a wide variety of perspectives, and that, at least, I have achieved. Inevitably, there is here some narrowing of the spectrum of possibility as a result of my own range of acquaintance and what the contributors may have read into my letters of solicitation (as well as the unfortunate circumstances of illness or overwork, which have lost for this volume several *other* perspectives). I have sought feminists, Marxists, new historicists, eccentrics, people very much committed to cultural studies—and, I confess, friends. And my not overtly articulated principle here was that the "aesthetic" cannot be understood as a single category; its history is too complex, its uses too various. The principle of multiplicity and variety, however, has its drawbacks when it comes to constructing a book. And it has taken me some time and several readings of each essay to induce from them inklings of order and relationship. In conclusion here, let me try to explain what I think this book is doing and account for how it is (beyond elements of inescapable arbitrariness) organized.

Overall, what I have discovered, happily for my understanding of this project, is that even the most academically and politically conservative of the essays share in a consensus that the aesthetic needs to be recuperated, re-understood, and that far from being a bad thing, ideologically complicit with all that elitist oppression, it had from its beginnings a very complex and potentially liberatory quality. Thus, the formalists and the revolutionaries agree at least on this point. The aesthetic matters. Everyone also agrees on the historically contingent nature of the aesthetic, and everyone refuses the language of the good, the true, and the beautiful, of eternal and universal verities, of the transcendent and the foundational. The problem is how to understand the aesthetic, with all its implications of value and all of its shady political history, as something valuable both politically and otherwise.

In the first section, I have paired essays by Arnold Rampersad and Myra Jehlen, two remarkable critics and scholars for whom the dichotomy between theory and texts is false and whose "theorizing" depends on what happens when they read well—that is, when they read their texts as intricately part of a complex historical context. Both of them are concerned with the way a too heavy pressure on questions of ideology, on exposure of the mystifications performed by literature, leads to something like hostility to literature among critics and graduate students. But it is obvious that while valuing literature and, in Myra Jehlen's focus, literary "greatness," both these critics manage to sustain their important engagement with political issues while at the same time valuing even that canonical literature that has, in recent years, been too often denigrated. Jehlen poses the question most acutely in her own essay in which she juxtaposes a very impressive history of the development of ideological criticism in the twentieth century to her later interest in the continuing "greatness" of Melville. The difficulties of that juxtaposition help frame the problems of this book.

In the second section, the book turns to the history of the idea of the aesthetic. In the light of the essays by Mary Poovey and Oscar Kenshur, it will be difficult to sustain some of the going truisms about the aesthetic—that, for instance, it is merely a diversion from or a disguise of the primacy of economic interests, or that it is linked to the tradition of empiricism rather than rationalism. Perhaps the odd woman out of this collection is Frances Ferguson's fascinating essay on De Sade and pornography. Ferguson is tracing a parallel development of aesthetics and pornography at the moment of their inception, and her essay should be seen, at least in part, as a revision of the history of the aesthetic that places its development in the context of developments in legal theory, particularly tort law, in the eighteenth century. Geoffrey Harpham's essay brings the history into the twentieth century and into the era of the postmodern, and works out its development and its crises through an extended and ingenious analogy to the Gulf War. In doing so he fruitfully complicates any notion of the ideological allegiances of the aesthetic, and at the same time suggests how difficult the connection between aesthetics and ideology is.

In the end, however, I believe that the most important thing this book can do, in forcing reconceptualization of the aesthetic, is push the pendulum back toward the formal elements that have for so long been denigrated as literary intellectuals complete their reaction to the excesses of the New Criticism. One of the dominant motifs of the essays collected here is the importance of the "formal." In effect, the book is a plea for a new kind of formalism, one that recognizes the ideological implications of the formal even as it values and deliberates over nuances of the text in ways that might, to vulgar eyes, seem like mere "formalism." Peter Brooks tackles the issue head on, and in doing so he goes a long way—as Derek Attridge does in his paper in the last section—toward identifying those qualities that give to literature as a field of study, parallel to but distinct from cultural studies, its special nature and justification. It is worth anticipating the essay by quoting briefly from Brooks:

> Students are only too willing to short-circuit the aesthetic, and to perform any kind of reading, including the ideological, that you indicate to them. What is more difficult for them—and hence more necessary—is to slow up the work of interpretation, the attempt to turn the text into *some other* discourse or system, and to consider it as a manifestation of the conventions, constraints, and possibilities of literature. Students need in their work on literature to encounter a moment of poetics—a moment in which they are forced to ask not only *what* the text means, but as well *how* it means.

The formal qualities of literature, those elements that relate most directly to its aesthetic quality, are precisely what a determinedly ideological criticism threatens to miss.

Maria DiBattista's paper, which takes some of the explicit positions of literary modernism seriously, might well be understood as a defense of some of the ideals of the aesthetic that have lost favor in the current critical world—particularly the ideals of impersonality and the refusal of political engagement. In working with writers like Virginia Woolf and Christopher Isherwood, who were clearly aware of the importance of the pressures to be

politically engaged, DiBattista dramatizes forcefully the price and the difficulty of achieving that tentative and incomplete impersonality that was the
ideal of modernist art and that, as I have argued, remains an aspect of the
aesthetic. Susan Wolfson's essay, which also insists on the major significance of the particulars of every text, is obviously also a defense of formal
criticism, but the formal becomes the political as well. She accepts Michael
Levinson's view that "Criticism must 'take up a position within but not *of*
the ideology [the work] seems to articulate' and in this position refuse seduction." But her argument is not to deny the connection of the aesthetic to
the ideological; it is to insist on its intricacy. Her essay becomes a kind of
example to prove her point that "no project of critical inquiry gains by
blunting its instruments of reading. To suspect formal complexities merely
as a threat to ideological clarity or to reduce such articulations to dubious
events of tired apparition and fabulous fusion, is, I think, to court unproductive simplifications of the interaction of aesthetics and ideology."
Working through the imperative of form along the lines of Brooks's earlier
argument, Wolfson, like William Keach, whose essay follows hers, shows
that the formal and the aesthetic were, for the Romantics, liberatory political efforts. Keach's essay, which is strongly sympathetic to the demystifying and ideological projects of contemporary criticism, nevertheless is
centrally concerned with the failure of Marxist analysis to be able to discuss
"form" adequately, to see it in its materiality. In their different ways, then,
each of these essays focuses on the centrality of form and yet remains alive to
the political and ideological tensions that help, in fact, to determine form.
(Wolfson and Keach's essays might well have taken their place in the "history" section of this volume because they both contribute importantly to
the history of aesthetics among the Romantics, and focus on "Romantic
ideology.")

In the last section, I wanted to veer off from formal questions back to
the question of ideology (which, as we have seen, we never entirely left).
Since I am interested in the complicated interactions of aesthetics and ideology and in trying to right what I consider a current imbalance in the relative
disregard of the aesthetic as a viable category, I have given the central section to questions of form. But I am happy, through the very different essays
of Derek Attridge, Regenia Gagnier, and Cheryl Wall, to return more directly to questions of ideology, which pick up several of the ideas in the
essays by Wolfson and Keach. Attridge, as my earlier quotations suggest, is
intent on working out the intricate connections between form and politics,
to try to show that it is, indeed, through the formal that the political gets
engaged. And in studying the work of Coetzee, Attridge argues that the
aesthetic is no conspirator in the strategies of the right but the very reverse.
Gagnier, whose interest in the formal is less central than Attridge's, also

claims that aesthetics (at least a certain kind of aesthetics) can become an aspect of liberatory politics. She usefully discriminates this kind of engaged aesthetics from the "decadent" kind that insists on the separation of art from practice. And finally, Cheryl Wall shows how the whole question of the relation between aesthetics and ideology is culturally determined. While the high modernists were resisting ideology, black writing, Wall points out, was "defined as having *only* ideological importance." Ironically, then, an increasing emphasis on the formal and ostensibly ornamental aspects of art becomes, in black writing, politically loaded. Through the writings of Zora Neale Hurston and Alice Walker, Wall traces an interesting and quite different trajectory in the interweavings of aesthetics and ideology and concludes this volume with a further confirmation of the complications of this difficult but important subject.

Thus the combined contributions to this volume offer a rich and varied view of how the aesthetic has operated historically, how it is presently conceived, and how it might or should be recuperated. They suggest, sometimes by indirection, sometimes quite explicitly, what is at stake in the very idea of the aesthetic these days. And what is at stake, I believe, is both personal and professional: the nature of the work critics do, the nature of the "discipline" under whose academic rubric most critics now make their livings. That is to say, I believe that to face head-on the question of the relation between aesthetics and ideology is not merely to write another interesting essay on another important topic, but to consider implicitly and expose quite vulnerably our own positions within the profession. It is to enter the critical wars in a distinctly uncomfortable way, ultimately unprotected by the depth of our scholarship or the cleverness of our intellectual maneuverings, by risking, in the ostensibly paradoxical efforts toward disinterest and community, to value once again those extraordinary experiences, provocations, and explorations that have always made literature central to the life of society.

Notes

1. This view is attributed to Walter Michaels by Brook Thomas in *The New Historicism and Other Old-Fashioned Topics* (Princeton: Princeton University Press, 1991), 162.

2. Fredric Jameson's *The Political Unconscious: Narrative as a Socially Symbolic Act* (Ithaca: Cornell University Press, 1981), has been enormously influential but in fact leads to a very different set of attitudes toward literature and in that respect has it seems to me had very little impact on the way preoccupation with ideology has manifested itself. Jameson's is a specifically Marxist and a self-consciously utopian narrative theory. Although he wants to escape the poststructuralist language of "master narrative," he begins his book by positing

one—"the collective struggle to wrest a realm of Freedom from a realm of Necessity" (19); and he builds his interpretive system on the assumption of that narrative. His method entails attention to the particularities of history and a self-conscious refusal to read old texts into our current histories and theoretical systems (except as they are part of the master narrative). His method entails a poetics, or a theory of narrative, and if his objective is in fact utopian, his attention to literature is justified by his sense that literature is itself the site of the utopian imagination (however repressed or "unconscious" it is). The new historicism, various as its manifestations might be, tends on the other hand to read literature much more judgmentally, much more as a mystification, much less as a creative myth of human possibility.

3. "Byron," *The Complete Prose Works of Matthew Arnold,* ed. R. H. Super (Ann Arbor: University of Michigan Press, 1973), 9:236.

4. In this respect, the deconstructive project, though often absorbed into the ideological projects, remains apart. For deconstructive criticism, language remains utterly central to every critical act, and, as Derek Attridge's essay here implies, and as much of Paul de Man's work affirmed, literary language is distinctive in its opacity, and rhetorical analysis remains a condition of all understandings of discourse. In a characteristic formulation, de Man writes: "For the statement about language, that sign and meaning never coincide, is what is precisely taken for granted in the kind of language we call literary. Literature, unlike everyday language, begins on the far side of this knowledge; it is the only form of language free from the fallacy of unmediated expression" ("Criticism and Crisis," in *Blindness and Insight: Essays in the Rhetoric of Contemporary Criticism* [New York: Oxford University Press, 1971], 17).

5. Stephen Greenblatt, *Renaissance Self-Fashioning: From More to Shakespeare* (Chicago: University of Chicago Press, 1980), 4–5.

6. I note that Brook Thomas, in *The New Historicism,* has a similar critique of Greenblatt's argument. See pp. 158–160.

7. Eve Kosofsky Sedgwick, *Between Men: English Literature and Male Homosocial Desire* (New York: Columbia University Press, 1985), 161.

8. D. A. Miller, *The Novel and the Police* (Berkeley: University of California Press, 1988), x.

9. Edward Said, *Culture and Imperialism* (New York: Alfred A. Knopf, 1993), 77. Further references are given in the text.

10. Terry Eagleton, *The Ideology of the Aesthetic* (Oxford: Basil Blackwell, 1990), 60.

11. Terry Eagleton, *Literary Theory: An Introduction* (Oxford: Basil Blackwell, 1983), 16.

12. Allan Bloom, *The Closing of the American Mind* (New York: Simon and Schuster, 1987), 252.

13. Bruce Robbins has called my attention to the way *Culture and Imperialism* treats the notion of "utopian space" inconsistently. Said's political engagement and belief that his analyses of literature allow for important political and social conclusions leads him to lament the apparent public irrelevance of literary study. Robbins, who has throughout his own important work—much influ-

enced, by the way, by Said—insisted on the culturally engaged nature of "professional" literary study, finds Said's notion of "utopian space" both inconsistent and inadequate.

14. At the time of writing this, I came across an essay by Louis Menand, "The Future of Academic Freedom." Menand points out the special vulnerability of "academic freedom" these days, not only because of the enormous external pressures coming from the right, but because of an "internal" pressure:

> The philosophical grounds on which the concept of academic freedom has traditionally rested are now regarded by many academics with skepticism. The notion that the pursuit of knowledge can be a disinterested, nonpartisan, apolitical endeavor, and that the goal of that pursuit should be, or can be, something called "the truth" about a subject, is not only not widely shared; it is quite specifically the target of a great deal of contemporary academic writing. The shorthand version of this attack is the slogan "All knowledge is political." Whether one subscribes to the slogan or not, I think it is true that the line separating "knowledge" from "ideology" has become increasingly hard to draw for many people in the humanities and social sciences these days, and that there are some academics who refuse to recognize the distinction altogether. (*Academe* 79 [May/June 1993]: 12).

The ironies of this position—that those who believe in principle in the political nature of all thought are the most likely to suffer from the breakdown of academic freedom, a concept they cannot credit—are multiple. Academic freedom implies that "intellectual inquiry is a neutral and disinterested activity," an aspect of that utopian space Said describes. From my point of view, any position that in the interest of theoretical and political consistency comes literally to reject ideas like academic freedom is in the long run self-deluded. There may be no such thing as disinterestedness; there may be no "utopian space." But the very mixed nature of knowledge, parallel to the mixed nature of literature, forces not only compromises but serious rethinking. Knowledge is not simply politics; literature is not simply ideology.

15. The problem of intellectual "free space" was brought home to me forcefully at a rather high-powered ACLS conference in the spring of 1993. There, a brilliant young theorist of law, justly appalled at the way the First Amendment has been invoked by critics from the far right to protect the "free speech" of racial slurs on campuses, made a very intelligent and complicated case to justify such things as "speech codes." Part of her argument depended on the fact that First Amendment rhetoric had been coopted by the right and had turned it into a very powerful conservative political force. In the course of the discussion that followed, reference was made from the floor to the famous "free speech" movement of the late 1960s, a movement, of course, emanating from the left. I was struck by the way the genuinely learned and brilliant law theorist was taken aback by that allusion, for her arguments had been constructed under the assumption that the First Amendment was a tool for the right. She confessed to not having thought of the historical case in which the First Amendment was a tool for the left, with whom her sympathies lay.

16. Eagleton, in *Ideology of the Aesthetic,* describes this development as part

of the middle-class inheritance of the "aesthetic" "from its superiors." This development, he suggests, made the aesthetic a potentially strong force of resistance both to the aristocracy and to the "spiritually impoverished" commercial, industrial life that the middle class had by and large adopted (36).

17. Bruce Robbins, *Secular Vocations* (London: Verso, 1993), 10.

18. Many contemporary theorists would explain this phenomenon in ways opposed to my use of it. That is, they might argue that the writing occurs within a large cultural system that is actually responsible for it so that intention is irrelevant since the text gets written by the culture and, of course, by the ideology of state.

19. As one ingenious and fascinating example, Wai-Chee Dimock's book on Melville shows how in his very overt antagonism to the "imperial," he in fact uses a language full of the "imperial" and implicitly buys into the idea of sovereignty and empire (*Empire for Liberty: Melville and the Poetics of Individualism* [Princeton: Princeton University Press, 1989]). "Melville will emerge, in my account, as something of a representative author, a man who speaks for and with his contemporaries, speaking for them and with them, most of all, when he imagines himself to be above them, apart from them, opposed to them" (6).

20. Raymond Williams, *Problems in Materialism and Culture* (London: Verso, 1982), 25.

I
Contingency and Value

ARNOLD RAMPERSAD

Values Old and New

CATHARINE STIMPSON'S question "Where is value now?" posed during the panel session at which this paper was first delivered, is timely and challenging.[1] As she has pointed out, many people are asking it. However, I myself am not one of those who regularly ask this question with reference to books. I am further provoked by one of her goading questions: "Is the yearning for textual value, be it ethical or aesthetic, valid?" If such yearning is not valid, then why should anyone read or write books—books, that is, that we would consider literature, as opposed to the flatly utilitarian, such as the Yellow Pages, or the glamorously utilitarian, such as a Mercedes Benz owner's manual? Also a little troubling is her question as to "what might feed our appetite for moral and aesthetic meaning without poisoning us with nostalgia." Nostalgia a poison? I had always thought that amnesia was the poison, or perhaps that unself-consciousness or unreflectiveness was the poison, of which the paralysis of amnesia was the major symptom and to which nostalgia was the original antidote. Nostalgia is probably the beginning of our cultivation of the past, our way of entry into a dialogue with and an understanding of history.

And yet Stimpson is surely correct in identifying a crisis of valuation in literary studies, in the very profession that used to see as its main reason for being the preservation of literature and the propagation of the array of values putatively inherent in its canon. I say a crisis even though the concept of inherent relativity has been a guiding force in literary appreciation and creation from time immemorial. This has been true, of course, for poets, who handsomely anticipated the relativist physics of Einstein. What brings the matter of devaluation into sharp focus here and now, however, is not its quizzical place beside the so-called eternal verities, as a kind of spice to highlight their sweetness or a foil to accentuate their light, but the way in our own time we have seen skepticism about value in literature, and the value of literature itself, become armed and dangerous within the profession. We now routinely deal with graduate students—future professors, I mean—who frankly refuse to read this and that, for various deeply felt reasons: in my own experience, almost scorning Shakespeare, definitely scorning Henry James, and Faulkner, and so on. Of course, I do not need to be reminded that the mainstream has traditionally scorned many of the writers who are central to my own scholarship. But to refuse to read Shakespeare, James, Faulkner, and other celebrated writers on radical socialist or feminist or cultural-nationalist grounds is really another matter. Are we simply answering scorn with scorn, like the dog in the manger? Or have we come on some grand proof, at last, of the devaluation of literature?

This general question of the value of books does to a large extent subsume the current debate over canon. (I regard canonization in itself as virtually instinctive; memory is surely the mother of all canons.) The idea in some quarters is assuredly that all books, like all men and women, are created equal, and that the choice by the authorities, whoever they might be, of some books over other books reflects not objective or even quasi-objective evaluations but assertions of power—patriarchal, imperial, repressive. An increasing number of the future teachers of literature clearly think so, and the consequences are going to be interesting. Nevertheless, that we would come to this pass in the profession was predictable, not simply because of the tradition of relativism I have alluded to but also because of the genuinely obnoxious political realities through which we have lived.

The walls of the profession, securely manned, once looked unbreachable, inevitable, a part of nature, much as the British once looked in India. The walls of the profession are not tumbling down, but they are distinctly dilapidated, in the root sense of that word; and the British are out of India. The analogy to colonialism is apt. The assault on value that seems to have reached its apex today began, in large respect, with Frantz Fanon's critique of decolonization, especially in his chapter "Concerning Violence" in *The Wretched of the Earth*. Fanon remains invaluable, I would suggest, but not simply as a definer of our own circumstances or as an unmediated guide to how we should proceed. Fanon's native assuredly can stand for the loose but increasingly potent alliance of the aggrieved who make up the most important single new force in the university today, where the teaching of literature is concerned. Against the native in Fanon is the settler, the colonizer, whose counterpart in our debate is you-know-who ("dead white males" is the disturbing phrase one heard far too often).

It is tempting to see the process of decolonization described by Fanon as easily translated into our own lives. The moment the native moves toward liberation, Fanon writes, is the moment that his master hands him over "to well-meaning souls who in cultural congresses point out to him the specificity and wealth of Western values."[2] However, the very mention of the term "Western values" produces in the native

> a sort of stiffening or muscular lockjaw. . . . When the native hears a speech about Western culture he pulls out his knife or at least he makes sure it is within reach. The violence with which the supremacy of white values is affirmed and the aggressiveness which has permeated the victory of these values over the ways of life and of thought of the native mean that, in revenge, the native laughs in mockery when Western values are mentioned in front of him. (43)

Under colonialism, the triumph of the master is complete when the native "admits loudly and intelligibly the supremacy of the white man's values. In the period of decolonization, the colonized masses mock at these very values, insult them, and vomit them up" (43).

According to Fanon, the native intellectual almost always plays a perfidious role by believing the idea "that the essential qualities remain eternal in spite of all the blunders men may make; the essential qualities of the West, of course. The native intellectual accepted the cogency of these ideas, and deep down in his brain you could always find a vigilant sentinel ready to defend the Greco-Latin pedestal" (46). Given a really bloody struggle for liberation, however, the native intellectual is brought radically down to the level of the people, as it were, and "this artificial sentinel is turned into dust. All the Mediterranean values—the triumph of the human individual, of clarity, and of beauty—become lifeless, colorless knickknacks. All those speeches seem like collections of dead words; those values which seemed to uplift the soul are revealed as worthless, simply because they have nothing to do with the concrete conflict in which the people is engaged" (46–47).

I would suggest that this scenario indeed reflects with almost uncanny accuracy the process of demoralization (call it radicalization if you will; but I think you have to be demoralized before you can be radicalized) that has swept and is sweeping hundreds, perhaps thousands, of future professors into the ranks of antihumanism even as they take up positions in schools of the humanities. The antihumanist or the *posthumanist* (pronounced *posthumous,* I am told) position can be immensely creative, but for many of these future professors antihumanism will amount to little more than the old philistinism. It seems to me that it takes an absolutely superior mind and spirit to both pursue the so-called demystification of literature and continue to love books. The relation of demystification to the *creation* of books is another matter, which I will set aside for the moment.

Although some of us like to think that the current talk about value represents the cleansing agency of brand-new political abrasives, this question of the absolute subjectivity of judgments of value was addressed a long time ago in our profession, and perhaps most adroitly by none other than Northrop Frye in *The Anatomy of Criticism*. "Value-judgements are subjective," he argues there, "in the sense that they can be indirectly but not directly communicated. When they are fashionable or generally accepted, they look objective, but that is all."[3] What we take to be the proven value judgment is only

> the donkey's carrot of literary criticism, and every new critical fashion . . . has been accompanied by a belief that criticism has finally devised a definitive technique for separating the excellent from the less excellent. But this always turns out to be an illusion of the history of taste. Value-judgements are founded on the study of literature; the study of literature can never be founded on value-judgements. (20)

One may object, in reference to this quotation and Catharine Stimpson's basic question, that Frye's words are not relevant here, in that our new certitude speaks not of "separating the excellent from the less excellent" but of doing away altogether with a term such as *excellence* in evaluating literature. However, if the impulse to rank books and to canonize some of them is correctly understood, an aspect of taste, then so is the impulse to say that value is gone from books or that all books have about the same value, really. On the latter score, one might say that what is involved is not so much taste as tastelessness, our suspicion of taste and our awareness of its abuses having deteriorated into a repudiation of the process of taste itself. The question could very well be, "Does taste still have a place in the world of reading, teaching, and writing books?" To some people, the accusation of tastelessness is a typical response to bourgeois conventionality; to others, just about everything comes down to a question of tastefulness or lack thereof.

"Every deliberately constructed hierarchy of values in literature known to me," Frye declares, "is based on a concealed social, moral, or intellectual analogy" (20). This point applies no matter what the approach:

> The various pretexts for minimizing the communicative power of certain writers, that they are obscure or obscene or nihilistic or reactionary or what not, generally turn out to be disguises for a feeling that the views of decorum held by the ascendant social or intellectual class ought to be either maintained or challenged. These social fixations keep changing, like a fan turning in front of a light, and the changing inspires the belief that posterity eventually discovers the whole truth about art. (23)

Frye does not, however, go on to argue that all books are created equal, or that moral or aesthetic considerations are irrelevant. Far from it. Instead, he takes care to distinguish between criticism as experience (as in Emily Dickinson's famous remark "If I feel physically as if the top of my head were taken off, I know this is poetry") and what we usually call literary criticism.

Concerning critical terminology, Frye accurately points out that it "can never recapture or include the original experience" (27) but only render it inexactly. And he wisely goes further, to bring to the fore the fact of celebrated mistakes of taste that have resulted from the attempt to bring "the direct experience of literature into the structure of criticism" (28). Even the best critics have blind spots (I myself recently heard a splendid critic, a lover of Stevens and Frost, frankly declare that the poetry of William Carlos Williams leaves him cold). Frye suggests both the need for openness to the variety of literature and the need to recognize that openness has itself to be tempered, disciplined: "To bring my own view that criticism as knowledge should constantly progress and reject nothing into direct experience would mean that the latter should progress toward a general stupor of satisfaction with everything written, which is not quite what I have in mind" (28). To which I would add only that a "general stupor" of *dis*satisfaction with everything written is probably even less desirable and helpful than the condition described by Frye.

This is not a question that one can settle simply with reference to Northrop Frye. When he writes that "the real concern of the evaluating critic is with positive value, with the goodness, or perhaps the genuineness, of the poem" and declares further that "such criticism produces the direct value-judgement of informed good taste, the proving of art on the pulses, the disciplined response of a high..y organized nervous system to the impact of poetry" (27), some readers today will immediately fasten on terms such as "informed good taste" and ask, what information? They may also ridicule the idea that the nervous system can be "highly organized" without the intervention of political and other prejudices, or that the pulses can prove anything about art that is beyond the jurisdiction of the head. I think we come here reasonably close to what may be the crux of the matter.

It is important, then, to look at what the more sophisticated thinkers among those associated with the new political and cultural forces have conjectured about such notions. One can hardly do better than look at the ideas of Cornel West, the author of *The American Evasion of Philosophy* and diverse essays. West is probably without equal in the creativity of his investigations of the relation between contemporary African-American culture and world political and cultural trends, especially as seen in the university and the arts. Surveying the ferment of change, West begins by identifying the existence of "a new kind of cultural worker . . . in the making, associated with a new 'politics of difference.'"[4] Among the distinctive features here he sees the urge "to trash the monolithic and homogeneous in the name of diversity, multiplicity, and heterogeneity; to reject the abstract, general, and universal in light of the concrete, specific, and particular; and to historicize, contextualize, and pluralize by highlighting the contingent, provisional, variable, tentative, shifting, and changing" (93). West knows that these "gestures" are not new "in the history of criticism or art." What makes them novel, "along with the cultural politics they produce," is what is considered difference. In respecting difference, one measures "the weight and gravity it is given in representation, and the way in which highlighting issues like exterminism, empire, class, race, gender, sexual orientation, age, nation, nature, and region at this historical moment acknowledges some discontinuity and disruption from previous forms of cultural critique" (93).

One inescapable result of the denseness operating not simply in West's rhetoric but also in the reality he describes (with general accuracy, I think) is this same question of the devaluation of literature that Stimpson had in mind. This is a later stage, the latest stage, if you will, of the process that Fanon described in the 1950s. Devaluation comes along with the defetishizing of literature, or "demystification," to invoke a term West prefers—one that troubles me. That his political and broad cultural arguments are relevant here is suggested by the term he ultimately prefers to "demystification," which is "prophetic criticism."

"Demystification" or "prophetic criticism," West argues,

> is the most illuminating mode of theoretical inquiry for those who promote the new cultural politics of difference. Social structural analyses of empire, exterminism, class, race, gender, nature, age, sexual orientation, nation, and region are the springboards— though not landing grounds—for the most desirable forms of critical practice that take history . . . seriously. Demystification tries to keep track of the complex dynamics of institutional and other related power structures in order to disclose options and alternatives for transformative praxis; it also attempts to grasp the way in which representational strategies are creative responses to novel circumstances and conditions. In this way, the central role of human agency (always enacted under circumstances not of one's choosing)—be it in the critic, artist, or constituency, and audience—is accented. (105)

An intellectual who would be nothing if not careful, West sees "deadly traps" in demystification, especially those of "reductionism, be it of the sociological, psychological, or historical sort. By reductionism I mean either one-factor analyses (i.e., crude Marxisms, feminisms, racialisms, etc.) that yield a one dimensionalism or a hyper-subtle analytical perspective that loses touch with the specificity of an art work's form and the context of its reception" (106). He writes of the dangerous tightrope (itself an amusing variant on the literary allusion) between "the Scylla of reductionism and the Charybdis of aestheticism."

West's work, as you may have seen, is marked by a conscious integrity; that is, it tries to confront not only its enemies but also its ignorant and fractious friends, of whom there are many. He lays down a challenge to his friends that will not be music to those who are tone-deaf:

> The existential challenge to the new cultural politics of difference can be stated simply: how does one acquire the resources to survive and the cultural capital to thrive as a critic or artist? By cultural capital (Pierre Bourdieu's term), I mean not only the high-quality skills required to engage in critical practices, but more important, the self-confidence, discipline, and perseverance necessary for success without an undue reliance on the mainstream for approval and acceptance. This challenge holds for all prophetic critics, yet it is especially difficult for those of color. (106)

Now this challenge is, in its own way, remarkably similar to that implicitly laid down by Frye to the person who would be a precise critic of literature. However they may differ politically, Frye and West yet are united in their common sense of the superfluidity of values and of the contingent nature of values as attributed to art and culture. Both men recognize an essentially indefinable human process in the creation and the evaluation of art and underscore the difficulty of accumulating the skills needed to understand and evaluate literature and other cultural production without falling into traps. I would venture to say that they both understand, unlike Fanon's native in the throes of decolonization, that certain Mediterranean values (such as democracy and the dignity of the individual), once experienced, become irresistible and cannot be denied except by a brutal repression that is fundamentally like the repression the native once endured at the hands of colonialism and imperialism.

In the extended passages from which I have been quoting, Frye and West both refer to Matthew Arnold, perhaps the principal arbiter of cultural meaning to have written in English, especially as that meaning is transmitted through formal education. Much of what is happening in our profession represents a struggle against the continuing persuasiveness to many people of Arnold's main ideas on education. Arnold, for example, holds a prominent place in William J. Bennett's landmark 1984 study, *To Reclaim a Legacy*. "Expanding on a phrase from Matthew Arnold," Bennett writes, "I would describe the humanities as the best that has been said, thought, written, and otherwise expressed about the human experience."[5] Many of us would probably agree with Richard Poirier's objection to this definition; he has called Bennett's description, in the context of the humanities, "the prose equivalent of a life-support system."[6]

Both Frye and West have come out of a contrary tradition, and while there are differences between them, they are united in an allegiance to pragmatism that we would do well to recognize. West, if not in the essay quoted then in his general work on William James, for which he is best known in philosophic circles, opts for a pragmatic approach to this question of value even as he seeks to avoid the inevitable charge, easily fatal in the bitterly contested ideological world in which we live, that pragmatism is a kind of opportunism. Compare West's words about the new cultural worker and James's at one point in lecture 2 of *Pragmatism*. For James, a pragmatist "turns away from abstraction and insufficiency, from verbal solutions, from bad *a priori* reasons, from fixed principles, closed systems, and pretended absolutes and origins. He turns towards concreteness and adequacy, towards facts, towards action, and towards power."[7]

This echo or resemblance of James in West helps us identify more than the genealogy of the latter's thinking on the matter. It may help us to see that the questioning of the value of literature raised by Stimpson is, in and of itself, absolutely healthy, a sign of vigor and vitality, and not proof of the death of civilization as we know it. For West's purpose is to link the dizzying and sometimes demoralizing cultural ferment of today to that continuing, radical critique of culture, of learning, of books that moves us, steadily or unsteadily, back from today's radicals and dissenters into the agitated history of cultural observation in America. The continuum moves backward through the philosopher of pragmatism, William James, and the fiction writer Gertrude Stein and the poets one can fairly associate with James, such as Stevens and Frost. It moves through and within the work of the greatest of American poets, Whitman, who deliberately summoned young men and women out of libraries and urged them to destroy their teachers; and back through Whitman to the radical philosopher of Concord, Emerson, who declares not only that "we have listened too long to the courtly muses of Europe" but also that "the only objection to *Hamlet* is that it exists."[8] In this gnomic form Emerson bespoke his hostility to works of art, even the greatest works of art, insofar as such works, through their remote, alienating prestige, interfere with our understanding of the rest of life—that is, of life itself. "For it is the inert effort of each thought," Emerson writes, "having formed itself into a circular wave of circumstance,—as, for instance, an empire, rules of an art, a local usage, a religious rite—to heap itself on that ridge, and to solidify, and hem in the life."[9]

In short, the opposition to a static view of culture and cultural activity possesses a heritage that its proponents should acknowledge and recognize as a source of power and encouragement. To make such an acknowledgment and such a recognition entails a more generous view of history than some of us will find possible. The fact that many "dead white men" have not only anticipated objections to hegemonic views of culture but also proposed disruption and heterogeneity as intrinsic to genuine culture will doubtless disappoint some. However, this is the kind of disappointment with which we should attempt to live, the kind that should deepen our confidence in the wisdom of our basic enterprise, properly, and not chauvinistically, understood.

Notes

1. Catharine Stimpson, "Where Is Value Now?" (Presidential panel, annual convention of the Modern Language Association, Chicago, December 1990).

2. Frantz Fanon, *The Wretched of the Earth,* trans. Constance Farrington (New York: Grove, 1968), 43.

3. Northrop Frye, *The Anatomy of Criticism* (Princeton: Princeton University Press, 1957), 20.

4. Cornel West, "The New Cultural Politics of Difference," in *Out There: Marginalization and Contemporary Cultures,* ed. Russell Ferguson, Martha Gever, Trnh T. Minh-ha, and Cornel West (Cambridge: MIT Press, 1990), 93.

5. William J. Bennett, *To Reclaim a Legacy: A Report on the Humanities in Higher Education* (Washington, D.C.: National Endowment for the Humanities, 1984), 3.

6. Richard Poirier, *The Renewal of Literature: Emersonian Reflections* (New York: Random House, 1987), 27.

7. William James, *Pragmatism* (Cambridge: Harvard University Press, 1978), 31.

8. Ralph Waldo Emerson, "The American Scholar," in *The Portable Emerson,* ed. Carl Bode (New York: Penguin, 1981), 70; Ralph Waldo Emerson, *Journals and Miscellaneous Notebooks,* ed. William Gilman et al. (Cambridge: Harvard University Press, 1982), 12:485.

9. Ralph Waldo Emerson, *Essays: First and Second Series* (London: Dutton, 1909), 169.

■ MYRA JEHLEN ■

Literary Criticism at the Edge of the Millennium; or, From Here to History

IN 1986, NOT VERY LONG ago measured under the aspect of the millennium whose end is also only seven years away as I write this, I introduced a collection of essays with an essay of my own that now seems strangely dated.[1] Yet I find its thesis as valid as ever. (In fact, a long portion of that essay constitutes the major part of this one because of its usefulness in laying out some of the issues of the volume as a whole.) The essays for which I wrote the introduction entitled "Beyond Transcendence" all demonstrated the method of "ideological" criticism. The paradoxical phrase, "beyond transcendence," referred both to the state of criticism, where I was implying that ideological criticism had superseded formalism, and to a definition of literature whose most powerful realizations penetrated history rather than escaping it. Art, I wanted to suggest, built its worlds inside the here and now, rather than elsewhere, beyond politics and society.

Now, in 1993, I have just completed another introduction to another collection, this one for the Melville volume in the series of New Century Views. As a group, these essays also understand literary vision as a way of seeing deeply into history, not beyond it. Indeed, if anything, their readings may be more politically informed than those of the first collection; nor is there anything conceptually incompatible between my two introductions. Yet I feel them to be significantly different, the second almost a rejoinder to the first, one of those rejoinders that begins, "I entirely agree, of course; there's just one thing . . ." What the "one thing" may be remains obscure, however, so long as I read the introductions separately; it grows a little more distinct upon reading the introductions together. So after the section reproduced from the first, I'll summarize the second to see how they do and don't come together.

I pick up "Beyond Transcendence" as it begins to survey the history of the concept or theory of ideological criticism. My intention in the essay was to show how this theory evolved toward a present definition newly congenial to literary analysis in its elevation of narrative to a commanding role over reality. [Beginning of section from "Beyond Transcendence."] The initial conception of ideological criticism, however, was mainly the work of Marxists for whom literature was not thus independent. This despite the fact that the term "ideology" had originally signified something like a system of self-defined and transcendent ideas. In the program of the French Revolution's Institut de France, ideology was the generic study of ideas that existed as universals in the realm of reason (rather than of history). Indeed, the savants of the Institut, established in 1795, represented Enlightenment idealism so well that they ran afoul of Napoleon's more immanent need to fortify his regime by restoring a degree of censorship and an established religion. To these reactionary moves, the ideologues, for whom the Revolution meant above all the right to think and speak freely, formed a liberal opposition that championed the embattled ideals of Enlightenment liberalism. Because these ideals were associated with a class, the bourgeoisie, their championship now came to represent a class attitude. Approximately fifty years after the coining of the term "ideology," Marx completed the reversal of its meaning when he denounced, as ideology, the self-serving "world view" of the middle class (which he believed the bourgeoisie had foisted on the proletariat). Ideology now meant "false consciousness," a system of beliefs about the world and one's relation to it that represented the interests of the dominant social class. The explication and exposition of this system were therefore crucial parts of political agitation: to change the world, the insurgents needed to prove that its present order was neither naturally good nor necessary.

Hence Marxist expositions of ideology have been efforts to find ways to expose its misrepresentations and false ideals, to strip away the lie and expose the liar. But this is an ambiguous mission for a literary critic, who thereby becomes, at least positionally, a sort of adversary of the work she or he analyzes. In practice, of course, ideological criticism has seldom been this simplistic and has sought to illuminate rather than merely to expose, to decode rather than debunk. Still, the possibility of reducing literary fictions into historical lies is there in the basic conflict between the notion of "false consciousness" and the root word "art," which, as Stephen Daedalus pointed out, extends into "artifice." In short, there is some basic opposition in intellectual impulse between those who erect imaginary worlds and those who seek to excavate the foundations of this one. As reading invites and may require a suspension of disbelief, criticism implies an appreciation of the writer's power to persuade the reader to that suspension. So long, then, as ideology essentially meant false consciousness, its relationship to reading and criticism—that is, to an engagement with the text that would value precisely its invention—remained problematical; though Marx himself and most Marxist critics understood very well the special value of literary creation.

In part this difficulty in dealing with literature, and with aesthetic issues generally, arose from the fact that Marx modeled his scientific analysis of society on the mechanistic and deterministic science of the nineteenth century. In that image, Marxism intended to discover an objective history ruled by the laws of causality. Ideology needed to be understood for its objective impact in permitting and even fueling the work of these laws, but as a subjectivity it was only an obstacle to be removed: an opiate. This definition of science, however, no longer prevails. In fact, the current definition essentially denies the possibility of objective knowledge. Thus, when the English Marxist Terence Eagleton sought to develop a "science of the text," he did not need to specify that his model was the science of relativity and quantum mechanics, which is neither absolute nor deterministic, on behalf either of the world or of the observer. In the abstract terms in which contemporary scientific ideas enter the general discussion, the change from nineteenth- to twentieth-century scientific models has invited an abrogation of the division between the evaluative, interpretive act and the facts it produces. Much as the dream life of the unconscious has come to be seen as a crucial aspect of consciousness, subjectivity now constitutes an inextricable part of our understanding of reality.

In the evolution of scientific Marxism and its concept of ideology, the Marxists of the Frankfurt Institute of Social Research (founded in 1923) might be described as a sort of interregnum, for they did not directly address the question of scientific models but rather moved to recast Marxism from a science into a social philosophy. In doing so, Max Horkheimer and his colleagues were perhaps reacting to post–World War I disillusionment with scientific authority as well as all totalizing absolutes. At any rate, putting aside the scientific Marxism inherited from the nineteenth century, they disengaged a cultural and philosophical Marxism with its own problems and possibly its own laws. The results of this emancipation were dramatic, though perhaps not fully evident until after World War II. In relation to a concept of ideology, the sense that Marxists were making social and cultural rather than scientific analyses broadened the examination of false consciousness into one of consciousness per se. "Today," Theodor Adorno would write, "ideology means society as appearance." In this formulation, ideology was a terminus of investigation rather than a pass-through to the reality it masked. The logic of this was much greater interest in literary and cultural forms, and in language as such.

Of course, the predecessors of the Frankfurt Marxists would not have denied the significance of language and form. The issue is not whether language matters, but how: how literary style and form participate in meaning. And although there is by no means a clear division between nineteenth- and twentieth-century Marxist views of this question, the wide-ranging debate in the thirties over the ethical and political value of modernism can be seen as expressing a disagreement over the nature of language and its relation to the material world. The most revealing antagonists in this debate are perhaps Georg Lukács and Walter Benjamin. Lukác's hostility to modernism (and in relation to Benjamin, to the experimental theater of Bertolt Brecht, which Benjamin greatly admired) and his endorsement of realism implement a Hegelian understanding of the way the mind engages history by seeking a reconciliation between the material and the ideal. As amended by Marx to make the material primary, this concept becomes still more committed to an external reality that it is the mission of art to illuminate, and not to supplant with its own imaginary world. But reality was at once more elusive and more malleable for Benjamin, who considered Brecht's use of the latest techniques in style and form "progressive" precisely in its experimentation, because that way the theater participated, in the same way as industrial innovation, in the radical reconstruction of history. Implicit in this view is the notion that language is not merely the vehicle, or even only the agent, but part of the material of historical process, more than an account of things, an aspect of the thing itself. In the same vein, Fredric Jameson has shown that Adorno sought through a "negative dialectic" to transform the dialectical method into a way of deconstructing the manifest (positive) content of established ideas in order to reveal the conditions in which they arose, and in which they might have taken other forms.

Thus the greater power these critics ascribe to language imparts more fluidity to the realm of the concrete as well. It is important to recognize that neither Benjamin nor Adorno stresses the subjective over the objective. Their alternative to an unmasking approach is not to remain within the realm of perception. By questioning realism as a literary mode and empirical content as the primary site of artistic meaning, and instead focusing on form via experimentation, both intended to move toward a more direct apprehension of the concrete. The paradox that is today virtually common sense—that the power to name is the power to know, but that conversely knowledge is limited by language—is already implied by the Frankfurt revision of the nature of art, and it represented then as it does now the enhanced reality of both form and its object. For although in the terms of this paradox the concrete is forever inaccessible, it achieves a greater autonomy in the measure of the power that language has to re-create it interpretively. More powerful and more autonomous, the concept of language developed by such ideological critics as Benjamin and Adorno is thus also more modest in defining its relation to the "real" world. On the other hand, in this revision, ideology becomes a newly important, indeed a crucial, category of knowledge, mediating terms—"subjectivity" and "external reality"—that are otherwise irreconcilable. This amounts really to a reversal of the earlier conception: Instead of obscuring reality, ideology now is just what in fact reveals it.

This reversal, whose process is exemplified here in the disagreement between Lukács and Benjamin over Brecht, is by now so widespread that it characterizes as well some more recent revisions of Marx that might be seen as moving in a direction opposite to that of the Frankfurt School, toward a more scientific Marxism. Although Louis Althusser, for instance, stresses the materialist economist Marx over the social historian, he also finds real substance in ideology where Marx saw "an imaginary assemblage . . . a pure dream, empty and vain, constituted by the 'day's residues' from the only full and positive reality, that of the concrete history of concrete material individuals materially producing their existence." For Althusser, this empty and vain negativity has become positive. Ideology is real, albeit "a non-historical reality," by which he means that it is "omnipresent, transhistorical," not composed of any particular content but rather the constant structure of social knowledge. In the same way Freud meant that the unconscious is eternal, Althusser proposes that "ideology is eternal," that is, always there as the "'representation' of the imaginary relationship of individuals to their real conditions of existence." Reflecting a radical transformation in conceptions of reality itself and in the role of language in relation to reality, the crux of the difference between Althusser and Marx lies in the fact that for Althusser the imaginary, like a dream for Freud, is its own reality, indeed, one that is not so much dependent "on the real conditions of existence" as more potently another account of them.

Along this line, the French critic Pierre Macherey (*A Theory of Literary Production*) carried the recognition of the substantive reality of ideological structures one step farther by his suggestion that the literary representation of ideology, in giving it the specific shape of this story or that drama, in turn enables the work to project, by juxtaposition, its own alternative structures. That is, the effort to embody an ideology in literature can expose some of its problematical or controversial aspects—for at some points, the work, becoming incompatible with the ideology it represents, falls silent. Having refused to take ideology's dictation, the work is left at those points without any language at all, and in its silences and ruptures, reveals the limits of the ideology. The literary form outlines ideological form within the work; and although the line is broken and in places disappears altogether, what is important in this context is that it is wholly formal, a

silenced and unconscious context paradoxically embodied in form. Ironically, if the objection to an older mode of ideological criticism was that it
tended to reduce meaning to message, this kind is so conscious of the un-
ceasingly creative meaningfulness of form that it is loath even to specify
meaning, and wants only to point in its direction and to indicate its condition and categories.

To be sure, Macherey continues to define ideology as an interested account intended to rationalize or bolster or win political power, and therefore as suppressive. It "exists because there are certain things which must
not be spoken of," namely the things that literature says by not-saying
them. But in this rendition, the presence of ideology in literature calls for an
even closer and more formal reading. As with the definition of ideology
described above, so too the analytical process has been almost reversed: we
are not to ask whether literature accords with history but are to read in order to discover history. Literature so considered is not about sensuous experience but about understanding and perception; and perception is about
structures, limits, and forms.

Indeed, this ideological formalism may be in danger of generating its
own reductionism. Far from there being any need to argue the unity of
form and content, it now seems rather that critics are in danger of ignoring
the more explicit content of a work as superficial or even as misleading. The
marriage of form and content has made them one, and that one is form. In
the structured literary universe, ideology is basically represented by available forms and their possible permutations, by styles and modes, in other
words the "mechanisms of aesthetic production" that generate the range of
possible ideological meanings. What all this seems to indicate is that writing
is a process of forms interacting and intersecting with forms; and that critical reading, however ideological, is essentially a formal exegesis of which
the elucidation of the content of literature is a byproduct. The work that
presents its conception of the world as natural through the apparent sponta-
neity of character and story conceals that way "its real ideological determinants," which it is the critic's task to reveal. The ideal and apparently
absolute imaginary world orbits an ideological star in a contingent universe.

So the word by which Destutt de Tracy and his eighteenth-century
confreres meant to indicate the study of the mind's eternal universe has
come down to us as in itself a historical system structuring the way the mind
interacts with nature and society to make and continuously remake a relativistic history. From its Enlightenment origin in a vision of infinitely free
ideas, "ideology" has become a term that mediates the finite entities of text
and context, and also of individual author and cultural history; that is, a
term that demarcates the limits of individualism and the imagination.

At the same time, however, the ideological dimension of a work is also the site or the means for at least a degree of imaginative freedom. Indeed, in Macherey's nice concept of literary silences that speak or hint of alternatives otherwise unimaginable, the literary encounter with ideology seems to produce a version of transcendence. Jameson stresses that Marxism offers not only a negative or demystifying but a positive, Utopian hermeneutic: even as an ideological analysis uncovers the political argument couched in apparently natural forms, it also aspires to transcend that opposition between ideology and ideal, and to project a Utopian "collective logic beyond good and evil." Insofar as the literary object of analysis is material, this kind of transcendence is perhaps rather an ultimate penetration to structural first principles. The alternative visions that succeed such a harrowing of the ideological underworld appear as shadows cast forward by history from the edge of this world. Thus they are not freely imagined in the old sense, nor do they construct new worlds. They only reveal that this one is finite and incomplete. Precisely by taking us to the limits of ideology, literature may offer a way to look a little beyond. The ideological analysis of literature would then be particularly perceptive even of literary "transcendence."

The Marxist tradition has been the primary context for the development of the concept of ideology, but both as word and as meaning it has a prior and concurrent independent history. Indeed, probably the best-known analysis of capitalist ideology was done by the sociologist Max Weber, who was not a Marxist, and his analysis implies a concept of ideology at least as powerful as the one projected by Marx. For whereas Marx had denounced ideology as mainly an apologia for the existing social system, Weber described it, in *The Protestant Ethic and the Spirit of Capitalism,* as the positive force that had enabled and inspired the emergence of a new system. In this guise, ideology early acquired a substance of its own, and became not only rationale but reason.

On one level, Marx's and Weber's definitions might be seen as two sides of a coin: rather than opposite definitions, only opposite perspectives. The Marxists, having adopted the perspective of the working class, would then be describing the way ideology deluded workers into quiescence, whereas Weber, looking at things from the standpoint of the middle class, sought to explain how it had acquired and maintained its hegemony. But in fact the two accounts are not entirely complementary, Weber's positive version of ideology going beyond Marx's negative, to add to instrumentality the capacity both for self-generation and for giving rise to history. Elsewhere, Weber explicitly criticized Marxists for what he described as their one-sided materialist conception of causality, which reduced ideology to a creature of economic interests.

He himself placed ideology at the origin of things. If men make history, ideologies make men. His examination of the history of capitalism starts not with the material formation of classes but with the making of individuals by "the influence of those psychological sanctions which, originating in religious belief and the practice of religion, gave a direction to practical conduct and held the individual to it." Although he did not claim that ascetic Protestantism had actually created economic capitalism, he did ascribe to it the power not only to abet but to enact material transformations. Thus for him, ideas, such as the one that hard work and simple living are pleasing to God, have the power to initiate economic activity and even to deter expected behavior. Weber stressed the irrationality of mortal beings accumulating wealth they would never consume, that indeed they intended never to consume, as the measure of the extraordinary power of the "spirit of capitalism" precisely to rationalize.

Weber's Protestant ideology was an autonomous system that "stood at the cradle of the modern economic man." In a formulation that epitomizes his difference with Marx, he found that Protestant asceticism had "created the force which was alone decisive" for the success of "the idea that faithful labour, even at low wages, on the part of those whom life offers no other opportunities, is highly pleasing to God," an idea that flowed from "the conception of this labour as a calling, as the best, often in the last analysis the only means of attaining certainty of grace." This translation of what Marx dubbed the "opiate" of religion that ensured the passivity of the oppressed proletariat, into the proletariat's positive inspiration to work hard and cheap, dramatizes the way, once thought is taken to be not only reproductive but productive, false consciousness itself may acquire a positive meaning.

The Weberian definition of ideology as a historical and cultural agent in its own right proved a congenial basis for the construction of subsequent definitions that also stressed the positive power of ideas. In his *Ideology and Utopia*, Karl Mannheim took Weber's concept to its logical conclusion by totalizing it so that it absorbed the entire universe of historical experience. All that we know, we know through the prism of ideology, he argued, "the thought of all parties in all epochs is of an ideological character." We had better, then, abandon "the vain hope of discovering truth in a form which is independent of an historically and socially determined set of meanings." The analysis of ideology is not an unmasking but a historical explanation of claims and attitudes that only present themselves as transcendent. Where for Weber ideology was a particular perspective among others, for Mannheim it became all-pervasive: "All historical knowledge is relational knowledge, and can only be formulated with reference to the position of the observer." Thus encompassing all social thinking and understanding, the study of ideology is really a "sociology of knowledge"; the analyst's goal is "to understand the narrowness of each individual point of view and the interplay between these distinctive attitudes in the total social process."

Mannheim's concept of ideology permits a material analysis that still realizes the substantiality of ideas and mental forms. But this reconciliation of thought and experience has its cost, or at least it runs a risk that Clifford Geertz dubbed "Mannheim's Paradox." The paradox is simply that if all knowledge is ideological, no analysis can rise above the level of its own ideology: it cannot then be fully analytical. For all his insistence that, despite the relative nature of all evaluation, one must still make moral and political judgments, Mannheim lacked firm ground on which to base such judgments. If all knowledge is relative, how can we even know that we know, let alone commit ourselves to it, as Mannheim continued to urge?

Geertz's conception of ideology might be considered in our context a third stage of non-Marxist descent. He proposed to resolve Mannheim's paradox, which had emerged from the totalization of Weber's ideology, by what amounts to a further totalization. Mannheim had argued that all knowledge was ideological. Geertz in essence suggested that ideological knowledge was its own universe, a universe of meanings that could be autonomously described and understood. He argued that Mannheim's concept of the sociology of knowledge was incompletely evolved, and implied as a next stage the sociology of meaning. "Meaning," as it replaced "knowledge," was a linguistic entity that was fully and stably apprehensible, because its components were wholly contained in the account itself. "Knowledge," on the other hand, was relational, and referred back continuously to a reality it never entirely comprehended and that thus, in any given account of things, always remained insurgent. One could say, in short, that knowledge is history while meaning is text.

This resolution of Mannheim's paradox does recuperate a conceptual terra firma and that way returns the possibility of some certainty (as the ground of judgment and decision) to Mannheim's ideology. But in exchange, Geertz's ideology jettisoned another aspect of the prior definition. To make the object of study "meaning" instead of "knowledge" may enable clear-sighted scholarship, but it does so by removing both the material and the scholar from the miasma of their own ongoing and effective historical involvement. The problem with this solution, even for literary criticism with which it would appear particularly congenial, is that in the process of restoring textual autonomy, it disconnects language from reality. The culminating transformation of ideology from objective lie to autonomous subjectivity (its ultimate rendition as language) has leapt right beyond its object, which was, precisely, the nexus of thought and reality, of literature and history—of knowledge and meaning. Significantly, the contributors to this collection, who represent a wide range of current modes of ideological analysis, seem to value an ideological approach precisely for the complications that trouble Geertz—its explicit political engagement and its aesthetic relativism. Geertz claims as an advantage of his definition that it "defuses ideology," that it removes the irony, as he saw it, of the ideologizing of ideology. Most of the essays gathered here move in the other direction to return to such considerations as the social or ethical value of a work in its time and the nature of the critic's own involvement in that judgment. For these critics, the attraction of an ideological analysis is precisely that it permits interested study of what has reemerged as interested art.

In that sense most contemporary ideological analysis does not deny but embraces its earlier opposition. When Daniel Bell announced the end of ideology about twenty years ago, he applauded this as signaling a new intellectual sophistication that saw through ideology as instrumental thinking meant to bring about "social change." Projections of the future generally sum up the past: published in 1960, *The End of Ideology* culminates the fifties the more tellingly for its blindness to the emerging sixties. But Bell did see clearly that the central purpose of ideology was to connect ideas to social action and that ideology represents not just meaning, but the realization of meaning in the world. In fact, at one remove, Geertz's concept too locates ideology in the world, for it is a system of thought that arises only in periods of historical transition during which social life departs from tradition and the community needs another way to rationalize its behavior. Thus, in effect, he too considers that the crux of this "cultural system" is its organization of social action. In the wake of a consensus, ideology orders the search for a new coherence. Science, he contends, organizes this search disinterestedly; ideology does so with commitment. The ideological critic may not be a political actor himself, in Geertz's terms, but political action is nonetheless his crucial concern; the real issue is whether the critic can ever, as Geertz would like to do, analyze the political nonpolitically. [End of section from "Beyond Transcendence."]

The rhetorical cast of the last sentence makes it evident that my exposition of an evolving notion of ideological criticism had not been agnostic. And I remain as convinced as ever that neither fictions nor their readers transcend politics. Yet, in writing the second introduction (to which I now turn), I began to think that even a non-transcendent literature might relate to its historical subjects in different modes, some more abstract and indefinite than others.

In particular, what prompted me to rethink transcendence was the observation that, as a group, the essays seemed to tacitly posit something about Melville's writing that they did not treat explicitly in their analyses.

Thus, even authors who would have categorically denied that literature could ever escape its times appeared to grant Melville a sort of transhistorical authority that seemed remarkably like what another generation of critics called "greatness" and projected as the content of transcendence. And reflecting its association with a notion of transcendence, this grant of authority came not as a conclusion of the essays but as their starting point or, even earlier, as a basic and unexamined premise.

Richard Chase, writing his preface to the *Melville* volume in the predecessor series *Twentieth Century Views* thirty years before, had been struck by the same observation. He began the preface by noting that, whatever disagreements of interpretation and judgement there were among the essays he had collected, "none of them thinks it necessary to defend [Melville's] greatness."[2] This seemed to Chase entirely natural, a transcendent greatness being for him the definition of a major work. He did not at all deny that this greatness had its political implications. On the contrary, animating his own interest in Melville was the explicit hope that the nineteenth-century author could serve the ailing cause of twentieth-century liberalism.[3] But this historical service would not require Melville to enter history. Chase's notion was that literature and history met in a world beyond history, speaking to one another in the language of universalities, using words like "freedom," "self," "individualism," and "nation," which Chase understood as themselves transcendent.

It would seem unlikely that the authors of the essays in the new collection could share Chase's notion of a "great" Melville. Today the words "freedom," "self," "individual," and "nation" are favorite illustrations of the way a culture falsely naturalizes its basic concepts and conceals their contingencies. In addition, many now argue that, since all we know of reality is a narrative, literary and historical narratives differ in style rather than in kind. When history is a form of literature, literature becomes a form of history; either way the literary imagination is wholly and inextricably engaged with society and politics. In what sense can we then imagine a distinct artistic achievement, art in its own terms? Yet it seemed to me clear, surveying the essays in my collection, that their authors did posit, by assuming it for Melville, just such an achievement. Artistic greatness seemed to have survived its fall from transcendence. Despite sharp criticisms of the way Melville dealt with the issues of his day—some critics found him duplicitous, compromising, confused and even cowardly—his literary standing remained as high as it was for Chase and his colleagues. Melville has remained canonical through the whole period of canon-busting, and to the canon-busters.

That the new readings never reconsider Melville's literary value cannot be because they address other subjects, since literary value—the effectiveness and vitality of a text—is unavoidably a subject in any critical reading. Opinions as to what constitutes literary value may differ widely but the issue is always present. For example, in the rereadings of nineteenth-century sentimental novels that in the seventies and eighties challenged established criteria of value, the argument was never and could never be that literary merit doesn't matter but rather that its evaluation was contingent upon a politicized esthetic that barred women's domestic fiction. Thus by not raising the issue of literary value in relation to their rereadings, the revisionist authors of the essays in the new *Melville* implicitly accede to Melville's established status.

Although I had read most of the essays I was collecting when they first appeared, I had never noticed this aspect of them until setting out to write my second introduction; and noticing it in the course of writing the latter formed the crux of its difference from the earlier. For seeing that, in the current criticism, a sense of Melville's "greatness" at once precedes and survives the most rigorous contextual readings led me to ponder the limits of a method that seven years earlier had appeared particularly penetrating. Of course, I had known then as well that an ideological analysis has its limits, in the sense that all approaches are limited. But I had not thought to mark those limits. Not marking the limits of one's own approach, on the other hand, is a serious flaw, and the graver when one's approach precisely denies the possibility of transcendence. It now occurred to me that I had fallen prey to Mannheim's paradox which, moreover, created still tighter constraints than I had seen. For by insisting that the understanding cannot escape the conditions in which it arises, Mannheim projects an understanding that actually falls short of its conditions. For self-consciousness never wholly comprehends the self; there are always more things in heaven and earth than can be dreamt of in anyone's philosophy.

In other words, the limits of historical understanding are narrower than those of events and experiences—which puts a new gloss on my old title, "Beyond Transcendence." For the point of this title turned on a claim that historical understanding actually exceeded the abstractions and universalities projected by the notion of transcendence. But when one considered the limitations of historical understanding itself, this incompleteness began to seem complementary to the partialities of formalism and of other approaches that claim the transcendence of art. Beyond all these approaches, the literary work retains an artistic value that, to invoke Wittgenstein's distinction, one can show or sense but not say. Obviously, literary works are themselves no more transcendent than any other form of perception. Still, what we call greatness, I suggested in the later introduction, is an exceptional plenitude of vision; while the critical recognition of greatness acknowledges the insufficiency of any reading. The essay writers who posited Melville's greatness without attempting to explain it recognized thus that their historical, cultural, and political explications would not account for all one finds in the works.

Ironically, given its title, "Beyond Transcendence," that essay did not acknowledge insufficiency even as it proposed an ideological criticism as still more encompassing then a purely aesthetic one. It could have acknowledged insufficiency without compromising, indeed strengthening, its historicism. It could have taken the high ground by arguing that literary visions can be said to transcend when they see past their immediate situations; the greatest transcending only from here to history. Having so argued, however, the essay would have come face to face with that transcendence, however partial, and would have had to recognize it as prodigious.

Why this recognition was apparent to me, indeed pressing when I came to write my second introduction, while it didn't arise as an issue when I wrote the first, seems to me an interesting question insofar as the answer may lie less within the evolving theory than outside it, in the context of its evolution. For, in short, the times have changed. They have changed in two opposite ways. On one side, the authority of the intellectual system of ideological analysis has been undermined by the catastrophic collapse of the social system with which it has been historically associated. As we saw earlier, the idea of ideological analysis has its roots in Marxism, and while many Marxist ideas still seem valid and important, Marxism, to put it moderately, has suffered a loss of authority over the last years. On the other side, the key concepts of ideological analysis now seem remarkably uncontroversial: the left and right in the field of academic criticism argue not so much over whether literature is political as over the content of the politics. Thus ideological criticism is beset by radical skepticism while, paradoxically, it is also less fundamentally embattled. Intellectually, this is a very good situation for a theory to inhabit, at once inspiring and permitting a reflexive stance that, precisely, can reveal the limits of the theory itself. And there or rather here, at those limits, ideological criticism reveals itself more imbricated with formalist and aestheticist approaches than was visible earlier. This imbrication seems to me all to the good and its generally obscured conjunctions particularly intriguing areas for critical exploration.

Notes

1. Myra Jehlen, "Introduction: Beyond Transcendence," in *Ideology and Classic American Literature,* ed. Sacvan Bercovitch and Myra Jehlen (New York:

Cambridge University Press, 1986). The section reprinted in this chapter is from pp. 4–14.

2. Richard Chase, ed., *Melville: A Collection of Critical Essays* (Englewood Cliffs, N.J.: Prentice-Hall, 1962), 1.

3. See Richard Chase, *Herman Melville: A Critical Study* (New York: Macmillan, 1949). Chase thought of this book as a direct contribution "to a movement which may be described . . . as the new liberalism" (vii).

II

Rewriting the History of the Aesthetic

"The Tumour of Their Own Hearts"

Relativism, Aesthetics, and the Rhetoric of Demystification

WHEN ONE THINKS about the history of aesthetics, the name Ralph Cudworth does not spring to mind. Of course, as a leading light of the seventeenth-century Cambridge Platonists, Cudworth is known to have had a profound influence on Anthony Ashley Cooper, the third earl of Shaftesbury, whose place in the history of aesthetics is unshakable. But unlike the more rhapsodic and essayistic Shaftesbury, Cudworth was a prolix writer whose erudite and interminable style of philosophizing prevented him from completing his magnum opus, *The True Intellectual System of the Universe,* and also no doubt prevented many eighteenth-century readers from appreciating his ideas. One might accordingly suppose that Cudworth must content himself with entering the history of aesthetics by proxy, through the mediation of Shaftesbury, the assimilated son, who spoke the language that the eighteenth century would understand.[1]

But the truth is that Cudworth's status as an aesthetician or protoaesthetician is impaired not only by the quaintness of his manner of philosophizing, but also because he does not greatly value the beautiful or notably concern himself with its analysis. Paradoxically, this makes him all the more interesting for our purposes. For although I do not seek to enshrine Cudworth in the history of aesthetics, I do wish to use him as an unlikely point of entry for an inquiry into the relationship between, on the one hand, the early modern concern with analyzing the beautiful, and, on the other hand, the current fascination—my own included—with analyzing how philosophical ideas serve political interests.

In contemporary theoretical debates, the notion that the aesthetic is that which gives art its value has tended to give way to the notion that such attribution of value itself serves political interests and therefore needs to be relativized and demystified. But by examining the early modern interplay between aesthetics and ideology—the ways in which seventeenth- and eighteenth-century appeals to the beautiful are manipulated in a complex discursive battle between competing conceptions of moral and epistemological authority—we will be able to see how the aesthetic was relativized and demystified well before it was given the status of the absolute against which other things are made relative. More significantly, we will see how the absolutization of the aesthetic served not to remove it from the hurly-burly of political strife, but rather to transform it into a powerful instrument for demystifying other ideas. This historical narrative, rather than a direct engagement with contemporary theoretical issues, will make up the bulk of the present essay. But contemporary theory fabricates its own historical narratives, and one of my aims is to suggest that theorists can avoid silliness only if they keep at least one eye on the events about which they are theorizing.

Cudworth will prove to be surprisingly helpful in this undertaking, not only because of the way he influenced Shaftesbury, but also because of the way he did not influence Shaftesbury, or more precisely, because of the way his relativization of the aesthetic resulted in problems that Shaftesbury, and the eighteenth century, would solve with an absolutization of the aesthetic. To understand the relationship between Cudworth and Shaftesbury in ideological terms, we will first need to see how Cudworth is reacting to Hobbes. Only then will we be able to see how Shaftesbury is trying to resolve philosophical and ideological difficulties that confronted both Hobbes and Cudworth.

This complex story could probably be told without any reference to the distinction between rationalism and empiricism. But since Cudworth is a Platonist who disparages claims to perceptual knowledge, and since the rise of aesthetics—especially British and Enlightenment aesthetics—is often associated precisely with perception, with corporeality, with the rise of science and with philosophical empiricism, one might be tempted to suppose that Cudworth remains outside of the history of early modern aesthetics precisely because he undervalues the corporeal and the perceptual.[2] One might also be tempted to suppose that the "ideology of the aesthetic" is a corollary of the "ideology of empiricism." These are suppositions that I wish to challenge, both because they distort the history of philosophy and because they distort the relationship between ideas and the ideological uses to which they are put. Thus, we cannot begin to rethink the relationship between aesthetics and ideology unless we first examine more closely the notion that the aesthetic is categorizable with respect to the alleged divide between rationalism and empiricism.

The relationship between Cudworth's conception of the beautiful on the one hand and the British empiricist tradition on the other may be illuminated if we compare Cudworth's views with those of Joseph Addison—a writer whose name comes readily to mind when we think about the rise of aesthetics as an adjunct to the rise of empiricism. Addison—who analyzes the beautiful as an idea in our minds caused by phenomena that it does not resemble—has been seen to embody the new philosophical and scientific attitude toward aesthetics.[3] Of course, in Addison, as in other writers, this affective analysis is applied to our perception of the beauty of nature as well as that of art. Indeed, Addison's analysis of natural beauty as ideas produced in us by things that are not in themselves beautiful may be seen to epitomize this new aesthetic:

> [God] has made so many Objects appear beautiful, that he might render the whole Creation more gay and delightful. . . . Things would make but a poor Appearance to the Eye, if we saw them only in their proper Figures and Motions: And what Reason can we assign for their exciting in us many of those Ideas which are different from any thing that exists in the Objects themselves, (for such are Light and Colours) were it not to add Supernumerary Ornaments to the Universe, and make it more agreeable to the Imagination? We are everywhere entertained with pleasing Show and Apparitions, we discover imaginary Glories in the Heavens, and in the Earth, and see some of this Visionary Beauty poured out upon the whole Creation; but what a rough unsightly Sketch of Nature should we be entertained with, did all her Colouring disappear, and the several Distinctions of Light and Shade vanish? In short, our Souls are at present delightfully lost and bewildered in a pleasing Delusion.[4]

In case it is not sufficiently clear that this account is based on Lockean sensationalism, and specifically on Locke's account of the ideas of secondary qualities, which are "produced by the operation of insensible particles on our senses," Addison goes on explicitly to acknowledge his debt to Locke:[5]

> I have here supposed that my Reader is acquainted with that great Modern Discovery . . . Namely, that Light and Colours, as apprehended by the Imagination, are only Ideas in the Mind, and not Qualities that have any Existence in Matter. . . . [I]f the *English* Reader would see the Notion explained at large, he may find it in

the Eighth Chapter of the Second Book of Mr. *Lock's* Essay on Human Understanding. (3:547)

I have allowed myself momentarily to shift my attention from the rationalist Cudworth to the paradigmatic empiricist critic Addison because the passage just quoted from "The Pleasures of the Imagination," despite its explicit appeal to Locke, has an exact counterpart in Cudworth's *Treatise Concerning Eternal and Immutable Morality:*

> Those corporeal Qualities, which they think to be such Real Things existing in Bodies without them, are for the most part fantastick and imaginary Things, and have no more Reality than the Colours of the Rainbow; and . . . therefore are not absolutely any Thing in themselves, but only relative to Animals. So that they do in a manner mock us, when we conceive of them as Things really existing without us. . . .
>
> Though it was not the Intention of God or Nature to abuse us herein, but a most wise Contrivance thus to beautify and adorn the visible and material World, to add Lustre or Imbellishment to it, that it might have Charms, Relishes, and Allurements in it, to gratify our Appetites; Whereas otherwise really in it self, the whole corporeal World in its naked Hue, is nothing else but a Heap of Dust or Atoms, of several Figures and Magnitudes, variously agitated up and down; so that these Things, which we look upon as such real Things without us, are not properly the Modifications of Bodies themselves, but several Modifications, Passions, and Affections of our own Souls.[6]

As in Addison's account, there is a disjunction between the naked reality of things out there, and the beauty that we perceive—the perception of beauty being caused by the operation of matter that does not resemble the ideas in our minds, but that, through the contrivance of God, is able to engender them.

Since I am not attempting to establish Cudworth's credentials as a proto-aesthetician, the question of his possible influence on Addison does not concern me. (Indeed, *Eternal and Immutable Morality* was not published until 1731, and I have no interest in trying to ascertain whether Addison saw the manuscript before its publication or gleaned its ideas indirectly.[7]) Cudworth's striking prefiguration of Addison's affective analysis of the beautiful serves my purposes by forcing us to hesitate before placing the aesthetic on one side of the conventional empiricist/rationalist dichotomy.[8] For Cudworth has all the defining characteristics of a rationalist: he does not believe that knowledge depends upon the senses, and indeed his analysis of

the beautiful in the passage that we have just examined may be seen to follow Plato and Descartes in demonstrating that what we apprehend through
the senses is either illusory or of secondary value. At the same time, however, Cudworth, without privileging the perceptual or the corporeal, and
certainly without being a Lockean, comes up with the same analysis that is
yielded by Addison's supposedly empiricist aesthetics.

But if we are going to take full advantage of Cudworth as a strangely
revealing locus in the relationship between aesthetics and ideology in early
modern Britain, we need to be aware not only of the way his analysis of the
perception of beauty throws into question the tidy link between the aesthetic and the empirical but also of the extent to which it is written with an
eye looking backward to Hobbes.[9]

Cudworth's central project in the *Eternal and Immutable Morality* is to
argue against moral relativism, that is, against the notion, forcefully articulated by Hobbes, that there is "nothing simply and absolutely" good,
against the notion that "these words of Good, Evill, and Contemptible, are
ever used with relation to the person that useth them: There being nothing
simply and absolutely so."[10] In order to argue against relativism, it was
necessary to argue against Hobbes, and indeed, the relativistic passage from
which I was just quoting is the one from which Cudworth himself quotes
shortly before he analyzes the illusory nature of corporeal beauty (287).

In the paragraph of *Leviathan* following the one from which I just
quoted, Hobbes buttresses his moral relativism by relating the English
words *good* and *evil* to the Latin words *pulchrum* and *turpe*:

> The Latine Tongue has two words, whose significations approach
> to those of Good and Evill; but are not precisely the same; And
> those are *Pulchrum* and *Turpe*. Whereof the former signifies that,
> which by some apparent signes promiseth Good; and the later,
> that, which promiseth Evil. But in our Tongue we have not so
> generall names to expresse them by. But for *Pulchrum*, we say in
> some things, *Fayre;* in others *Beautiful*, or *Handsome*, or *Gallant*, or
> *Hounourable*, or *Comely*, or *Amiable;* and for *Turpe, Foule, De-
> formed, Ugly, Base, Nauseous*, and the like, as the subject shall re-
> quire; All which words, in their proper places signifie nothing
> else, but the *Mine*, or Countenance, that promiseth Good and
> Evil. (121)

In tying the concept of goodness to that of *pulchrum*, Hobbes is rein-
forcing his claim that goodness is merely relative by linking goodness to the
merely beautiful. When Cudworth writes that our perception of the beautiful does not correspond to anything inherent in external objects, but is only
"relative to Animals," serving "to gratify our Appetites," he is speaking in

very Hobbesian terms, and is granting Hobbes's claim that beauty is not absolute. At the same time, however, by linking the illusory nature of the beautiful to the nakedness of the corporeal world, Cudworth would seem to be turning the tables on Hobbes—that is, by attributing the relativity of the beautiful not to the perspectival nature of goodness but to the insubstantiality of phenomenal reality. Whereas Hobbes employs the materialist's technique of explaining values in mechanistic terms, Cudworth is transforming the materialist critique of values into a critique of the relative inadequacy of the material world as a source of knowledge. For although Cudworth is an atomist with respect to the structure of the physical world, he is certainly not a materialist, and his very embrace of Hobbes's devaluation of the beautiful serves his philosophical goal of saving goodness from the clutches of relativism.[11] Cudworth is able to agree with Hobbes not only that beauty is relative, but even that there is no "common Rule of Good and Evil to be taken from the Nature of the Objects themselves" (quoted in Cudworth, 287). But in Cudworth's discourse, Hobbes's words no longer point to the relativity of goodness, but merely to the inadequacy of the physical world as a source of moral knowledge. For Cudworth, goodness is not relative to anyone's perceptual apparatus or appetites; it is absolute, eternal, and immutable.

▪   ▪   ▪

What does all of this logical and rhetorical interplay between the beautiful and the good, and the relative and the absolute, have to do with ideology? First, Hobbes's relativization of goodness is a central element of his argument for submission to the undivided sovereignty of the state. A problem that concerns him throughout *Leviathan* is that "the most frequent pretext of Sedition, and Civil Warre, in Christian Common-wealths" (609) has been men's claim that their actions have been commanded by God and are therefore good, and that the failure to perform those actions would have been evil and would have resulted in damnation.

Virtually no one in seventeenth-century Europe, not even the "atheistical" Hobbes, could directly challenge the view that salvation is humanity's chief concern, and that if there were a conflict between God's commands and those of the state, religion must take precedence. Accordingly Hobbes must link his insistence that the sovereign is to be obeyed with the assurance that political obedience does not endanger one's soul: "This difficulty of obeying both God, and the Civill Soveraign on earth, to those that can distinguish between what is *Necessary* and what is not *Necessary* for their *Reception* into the Kingdome of God, is of no moment. For if

the command of the Civill Soveraign bee such, as it may be obeyed, without the forfeiture of life Eternall; not to obey it is Unjust" (610). Hobbes's
general strategy, accordingly, is to argue that the proper way to fulfill one's
duty to God is precisely by obeying the sovereign, and that the attempts of
the Puritan revolutionaries—Hobbes's Enthusiasts—to construe God's
commandments as requiring rebellious disobedience of secular authority,
are based on a false understanding of God's will. [12]

   In unmasking false understandings of Divine will that serve as pretexts
of sedition, Hobbes engages several theological and philosophical issues,
ranging from principles of exegesis to questions of inspiration and moral
epistemology. He needs, for example, to challenge the Enthusiasts' method
of biblical interpretation on the ground that it is skewed and self-serving:
"They that insist upon single Texts without considering the main Designe,
can derive no thing from them cleerly; but rather by casting atomes of
Scripture, as dust before mens eyes, make every thing more obscure than it
is; an ordinary artifice of those that seek not the truth, but their own advantage" (626). Since the sectarian revolutionaries appealed to private revelation, or inspiration, both to justify their interpretation of Scripture and to
justify claims to direct knowledge of God's wishes, Hobbes's challenge to
the Puritan ideology must address such claims. Although Hobbes's critique
of private revelation includes the charge that sometimes lucky discoveries
are falsely attributed to the personal intervention of God (141), he is more
interested in establishing a general principle whereby claims to prophetic
authority among a sovereign's subjects amount to usurpation:

> For when Christian men, take not their Christian Soveraign, for
> Gods Prophet; they must either take their owne Dreams, for the
> Prophecy they mean to bee governed by, and the tumour of their
> own hearts for the Spirit of God; or they must suffer themselves to
> bee lead by some strange Prince; or by some of their fellow sub-
> jects, that can bewitch them . . . into rebellion, . . . by this
> means destroying all laws, both divine, and humane, [reducing]
> all Order, Government, and Society, to the first Chaos of Vio-
> lence, and Civill warre. (469)

   From the brief exposition that I have offered thus far, it becomes clear
that Hobbes's strategy is to challenge any claims to moral knowledge that
threaten the authority of the sovereign. Seen in this light, Hobbes's moral
relativism may appear to be merely an aspect of a larger ideological pattern.
He attempts to undermine the sectarian radicals not simply by challenging
their arrogation of special cognitive authority based on claims to private
revelation, but by subsuming their moral errors under a broader tendency
of human nature: "Men judge the Goodnesse, or Wickedness of their own,

and of other men's actions, and of the actions of the Common-wealth it self, by their own Passions; and no man calleth Good or Evill, but that which is so in his own eyes, without any regard at all to the Publique Laws" (697). Those who fail to recognize the relativity of their notions of moral goodness may, in the mistaken belief that they are obeying a higher authority than that of the state, promote sedition and civil war.

Once we have placed this use of moral relativism in its ideological context, it may seem something of an overstatement to call Hobbes a relativist. After all, even as he demystifies the moral epistemology of the political subject, he gives normative status to the imperative to obey the sovereign. And he does not treat this imperative as merely relative to the political strategies of royalism, but as rooted in natural law. Moreover, on occasion Hobbes even goes so far as to talk about natural law as eternal and immutable.[13] It is not my purpose, however, to decide whether Hobbes is essentially a relativist, or whether his relativistic pronouncements are reconcilable with his appeals to immutable principles of natural law. I am interested in explaining why Hobbes would have seemed a relativist in Cudworth's eyes, and for this purpose it is necessary to look not merely at Hobbes's statements regarding the self-interestedness of moral perspectives, but also at his conflation of power and moral authority.

From Cudworth's point of view, Hobbes is a relativist not simply because of the way he analyzes the imaginary obligations concocted by fanatical subjects, but also because of the way he talks about moral duty and obedience. For Hobbes, our duty to obey God is grounded in God's omnipotence, specifically, his power to force our obedience: "To those therefore whose Power is irresistible, the dominion of all men adhaereth naturally by their excellence of Power; and consequently it is from that Power that the Kingdome over men, and the Right of affecting men at his pleasure, belongeth Naturally to God Almighty; not as Creator, and Gracious; but as Omnipotent" (397). From the idea that we obey God simply because God has the power to enforce obedience, it is but a short step to the notion that God's commandments are purely a function of his will. But this, ironically, is precisely the position of Hobbes's Enthusiastic enemies.[14] The Enthusiasts' conception of morality is that of a religious duty imposed by God; goodness for them is a matter of actions that are performed in obedience to God's will. For Cudworth, on the other hand, the fact that a moral imperative is willed by God does not, in itself, give the imperative absolute validity. Cudworth's argument is precisely that if moral truths, or other truths, were merely creations of God's will, they would be *relative* to his momentary disposition and hence arbitrary. Truth so conceived is unstable, and appeals to such truths are depicted by Cudworth in terms that would have a powerful political charge for his readers:

Now it is certain, that if the Natures and Essences of all things, as to their being such or such, do depend upon a Will of God that is essentially Arbitrary, there can be no such thing as *Science* or *Demonstration,* nor the Truth of any Mathematical or Metaphysical Proposition be known any otherwise, than by some *Revelation* of the Will of God concerning it, and by a certain Enthusiastic or Fanatick Faith and Perswasion thereupon, that God would have such a thing to be true or false at such a time, or for so long. And so nothing would be true or false *Naturally* but *Positively* only, all Truth and Science being meer Arbitrarious things. (33–34)

Cudworth is not invoking the dangerous Enthusiasts and Fanatics merely to add rhetorical force to his abstract argument regarding the necessity of immutable truths; his abstract argument is showing what is politically dangerous about the Enthusiasts' conception of morality. For if morality were the product of God's will, then it would be unavailable to human reason and accessible only through revelation. And those who sought to appeal to revelation for their own fanatical and seditious purposes would be able to enlist a capricious God to support their designs. In doing so, they would be projecting their own conceptions of truth upon God, treating their own willfulness as God's willfulness. Thus for Cudworth, the rejection of the fanatical conviction that one has private knowledge of God's will is closely tied to the rejection of the belief that the goodness commanded by God is merely a creation of his will. And insofar as a legislative conception of morality is seen as a higher-order relativism, and insofar as Hobbes accepts such a view, Hobbes's attack on sectarian fanaticism would, from Cudworth's perspective, suffer from the same dangerous weakness as the doctrines of the fanatics themselves, namely, a failure to ensure stability by giving morality a transcendent status.

▪ ▪ ▪

Our analysis has brought us to a point at which we can begin to see the extent to which both Hobbes and Cudworth, when viewed in ideological terms, turn out to be on the same side. Indeed, although Cudworth's philosophy presents itself as a pious attempt to refute Hobbes, and hence to defend Christianity against the encroachments of atheism, both the relativism of *Leviathan* and the moral rationalism of the *Eternal and Immutable Morality* are in fact part of the seventeenth-century development of secular ethical theory that would culminate in the great efflorescence of secular ethics in the eighteenth century.[15] In this general movement, Cudworth's reaction to Hobbes may be seen to grow out of earlier deistic positions. Whereas Hobbes attempts to preclude appeals to private revelation by reducing moral epistemology largely to the functioning of individual appetites and desires, the deists attempted to make moral truth so universally accessible as to leave no room for fanatical appeals to private revelation. For seventeenth-century deists, it was enough to claim that the fundamental commandments of God are inscribed in every human heart, that there were no additional commandments that needed to be obeyed for the sake of one's salvation, and hence that no religious group can appeal to revelation or inspiration to justify transgressing the public order.[16] Cudworth and other Cambridge Platonists shared with the deists this reliance on natural as opposed to revealed religion, but they further stipulated that these moral truths had a status that was independent of the divine will. In making morality and justice independent of any legislating will, whether human or divine, Cudworth, for all his anti-atheistic rhetoric, enlarges the gap that Hobbes had opened between religion and morality.

Cudworth does this, I am suggesting, in order to avoid the pitfalls that threaten the political efficacy of the Hobbesian philosophy, and thereby to render stronger and more palatable Hobbes's own attack on sectarian fanaticism. In rejecting both the moral relativism of Hobbes and the legislative conception of divine morality as merely a higher-order relativism, Cudworth is attempting to shore up the argument that would prevent revolutionaries from appealing to private conscience, revelation, or divine will in order to justify disruptions of public order. Thus Cudworth's high road leads to the same ideological destination as did Hobbes's low road, but it does so while attempting to avoid the corrosive and self-defeating implications of Hobbes's relativism.

The high road of eternal and immutable morality, however, while attempting to avoid the pitfalls of Hobbes's low road, is not without pitfalls of its own. One significant difficulty was pointed out by J. A. Passmore: "The laws of the State are neither eternal nor immutable; and whatever morality we take to be eternal and immutable, it will be easy enough to point to occasions on which adherence to it conflicts with the precepts of a particular sovereign."[17] For Hobbes, as Passmore goes on to observe, this made eternal and immutable morality no better than divinely ordained morality: for "unless morality is identical with the decrees of the sovereign, there will be a conflict of moralities within the community, of the kind which leads inevitably to civil disorder and warfare."

Thus although Hobbes and Cudworth are united in rejecting the Enthusiasts' "pretexts of sedition," they employ antithetical theories, each of which is in danger of undermining itself and justifying sedition.[18] Hobbes's alternative to the Enthusiasts' conception of morality would make goodness indistinguishable from the authority of the state, but his project is threatened both by the obvious difficulty that his moral relativism may leave state authority without any convincing transcendent underpinnings, and by Cudworth's charge that to make morality the function of human or divine will is to encourage sedition and chaos. Cudworth's alternative provides a transcendent basis for morality, but raises the danger that transcendent goodness may not be consistent with positive laws promulgated by the state. Thus both alternatives to the Puritan ideology leave an uncomfortable gap between the state's authority to preserve order and the principles that legitimate that authority.

There is at least one other gap in Cudworth's moral epistemology that is of great interest for our purposes. If God's will is not the source of morality, and revelation is not the exclusive medium through which moral knowledge is apprehended, there is a pressing need to be able to characterize that which is good. When we rationally apprehend transcendent goodness, what is it that we are contemplating? What does it look like? What are the criteria by which we recognize it?

In the tradition stemming from Descartes, the criterion for recognizing truth is clarity and distinctness. But Descartes is an uncomfortable authority for Cudworth. For one thing, Descartes ultimately requires God as the guarantor of the truth of that which is clearly and distinctly known; Cudworth—fundamentally opposed as he was to anchoring truth in the will of a divinity—was perhaps the first philosopher to offer a critique of the Cartesian circle.[19] More specifically, Descartes's rationalism had made no attempt to separate moral truth from the divine will, and indeed Descartes had been the most conspicuous recent defender of the view that Cudworth found so uncongenial, namely that *"Moral Good and Evil, Just and Unjust* must needs depend upon the Arbitrary Will of God" (Cudworth 27).[20] But even if Cudworth had been willing to set aside his quarrels with Descartes in order to claim that that which is good is that which is clearly and distinctly known to be good, it is doubtful that such a clarification would have proved terribly illuminating. It has been charged that "all [Cudworth's] position amounts to is the assertion that if something is moral, then it necessarily has the property of morality; in other words, what is moral is moral."[21] And it is hard to imagine that the claim that what is moral is that which is clearly and distinctly known to be moral would have been able to deflect charges that Cudworth's moral rationalism is tautological.

▪   ▪   ▪

I have suggested that Hobbes and Cudworth represent crucial stages in the development of secular ethical theories, a development at least partly attributable to the fact that appeals to revelation as the source of moral knowledge had, at least since the Protestant Reformation, resulted in discord, violent disorder, regicide, and revolution. The broadest and most conspicuous trends in eighteenth-century moral theory would take as their point of departure the anti-Hobbesian appeal to a conception of morality as universally accessible and universally true, and its corollary, the conception of a more benign human nature that recognizes eternal moral truth and acts in accordance with it. In developing the principles of Cudworth (and the other Cambridge Platonists), the eighteenth century would not ignore the two difficulties that I have just outlined, but would attempt to resolve them. And the theoretical strategy by which this would occur would involve a redefinition of the relationship between relativism and aesthetics that, in turn, will throw an interesting light on our inquiry into the relationship between aesthetics and ideology.

Cudworth's first difficulty, it will be recalled, was that eternal moral laws might run afoul of positive law, and hence that the doctrine of eternal and immutable morality might threaten the public order. Put another way, the appeal to transcendent moral principles, while eschewing relativism, ran the danger of relativizing the political subject's obligation to submit to the authority of the state. For seditious people could just as easily appeal to eternal and immutable principles as to the will of God, and as long as positive law might not be in accord with eternal law, there was the danger that seditious behavior would be justified by appeal to the very principles that had been set forth to oppose it.

The second difficulty, involving the criterion for moral knowledge, can also be understood as a paradoxical consequence of the attempt to avoid relativism. For it is precisely because eternal and immutable moral principles are, by definition, good in themselves and not good relative to something else, that it becomes difficult to define those principles in any terms that are not tautological.

The way eighteenth-century moral rationalists (and moral-sense theorists) would try to avoid both of these difficulties was by finding a criterion that allows us to characterize goodness with reference to something other than goodness itself (yet without impairing the status of goodness as eternal and immutable), and that, at the same time, allows us to recognize that a stable and orderly society is good by definition. The phenomenon that would serve this important role was the one that both Hobbes and Cudworth had seen fit to relativize, namely the beautiful. In a word, the eighteenth century would find it useful to absolutize the beautiful and tie it closely to the good:

The case is the same in the mental or moral subjects as in the ordinary bodies or common subjects of sense. The shapes, motions, colours, and proportions of these latter being presented to our eye, there necessarily results a beauty or deformity, according to the different measure, arrangement, and disposition of their several parts. So in behaviour and actions, when presented to our understanding, there must be found, of necessity, an apparent difference, according to the regularity or irregularity of the subjects.[22]

This passage is from Shaftesbury, the writer who most conspicuously marked the transition between Cudworth's conception of eternal and immutable morality and the fully elaborated moral theories of Cudworth's eighteenth-century descendants. We saw in the first section of this essay that Hobbes and Cudworth had, for their separate purposes, treated the beautiful as relative to the eye of the beholder. Hobbes had said that the case of goodness was like that of the beautiful, and hence that moral opinions were no more objectively grounded than aesthetic tastes. Cudworth had accepted the relativity of aesthetic taste, but had attempted to differentiate the good from the beautiful. Shaftesbury goes back to Hobbes to the degree that he ties the fate of the good to that of the beautiful. But instead of having each undermine the objectivity of the other, Shaftesbury has each point to the intrinsic value of the other, thus allowing the perception of beauty to serve as the criterion for the recognition of the good.[23] Moreover, since good actions, in their very beauty, resemble the order of the universe as a whole and the order of society, eternal and immutable morality would seem to be deprived of its subversive potential. For it is beauty itself that links personal morality to social obligation, as Shaftesbury observes: "This . . . is certain, that the admiration and love of order, harmony, and proportion, in whatever kind, is naturally improving to the temper, advantageous to social affection, and highly assistant to virtue, which is itself no other than the love of order and beauty in society" (1:279).

When we include Shaftesbury in the philosophical and ideological narrative that I have been setting forth, it becomes all the more difficult to adhere to the view that the rise of aesthetics is rooted in a rejection of rationalism in favor of the bodily and the perceptual. As Ernst Cassirer correctly observed many years ago, Shaftesbury represents a culmination of Cudworth's moral rationalism, an extension of the argument for the existence and significance of that which is good in itself.[24] The conventional assumption about the nature of the aesthetic is at least partly nurtured by the fact that handbook histories of philosophy tend to distinguish between rationalism and empiricism on the basis of opposing modes of cognition—abstract intellection versus sensory experience. In point of fact, however,

insofar as rationalism is a useful historical category, it is much more concerned with the nature of truth than with the physical or mental faculty that
apprehends it; the crucial thing about Shaftesbury's ethics and his aesthetics
is that their objects are eternal and immutable. It is true that rationalism traditionally, from Plato through Descartes, disparages the senses as a mode
of cognition, but this attitude—as in Descartes's famous ball of wax
example—is premised on the notion that the senses are incapable of apprehending that which is primordial and unchanging. The fact that Shaftesbury and his followers in the eighteenth-century moral sense school make
the universal and the primordial accessible through a kind of sense
perception—or through a process of reflection vaguely analogous to sense
perception—does not mean that rationalism is being rejected in favor of the
corporeal, but rather that rationalism is appropriating a mode of cognition
that it had sometimes excluded from its province.[25]

▪   ▪   ▪

It may seem as if my analysis thus far amounts to no more than an exercise
in intellectual history, and falls far short of any fundamental analysis of the
relationship between aesthetics and ideology. After all, I have not challenged the notion that early aesthetic ideas are amenable to an ideological
analysis whereby they can be shown to be serving sectional interests. All I
have done is to suggest that the aesthetic may not be what it has been taken
to be—namely, an offshoot of empiricist epistemology—and, implicitly,
that its ideological usefulness may have had less to do with bourgeois individualism and capitalism than with the attempt to undermine the religious
justification for overturning the social order.[26] But it is my conviction that
careful historical analyses of the way ideas are put to ideological uses does
have implications for our theoretical understanding of ideological criticism,
and in the specific issue at hand, I would argue that there is more to the role
of the aesthetic than its capacity to serve ideological purposes.[27]

As I have argued elsewhere there are two main problems with ideological criticism as it is generally practiced today.[28] First, it tends to be
premised—if only surreptitiously—on the science/ideology dichotomy
according to which a given symbolic structure is treated as *either* ideological
(and therefore reducible to its legitimating function) *or* as science (and
therefore providing the vantage point from which ideological criticism can
be carried out). Secondly, ideological criticism tends to treat the relationship between a symbolic structure and its ideological use as intrinsic and
transhistorical. That is to say, the symbolic structure is seen to have a natural and unalterable connection to its legitimating function.

Historical analysis serves to undermine these assumptions by showing that symbolic structures change their ideological valences through processes of what I call intellectual co-optation.[29] In this way the ideological use of an idea can be altered or reversed. Historical analysis also shows that nothing is essentially ideological or essentially scientific, but that the designations "science" and "ideology" indicate merely how a given symbolic structure is being perceived or how it is being used.

The relevance of all this to the relationship between aesthetics and ideology starts to become clear when we recognize that in performing an ideological analysis of Hobbes—and the other participants in the ideological battles of the period—we are simultaneously observing how they are carrying out ideological critiques of their enemies. It is Hobbes's view that the revolutionary fanatics were not innocently mistaken when they appealed to the will of God to justify sedition, but that they were willfully mistaken. As we saw in the passage on biblical interpretation quoted above, the Enthusiasts are seen as "those that seek not the truth, but their own advantage," and Hobbes would apply the same sort of critique to other attempts to justify political disobedience. Hobbes's deployment of relativism thus is part of an attempt to demystify what he takes to be the Enthusiasts' self-serving attempts to provide moral and epistemological legitimations for their political appetites. To this degree, it is not merely an epistemological critique that serves Hobbes's political purposes, but it is simultaneously an ideological demystification of Hobbes's enemies. Insofar as we ourselves are examining the political function of Hobbes's abstract philosophical ideas, we are treating as ideology what Hobbes is treating as science.

When we recognize that Hobbes's deployment of relativism is part of an ideological critique of the Enthusiasts, then we can see that his ideological critique itself falls prey to a problem that has always bedeviled critiques that reduce the claims of one's enemies to a function of their material interests—or, in Hobbes's terminology, to their appetites and passions: how do you exempt yourself from the process by means of which you demystify someone else's claims to moral knowledge? How, in a word, do you legitimate the position from which you are demystifying the legitimations of your enemies?

If we take the problems that we earlier presented as epistemological, and recast them in terms of a threat to the effectiveness of ideological critique itself, then we can see that the issues confronting Hobbes are quite similar to the issues confronting ideological criticism today: how can one demystify the ideas that legitimate the social order, without providing an epistemological grounding for the technique that carries out the demystification?

If we try to maintain a double perspective that sees Hobbes's theoretical

difficulties as difficulties also for the self-legitimization of ideological critique, then we can see how the emergence and refinement of the principle of
eternal and immutable morality provides a grounding for the ideological
critique of one's enemies. Seen in this light, Shaftesbury's grafting of the
eternally beautiful onto Cudworth's conception of eternal and immutable
morality is more than a solution to Cudworth's failure to provide a criterion
for recognizing that which is good in itself or his difficulty in bridging the
disjunction between moral duty and social responsibility: it stands as an
eighteenth-century solution to Hobbes's problem of finding an epistemological anchor for his ideological critique. For if one uses eternal and
immutable principles as the vantage point from which one attacks transitory and self-serving attempts to justify evil actions, then one is establishing
for oneself the "science" that will be used to demolish the "ideology" of
one's enemies. The anti-Hobbesian and anti-relativist version of ideological critique that was adopted by the Enlightenment, I would maintain, uses
the concept of rationally (or perceptually) apprehensible goodness and
beauty as a touchstone for the rejection of narrow and self-serving supersti-
tion and fanaticism, and this broad cultural movement may be seen as an
extension of Cudworth's ostensibly quaint and esoteric reaction to Hobbes.

But insofar as it attempts to provide a solid underpinning for ideological critique, the aestheticized conceptions of that which is good in itself need
not serve steadfastly as a defense of the status quo. Just as the same symbolic
structure can perform a legitimating function and carry out an ideological
critique of others' legitimations, a symbolic structure that in one context
attacks the fanaticism that threatens social stability from below can in another context attack the legitimations of those in authority. In the French
Enlightenment—where claims to special knowledge of the divine will were
associated less with the threat of sectarianism and sedition than with what
was perceived as the entrenched theocratic despotism of the Ancien
Régime—the accessibility of the true and immutable (and, following
Shaftesbury, beautiful) principles of morality could be used to attack
tyranny.

Such a transformation in the ideological and counterideological potency of aestheticized true and immutable morality occurs in Montesquieu's *Lettres persanes*.[30] This celebrated combination of epistolary fiction
and philosophical epistles culminates in a rebellion of wives in Usbek's
seraglio back in Persia. The rebellion has been sparked by Roxane, who justifies herself by using the very language of republicanism that Usbek himself, in his role as philosopher, had employed earlier in the book. This
republicanism, in turn, is premised on a moral psychology according to
which citizens are capable of acting virtuously without being constrained to
do so by a higher political authority. In the fable of the Troglodytes, the

man who is appointed king of the previously autonomous people laments that, in giving up their political freedom, the Troglodytes are giving up their moral autonomy: "Not having a ruler, you have to be virtuous in spite of your selves: otherwise you would not be able to survive, and would fall into the miseries of your ancestors. But this yoke weighs too heavily upon you; you prefer to submit yourselves to a prince and to obey his laws, which will be less strict than your own morality" (no. 14).[31] To presuppose that one can be a virtuous citizen without being guided or constrained by institutions requires not only that goodness can be achieved without being coerced, but that moral knowledge can be obtained independently of the dictates of positive law. But this is not enough. It is important for Montesquieu, as it had been for Cudworth and Shaftesbury, to keep this moral knowledge independent of divine commands. For in the seraglio, and, indeed, throughout the *Lettres persanes,* appeals to revelation are used to legitimate narrow superstitions, tyranny, and bigotry; true moral knowledge resides in the eternal and immutable principles of goodness, principles that transcend the divine will:

> Justice is a relationship of fitness which actually exists between two things. This relationship is always the same, no matter who contemplates it, whether it be God, or an angel, or, finally, a man. . . . Thus, even if there were no God, we would still be obliged to love justice, obliged, that is, to try to resemble this being of whom we have so noble a conception, and who, if he existed, would necessarily be just. Even if we were free of the yoke of religion, we would still be obliged to submit to that of equity. (no. 83)

To the extent that this view of justice is recognizable as a relationship of fitness (*rapport de convenance*), it is part of what I have called the aestheticization of Cudworth's conception of morality. Justice is eternal and immutable, it transcends God's will, and it is recognized aesthetically, by dint of its harmonious structure. The deployment of this aestheticized conception of absolute justice as a weapon against political structures that legitimate themselves—as does Usbek's regime in the seraglio—by appeal to the dictates of revealed religion marks a pivotal moment at which the aesthetic takes its role in the ideological critique of established authority.

Hobbes was right to fear the consequences of detaching morality from positive law and sovereign authority. For if one can claim to have moral knowledge that is independent of positive law, then, potentially, one can claim to have moral knowledge that is subversive of positive law. Cudworth's attempt to use the eternal and immutable truths of morality to provide a stronger foundation for social order than Hobbes had been able to provide with his moral relativism thus gives way to the demystification of political authority's attempt to legitimate itself. This occurs not because of the weakness of Cudworth's arguments, and not because the eternal and immutable truth, or aesthetic harmony, is intrinsically subversive, but because moral epistemology, and aesthetics, and all the other weapons in the arsenal of ideas can change their ideological valences: they can stop being the object of ideological analysis, and can become the epistemological grounding of ideological analysis. Ideological critique, at least as far back as Hobbes, undertakes to show that what purports to be good actually operates in the service of interests. What Cudworth adds to the rhetoric of demystification is the claim that one speaks from the perspective of that which is good in itself. And with Shaftesbury and his followers, the aesthetic becomes the banner that identifies the armies fighting on the side of the eternally good.

To the extent that the appeal to the apprehensibility of that which is good and beautiful in itself takes on its historical role as an enabling principle of ideological analysis, and to the extent that my analysis of the rhetoric and logic of this development attempts to uncover the ideological dimension to the historical rise of aesthetics, it might seem as if I have been engaging in a highly paradoxical enterprise. For on the one hand, I may seem to have "unmasked" aesthetics by showing how it was used to serve interests, while on the other hand the unmasking may seem to deprive the very enterprise of ideological criticism of its potency by demystifying the principles on which it is grounded. Hence, if my critique is cogent, it might seem, by dint of its very success, to undermine itself.

To ears accustomed to the rhythms of contemporary theory, this paradoxical formulation might have a soothingly familiar ring to it. But in fact, once we recall that we have dispensed with the science/ideology dichotomy, the paradox dissolves. For the fact that the aesthetic came to serve a particular function in the development of ideological analysis, and the fact that this function is revealed through ideological analysis itself, does not necessarily undo the aesthetic as a grounding for such analysis, or even as a way of valorizing the beautiful. For to see that a symbolic structure emerged in a specific historical situation to serve a specific ideological role does not necessarily deprive it of its cogency or intellectual potency.

Indeed, in the context of contemporary theoretical discourse, the truly paradoxical position is the one occupied by those who, like Hobbes, attempt to carry out the critique of the epistemological claims of others while at the same time grounding their analyses in relativistic theories. On the other hand, Shaftesbury's solution to the self-defeating or self-refuting positions of Hobbes and Cudworth is one that, for all its historical embeddedness, may continue to hold us in thrall. It may be, in a word, that our own demystifications actually rely, however surreptitiously, upon the power of the aesthetic. It may also be that we, like Montesquieu, will find it useful to embrace the aesthetic while putting it to our own uses. For we may ultimately decide that the reason we undertake ideological analyses of the symbolic structures that make up the fabric of our history is that we are motivated by principles that we find beautiful and valuable in themselves. And we may ultimately wish not to suppress this fact as sentimental and embarrassing, but to theorize these principles and make them an explicit part of our arguments.

Notes

1. Cf. Ernst Cassirer, *The Platonic Renaissance in England,* trans. James P. Pettegrove (New York: Gordian Press, 1970), 159–160: "Repetitions and excursions and demonstrations and polemical digressions pile up higher and higher as the book [Cudworth's *True Intellectual System*] goes on. By adopting this manner of writing the Cambridge School had, so to speak, sealed its literary fate; it had shut itself up in the scholar's study. . . . That it did not remain in this isolation, but, though rather late, rejoined and gave a certain direction to the intellectual life of the world at large—this the Cambridge School owes to the one great writer who took sides with it, and defended its central convictions with all the splendour of his poetic and rhetorical diction. It is principally Shaftesbury who saves the Cambridge School from the fate of a learned curiosity."

2. For an example of the general attitude toward science and Enlightenment aesthetics, see Jacques Chouillet, *L'Esthétique des Lumières* (Paris: Presses Universitaires de France, 1974), 6: "Il n'existe, dans l'esprit des Lumières, aucun domaine qui échappe à la réflexion scientifique, pas même celui des données sensorielles, jusqu'ici réservé aux poètes, aux musiciens et aux peintres."

3. Cf. Lee Andrew Elioseff, *The Cultural Milieu of Addison's Literary Criticism* (Austin: University of Texas Press, 1963), 146: "Just as the natural philosophy is capable of discovering efficient causes only, so the degree of naturalness in art, or faithfulness of representation, can be discovered only through a study of the affective workings of the art upon the observer."

4. Joseph Addison, *Spectator,* ed. Donald F. Bond (Oxford: Oxford University Press, 1965), 3:546.

5. John Locke, *Essay Concerning Human Understanding,* ed. John Yolton, 2 vols. (London: Everyman, 1964), 2.4.13.

6. Ralph Cudworth, *Treatise Concerning Eternal and Immutable Morality* (London, 1731), 294–296. Further references in the text are to this edition.

7. Cudworth's daughter, Lady Masham, who diligently defended her father's philosophical reputation, as well as his Christian orthodoxy, by means of epistolary intercessions with leading critics of his work, is also known to have been generous in making his manuscripts posthumously available to Locke and several other intellectual luminaries.

8. It may also move us to question the usefulness of the dichotomy itself, but that project lies outside the parameters of this essay.

9. John Tulloch wrote of Cudworth's relationship to Hobbes: "He [Cudworth] is the reactionary creation of [Hobbes], in the shadow of whose speculations all his own live and move. If the *De Cive* and *Leviathan* had never been written, neither, probably, would have *The True Intellectual System of the Universe* nor the treatise on *Immutable Morality*" (John Tulloch, *Rational Theology and Christian Philosophy in England in the Seventeenth Century*, 2 vols. [Edinburgh, 1872], 2:293). There are no doubt whole libraries of seventeenth- and eighteenth-century works about which the same could be said.

10. Thomas Hobbes, *Leviathan*, ed. C. B. Macpherson (Harmondsworth: Penguin, 1968), 121. Further references in the text are to this edition.

11. Elsewhere in the *Eternal and Immutable Morality*, Cudworth begins to talk about beauty as relational and as apprehended by the intellect. But he declines to press the point, "because many will be ready to say here, that Beauty is nothing but a fancy neither, and therefore cannot argue any reality in these Schetical things" (161). Cf. Ralph Cudworth, *The True Intellectual System of the Universe* (London, 1668), 881, where Cudworth employs the plenitude theodicy that justifies divine providence in creating the beautiful variety of the universe.

12. See Hobbes, 612: "The laws of God . . . are none but the Laws of Nature, whereof the principall is . . . a commandement to Obey our Civill Soveraigns."

13. See Hobbes, 323–324. See also Thomas Hobbes, *De Cive: The English Version*, ed. Howard Warrender (Oxford: Clarendon Press, 1983), chap. 3, sec. 29. The notion of immutable and eternal truth as prior to God's will had been introduced into Anglican doctrine by Richard Hooker. On the growth of English rationalism and its antagonism to nominalistic conceptions of morality, I have been aided by Frederick Beiser's forthcoming *Faith in Reason: The Defense of Reason in the Early English Enlightenment* (Princeton: Princeton University Press) which Professor Beiser has kindly shown me in manuscript.

14. Cf. Beiser, *Faith in Reason*, chap. 4, on "The Birth of Rational Theology and the End of the Protestant Tradition": "What, indeed, was the God of Hobbes but the God of Calvin spelled in materialist terms? It is in just this respect that it becomes impossible to separate the Cambridge Platonists' reaction against Calvin from their reaction against Hobbes."

15. The first and only part of Cudworth's unfinished magnum opus, *The True Intellectual System of the Universe*, has as its subtitle, *Wherein All the Reason and Philosophy of Atheism Is Confuted; and Its Impossibility Demonstrated*.

16. On the ideological uses of deism see chapter 2 of Oscar Kenshur, *Dilemmas of Enlightenment: Studies in the Rhetoric and Logic of Ideology* (Berkeley: University of California Press, 1993).

17. J. A. Passmore, *Ralph Cudworth: An Interpretation* (Cambridge: Cambridge University Press, 1951), 45.

18. Perez Zagorin, "Cudworth and Hobbes on Is and Ought," in *Philosophy, Science, and Religion in England, 1640–1700*, ed. Richard Kroll, Richard

Ashcraft, and Perez Zagorin (Cambridge: Cambridge University Press, 1991), 128–148. In stressing a shared concern with the danger of sectarian sedition—a concern that connects Cudworth to Hobbes and, as will be seen later in my analysis, to Shaftesbury as well—I am pointing to an ideological regularity that underlies not only differences in moral and aesthetic theory, but also differences in attitudes toward political sovereignty. Thus those who opposed Hobbes's materialism and moral relativism were likely also to oppose his defense of royal absolutism, and might well wish to accord at least some degree of sovereignty or autonomy to Parliament or to the Church of England. A more thorough and full-bodied analysis of the ideological dimensions of aesthetic and moral theory would have to include abstract theories of sovereignty and concrete party politics, and would have to consider whether, in given cases, the appeal to immutable morality serves as a counterpoise to royal authority that at the same time attempts to avoid the implication that it is courting sedition. For a close analysis of a complex attempt to use moral rationalism to attack the exercise of royal and ecclesiastical authority (in France), while at the same time avoiding the charge of sedition, see chapter 3 of my *Dilemmas of Enlightenment,* on Pierre Bayle's *Commentaire philosophique.*

19. Passmore, *Ralph Cudworth,* 9.

20. For Cudworth's extended discussion of the moral theory of "that ingenious Philosopher Renatus Des Cartes," see Cudworth, *Eternal and Immutable Morality,* 27–32.

21. Zagorin, "Cudworth and Hobbes," 132. Zagorin credits John Tulloch with first raising the charge of tautology. Although I believe that Zagorin gives the wrong page reference, Tulloch may be interpreted as raising such a critique elsewhere in his text. (See Tulloch, *Rational Theology,* 2:285.)

22. Anthony Ashley Cooper, third earl of Shaftesbury, *Characteristics of Men, Manners, Opinions, Times,* ed. John M. Robertson (Indianapolis: Bobbs-Merrill, 1964), 1:251. Further references in the text are to this edition.

23. This mechanism is, of course, a Platonic one, but if we content ourselves with the internalist habit of attributing a conjunction of ideas to historical precedent or to the workings of a philosophical tradition, then we might have difficulty explaining why the Cambridge Platonist Cudworth, in the way that we have been examining, saw fit to dislodge the beautiful from its lofty Platonic perch, and why it was so important for Shaftesbury to restore it.

24. Cassirer, *Platonic Renaissance,* 159–198.

25. Barbara Stafford has recently demonstrated the extent to which aesthetic ideas and a wide range of representational practices in the Enlightenment were informed by rationalistic philosophy. Barbara Maria Stafford, *Body Criticism: Imaging the Unseen in Enlightenment Art and Medicine* (Cambridge: MIT Press, 1991).

26. On bourgeois individualism and capitalism, see Terry Eagleton, *The Ideology of the Aesthetic* (London: Basil Blackwell, 1990), 1–3.

27. For an extended attempt to show the interrelationship between historical analysis and the theory of ideology, see Kenshur, *Dilemmas of Enlightenment.*

28. Ibid., chap. 1.

29. Ibid.

30. Baron de Charles Louis de Secondat Montesquieu, *Lettres persanes,* in *Oeuvres complètes,* ed. Roger Callois, 2 vols. (Paris: Pléiade, 1949).

31. In citing Montesquieu, I give the number of the letter rather than the page. Translations are my own.

■ MARY POOVEY ■

Aesthetics and Political Economy in the Eighteenth Century

The Place of Gender in the Social Constitution of Knowledge

IN HER 1988 INTERROGATION of literary-critical business-as-usual, Barbara Herrnstein Smith invokes an opposition with considerable currency in contemporary academic circles.

> On the one hand there is the discourse of economic theory: money, commerce, technology, industry, production and consumption, workers and consumers; on the other hand, there is the discourse of aesthetic axiology: culture, art, genius, creation and appreciation, artists and connoisseurs. In the first discourse, events are explained in terms of calculation, preferences, costs, benefits, profits, prices, and utility. In the second, events are explained—or, rather (and this distinction/opposition is as crucial as any of the others), "justified"—in terms of inspiration, discrimination, taste (good taste, bad taste, no taste), the test of time, intrinsic value, and transcendent value.[1]

Smith mobilizes this familiar opposition for two related reasons. First, like many other liberal-pluralist literary critics, Smith wants to underscore the ideological dimensions of "aesthetic axiology." The sudden proliferation of graphical markers in the last sentence of this passage—the dashes, parentheses, solidus, and scare quotes—signals Smith's conviction that the claims made by aesthetics are ideological, in the sense of being rationalizations, if not downright lies. Second, again like other pluralists, Smith wants to demonstrate that the opposition between "economic theory" and "aesthetic axiology" is actually an effect *of* aesthetic ideology. Smith argues that aesthetic value is not different in kind from economic value but the "product of the dynamics of an economic system," which acquires its apparent autonomy by denying its own conditions of possibility. This affiliation explains the tendency of the two discourses to "drift toward each other" and mandates that practitioners of each constantly reinforce their separation.[2] It also suggests that what Smith calls the "double discourse of value" could be demystified if literary critics exposed in the false consolations of aesthetics the hard truths of the market.[3]

While I agree with Smith's central point that the institutionalized opposition between economic theory and aesthetics is the effect of an ideological maneuver, not an accurate reflection of two discrete kinds of objects (or knowledge), I disagree with the suggestion that the perpetrator of this ruse was exclusively—or even primarily—"aesthetic axiology." The implication of Smith's argument is that economic "dynamics" are real, even if economic theory sometimes fails to capture those dynamics accurately. In contrast to economic explanations, aesthetic axiology generates "justifications" about a realm that is not real, both in the sense that it is not—as its defenders claim—autonomous, and in the sense that its "truths" are merely rationalizations. The bias toward economics implicit in Smith's argument reflects in part her own institutional position as a (self-consciously irreverent) professor of literature. Partly, however, it reflects the bias of her chosen argumentative mode. Arguing philosophically rather than historically, Smith tends to repeat the discursive division and reification she also criticizes. A properly historical analysis would uncover not some truth of economics behind the self-justifications of aesthetics but the process by which the appearance of autonomous realms was generated from what was actually a continuum of human activity. Such an analysis would also reveal, alongside aestheticians' disavowal of the economic dimension of their work, economists' dependence upon and erasure of an aesthetic component in their theory.

This essay is intended as a contribution to such a history. In it, I have two purposes. First, I want to complicate the assumption of many literary critics that economic theory is the repressed truth of aesthetics by demonstrating that the reverse is also true. Second, I want to show that the social constitution of knowledge to which this discursive split contributed also performed ideological work apparently unrelated to aesthetics and economics. This ideological work involves the enforcement of a set of truisms about gender. I conclude this essay with Mary Wollstonecraft because she was the first to recognize that one of the devastating effects of the modern constitution of knowledge was the cultural denigration of women *alongside* (and as part of) the valoration of aesthetic beauty.

■ ■ ■

In 1776, Adam Smith offered what many considered to be the conclusive contribution to a debate that had preoccupied British philosophers for the entire eighteenth century. This debate concerned the relationship between commerce or wealth and what contemporaries called virtue. The central question in this debate was whether the economic activity that had accelerated dramatically after 1688 was compatible with good citizenship and moral rectitude. This question became more pressing in the course of the eighteenth century because economic activity increasingly involved mobile property (like capital and credit) rather than real estate.[4] Smith's solution to this question drew upon four principles, which he presented as "laws" of human nature and the market. These principles can be summarized as follows: (1) money, as a universal equivalent, can be substituted for any other object of desire; therefore, (2) the universal desire of all individuals is for (monetary) advantage or gain; (3) monetary exchanges are politically neutral; and therefore, (4) free trade is conducive to personal liberty.[5] These principles yoked individual interest to national prosperity by reducing "interest" to the single desire for economic improvement, by arguing that overall production is automatically generated by aggregate demand, and by disciplining the individual desire for gain by the twin mechanisms of an external, invisible "hand" and an internal differentiation within desire that separates wasteful "luxury" spending from productive saving. In short, Smith reconciled commerce and virtue by presenting all individuals as structural equivalents who conduct self-serving transactions in a world providentially arranged to make even competition serve the common good. Not unexpectedly, this solution was less an exact description of the real society in which Smith lived than a creative reworking of history and theory in the terms available to Smith in 1776.[6] In the 1770s, and especially for a Scotsman, the terms considered appropriate to the problem of commerce and virtue came from the discourse of which Adam Smith was a university professor—moral philosophy.

It is important to return Smith's *Wealth of Nations* to the discourse from which political economy emerged because doing so restores to what would eventually become the "science" of economics its foundational status as a subset of ethics. It also realigns political economy with the discourse from which it was only imperfectly differentiated in the course of the eighteenth century—aesthetics. In what follows I will be making a generic argument about this consubstantiality. I will argue that the generic continuity of political economy and aesthetics underwrites the persistence in one discourse of concerns and metaphors that increasingly seemed to belong to the other. Because political economy and aesthetics were once part of the same discourse, in other words, and because their separation was never complete, each discourse continued to haunt the other in the form of vestigial traces. Indeed, even once they were consolidated as generically discrete, each discourse continues to make visible issues and formulations that are still active but no longer definitive in what was once its other half.[7]

Moral philosophy has its own complex history, of course, which includes its originary consubstantiality with natural philosophy in the seventeenth century and the gradual disarticulation in the eighteenth century.[8] The traces of this common origin linger in the eighteenth-century discipline as it was institutionalized especially in Scottish universities. They can be identified both in moral philosophy's claim to provide a comprehensive, Newtonian science of society and human nature and in the heterogeneous range of subjects the discipline encompassed. Alongside economic processes, moral philosophers like Adam Ferguson, Francis Hutcheson, David Hume, and Adam Smith addressed social issues, marriage and family relations, religion, international relations, elementary jurisprudence, primitive customs, ethics, aesthetics, the principles of government, and the history of institutions.[9] The relationship between commerce and virtue was especially prominent in this social science because for Scotsmen struggling with the 1707 Union, the challenge was to partake of England's commercial buoyancy without succumbing to excesses like the South Sea Bubble. With the Highlanders on one side, reminding them of the "barbarism" of feudal society, and London's "stockjobbers" on the other, incarnating modern, conscienceless greed, Scottish moralists sought to discover "laws" that would legitimize commerce without opening the floodgates to abuse.[10]

For my purposes, the most important feature of the various solutions advanced by moral philosophers to reconcile virtue and commerce is their common recourse to what we would call an aesthetic vocabulary. Working from the philosophical essays of Anthony Ashley Cooper, third earl of Shaftesbury, Scottish moral philosophers developed two models capable of providing self-interested (implicitly commercial) activity with an ethical base, both of which incarnated aesthetic principles. The first of these emphasized proportionality or "fit." The second formulation proposed a "disinterested" relationship between the spectator and worldly objects. As we will see, these two formulations were implicitly at odds with one another, and the second was implicitly antithetical to commercial growth. While their dissonance was eventually emphasized in the disciplinary breakup of moral philosophy, however, for the first half of the century these two formulations coexisted in an unstable compound whose theoretical volatility Adam Smith was fully to exploit.

The notion of proportionality or fit as it was developed by Shaftesbury applied both to the harmony of parts within any given system or object and to the correspondence between the human spectator and the outside world. "Taste" or "sense" is the faculty that links the two, and that thereby enables an individual to align his actions to the orderly beauty of the world. Because Providence was assumed to preside over both the world and the individual, virtue and pleasure were thought naturally to follow from perceiving and reproducing God's harmony. "Thus the wisdom of what rules, and is first and chief in Nature," Shaftesbury proclaims, "has made it to be according to the private interest and good of every one to work towards the general good. . . . So that virtue, which of all excellences and beauties is the chief and most amiable . . . is found equally a happiness and good to each creature in particular, and is that by which alone man can be happy, and without which he must be miserable."[11] In response to Bernard Mandeville's assault on Shaftesbury's optimism, Francis Hutcheson, Shaftesbury's disciple and Adam Smith's teacher, reiterated this argument about the harmonious relationship between virtue and self-interest in 1725. "Self-love is really as necessary to the good of the whole as benevolence; as that attraction which causes the cohesion of the part, is as necessary to the regular state of the whole as gravitation."[12]

The notion of "disinterestedness" originated in Shaftesbury's distinction between actions motivated by an agent's concern for his own well-being and a noninstrumental attitude—that is, a stance concerned neither with consequences nor with actions. "Disinterestedness" in Shaftesbury's work involves "a mode of attention and concern" that renders the virtuous man a spectator and the object, whether natural or made, the self-sufficient end of the contemplative gaze.[13] Disinterestedness therefore preserves virtue in the individual at the same time that it emphasizes the autonomy and noninstrumental nature of the observed object. In so doing, at least according to Joseph Addison, the disinterested gaze augments the pleasure that the "Man of a Polite Imagination" derives from the world. In his *Spectator* essays on the imagination and art, Addison characterized the "Man of a Polite Imagination" as feeling "a greater Satisfaction in the Prospect of Fields and Meadows, than another does in the Possession." As Addison's next sentence suggests, the desire to possess, which is the motor of commerce, does not wholly disappear from aesthetic contemplation; it simply undergoes the sea change of metaphor. Here is Addison again: "It [aesthetic contemplation] gives him, indeed, a kind of Property in every thing he sees, and makes the most rude uncultivated Parts of Nature administer to his Pleasures."[14]

Addison's elaboration of aesthetic contemplation functioned to admit into the behavior that Shaftesbury associated specifically with leisured gentlemen men of a more middling rank—men for whom possession would have been linked to commerce, not inherited property. In so doing, it is part of the series of rhetorical and institutional moves by which men of the middle class (and often from the geographical "fringes") sought to rival aristocratic prerogative by claiming a superior social role as moral conscience for the nation.[15] In 1747, this claim was given institutional expression at Trinity College, Dublin. In meetings of "the Club," a young Irishman worked out many of the problems that had long occupied moral philosophers not in philosophical or "scientific" language but in terms derived from the "more refin'd elegant and usefull parts of Literature." In debate, Edmund Burke specifically announced the superiority of poetry to philosophy; in the process, he further elaborated the difference between what was gradually beginning to appear as two different kinds of knowledge. Here is a summary of Burke's speech:

> That the provinces of Phill: & poetry are so different that they can never coincide, that Phil: to gain its ends addresses to the understanding, poetry to the imagination wch by pleasing it finds a nearer WAY to the heart, that the coldness of Philosophy hurts the imagination & taking away as much of its power must consequently lessen its effect, & so prejudice it. That such is the consequence of putting a rider on Pegasus that will prune his wings & incapacitate him from rising from the ground.[16]

When Burke finally published his *Enquiry into . . . the Sublime and Beautiful* in 1757, he specifically opposed these "speculations, upon the humbler field of the imagination" to the "severer sciences."[17] In his 1761 *Elements of Criticism,* Henry Home, Lord Kames, repeated this distinction when he characterized his typology of the "fine arts" by reference to the opposition between pleasure and utility. "The fine arts are intended to entertain us, by making pleasant impressions; and, by that circumstance, are distinguished from the useful arts," Kames wrote.[18] While such protodisciplinary differentiations generally emphasized the object each "science" took for its analysis, the distinction was also sometimes made in terms of the relationship the subject established to the object. Whereas aesthetic contemplation was increasingly figured according to Shaftesbury's model of "disinterestedness," political economy dealt with the individual's acquisitive relation to the world, and, by extension, to the use or end that objects, once possessed, were made to serve.[19]

What eventually became a disciplinary split between aesthetics and political economy was therefore initiated partly by prizing apart the two models with which Shaftesbury had figured the relationship between individual interest (or commerce) and social good (or virtue). It is also important to note, however, that neither the disciplinary split nor the intellectual division of labor that underwrote it was formalized before the end of the century. We see this in the fact that theorists of both discourses continued to deploy the same vocabulary, even when they intended to reinforce the difference between the two enterprises. Thus Edmund Burke insisted that, even though his disquisition on "taste" was not one of the "severer sciences," it nevertheless uncovered inherent "laws," just as Adam Smith claimed to discover the "laws" of the economy.[20] We also see the persistence of common interests in the specifically *causal* formulations of the relationship between aesthetic contemplation and commercial success offered in the 1750s and 1760s. Lord Kames suggested in 1761, for example, that "to prevent or retard . . . fatal corruption, the genius of an Alfred cannot devise any means more efficacious, than the venting opulence upon Fine Arts; riches employ'd, instead of encouraging vice, will excite virtue."[21] David Hume similarly argued that "refinement in the arts" goes hand-in-hand with individual "industry" and national economic productivity: "The encrease and consumption of all the commodities, which serve to the ornament and pleasure of life, are advantageous to society; because, at the same time that they multiply those innocent gratifications to individuals, they are a kind of *storehouse* of labour, which, in the exigencies of state, may be turned to the public service."[22]

The dynamic interrelation of issues and metaphors that once belonged to a single discourse but were gradually being divided between two is nowhere clearer than in the work of Adam Smith. Indeed, what scholars have called "the Adam Smith Problem"—the apparent discontinuity between his *Theory of Moral Sentiments* and *The Wealth of Nations*—dissolves when one recognizes that the two texts both address the characteristic concerns of moral philosophy *but differently*. The difference between the two reflects the contemporary tendency to separate these concerns *and* the inertial force of their common generic origin.[23] We see traces of the common origin in the attention Smith pays in both texts to the problem of wealth and virtue. As we have already seen, by the time that Adam Smith revised his essays on ethics for his 1759 *Theory of Moral Sentiments,* the problem of reconciling virtue and commerce was typically formulated in terms of the relationship between the subject and its object, and, as we have also seen, the two theorists who most directly influenced Smith—Hutcheson and Hume—proposed a version of Shaftesbury's aesthetic model to describe this relationship. Smith, in turn, adapted this paradigm so as to emphasize proportion (which he calls "propriety") and imaginative identification (which he calls "sympathy"). We recognize the virtue of an action, Smith explains, by the harmony between the means exerted and the end obtained; we recognize the virtue or appropriateness of another's emotion by the harmony between the emotion we perceive and that which we feel. Thus sympathy, which is both the motor of social relations in Smith's *Theory of Moral Sentiments* and the faculty of moral judgment, is a sense that registers virtue as the formal properties of proportion, fitness, and harmony.

This aesthetic dimension also appears in *The Wealth of Nations,* but because Smith conceptualizes his subject at a different level of abstraction, proportion or harmony appears at the level of the aggregate, not the individual. Here we can see that giving a single formulation two different emphases produces two separate problematics. In both texts, Smith assumes that human beings are by nature dependent. In the *Moral Sentiments,* Smith fills the lack that dependence entails through individual imaginative exchanges; sympathy or admiration therefore becomes the object of universal desire.[24] In *The Wealth of Nations,* Smith fills this lack by means of very concrete exchanges, which *seem* to be individualistic as well. "Man has almost constant occasion for the help of his brethren," he writes; "give me that which I want, and you shall have this which you want. . . . It is not from the benevolence of the butcher, the brewer, or the baker, that we expect our dinner, but from their regard to their own interest."[25] The object of desire in this scenario is money, because, as a universal equivalent, it can further the self-interests of butcher, brewer, and baker alike. While the exchanges Smith describes in *The Wealth of Nations* seem to be as individual and immediate as the admiring relation between two friends, however, they actually occur at the level of society as a whole, not at the level of individuals. In the complex society Smith describes, one buys bread not from the farmer who grows the wheat but from the baker who runs the store; one tenders in exchange not the products of one's labor but the universal equivalent. In the revision that produces *The Wealth of Nations,* then, Smith abstracts proportion or harmony and relocates it in the economy as a whole.

But how, we still might ask, does aesthetic contemplation, which implicitly governs the subject's relation to the object in Smith's *Moral Sentiments,* become the desire to possess, which, by 1776, Smith represents as the individual's *only* motivation? Smith lays the groundwork for this transformation in a passage from the earlier text that describes the relationship between imaginative contemplation and action:

> If we consider the real satisfaction which [wealth and greatness] are capable of affording, by itself and separated from the beauty of that arrangement which is fitted to promote it, it will always appear in the highest degree contemptible and trifling. But we rarely view it in this abstract and philosophical light. We naturally con-

found it in our imagination with the order, the regular and harmonious movement of the system, the machine or economy by means of which it is produced. The pleasures of wealth and greatness, when considered in this complex view, strike the imagination as something grand, and beautiful, and noble, of which the attainment is well worth all the toil and anxiety which we are so apt to bestow upon it.

And it is well that nature imposes upon us in this manner. It is this deception which rouses and keeps in continual motion the industry of mankind. It is this which first prompted them to cultivate the ground, to build houses, to found cities and commonwealths, and to invent and improve all the sciences and arts, which ennoble and embellish human life.[26]

In this passage, Smith discounts the "real satisfaction" afforded by wealth as "trifling"; by contrast, imaginative satisfaction is deceptive but "grand." Paradoxically, however, imaginative gratification is sufficiently attractive to rouse the spectator—both in the sense of inspiring in him a kind of sympathetic activity (he wants to imitate so as to be a part of the economic machine) and in the sense of animating the desire to possess and thus the willingness to toil and worry—even though the material reward, presumably, will be "trifling" again.

This transformation of aesthetic contemplation into acquisitive desire is completed in *The Wealth of Nations*. Essentially, Smith effects this transformation by emphasizing the difference between Shaftesbury's two aesthetic models. One of these models—that which emphasized proportionality or fit—was explicitly grounded in a very material referent, the bodily "structure" of male and female animals. Shaftesbury is explicit about this: "If therefore in the structure of this or any other animal, there be anything which points beyond himself, and by which he is plainly discovered to have relation to some other being or nature besides his own, then will this animal undoubtedly be esteemed a part of some other system. For instance, if an animal has the proportions of a male, it shows he has relation to a female. And the respective proportions both of the male and female will be allowed, doubtless, to have a joint relation to another existence and order of things beyond themselves."[27] Shaftesbury's other aesthetic model—that which emphasized disinterest—stressed the imaginative or metaphorical nature of harmony; one does not have to possess or even touch an object to enjoy it. As we have just seen, Smith emphasizes the second of these two models in his *Theory of Moral Sentiment*. In that text imagination plays a central, indeed, *the* central role in desire. This is also true in the *Wealth of Nations,* but as we have also just seen, in the later text the body returns. Even here, however, Smith assigns the body a very equivocal role. On the one hand, Smith takes the body as the explicit model for human dependency; on the other hand, he discounts bodily needs as ruthlessly as he discounted "real satisfactions." "The desire of food is limited in every man by the narrow capacity of the human stomach," Smith explains; "but the desire of the conveniencies and ornaments of building, dress, equipage, and household furniture, seems to have no limit or certain boundary" (*WN*, 164). In this statement, Smith rewrites Shaftesbury's distinction between the referents that ground desire as a distinction *within desire itself.* That is, whereas Shaftesbury had derived harmony from both the physical world (the body) and imaginary correspondences, Smith distinguishes between the two referents and represents this difference as the difference between two kinds of desire. Thus later in *The Wealth of Nations,* Smith elaborates his double definition of desire: "The principle which prompts to expence, is the passion for present enjoyment; which, though sometimes violent and very difficult to be restrained, is in general only momentary and occasional. But the principle which prompts to save, is the desire of bettering our condition, a desire which, though generally calm and dispassionate, comes with us from the womb, and never leaves us till we go into the grave" (*WN*, 324).

The distinction within desire, which Smith has carried over from the double aesthetic model in moral philosophy, constitutes one of the most important principles of *The Wealth of Nations.* On the one hand, separating desire from the body enables Smith to free the economy from need and therefore to represent economic growth as infinitely expansive.[28] At the same time, this separation allows him to hold at bay the bugbear of "luxury," which was also conceptualized as desiring more than one needs.[29] On the other hand, however, retaining the body as the implicit ground of dependence permits Smith to prevent desire from being simply imaginative; and retaining proportion, to which the body was originally linked, enables him to explain the "fit" between consumption and production. The persistence of Shaftesbury's double aesthetic model, which Smith ensures when he divides desire in two, means that these formulations remain available to Smith as he tries to conceptualize the economy as something that both is and is not like a work of art.

If Smith's *Wealth of Nations* precipitated out economic issues without wholly purging political economy of its aesthetic concerns, then aesthetics underwent an equivalent transformation at midcentury. Like political economy, aesthetics retained both a model of acquisitive desire and a paradigm of disinterested contemplation, but the priority of the two was reversed. Significantly, moreover, even though contemplation increasingly displaced possession in theories of taste and art, the material referent in which Shaftesbury grounded proportion also appears in midcentury aesthetics in such a way as to trouble the very idea of "disinterest." To see this, we must examine in more detail Burke's 1757 *Enquiry*.

When Burke describes the aesthetic appreciation of beauty, he does so by distinguishing a contemplative mode that he calls "love" from an acquisitive relation to the object, which he designates "desire or lust." Lust, according to Burke, "is an energy of the mind, that hurries us on to the possession of certain objects."[30] "Lust" therefore defines the aesthetic stance by *opposition,* since it obviously threatens both contemplation and disinterest. But Burke is not done with sex, and the further use to which he puts Shaftesbury's paradigmatic instance of proportion reveals that aesthetics has carried over a function once performed by moral philosophy and now disclaimed by political economy. This function is discrimination, which Burke introduces when he derives the foundational concept of beauty. As Burke defines it, discrimination entails both differentiation (the apprehension of features that distinguish one object from another) and evaluation (the ranking of different objects according to some quality or property). The differences among objects, in Burke's account, register in the observer as preferences. Unlike male animals, Burke explains, who indiscriminately pursue any female for copulation,

> man . . . connects with the general passion [of sexual desire], the idea of some *social* qualities, which direct and heighten the appetite which he has in common with all other animals; and as he is not designed like them to live at large, it is fit that he should have something to create a preference, and fix his choice; . . . The object therefore of this mixed passion which we call love, is the *beauty* of the *sex*. Men are carried to the sex in general, as it is the sex, and by the common law of nature; but they are attached to particulars by personal *beauty*. I call beauty a social quality; for where women and men . . . give us a sense of joy and pleasure in beholding them . . . they inspire us with sentiments of tenderness and affection towards their persons.[31]

Burke's derivation of "preference" and, by extension, society, from men's sexual attraction to beauty has profound implications. First, in mapping discrimination onto sexual relations, Burke adopts the sexed subject as the tenor and vehicle for aesthetic judgment.[32] That is, the difference of sex, as it appears in Burke's distinction between a feminized beauty and the masculine sublime, becomes the basis for distinctions within aesthetics as well as between aesthetic contemplation and acquisitive desire. More importantly, however, deriving preference from sexed beauty renders a man's relation to an aestheticized reading of sex and an eroticized reading of difference the basis for social distinctions and discrimination. Thus sexual difference, which exists in nature, becomes the fundamental organizing dichotomy of a semantic system that produces distinctions—and therefore discriminations—in excess of the natural, originary difference. Burke's use of (hetero)sexual relations to organize difference and judgment therefore restores the body to the center of desire but not simply as a referent or anchor of need. Instead, the sexed body and its aestheticized excess—beauty—becomes the occasion and mandate for differentiation, for judgment—indeed, for meaning itself.

Burke's genealogy of discrimination is part of an elaborate account of how individuals make judgments about the world and why they react the way they do to danger and beauty both aesthetic and real. Accounting for discrimination in the subject and tabulating differentiations in the world are the two faces of what was once the central ethical function of moral philosophy: making judgments, judging difference. By the 1770s, this function seems to have been relegated almost completely to aesthetics. Political economy, by contrast, sought to deny difference and therefore to bracket discrimination: every individual, Smith proclaimed, is an incarnation of *homo economicus;* every exchange can be (and is) translated into the universal equivalent. Despite the fact that political economy seems to privilege norms over individuals, however, and therefore to leave discrimination to aesthetics, Smith's "science" continued to assume and to produce discriminations as the condition that made its "laws" work. Indeed, the foundational asymmetry that emerges so clearly in Burke's use of sex points to the constitutive asymmetry that political economy simultaneously assumed and denied. Despite the fact that Smith explicitly asserts that all individuals are structural equivalents in the market, that is, he assumes that certain "natural" barriers restrict the ability of some to achieve economic (not to mention social and political) equality with others. Significantly, but not unexpectedly, Smith uses sexual difference as the paradigmatic example of natural—read, unalterable—inequality. Because everyone recognizes the inferiority of women, Smith notes in passing, inequality must be written in nature at large.[33] Aesthetics, meanwhile, also anchored the knowledge its practitioners generated in a constitutive paradox that dealt symbolically with gender. As aesthetic principles were articulated in Sir Joshua Reynolds's *Discourses on Art,* the act of discrimination prevailed in the artist, but this faculty was directed toward distinguishing between the "excrescences" that characterized all objects and the ideal form that lay behind these irregularities. This aesthetic emphasis on norms made the artist's perception (or even his imagination)—not the female body—the origin of true, that is, ideal, beauty.[34]

By the 1790s, the gulf between aesthetics and political economy seemed unbridgeable. In 1790, Archibald Alison identified the "man of business" as one example of an individual who lacked the "aesthetic attitude"; and in 1798, Thomas Robert Malthus published his *Essay on the Principles of Population,* which renounced the metaphor of proportion as a description of the relationship between natural production and human demand.[35] The breakup of moral philosophy generated a number of important effects. Among these were two models of desire (the one "disinterested," the other acquisitive); two kinds of objects (the one infinitely nuanced, the other universally reducible to a single equivalent); two kinds of value (the one formulated as "quality," the other theoretically tabulated by quantity); and two kinds of knowledge (the one objective and masculine, the other subjective and feminine). Subsequent decades were to witness both the institutionalization of these oppositions and theoretical elaborations of the difference between "art" and "science"—albeit sometimes in versions that strained the distinction theorists were trying to reinforce.[36] Even as the differences between the two discourses were codified, however, traces of their originary relationship persisted. In 1792, Mary Wollstonecraft identified this relationship—and its imperfect effacement—as one source of the social discrimination that kept women second-class citizens even in a period of democratic dreams.

■ ■ ■

In chapter 9 of the *Vindication of the Rights of Woman,* Mary Wollstonecraft somewhat surprisingly links political inequality to sexual decadence and argues that the root cause of both is "the respect paid to property." "From the respect paid to property flow, as from a poisoned fountain, most of the evils and vices which render this world such a dreary scene to the contemplative mind," Wollstonecraft explains. "For it is in the most polished society that noisome reptiles and venomous serpents lurk under the rank herbage; and there is voluptuousness pampered by the still sultry air, which relaxes every good disposition before it ripens into virtue."[37] Read in the context of the debates I have thus far traced, this passage has a double resonance. First, the association Wollstonecraft makes between "polished society" and "voluptuousness" reveals the fact that, in addition to echoing Thomas Paine's *Rights of Man,* the *Vindication* also contributed to the eighteenth-century debate about wealth and virtue.[38] Second, Wollstonecraft's reference to the "contemplative mind" suggests that she is assuming—or would like to assume—an aesthetic, in the sense of "disinterested," stance. "Disinterest," she hopes, will enable her to avoid the charges of special pleading with which her contemporaries dismiss personal complaints. "I call with the firm tone of humanity," she writes; "I plead for my sex—not for myself" (*VW,* 3).

I will return in a moment to the problems generated by

Wollstonecraft's attempt to mobilize aesthetic terms for a political argument. First, I need to examine in some detail her contribution to the debate about wealth and virtue, which draws directly on the (denied) relationship between aesthetics and political economy. Wollstonecraft's complaint that commerce has debased virtue focuses on two properties of market logic that were marginalized in Smith's political economy but adumbrated in Burke's aesthetics. The first is the fetishization of sexual difference. As we have just seen, political economy sought to discount this difference in constructing *homo economicus* at the same time that Smith used the difference Burke and others assumed to ground other kinds of inequality.[39] Wollstonecraft picks up not only the asymmetry Smith denies but also the implications of Burke's assumption that sex is both foundational *and* subject to the aesthetic elaboration of beauty. Wollstonecraft charges that aestheticizing women's bodies, as Burke does, underwrites a sexual double standard both because sex is assumed to be the only difference that matters *and* because anatomy is assumed to be apprehended only through erotic desire. Burke's aestheticized reading of sexual difference has been institutionalized in modern society, Wollstonecraft continues—by an education that limits women's attention to their bodies, by "novels, music, poetry, and gallantry" that tend to make women "creatures of sensation" (*VW*, 61), and by the "sensual homage paid to beauty" (*VW*, 47) that reinforces women's hunger for immediate gratification and for power in the only available form. "To their sense, are women made slaves," Wollstonecraft laments, "because it is by their sensibility that they obtain present power" (*VW*, 61). "Present power," of course, turns out to be illusory, for the aestheticized "sensibility" that makes women attractive actually belongs to a market dynamic in which women are not the consumers but the commodities that are bought and sold. "To rise in the world, and have the liberty of running from pleasure to pleasure, [women] must marry advantageously, and to this object their time is sacrificed, and their persons often legally prostituted" (*VW*, 60).

If the fetishization of sexual difference subjects women to civil and social inequality and to the logic of the market, then it also subjects men—and, thus, by extension, women again—to the dynamic of discrimination that Burke identified but did not explore. The second focus of Wollstonecraft's complaint, this dynamic answers to a model of desire that eluded Adam Smith. Unlike Smith, who claimed to assimilate desire to the imagination, Wollstonecraft reads desire as Burke does—through the sexed body. When Wollstonecraft examines desire, then, she sees not a self-generating, limitless drive, but an appetite that swells and then expires. She sees, in other words, male sexuality, which, mocking Burke, she characterizes as "love": "Love, considered as an animal appetite, cannot long feed on itself without expiring," Wollstonecraft observes (*VW*, 73).[40] Because male sexual arousal constitutes Wollstonecraft's prototype for desire, commerce and virtue will coexist only if desire is continually regenerated, not disciplined, as Smith imagined. The solution devised for the problem of satiety has energized the economy, Wollstonecraft admits, but it has proved disastrous for virtue, for the only stimulus capable of rousing a "sated appetite" is Burke's eroticized aesthetics of deferral and variety. "Passion [is] naturally increased by suspense and difficulties," Wollstonecraft writes; but while this may lead men to work and save for future well-being, it generates a morality founded on duplicity: to enhance "suspence" and elaborate "difficulties," viragos masquerade as virgins and modesty becomes a sexual lure. Morality, in other words, acquires some of the properties of a work of art; it conceals the artistry behind the appearance of "nature," and it defers the gratification that it promises to award. The solution of variety is equally ruinous to virtue, for the "epicure" requires such exotic tidbits to rouse his appetite that the bounds of nature may even be transgressed: so "depraved" can the appetite become that "the lustful prowler . . . refines on female softness. Something more soft than woman is then sought for; till, in Italy and Portugal, men attend the levees of equivocal beings, to sigh for more than female languour" (*VW*, 30, 138).

If men sigh for "more than female" charms—that is, for other men— then the dynamic by which heterosexual desire is regenerated is also capable of elaborating desire—that is, of producing varieties of desire alongside varieties of stimulation. This is the most far-reaching insight of Wollstonecraft's *Vindication,* and, although it follows directly from Burke's derivation of discrimination from an aestheticized reading of sex, Wollstonecraft pursues this observation with an ardor Burke did not.[41] In order to appreciate Wollstonecraft's analysis, we need to turn briefly to another conjuncture of economics and "beauty" that was almost completely overlooked by theorists like Smith and Burke. This conjuncture, which embraced concerns about social emulation, ambition, and commodification —in short, the relationship between wealth and virtue—was (and is) captured by the term "fashion."

Even though it generally escaped the notice of theorists, fashion was a topic of much discussion in the popular press throughout the long eighteenth century.[42] Like the debates about credit, discussions of fashion often carried anxieties about the economic and epistemological instability of modern society.[43] Commentators like Daniel Defoe, for example, conceptualized fashion as a highly unstable and unpredictable player in the roulette of personal prosperity and cautioned young tradesmen against the "eager resolved pursuit of that empty and meanest kind of pride, called imitation."[44] Necessary but of dubious morality, fashion—again like credit— was also often associated with women, either because "the Changeable

Foible of the Ladies" was considered the source of revolutions in style or because women like Alexander Pope's Belinda were thought to exacerbate England's consumption of what Defoe called "Foreign Trifles."[45]

Whatever doubts were expressed about the ethics of fashion, no one questioned its power, especially after the commercial triumph of Josiah Wedgwood in the 1760s.[46] For my purposes, the significance of Wedgwood's production and marketing innovations is that they made visible to analysts like Mary Wollstonecraft a dynamic of desire that Adam Smith implied but never formulated. According to Smith's model, desire is simply limitless by nature; assimilated explicitly to the imagination and only implicitly to the body, desire—and hence economic demand—marches to its own, apparently indefatigable drummer. Yet *because* Smith retains this aesthetic model of desire in order to check frivolous expenditure, he also implies that desire is separable from all real (as opposed to imaginary) objects. If this were really true, then we would have a purely contemplative—that is, a purely aesthetic—economy in which possession and property were simply metaphors; we would have, in other words, Addison's "Man of a Polite Imagination" who looked and did not buy. Smith retained the *other* model of proportionality, which is grounded in the body, in order to prevent this collapse into metaphor, to anchor Addison's *theoretical* rationale for middle-class virtue in an *economic* argument that assumes the virtue of commerce. Smith never theorized the implications—or the limitations—of this move, however. What theories of fashion add to Smith's model of self-generating, self-sustaining, and theoretically self-sufficient desire is an account of an external agent that generates, sustains, and elaborates desire. Early in the eighteenth century, this agent was often figured as "woman," but by the end of the century it had begun to appear in another guise—as the reified market that Adam Smith abstracted from individual exchanges. As early as 1747, *The London Tradesman* was urging tradesmen to take the initiative, to exercise their "quick Invention for new Patterns . . . to create Trade."[47] By the end of the century, as the example of Wedgwood suggests, fashion was being consciously manipulated to *produce* desire precisely by generating infinitely discriminated products whose meanings were exclusively differential and social.[48]

What the logic of fashion gradually began to expose, then, is the persistence of aesthetic concerns within economic exchanges, and the persistence of a market logic in the domain of beauty or art. Especially as it was equated with ideas about what makes a woman beautiful, the dynamics of fashion revealed that what contemporaries were increasingly presenting as two different discourses did not describe different realms at all: fashion simultaneously solicited everyone's participation in a single kind of exchange, as political economy foretold, and ruthlessly adjusted that participation to a *social* calculus of desire produced by advertisers and manufacturers. While this corresponded to the logic Burke described, however, the connection between discrimination and the market was rarely explored in the late eighteenth century because the providential underpinnings that anchored ideas about harmony, beauty, and taste were so crucial to epistemological security. Indeed, with a few exceptions, theorists of the economy and of art tended to widen rather than close the distance between the two realms—with the consequences we all know so well.[49]

We are now in a better position to understand the implications of Wollstonecraft's charge that a "polished society" breeds "noisome reptiles" and serpents of vice. At one level, she is obviously issuing a series of familiar charges: that where wealth reigns, "poverty will become more despicable even than vice," principle will be sacrificed to greed, and independence will be traded for patronage. But at another level, Wollstonecraft's complaint exposes what fashion also showed: that the *apparent* separation of ethics and the economy, the apparent divorce of aesthetics from politics and the economy, and the apparent discovery of two separate sets of natural laws were all contributing to mask and produce the constitutive dynamic of market society—the relationship between the production of discrimination at the level of meaning or sign and the enforcement of discrimination at the level of power.[50] To see Wollstonecraft's complaint more clearly, we have only to look at her scathing denunciation of Rousseau.

Like Burke but more so, Rousseau incarnates "refined licentiousness" for Wollstonecraft (*VW*, 90). Like Burke but more so, Rousseau eroticizes sexual difference, then derives an aestheticized taxonomy of beauty for the fetishized female body. While the consequences of Rousseau's idolatry are debasing for women, however, they also betray a crucial fact about the society that reproduces itself by means of this dynamic. Rousseau's transgression, Wollstonecraft explains, was not consuming women, as Adam Smith's model of desire might predict. Instead, Rousseau's transgression did not involve consumption at all. Because he was so fastidious—because he was, in society's terms, so virtuous—Rousseau converted his lust into "sensibility" and fantasized when he might have loved.

> Even his virtues . . . led him farther away; for, born with a warm constitution and lively fancy, nature carried him toward the other sex with such eager fondness, that he soon became lascivious. Had he given way to these desires, the fire would have extinguished itself in a natural manner; but virtue, and a romantic kind of delicacy, made him practise self-denial; yet, when fear, delicacy, or virtue, restrained him, he debauched his imagination, and reflecting on the sensations to which fancy gave force, he traced them in the most glowing colours, and sunk them deep into his soul. (*VW*, 91)

Writing about instead of enjoying the female body, Rousseau proves that possession is less gratifying than fantasy. At the same time, he demonstrates that fantasy is more productive than acquisition, for through writing, Rousseau incites in others the desire he refuses in himself, only now sexual desire is translated into the desire to possess a simulacrum of the desirable object—a novel, not the woman who inspired Rousseau to write. As active agents, women are excluded from this economy. As recipients of Rousseau's inscribed desire, readers (both male and female) imagine intellectual improvement when they have really only experienced aesthetic titillation. "So warmly has [Rousseau] painted, what he forcibly felt," Wollstonecraft continues, "that, interesting the heart and inflaming the imagination of his readers; in proportion to the strength of their fancy, they imagine that their understanding is convinced when they only sympathize with a poetic writer, who skillfully exhibits the objects of sense, most voluptuously shadowed or gracefully veiled—And thus making us feel whilst dreaming that we reason, erroneous conclusions are left in the mind" (*VW*, 91).

The point, for Wollstonecraft, is that the "erroneous conclusions" with which writers like Rousseau infect their readers are the discriminations by which men like Rousseau retain power. At the heart of this semiotic system of discriminations is the difference upon which Burke anchored aesthetics: women are "the sex"; men discriminate among women and so found civilization. Beyond this we have all the other discriminations that actually tie women to their bodies but do so simply as effects of a system that infuses differentiation with social meaning while claiming to reflect universal beauty and desire.

Despite Wollstonecraft's powerful analysis of Rousseau and Burke, the complexities inscribed in the corrective she tried to administer vitiate the solutions she is able to devise. We see this first in the ambivalence Wollstonecraft repeatedly voices toward the faculty most consistently associated with aesthetics—the imagination. On the one hand, Wollstonecraft celebrates what she calls "the romantic passion, which is the concomitant of genius" (*VW*, 31–32). On the other hand, she worries that a "lively heated imagination" may "revel" in "unnatural and meretricious scenes" from novels, producing in women a "vitiated taste" as debased as that which draws men to illicit sex (*VW*, 74, 185). The only solution Wollstonecraft can imagine for the problem the imagination presents in a world of eroticized objects is a dynamic in which "disappointed hope" schools desire into another version of disinterested contemplation—a contemplation that focuses not on the pleasures of this world, whether imaginary or bodily, but on the promise of a world to come.

> When, in the lapse of time, perfection is found not to be within reach of mortals, virtue, abstractedly, is thought beautiful, and

wisdom sublime. Admiration then gives place to friendship, properly so called, because it is cemented by esteem; and the being walks alone only dependent on heaven for that emulous panting after perfection which ever glows in a noble mind. . . . The powers of the soul that are of little use here, and, probably, disturb our animal enjoyments, even while conscious dignity makes us glory in possessing them, prove that life is merely an education, a state of infancy, to which the only hopes worth cherishing should not be sacrificed. (*VW,* 108–109)

The second sign of the complexities generated by the imbrication of aesthetics and erotics is Wollstonecraft's ambivalence toward the female body and sexuality in general. On the one hand, she repeatedly both voices and alludes to the desires that women feel. On the other hand, she excoriates women for what she calls "nasty customs" and "bodily wit" and she chides Frenchwomen in particular for their "brutal excesses" (*VW,* 128, 137). Once more, the solution Wollstonecraft imagines is another form of aestheticized behavior—the endless deferral of sexual gratification, not in order to prolong or enhance excitation, but to escape altogether sexuality's cruel logic. Do not "obstinately determine to love . . . [your husband] to the end of the chapter," Wollstonecraft warns, lest you become the "fond slave" of a "suspicious tyrant, who contemptuously insults the very weakness he fostered" (*VW,* 120).

These manifestations of ambivalence and theoretical uncertainty are both elaborations of the impossible position assigned to women by an aesthetics that retained yet denied its relationship to political economy. For, on the one hand, the aesthetic paradigm developed by Burke takes the female body as the paragon of beauty and the sexual "fit" between (heterosexual) bodies as the incarnation of providential proportion; in so doing, it elevates woman to the status of nature's most perfect specimen, but it also constructs her as an object, which, like any other object in a market society, can be represented by the universal equivalent and exchanged according to its rules. On the other hand, the aesthetic stance articulated as an alternative to the acquisitive relation to objects—disinterested contemplation—positions women as objects to be appreciated imaginatively; in so doing, it leaves no room for expressing the sexual desires that aesthetics also inscribes *in* the woman so that she can fulfill the task of inciting male desire.[51]

The imperfect separation of eighteenth-century political economy and aesthetics and the role played by gender in this process have also marked the disciplines descended from these discourses. As nineteenth-century political economists elaborated the "laws" of an "autonomous" economy, they retained the sexual asymmetry Smith assumed in *The Wealth of Nations.* Thus Malthus, Ricardo, and Senior excluded non-waged labor—signally childcare and housework—from accounts of national productivity and value. By the same token, most theorists constructed political representation and economic opportunity according to a model that both assumed the inequality of the sexes and justified this assumption by theories of "virtual" representation and the "family wage" that incarnated the aesthetic principle of synecdoche. Similarly, (mostly male) theoreticians of the imagination, beauty, and art struggled to marshal prestige for a discourse increasingly constructed as "feminine" and as "above" market logic. For some writers, like Percy Shelley, this meant celebrating the "universality" of aesthetic value and representing the poet as "unacknowledged legislator of the world." For others, like Charles Dickens, it meant exaggerating the artist's freedom from waged slavery by elaborating the writer's likeness to the virtuous housewife, who was increasingly celebrated as the incarnation of England's national superiority.[52]

In this century, the academic institutionalization of these kinds of knowledge as if they represented autonomous realms has further reified what originated as a discursive division. In so doing, it has also both encouraged the development of interpretive strategies that serve further to separate economic from aesthetic knowledge and generated the kind of nostalgia that we see in Barbara Herrnstein Smith's account. These developments undeniably affect the way that professional literary critics and economic theorists understand and conduct our business today, and it would be foolish to pretend that the discursive division could be wished or willed away. It is equally shortsighted, however, simply to accept this division as natural. One way to remember the originary relationship between these two discourses—and to measure the toll exacted by their division—is to tease from each its past and present entanglements with gender.[53] As Mary Wollstonecraft remarked two centuries ago, the violence by which the disciplines separated lingers still as contradictions inscribed in the figure of woman and the difference of sex.

Notes

1. Barbara Herrnstein Smith, *Contingencies of Value: Alternative Perspectives for Critical Theory* (Cambridge: Harvard University Press, 1988), 127.

2. Ibid., 33.

3. My analysis of Smith is indebted to John Guillory, *Cultural Capital: The Problem of Literary Canon Formation* (Chicago: University of Chicago Press, 1993), 296–297.

4. The most influential analyst of this debate is J.G.A. Pocock. See his *The Machiavellian Moment: Florentine Political Thought and the Atlantic Republican Tradition* (Princeton: Princeton University Press, 1975), especially chaps. 13 and 14, and "The Mobility of Property and the Rise of Eighteenth-Century

Sociology," in his *Virtue, Commerce, and History: Essays on Political Thought and History, Chiefly in the Eighteenth Century* (Cambridge: Cambridge University Press, 1985), 103–124. See also Istvan Hont and Michael Ignatieff, eds., *Wealth and Virtue: The Shaping of Political Economy in the Scottish Enlightenment* (Cambridge: Cambridge University Press, 1983).

5. The summary follows the argument of William M. Reddy, *Money and Liberty in Modern Europe: A Critique of Historical Understanding* (Cambridge: Cambridge University Press, 1987), 87.

6. On the limits of Smith's empiricism, see T. C. Smout, "Where Had the Scottish Economy Got To by the Third Quarter of the Eighteenth Century?" in Hont and Ignatieff, *Wealth*, 45–72; and Philip Mirowski, "Adam Smith, Empiricism, and the Rate of Profit in Eighteenth-Century England," *History of Political Economy* 14, no. 2 (1982): 178–198.

7. A provocative discussion of the breakup of moral philosophy can be found in Guillory, *Cultural Capital*, chap. 5.

8. For a related discussion of natural philosophy, see Julian Martin, *Francis Bacon, The State, and the Reform of Natural Philosophy* (Cambridge: Cambridge University Press, 1992), especially chap. 6.

9. This list is derived from Gladys Bryson, *Man and Society: The Scottish Inquiry of the Eighteenth Century* (1945; rpt. New York: Augustus M. Kelley, 1968), 4. See also Guillory, *Cultural Capital*, chap. 5.

10. See Pocock, "Hume and the American Revolution," in *Virtue*, 125–142; David McNally, *Political Economy and the Rise of Capitalism: A Reinterpretation* (Berkeley: University of California Press, 1988), chap. 4; and introduction to Bryson, *Man and Society*. Howard Caygill briefly discusses the relationship between moral philosophy and the Glorious Revolution of 1688 in *Art of Judgement* (Oxford: Basil Blackwell, 1989), 41–42.

11. Anthony Ashley Cooper, third earl of Shaftesbury, *Characteristics of Men, Manners, Opinions, Times,* ed. John M. Robertson (1711; Indianapolis: Bobbs-Merrill Co., 1964), 338. Helpful discussions of Shaftesbury's work include Caygill, *Art,* 44–50; and Robert Markley, "Sentimentality as Performance: Shaftesbury, Sterne, and the Theatrics of Virtue," in *The New Eighteenth Century: Theory, Politics, English Literature,* ed. Felicity Nussbaum and Laura Brown (New York: Methuen, 1987), 210–230. John Barrell describes Shaftesbury's treatment of the relationship between aesthetic contemplation and virtue in terms of a split within the "civic humanist theory of the fine arts"—that is, between public and private modes of activity. See " 'The Dangerous Goddess': Masculinity, Prestige, and the Aesthetic in Early Eighteenth-Century Britain," *Cultural Critique* 12 (Spring 1989): 128–129.

12. See Francis Hutcheson, *Inquiry Concerning the Original of our Ideas of Virtue or Moral Good* (1725; quoted by Bryson in *Man and Society,* 215).

13. For two important discussions of the concept of disinterestedness, see Jerome Stolnitz, "On the Origins of 'Aesthetic Disinterestedness,' " *Journal of Aesthetics and Art Criticism* 20, no. 2 (1961): 131–143; and Martha Woodmansee, "The Interests in Disinterestedness: Karl Phillipp Moritz and the Emergence of the Theory of Aesthetic Autonomy in Eighteenth-Century Germany," *Modern Language Quarterly* 45 (1984): 22–47.

14. *Spectator* 411 (June 21, 1712), in *The Spectator,* ed. Gregory Smith (London: Dent, 1970), 3: 278.

15. See Markley, "Sentimentality as Performance," 213–217. Barrell's observations on bourgeois critics in the generation after Shaftesbury are relevant here; see "'The Dangerous Goddess,'" 131.

16. Quoted in the introduction to Edmund Burke, *A Philosophical Enquiry into the Origin of Our Ideas of the Sublime and Beautiful,* ed. J. T. Boulton (1757; Notre Dame, Ind.: University of Notre Dame Press, 1968), xix–xx.

17. Burke, *Enquiry,* 6.

18. Henry Home, Lord Kames, *Elements of Criticism,* rev. ed., ed. James R. Boyd (New York: A. S. Barnes and Co., 1858), 29–30.

19. As John Guillory has pointed out, in order for an object to have an aesthetic function, it must first be classified *as* an aesthetic object. This is true because one function (or effect) of classification is to designate certain effects (and not others) *as* the definitive effects: "It is thus no refutation of the specificity of the aesthetic that a work of art might be used in some non-aesthetic context; or that an object not produced as a work of art can be so regarded in a later social context than the context of its production. The relevant consideration is the specific social functions of objects produced or received in a given historical context *as* works of art, since it is only as works so classified that they can have certain *other* social functions" (*Cultural Capital,* 295).

20. "If Taste has no fixed principles, if the imagination is not affected according to some invariable and certain laws, our labour is like to be employed to very little purpose; as it must be judged an useless, if not an absurd undertaking, to lay down rules for caprice, and to set up for a legislator of whims and fancies" (Burke, *Philosophical Enquiry,* 12).

21. Kames, *Elements of Criticism* (1761; rpt. New York: Garland, 1972), 1: vii.

22. David Hume, "Of Refinement in the Arts," in *Essays Moral, Political, and Literary,* ed. Eugene F. Miller (Indianapolis: Liberty Classics, 1985), 272. It is important to note that Hume eventually concluded that the laws of taste cannot be ascertained by scientific means but only by the test of time—that is, by the verdict of critics throughout the ages.

23. On the Adam Smith problem, see the following: Jacob Viner, "Adam Smith and Laissez-Faire," in *The Long View and the Short: Studies in Economic Theory and Policy,* ed. Jacob Viner (Glencoe, Ill.: Free Press, 1959), 213–245; Ralph Anspach, "The Implications of the *Theory of Moral Sentiments* for Adam Smith's Economic Thought," *History of Political Economy* 4 (1972): 176–206; A. W. Coats, "Adam Smith's Conception of Self-Interest in Economic and Political Affairs," *History of Political Economy* 7 (1975): 132–136; T. W. Hutchison, "The Bicentenary of Adam Smith," *Economic Journal* 86 (September 1976): 481–492; Albert O. Hirschman, *The Passions and the Interests: Political Arguments for Capitalism before its Triumph* (Princeton: Princeton University Press, 1977), 108–10; Jeffrey T. Young, "The Impartial Spectator and Natural Jurisprudence: An Interpretation of Adam Smith's Theory of the Natural Price," *History of Political Economy* 18 (1986): 365–382; Jerry Evensky, "The

Two Voices of Adam Smith: Moral Philosopher and Social Critic," *History of Political Economy* 19 (1987): 447–468; Syed Ahmad, "Adam Smith's Four Invisible Hands," *History of Political Economy* 22 (1990): 137–144; J. Ronnie Davis, "Adam Smith on the Providential Reconciliation of Individual and Social Interests: Is Man Led by an Invisible Hand or Misled by Sleight of Hand?" *History of Political Economy* 22 (1990): 341–352; Nathan Rosenberg, "Adam Smith and the Stock of Moral Capital," *History of Political Economy* 22 (1990): 1–17.

24. Adam Smith, *The Theory of Moral Sentiments,* new ed. (London, 1853; rpt. New York: Augustus M. Kelley, 1966). See especially p. 166 (pt. 3, chap. 2).

25. Adam Smith, *An Inquiry into the Nature and Causes of the Wealth of Nations* (1776; rpt. New York: Modern Library, 1937), 14. All future references will be cited in the text with the abbreviation *WN*.

26. Smith, *Moral Sentiments,* 263–264 (pt. 4, chap. 1). For relevant discussions of Smith, see Caygill, *Art of Judgement,* 85–98; and Guillory, *Cultural Critique,* 305–312.

27. Shaftesbury, *Characteristics,* 245.

28. On the idea that need follows from rather than grounds exchange in Smith's work, see Guillory, *Cultural Capital,* 315–317.

29. See Pocock, *Machiavellian Moment,* 430–431, 444–445. Smith was explicitly hostile to luxury, which he denigrated as "childish." See *Wealth of Nation,* 331, 332, 388, 389, 391, 414. For a survey of the concept of "luxury," see John Sekora, *Luxury: The Concept in Western Thought, Eden to Smollett* (Baltimore and London: The Johns Hopkins University Press, 1977).

30. Burke, *Enquiry,* 91.

31. Ibid., 42–43.

32. Peter de Bolla makes the following observation about what he calls the discourse on the sublime: "The discourse on the sublime produces and examines subjectivity in gender-specific terms. . . . The discourse on the sublime is faced with a product of its own analysis, which we will label here as the sexed subject, with which it is both uncomfortable—an unwanted product—and hopelessly drawn to, fascinated by. The discourse on the sublime recognizes this sexed subject, but refuses to theorize it." In a note, de Bolla explains "sexed subject": "The complex of relations articulated by the difference of gender: attitudes and figurations of the differences between male desire and female objectification, economies of sexuality split into masculine demand and female objectification" (*The Discourse of the Sublime: History, Aesthetics, and the Subject* [Oxford: Basil Blackwell, 1989], 56; 56 n. 28). John Barrell also discusses the slide within aesthetics toward a rhetoric of masculine sensuality. See "'The Dangerous Goddess,'" 127–131.

It should be noted that Shaftesbury's use of sex as the paradigm for proportion played such a prominent role in Kames's aesthetics that his Victorian editor found it necessary to omit material "objectionable on account of its indelicacy." Kames's references to sex, according to Boyd, had thus far rendered the *Elements* unfit for course adoption "as a text-book, especially in female seminaries" (Kames, *Elements of Criticism,* 4).

33. In his discussion of primogeniture, Smith explains: "That the power, and consequently the security of the monarchy, may not be weakened by division, it must descend entire to one of the children. To which of them so important a preference shall be given, must be determined by some general rule, founded not upon the doubtful distinctions of personal merit, but upon some plain and evident difference which can admit of no dispute. Among the children of the same family, there can be no indisputable difference but that of sex, and that of age. The male sex is universally preferred to the female; and when all other things are equal, the elder every-where takes place of the younger. Hence the origin of the right of primogeniture, and of what is called lineal succession" (*Wealth of Nations*, 362).

For a discussion of Smith's treatment of women, see Jane Rendall, "Virtue and Commerce: Women in the Making of Adam Smith's Political Economy," in *Women in Western Political Philosophy: Kant to Nietzsche,* ed. Ellen Kennedy and Susan Mendus (New York: St. Martin's Press, 1987), 44–77.

34. By long study and diligent comparison of individual objects, Reynolds writes, the artist "acquires a just idea of beautiful forms; he corrects nature by herself, her imperfect state by her more perfect. His eye being able to distinguish the accidental deficiencies, excrescences, and deformities of things, from their general figures, he makes out an abstract idea of their forms more perfect than any one original; and what may seem a paradox, he learns to design naturally by drawing his figures unlike any one object. This idea of the perfect state of nature, which the Artist calls the Ideal Beauty, is the great leading principle, by which works of genius are conducted" (Sir Joshua Reynolds, *Discourses on Art,* ed. Robert R. Wark [New Haven: Yale University Press, 1975], 44–45). Reynolds's discourses were delivered to the members of the Royal Academy between 1769 and 1790. For a relevant analysis of Reynolds, see Naomi Schor, *Reading in Detail: Aesthetics and the Feminine* (New York: Methuen, 1987), chap. 1.

35. Archibald Alison, *Essays on the Nature and Principles of Taste,* 4th ed. (Edinburgh, 1815), 1:95.

36. In 1805, for example, the first professorship of political economy was established in England, at the East India College at Haileybury. Robert Malthus was appointed to this position. For an attempt to distinguish between the "science" of economics and the "art" of political economy, see, for example, Nassau Senior's *Industrial Efficiency and Social Economy* (New York: Henry Holt and Co., 1928), 1:3–44.

37. Mary Wollstonecraft, *A Vindication of the Rights of Woman,* ed. Carol H. Poston (New York: Norton, 1975), 140. All subsequent references to this edition will be cited in the text by page number with the abbreviation *VW.*

38. While it differs in emphasis, my interpretation of Wollstonecraft's work is indebted to David Simpson's *Romanticism, Nationalism, and the Revolt Against Theory* (Chicago: University of Chicago Press, 1993). Simpson argues that Wollstonecraft's genius consists in the fact "that she has managed to situate the condition of women exactly in the vocabulary criticizing the decline of civic virtue within commercial economies, one of the major ethical discourses of the

eighteenth century. This removes the 'woman question' from any potentially single-issue status and embeds it within a general analysis of the negative effects of a surplus (luxury) economy. Women are classified with monarchs, the rich, and soldiers in suffering the psychological and intellectual enfeeblement consequent upon worship of social distinction and the urge to novelty. By implication it is only when the institutions maintaining these inequities are removed that women, along with the others, will break free from their oppression —an oppression that is not just instrumental and crudely coercive but also internal and self-imposed" (107–108).

39. For a discussion of the reformulation and normalization of sexual difference during the eighteenth century, see Thomas Laqueur, *Making Sex: Body and Gender from the Greeks to Freud* (Cambridge: Harvard University Press, 1990), especially chaps. 3 and 4.

40. Cf. "Love, from its very nature, must be transitory" (*VW*, 30). See also pp. 50, 65, 119.

41. One reason that Burke did not pursue this line of thinking may well be that the Foxite Whigs, whose spokesperson he had become by 1790, epitomized for many contemporaries exactly the kind of effeminacy Wollstonecraft denigrates here. See Peter Mandler, *Aristocratic Government in the Age of Reform: Whigs and Liberals 1830–1852* (Oxford: Clarendon Press, 1990), 18, 45.

42. Historians have only recently begun to take fashion seriously. Now, however, debates about the rage for cheap Indian fabrics in the 1680s and 1690s have been identified as the origin of Smith's model of acquisitive desire, and what historians have called "emulative spending" has been credited with fueling the takeoff of the Industrial Revolution. For the former, see Joyce Appleby, "Ideology and Theory: The Tension between Political and Economic Liberalism in the Seventeenth Century," *American Historical Review* 81 (1976): 499–515; and Appleby, *Economic Thought and Ideology in Seventeenth-Century England* (Princeton: Princeton University Press, 1978). For the latter, see Neil McKendrick, "Home Demand and Economic Growth: A New View of the Role of Women and Children in the Industrial Revolution," in *Historical Perspectives: Studies in English Thought and Society in Honor of J. H. Plumb,* ed. Neil McKendrick (London: Europa, 1974); and McKendrick, "The Commercialization of Fashion," in *The Birth of a Consumer Society: The Commercialization of Eighteenth-Century England,* ed. Neil McKendrick, John Brewer, and J. H. Plumb (Bloomington: Indiana University Press, 1985), 34–98. See also Dorothy Davis, *A History of Shopping* (London: Routledge and Kegan Paul, 1966), especially chaps. 8 and 10, and the essays collected in John Brewer and Roy Porter, eds., *Consumption and the World of Goods* (London and New York: Routledge, 1993).

Ironically, one of Burke's reviewers, Payne Knight, charged that Burke took his model of "timeless" beauty from a fashion that briefly prevailed among women at midcentury. See *Analytical Inquiry* 3:1 (1757): 34.

43. For provocative discussions of credit, see Pocock, "Mobility of Property"; Julian Hoppit, "The Use and Abuse of Credit in Eighteenth-Century England," in *Business Life and Public Policy: Essays in Honour of D. C. Coleman,* ed.

Neil McKendrick and R. B. Outhwaite (Cambridge: Cambridge University Press, 1986), 64–78; and John Brewer, "Commercialization and Politics," in McKendrick, Brewer, and Plumb, *Birth of Consumer Society,* 197–262.

44. Daniel Defoe, *The Complete English Tradesman* (1726; rpt. Glouster: Alan Sutton, 1987), 86.

45. Quoted in McKendrick, "Commercialization of Fashion," 50. On Pope, see Louis A. Landa, "Pope's Belinda, The General Emporie of the World, and the Wondrous Worm," *South Atlantic Quarterly* 70 (1971): 215–235. On Swift's attitudes toward women and fashion, see Laura Brown, "Reading Race and Gender: Jonathan Swift," *Eighteenth-Century Studies* 23 (1990): 424–443. On Mandeville's treatment of women and fashion, see Laura Mandell, "Bawds and Merchants: Engendering Capitalist Desires," *ELH* 59 (1992): 107–123.

46. See Neil McKendrick, "Josiah Wedgwood and the Commercialization of the Potteries," in *Birth of a Consumer Society*, ed. McKendrick, 99–145.

47. Quoted in McKendrick, "Commercialization of Fashion," ibid., 50.

48. Neil McKendrick argues that by the end of the century "the competitive, socially emulative aspect of fashion was being consciously manipulated by commerce in pursuit of increased consumption. This new fashion world was one in which entrepreneurs were trying deliberately to induce fashionable change, to make it rapidly available to as many as possible and yet keep it so firmly under their control that the consuming public could be sufficiently influenced to buy at the dictate of *their* fashion decisions, at the convenience of *their* production lines. Those fashion decisions were increasingly based on economic grounds rather than aesthetic ones, on the basis of what the factories could produce and on what the salesmen could sell rather than on what the French court dictated" (ibid., 43).

49. Samuel Johnson was among the few writers who openly explored the imbrication of authorship in market relations.

50. This analysis is indebted to a number of contemporary theorists of fashion and aesthetics. See, for example, Jean Baudrillard, "Sign Function and Class Logic," "The Ideological Genesis of Needs," "Fetishism and Ideology: The Semiological Reduction," and "Beyond Use Value" in *For a Critique of the Political Economy of the Sign,* trans. Charles Levin (St. Louis: Telos Press, 1981), 29–62, 63–87, 88–101, 130–142; Schor, *Reading in Detail,* especially chap. 5; and Roland Barthes, *The Fashion System,* trans. Matthew Ward and Richard Howard (New York: Hill and Wang, 1983).

51. The double bind in which an eroticized aesthetics places women in particular helps explain why, for Wollstonecraft, the use of an aesthetic formulation undermined her political argument rather than advancing it. For Burke, by contrast, who was not hampered (in the same way) by its gendered meanings, the aesthetic vocabulary could be invoked to justify a political program. Thus, Burke argued that the high Whigs were fit to represent the common people in Parliament because the great wealth of the former rendered them "disinterested." Not incidentally, Burke argued that their education in the liberal arts (especially poetry) qualified (male) Whigs to govern. See Mandler, *Aristocratic Government,* 19–20.

52. See my *Uneven Developments: The Ideological Work of Gender in Mid-Victorian England* (Chicago: University of Chicago Press, 1988), chap. 4.

53. Recent studies that illuminate this relationship include Christine Battlesby, *Gender and Genius: Towards a Feminist Aesthetics* (London: Women's Press, 1989); de Bolla, *Discourse of the Sublime;* Rita Felski, *Beyond Feminist Aesthetics: Feminist Literature and Social Change* (Cambridge: Harvard University Press, 1989); Schor, *Reading in Detail;* Simpson, *Romanticism* (particularly chap. 6); and Kathy Alexis Psomiades, "Beauty's Body: Gender Ideology and British Aestheticism," *Victorian Studies* 36 (1992): 31–52.

■ FRANCES FERGUSON ■

Justine; or, The Law of the Road

IN THE WAKE of the New Criticism and its emphasis on taking the poem, the story, the novel as the unit of analysis, literary criticism has recurrently found itself asking a set of questions that center on literature in its relation to what is, if not real, then at least nonliterary. It has seemed important, in other words, to identify the kind of work literature does and to ask how it relates to its messages. And nowhere have those questions seemed more urgent than in two apparently quite different types of studies—the accounts of the emergence of aesthetics and of the emergence of pornography.[1]

On the one hand, it has seemed that aesthetics and pornography were completely distinct, as in Theodor Adorno's account of the eighteenth century's (and specifically Kant's) relegation of art and pornography to separate spheres.[2] If pornography was pornography by virtue of its insistent materialism and its appeal to affect, art was art by virtue of what came to be seen as the sublimation that formalism effected, the claim that art necessarily detached itself from the world and its representations. On the other hand, it has seemed to other critics that affectivism linked pornography and aesthetics: while the two might have different objects of representation, a similar emphasis on reception and affect suggested their affinities, as some arguments found affective recognition so important to the constitution of art objects and pornography alike that their relative explicitness or inexplicitness did not matter.[3]

The following account of Sade's *Justine* offers a reading of that novel in the service of an hypothesis about pornography and aesthetics—namely, aesthetics and pornography can emerge as distinct spheres of philosophical speculation and legal regulation only in relation to the question of civil society as it emerges in the eighteenth century. Many histories of aesthetics trace the abandonment of reference and reality in the emergence of the formalist argument for art, and many histories of pornography document what might look like the relatively steady advance of laws repressing sexuality and its expression in pornography and the various "victimless" crimes. Both sets of tendencies, however, obscure at least as much as they reveal (and do so for what is fundamentally the same reason—that they conceive art and pornography as involving epistemological transactions in which someone produces a discrete object with implicit or explicit messages that are more or less effectively received). Between the view that formalist aesthetics increasingly identifies art as the anti-didactic because it speaks in terms so formal as not really to have a message and the view that pornography's value lies in its speaking to a sexuality that never needs to be learned, there lurks a view that we have insufficiently attended. It is that the evolution of civil society in the eighteenth century did not—or did not merely—extend democracy and replace monarchs with republics; it also created society as a whole that was simultaneously more and less than the sum of its parts. Civil society, in other words, is not mass society by virtue of disseminating its products and its privileges more widely. Rather, civil society, in its extension of education to the many rather than the few, in its suggestion that art might serve as an anti-type to property, in its rediscovery of pornography, enables us to see the obsolescence of privacy even in the rise of protections for it, or the evacuation of individualism even in its triumph.

I should like to make three basic points regarding Sade's pertinence to these issues. First, I will argue that *Justine* is an example of pornography that does not so much challenge the law *tout court* as contribute a very specific position to the extensive eighteenth-century discussions of it. Second, I will suggest that Sade does not punish Justine as relentlessly as he does in the novel just for the sake of being true to his character or nature (being Sade and therefore sadistic), but rather because he is implicitly making an argument that the very practices of domination and subordination that we take to be crucial to Sade and sadeanism have already been replaced by the dissemination of punishment through society. And third, I will indicate the ways in which my reading of Sade involves a critique of the Foucauldian account of modern social organization.

Justine, published in 1791, epitomizes Sadean monotony, if monotony involves the relentless consistency of the elements of the novel. In saying this, however, I do not mean to talk about the fact that the same thing arguably happens over and over again—though it does, as Justine goes from one miniature world to another, falling victim to one tyrant after another, tyrants who are able to enforce their wills through either explicit or implied force. Rather, it is that the repetitiveness of the various scenes in Sade's novel precludes there being anything like plot, if plot is understood to involve anything like additive action. To state the obvious, *Justine* is a picaresque novel.[4] Yet *Justine* is not, I would argue, just another eighteenth-century picaresque, an example of the early novel's commitment to looking as if it were not yet art and were still preoccupied with the notion of imitating real and realistic narrative. Nearly fifty years after *Tom Jones,* it repudiates the kind of novelistic advance that had enabled Fielding to produce the apparently random, episodic plot as the infinitely determined one when Tom wandered long enough to be brought to the point of thinking that he was about to marry his mother, so that all roads might look as though they ended in the archetypal signature of plot that marked literature as literature. Moreover, it repudiates the artistic advance of well-formed plot in part by having Justine continually resume her original attitude, with her disposition to future action always looking uninfluenced by her own past. If Fielding had made the picaresque accommodate the modest recognitions of a virtually ineducable character (Tom), Sade insisted upon the episodic nature of his plot in part by preventing Justine from making any connections that seem to rise much above the level of the merely grammatical.

The novel *Justine,* that is, manages to be resolutely picaresque not merely because it employs the device of the journey but also, and primarily, because the character Justine never seems to recognize any resemblances between one episode and another, never seems to adapt what she might have learned from one situation to another. I think particularly here of the ending of the novel, which features Justine providing a capsule summary of the novel's incidents as if she saw the elements of her cumulative history in explicitly causal terms but still could not apply them to the future.

> During my childhood I meet a usurer; he seeks to induce me to commit a theft, I refuse, he becomes rich. I fall amongst a band of thieves, I escape from them with a man whose life I save; by way of thanks, he rapes me. I reach the property of an aristocratic debauchee who has me set upon and devoured by his dogs for not having wanted to poison his aunt. From there I go to the home of a murderous and incestuous surgeon whom I strive to spare from doing a horrible deed: the butcher brands me for a criminal; he doubtless consummates his atrocities, makes his fortune, whilst I am obliged to beg for my bread. I wish to have the sacraments made available to me, I wish fervently to implore the Supreme Being whence howbeit I receive so many ills, and the august tribunal, at which I hope to find purification in our most holy mysteries, becomes the bloody theater of my ignominy: the monster who abuses and plunders me is elevated to his order's highest

honors and I fall back into the appalling abyss of misery. I attempt to preserve a woman from her husband's fury, the cruel one wishes to put me to death by draining away my blood drop by drop. I wish to relieve a poor woman, she robs me, I give aid to a man whom adversaries have struck down and left unconscious, the thankless creature makes me turn a wheel like an animal; he hangs me for his pleasure's sake; all fortune's blessings accrue to him, and I come within an ace of dying on the gallows for having been compelled to work for him. An unworthy woman seeks to seduce me for a new crime, a second time I lose the little I own in order to rescue her victim's treasure. A gentleman, a kind spirit wishes to compensate me for all my sufferings by the offer of his hand, he dies in my arms before being able to do anything for me, I risk my life in a fire in order to snatch a child, who does not belong to me, from the flames; the infant's mother accuses and launches legal proceedings against me, I fall into my most mortal enemy's hands; she wishes to carry me off by force and take me to a man whose passion is to cut off heads: if I avoid that villain's sword it is so that I can trip and fall under Themis'. I implore the protection of a man whose life and fortune I once saved; I dare expect gratitude from him, he lures me to his house, he submits me to horrors, and there I find the iniquitous judge upon whom my case depends; both abuse me, both outrage me, both accelerate my doom; fortune overwhelms them with favors, I hasten on to death.[5]

If its heroine's name begins to identify the novel with the justice that Justine continually says she doesn't get, the novel's commitment to its picaresque mode locates its view of justice. For the picaresque here announces itself as the principle of geographical relativism, the view that the one transcendental rule is that laws are always local. This version of the law of the road represents might as making right within the domain that it can oversee. And if the initial joke of the novel is that Justine keeps failing to "learn," to carry over from one experience to another, the joke on the joke is that she is the purest geographical relativist of the novel: only she imagines that the sun might not rise tomorrow, only she believes that there might be a genuinely sympathetic individual over the horizon.

The argument in favor of geographical relativism had, of course, been put forth most famously by Montesquieu, in *L'esprit des lois* (1748), and its care in outlining its account of government as a functional equivalent of collective intention established it as a particularly important moment in the eighteenth century's emerging debate between intentionalism and consequentialism in law. Although it deserves a lengthier account than I can give it here, its undisputed importance seems to me a function of its incarnation of a "mentality" position, the view that individuals may not have intentions but that the groups in which individuals exist have intentions for them. As in Max Weber's later understanding of the Protestant spirit, the group, the geographically and culturally constituted state, functions as a disembodied individual, a repository of individual traits expanded and overblown by virtue of the fact that mere individuals don't have to be their bearers. As a compromise formation between transcendentalism and absolute individualism, it suggested that laws and customs must inevitably extend past the individual; as a hybrid between intentionalism and consequentialism, it insisted that individual intentions were always the consequence of a social organization. Like a form of the weak social constructionist argument that is frequently attributed to Foucault, Montesquieu's description of governmental organizations keeps funding itself through the discovery of the identities of terms that might be opposed: the individual is collective within a particular locale.[6]

I take *Justine*'s concern with law and government to involve a purification of the position of geographical relativism. Thus, Justine's imagining that the laws might really be local and therefore different over the next hill. Thus, the prominence of the sovereign individual in Sade's work. If picaresque law is the non-transcendental law of geographical relativism, it is also the law of the non-general will. Sovereignty, that is, must be individualizable, even if that sovereignty can only realize itself through an intensification of the policing powers of an individual subordinating all others to his will.

Another way of putting this point would be to say that Justine's plight, her repeated victimization, challenges the eighteenth-century project of democratizing action, the century's obsession with the question of how a government can be capacious enough to accommodate more than one set of intentions. It makes, that is, a simultaneous claim that intentions may constitute one's—specifically Justine's—sense of conscience *and* that intentions are irrelevant to anyone except oneself. Moreover, a distinctly utilitarian line of reasoning enables Sade to demonstrate that Justine's being an orphan, being deprived of a certain protection afforded by the alliances and the privacy of family life, immediately increases the likelihood that other people will see her less for her intentions than for her body. Strangers may not, in other words, understand what she means by virtue, but they continually find something to do with her body. As Dubourg, the rich man from whom she initially seeks aid, says, "The thing which least flatters men, that which makes the least favorable impression upon them, for which they have the most supreme contempt, is good behavior in your sex; . . . what does the virtue of women profit us! It is their wantonness which serves and amuses us; but their chastity could not interest us less" (470).

Justine as a picaresque novel forces the orphaned Justine to travel, and travel looks as though it ought to teach her a particularly intense version of Montesquieu's account of laws: that right and wrong are less ethical terms than geographical ones, dependent less upon what you do than upon where you are. Yet while Montesquieu had imagined that one could produce an empirical catalog of types of governments and the kinds of actions that each might favor without imagining an ideal type that all individuals ought to attain, Sade implicitly attacks even the notion of government that is local rather than transcendental as itself too strongly committed to intention. Sade produces a narrative that, as I suggested earlier, enlists Justine in a cartoonlike commitment to the primacy of her intentions. It does not matter, in her view, that her body has been through the proverbial wars. She can, she thinks, preserve a mental chastity. Thus, even after her body has been ravaged, she implores Saint-Florent to rescue her from the band of robbers, imagining her honor as the "unique treasure" that she has salvaged from her wreck of her body. She can recount being obliged to satisfy the wishes of a gang of robbers and gloss it with the remark that "at least my honor was respected even though my modesty assuredly was not" (486). As Rodin and Rombeau use her own argument against her and say that her conscience will remain unsullied through their rape because they promise that she "will have been vanquished by force" (556), as they brand her with the mark of the whore, she affirms cheerfully, "Whatever had been my trials until that time, at least I was in possession of my innocence" (557). Severino the monk can introduce her into the monastery as "one of the veritable wonders of the world, a Lucretia who simultaneously carries upon her shoulder the mark stigmatizing girls who are of evil repute, and, in her conscience, all the candor, all the naivete of a virgin" (564). She reapplies the taunts of others as if they were comforting: she cherishes what Dubois the procuress calls her "sentimental chastity" (705). Like a strange variation on high Calvinist antinomianism and its claim that election constitutes a spiritual state that may go so far as to nullify the significance of individual acts, Justine's chastity is "sentimental" in its refusal to acknowledge acts that she has not meant to commit. Her position is, in the first place, completely plausible. If the mere physical act of sexual intercourse, regardless of the intention to have intercourse, counted as an action, we would not have the notion of rape, and the corollary notion of a rape victim. It is not, then, that Justine is entirely absurd to imagine that her virtue is not compromised by acts she was coerced into committing. Western criminal law constantly relies upon just such a distinction; it is intention that sorts the criminal from the innocent, the criminal from the victim.

Yet even though Nietzsche characterized Western law as having increasingly abandoned the Greek moral understanding of "the value or disvalue of an action . . . from its consequences," the outcomes of one's actions, the history of law in the eighteenth century defines a different trajectory altogether.[7] Kant, certainly, was perfecting the intentionalist argument for ethical action by suggesting that one entered into the equivalent of an illusory contract with oneself in the absence of any sense of inevitable reward and in the absence of any sense of inevitable contractual exchange with anyone else.[8] Yet the burden of legal consequentialism in the work of figures like Cesare Beccaria and Jeremy Bentham was an assertion of the irrelevance of intention.[9] If the intentionalist approach to law and morals involved hating the sinner who could mean to commit a particular act, the consequentialist approach eliminated the criminalization of apparently ignoble states of mind by asking if the practices they involved really resulted in harm to anyone. (Thus, Bentham's famous defense of usury that freed it from its socioreligious history and identified it instead in terms of its productive effects.)

Justine's particular spin on these issues is to foreground the question of bodily liability. For if Justine is continually being falsely accused and framed for the very crimes she refuses to collaborate in, her vulnerability to framing comes from the fact that she keeps being physically located at the scenes of crimes, and that her physical presence has infinitely more weight than her statements of her intentions and her innocence. Her refusal to participate in crimes becomes the immediate cause of her being accused of crimes. Moreover, false accusation is only the simplest version of Justine's problem with her body, as she becomes what she calls "criminal through virtue." And "virtuous criminality," Sade's most brilliant stroke in the novel, involves Justine in committing a crime to cover the tracks of an innocence that looks like guilt. As Monsieur du Harpin, the avaricious thief, brings charges against her to "be rid of a creature who, through possession of his secret [thievery], had become his master" (479), the novel lays down its key pattern. Justine sees herself "upon the brink of having to pay with my life for having refused to participate in a crime" (479); and then she knowingly witnesses an arson at the Conciergerie in which "many people" are burned (480). Now Dubois the arsonist who arranges the actual torching of the Conciergerie glosses the matter by simply suggesting that virtue suffers while crime pays: "A misplaced delicacy led you to the foot of the scaffold, an appalling crime rescued you from it" (480). Yet that simple reversal, the neat chiasmus in which good intentions produce bad consequences and vice versa, may epitomize Dubois's views, but it by no means captures the extent and complexity of the matter. For the trick of the plot is continually to take an innocent and turn her out as a criminal, and to do so without ever corrupting her mind—and, indeed, *without so much as needing to corrupt her mind*.

This is to say that *Justine* lays down the law of recruitment for pornography by virtue of making the process of registering and obscuring intentions continually complicit in the process of committing new crimes. Justine, that is, may take comfort in the fact that her performing as a slave or a servant exonerates her of having acted willingly (640), but that very process of self-examination enables her to function as an increasingly effective tool of destruction. In describing her encounter with Coeur-de-fer and his band of robbers, this seems like merely a matter of choosing the lesser of two evils: faced with the possibility of being forcibly sodomized or vaginally raped, she remembers, "I was going to abandon myself and become criminal through virtue" (490); and only the coincidental arrival of travelers for Coeur-de-fer to rob saves her from choosing against one crime not by actually choosing but merely by appearing to choose the other.

Justine is put in an increasingly problematic position. Her being a slave by virtue of being an unprotected woman establishes her as repeatedly dependent and as necessarily being repeatedly a "sneak in bondage" (647). But it is not merely that she accepts the appearance of complicity in crime in order to avoid committing a crime, as when she agrees to aid the Comte de Bressac in his plot to kill his aunt precisely so that she will be able to save the woman. Refusing to collaborate with the Comte would not save his aunt; appearing to collaborate enables Justine to have the chance of performing a virtuous action by means of her very appearance of perfidy. But Sade has Justine commit to consciousness that her virtuous motives must, perforce, commit her to the vicious action of lying: "*Le parjure est vertu quand on promit le crime,* one of our tragic poets has said; but perjury is always odious to a delicate and sensitive spirit which finds itself compelled to resort to it. My role embarrassed me" (526). The embarrassment of conscious duplicity, however, will become the least of her difficulties. For her efforts to enlist herself in behalf of other unfortunates and to create leagues of women— from Madame de Bressac to Rosalie in the convent, to Madame de Gernande, the wife of the bloodsucking Count, to Suzanne, sister and mistress of Roland the counterfeiter—will be punished and will multiply the sufferings of the very victims she intended to aid. The lie that she sees herself enlisted to produce continually enlists her as part of the project of torture. And never having intended any wrong itself becomes part of the extension of the wrong.

Toward the end of the novel one reaches the apogee of this pattern, and Justine's double agency ceases to involve the contradiction between what one says and what one really means to do and involves instead conspicuously deficient intention. Justine, having taken refuge from the pursuing Dubois in an inn in Villefranche, wakes to find the inn in flames and everyone around her in panicky flight. She hastens from the inn with a woman with whom she has recently joined forces on the road and at this point I remember that my conductress, more concerned for her own than for her child's safety, has not thought of preserving it from death; without a word to the woman, I fly to our chamber, having to pass through the conflagration and to sustain burns in several places: I snatch up the poor little creature, spring forward to restore her to her mother: I advance along a half-consumed beam, miss my footing, instinctively thrust out my hands, this natural reflex forces me to release the precious burden in my arms . . . it slips from my grasp and the unlucky child falls into the inferno before its own mother's eyes; at this instant I am myself seized. (713)

If Justine has regularly reassured herself that, as a servant or a slave, she never acted willingly in anything whatsoever, the meddlesome commitment to virtue that makes her more solicitous of the child than its own mother here emerges with considerable clarity. No one has made her pick up the child; and, even if a "natural reflex" forced her "to release the precious burden in [her] arms," no one has made her drop the infant.

This "crime" is the one Justine stands accused of as she relates her story to her long-lost and recently refound sister Juliette and her lover Monsieur de Corville. But it is an especially peculiar crime in a novel obsessed with an analysis of the rewards and punishments of crime. On the one hand, the novel has repeatedly challenged the wisdom of a criminal law that can, in the process of trying to discourage the crime of robbery with capital punishment, actually provide an incentive for a robber, who already potentially stands under a capital sentence, to commit murder as well.[10] On the other, it is difficult to see what kind of disincentive, what kind of exemplary punishment, one might offer to discourage the crime of tripping and falling, the misdeed of dropping and breaking.

For in a novel in which there are many intentional crimes that Justine herself may not have intended, Justine's abortive rescue—the good deed–cum-murder—is the first purely unintended harm. And its occurrence marks an important shift in the understanding of the law and its relationship to Sadean pornography. For the ultimate rebuke to Justine's virtuous intentions is not that other people interfere with her ability to effect them but that a thoroughgoing consequentialism would begin to erode the value of that virtue. That is, the eighteenth century's major contribution to Western law would occur less in the form of any codification of the law than in the evolution of a law of torts to supplement the criminal law. Here, in making this claim, I am of course employing a concept that would not necessarily have had a clear definition for Sade, since the law of torts emerged irregularly throughout the eighteenth and nineteenth centuries and would receive its first histories only in the 1920s in England and America. Suffice it to say, however, that the tort law came into being largely as what one can think of as a law of the road. It did not rely upon the justice or honor of thieves (the assumption that might makes right); but, on the other hand, it almost completely bypassed a transcendental argument that implicitly established some version of contract—or an appeal to the durability of intentions—as the basis of law. Rather, as an essential complement to mercantilism, it emphasized a law of physical persistence over time and space. Against the credit economy's emphasis on relating individuals and their rights and obligations to the property that gave them incentives for character, for stability of disposition, the very circulation of goods in the mercantile economy produced an argument that ultimately had little to do with the notion of the value of the goods. For the tort law assigned a liability for possession that matched and perhaps overmatched its privileges as it came to hold persons responsible for their effects and for the effects of their objects. The paradigmatic early cases established a law of the road by claiming that a person's carriage did not cease to be his or her carriage even when it was out of his or her control. In the eighteenth century's early versions of the laws which presently require us to carry insurance against the damages we might unwillingly and unwittingly commit against others, it might be a defense against the criminality of our intentions that we could have no motive for doing harm to someone we didn't know (and thus had no feelings about) if we saw no possibility of gain to ourselves. The logic of causation, however, operated to emphasize the material persistence of persons and objects at the expense of intentions. Not only was ignorance of the law, in the materialist account of the tort law, no excuse; one could never really be anything but ignorant of the law so long as the future remained invisible. And thus the notion of rewards and punishments for actions—indeed, the very notion of actions—was considerably refashioned.

One way of describing the effect of the tort law would be to say that it mistakenly tries to assert social control over the accidents of fate. But it seems to me that one major element—both cause and effect—of the tort law is to demonstrate the limits of quietism, or the activity even of inaction. If the existence of the tort law exposes the luck of morality, what Bernard Williams has called the "moral luck" of those of us who are able to have relatively clear consciences because our cars have not gone out of control and accidentally caused us to kill or maim anyone lately, it is especially important for funding the errors of omission as well as the errors of commission.[11] Tort law, that is, makes incapacity count as an action.

That Justine should have begun to do harm as the unwilling servant or instrument of others, that she should have ended by being able to have avoided doing harm, thus begins to clarify certain otherwise mysterious elements of Sade's novel. They are, moreover, issues worth addressing because they speak to the question of Sadeanism—its sadism, its masochism—quite directly. These are, first, Sade's strong argument against contract because contract presupposes an equality that can never exist; and, second, his handling of the question of punishment.

In the episode involving the Count de Gernande, serial vampire to a succession of wives, Gernande delivers himself of an eloquent denunciation of the illogic of contract in marriage (and far more so in the civil state). "How are you justified," he asks Therese/Justine, "in asserting that a husband lies under the obligation to make his wife happy? . . . The necessity mutually to render one another happy cannot legitimately exist save between two persons equally furnished with the capacity to do one another hurt and, consequently, between two persons of commensurate strength. . . . I can agree not to employ force against him whose own strength makes him to be feared; but what could motivate me to moderate the effects of my strength upon the being Nature subordinates to me?" (645). A passage that lends itself to support the claim that sadomasochistic contract is not a particularly Sadean notion, it seems to enlist itself on the side of an insistent assertion of the physically enforceable will. Yet it follows on a description of Gernande that correlates his merciless practices with his incompetence or incapacity. "It was then I noticed [Therese relates], not without astonishment, that this giant, this species of monster whose aspect alone was enough to strike terror, was howbeit barely a man; the most meager, the most minuscule excrescence of flesh or, to make a juster comparison, what one might find in a child of three was all one discovered upon this so very enormous and otherwise so corpulent individual" (641). What seems to me to be suggested by the various elements of the Gernande episode is what one might think of as a theory of progressive action, on an analogy with a theory of progressive taxation. In the progressive legal economy, one should only be expected and required to act according to one's ability to act. As Clement has repeatedly declared to Therese/Justine during her incarceration in the monastery, "it is the most barbarous and stupid intolerance to wish to fly at" the throat of the singular and extravagant individual, who is "no more guilty toward society . . . than is . . . the person who came blind and lame into the world" (602).

Taken alone, Clement's arguments might simply be taken as advocacy of pluralism (with sexuality made the paradigm of what it might mean for the senses to be abled or disabled, functional or dysfunctional); taken alone, Gernande's repudiation of contract might seem to continue its claim that the freedom to act is fundamentally asymmetrical and unequalizable. Together, and together with the account of the "fatal apathy" of Gernande as an epitome of "the true libertine soul" (644), these views indicate the massive changes that the logic of the law of torts effects upon the body of the criminal law. While it may be difficult, even to the point of impossibility, for an individual to perform a virtuous action, to satisfy a contract implicit or explicit, Sadean sadism is the process of recognizing harm to another as a kind of prosthetics of agency. The unlovable and the incompetent may have no positive capacity to please, that is, but harm is something one can accomplish without charm or resources—"apathetically."

Indeed, all the mechanisms of the Benedictine monastery suggest how far apathy may be from asceticism. For the trick of the monastery involves not merely converting the young women who have been abducted at the monks' behest into the servants of their pleasures; it includes a transfer of agency so extreme that the young women's actions are completely detached from their intentions. This is, in the first place, a matter of their facing up to the inevitability of their fates, to the "impunity guaranteed [the monks] by this impregnable retreat" (580). As young women who are bereft of observers, of people who will sound any alarm at their disappearance, they are transported into an enclosure whose rules contradict their wills so thoroughly that their wills become obviously irrelevant, and, indeed, "all resistance" comes to seem "pure affectation, pretense, and useless" (567).

In the moment that resistance comes to be defined as "feigned" whether one means it or not, the importance of the notion of the class in Sadean pornography becomes clear. The regimentation of the Monastery of Saint Mary-in-the-Wood, that is, may involve an interest in imposing discipline, in producing an arbitrary system that is inflexibly maintained, but even more importantly the regimentation assembles groups of people—four classes of four women each, twelve procuresses who provide twelve young women a year for the monks, circles of debauchees—so as to transfer agency. Thus, the penal code of the monastery must be detailed to each new inmate, but the code is one that is arbitrary not by contrast with some standard of naturalness but because one has no way of conforming to it. Some offenses are punishable even though they have occurred "either through misunderstanding or for whatsoever may be the reason" (581); and if others, such as pregnancy, are punishable, their remedies (abortion) are as well.[12] As Omphale, the "superintendent" who explains the system to Therese/Justine, makes clear, the monks are interested only in sexuality as infinitely repeated rape, sexuality always separated from consent.

> "They do not absolutely confine themselves to virgins: a girl who has been seduced already or a married woman may prove equally pleasing, but a forcible abduction has got to take place, rape must be involved, and it must be definitely verified . . . ; they wish to be certain their crimes cost tears; they would send away any girl

who was to come here voluntarily; had you not made a prodigious defense, had they not recognized a veritable fund of virtue in you, and, consequently, the possibility of crime, they would not have kept you twenty-four hours." (587)

And, in the ultimate conceit for the monastery's dislocation of the will, the young women who have been abductable by virtue of not being watched are required to maintain a constant vigil, to become "Girls of the Watch," each of whom "must remain awake all night throughout the whole of the term she spends with her master" and each of whom is made responsible and punishable for his every action and inaction—"who is always wrong, always at fault, always beaten" (585). The perfection of the monks' power, in other words, is that they can inflict suffering even in their sleep (611). And whatever deterrent effect might be achieved by a system of punishment that seeks to make the law an incentive system to individual action must contend with the transfer of both actions and their consequences.

Sadean pornography, in the account I'm giving of *Justine,* is thus important for establishing the notion of class action. But unlike the notion of class as an economic group defined by a relationship to the means of production, and unlike the notion of class as a group assembled through a classification of similar individuals or similar aims, class here functions as a conspicuously self-divided term. The Sadean enclosure, that is, operates not just to seal an individual from any world outside it but (like the parentheses that identify a mathematical grouping or class) also to create the possibility of distributing action among the members of the group.

For what Sade describes in *Justine* is neither sadomasochism as a plausible version of sexual contract (establishing a class of sexual deviants) nor sadomasochism as what Lacan identifies as the opposite of the categorical imperative—an individual's right to demand unremittingly that others supply one's needs, one's desires (in which class domination and class subordination provide the model).[13] Instead, an enclosure creates a class less as a conceptual term, an epistemological statement, than as a tool for the redistribution of the consequences of action. As the tort law supplements the criminal law, there is no mere extension of the old law of the servant which held a master accountable for the acts that a servant had committed at his behest. Instead, the tort law identifies everyone except the sovereign individual (who becomes increasingly rare, increasingly elusive) as a servant to the very idea of the civil state, the law of society that is always verging on putting one in the wrong, by holding one accountable less for intentions than for consequences—or by holding one accountable for both simultaneously. And it is the simultaneity of these dual regimes of law that makes it particularly difficult to track their operations precisely, since the triumph of utilitarian legal arguments did not so much replace intentionalism with consequentialism as insist upon applying both at once. Acts that had long been criminal, such as murder and theft, remained criminal and found punishments that were designed to be disincentives; thus, Sade is able to present the counterfeiter Roland as the perfected criminal not so much because he commits more crimes or more serious ones than other characters as because he has unleashed the power of the legal system of disincentives. Loving being punished, having himself hanged for pleasure, his every action is charmed, and he can exist within a happy orbit of intentions in which even what he hasn't chosen seems like a reward. In the tort law's distribution of rewards and punishments, he becomes a sovereign individual less through strength of will than through an accident of adaptation that enables him to experience punishment as a reward.

Thus, though Sadean criminality has recurrently been seen as a conscious violation of conventional morality, I think that the existentially thrilling account of the Sadean hero who chooses his necessity and demands the punishment that others might impose on him is fundamentally flawed. For whatever else Sade may have been doing (and whether or not he liked what he was describing), he was providing one of the most effective ways of identifying the way in which the tort law funded a host of new forms of action.

To some extent, my view of the tort law coincides with Foucault's account of the disciplinary society, with its particular reliance on Bentham's Panopticon as an emblem of the importance of visibility.[14] Within the various Panoptic structures of society, Foucault's argument says or implies, certain kinds of technological efficiencies occur. A Panopticon, by giving one superintendent a central position from which he can view a host of people, replaces the relative cumbersomeness of a social contract model of society (with one-to-one agreement providing a paradigm for the agreement of many) with the control of many by one. With an architectural gesture, the Panopticon resolves a basic dilemma of the law—why it is that, when those who have been taken to be criminals assume the majority, they don't simply overtake the minority and make criminality the new law. The superintendent's impersonality, his having no personal views of those he supervises, minimizes the contractual nature of the interaction, and being visible is increasingly detached from the notion of potentially verifiable contractual agreement.

A great deal is almost instantaneously plausible about this version of Foucault. Yet its particular way of treating the relationship between penality and social action tends to make surveillance seem a sufficient consequence in itself, as if the expansion of visibility were itself a regulative process.[15] In this form, the Foucauldian account suggests how changing the odds of detecting a crime might act as a disincentive to further crime; and self-surveillance appears as an individual's tendency continually to represent probability as inevitability, likelihood as event. Yet what seems mistaken about this account is that it fails to register how fundamentally the consequentialism of the law of torts precipitated a reconfiguration of both action and its evidence. As much as Bentham wanted to have the Panopticon built, as much as he favored the reduction of the law to statute (what could be known in advance of action) rather than common law (what was always in danger of being invented on the spot by judges), his work on morals and legislation is important for having supplemented the anticipatory causation of intentional action with the retrospective causation of consequential effect. And in that maneuver, he underwrote the tort law as a law of class that does not know itself because of being observed but recognizes itself as action because of what it has done. Thus, certain kinds of involuntary action—the damage caused by your property run amok that I mentioned earlier—come to count as moral action; indeed, certain kinds of omission become actions, as when the eighteenth-century law identifies professional misconduct as one of the earliest examples of a tortious harm. In this process, the Panoptican is merely one case of what it means for there to be such a thing as class formation. Like Wesleyan Methodism, with its introduction of the twelve-person class, like the Lancasterian schoolroom, with its creation of large numbers of small grade-levels for classes, the Benthamite account of causation produces class actions. While all of these social structures have been seen as implementing social conformity and establishing oppressive disciplinary regimes in every conceivable direction, they are, instead, crucial in making action look as though it were only possible through other people. (The examinations in a Lancasterian classroom, for instance, continually correlate your achievement with that of other people; indeed, they speak the message of class even as they ostensibly inaugurate the expansion of education beyond the ranks of the aristocracy and the gentry by making your class standing depend not merely on your knowledge but also on someone else's failure or lapse of knowledge.)

This is as much as to say that Sadean pornography joins Benthamite consequentialism and a host of class-forming practices in eighteenth-century civil society to make actions more visible in relation to other people than in relation to individual intention. The importance of the visibility of pornography is, thus, not that it assaults the eyes (and claims that sight is the most involuntarily transmissible sense), not that it offends the public good, the public interest, the public morals. Rather, it is that *Justine* presents pornography as the model of action in which morality is very imperfectly assimilable to rules of conduct, codes of behavior that may be taught. For pornography, in this view, commits itself less to affect (the production of further responses and consequences) than with effect (the manifestation of the visible consequences of what one has already done). As *Justine* keeps telling its heroine, "There's no justice," or "Now look what you've done."

This particular account of Sadean pornography, as instanced by *Justine*, suggests how important it may be to revise what has now come to be a conventional antithesis between Kant and Sade, aesthetics and pornography. As I have argued elsewhere, the Kantian sublime founds Kant's version of idealist aesthetics on the insistence that aesthetic experience essentially involves a reconfiguration of our notion of objects. [16] From the moment that Kant distinguishes the sublime from the beautiful principally on account of its being natural, not having been produced by human beings for human beings, the aesthetic appreciation of nature becomes something quite distinct from a *recognition* or *understanding* of objects. The aesthetic appreciation of what was never made to be appreciated, that is, eliminates the need—and, indeed the possibility—for certain kinds of justification and explanation; it cares less about evaluating a beech tree, for instance, as a specimen of beech trees than about producing what one can only call a new object from what may be accidental or transitory or incidental features of the old.

The account of the sublime, in other words, enables Kant to make the aesthetic the vehicle for the notion of ontological relativity. What I have been arguing about Sadean pornography in the case of *Justine* is that it provides a similarly relativized account of what an action might be, to correspond with Kant's relativized account of what an object might be. As civil law in the eighteenth century increasingly supplements the criminal law's emphasis on intention with an emphasis on consequence, it reconfigures even the notion of personal intentions and individual character by making the material persistence of the body of the messenger (Justine and her equivalents) override any message that she might want to deliver.

Thus, pornography and aesthetics, however strongly they have been distinguished from one another as the most material and most immaterial poles of our experience of representations, are not nearly so much opposed as similar. They are similar in their shared commitment to the interimplications of medium and message, and to the ways in which those interimplications enable the reconfiguration of both objects and actions by expanding the role of effects in defining them. They are similar, that is, in making effects so much more important than intentions that the aesthetic can lay claim to a pleasure that was never meant (since the sublime is, in Kant's view, concerned only with a pleasure in what was never designed for our perception or our pleasure) and the pornographic can attach blame to a harm that was never intended (since the pornographic is, in Sade's view, concerned only with the physical and "unsentimental" effects of one's actions). This is as much as to say that the relativity that both Kantian aesthetics and Sadean pornography attach to objects and actions conspicuously erodes the abilities of either aesthetic objects or pornography to "express" either personal or ideological commitments, because the effective meaning of such objects and actions is no longer in the eye of the maker or the beholder.

Notes

1. I give here only a very abbreviated set of references to indicate something of the extent of the concern with these issues. Some of the most recent relevant discussions appear in John Barrell, *The Political Theory of Painting from Reynolds to Hazlitt: The Body of the Public* (New Haven: Yale University Press, 1986); Terry Eagleton, *The Ideology of the Aesthetic* (Oxford: Basil Blackwell, 1990); my own *Solitude and the Sublime: The Aesthetics of Individuation* (New York: Routledge Chapman and Hall, 1992); and much of the work of Paul de Man and Frederic Jameson. Both feminist and gay studies have prompted renewed interest in the development of pornography; and the most influential positions have developed in either sympathetic or hostile response to the work of Michel Foucault, whose emphasis on the discursive structures of sexuality has importantly altered the view that social regulation constantly provides incentives to action by iterating the acceptable and the taboo, and Catharine A. MacKinnon, whose anti-pornography position has drawn considerable fire from anti-censorship feminists as a restraint on freedom of expression.

2. Adorno speaks of aesthetic autonomy as having involved art's emancipating "itself from cuisine and pornography, an emancipation that has become irrevocable," in *Aesthetic Theory,* tr. C. Lenhardt, ed. Gretel Adorno and Rolf Tiedemann (New York: Routledge and Kegan Paul, 1984), 18.

3. See particularly Leo Bersani, "Sexuality and Esthetics" in *The Freudian Body: Psychoanalysis and Art* (New York: Columbia University Press, 1986), 29–50, and D. A. Miller, *The Novel and the Police* (Berkeley: University of California Press, 1988) for unusually able accounts of an affective position.

4. Roland Barthes has drawn attention to the novel as picaresque in *Sade, Fourier, Loyola* (Berkeley: University of California Press, 1976), 149.

5. Donatien-Alphonse-François, Marquis de Sade, *Justine, Philosophy in the Bedroom, and Other Writings,* tr. Richard Seaver and Austryn Wainhouse (New York: Grove Press, 1965), 736–737. Further references in the text are to this edition. Until the Pléiade edition of Sade is complete, the best available French text of the novel is Annie Le Brun and Jean-Jacques Pauvert, eds., *Oeuvres complètes du Marquis de Sade,* vol. 3: *Justine, ou les Malheurs de la vertu* (n.p.: Pauvert, 1986), 306–307.

6. Charles Secondat, Baron de Montesquieu, *The Spirit of the Laws,* tr. Thomas Nugent (New York: Hafner Press, 1949).

7. Friedrich Nietzsche, *Beyond Good and Evil*, tr. Walter Kaufmann (New York: Random House, 1966), 43–44.

8. See particularly the discussion of "duties to oneself as such" in Immanuel Kant, *The Metaphysics of Morals*, tr. Mary Gregor (Cambridge: Cambridge University Press, 1991), 214ff.

9. Cesare Beccaria, *On Crimes and Punishments*, tr. David Young (Indianapolis: Hackett Publishing Company, 1986). Bentham's account of the "principle of utility," however much it has been seen to be committed to crass materialism, is in fact rather a statement of the primacy of consequentialism; see particularly his account of pleasure and pain that transmutes them from individualistic terms into the basic terms for identifying consequences. Jeremy Bentham, *The Principles of Morals and Legislation* (New York: Hafner Press, 1948), 8ff.

10. Dubois's claim is that "the law's to be blamed for these crimes . . .; so long as thieves are hanged like murderers, thefts shall never be committed without assassinations. The two misdeeds are punished equally; why then abstain from the second when it may cover up the first?" (Sade, *Justine*, 491.)

11. Bernard Williams, *Moral Luck: Philosophical Papers 1973–1980* (Cambridge: Cambridge University Press, 1981), 20–39.

12. "Upon the day the surgeon confirms the existence of a pregnancy, one hundred strokes are administered" (Sade, *Justine*, 581); but we—and Therese/Justine—are also told that the detection of contraceptives or abortifacients will provoke Antonin's wrath (586).

13. Jacques Lacan, "Kant with Sade," tr. James Swenson, *October* 51 (Winter 1989), 55–75.

14. Michel Foucault, *Discipline and Punish: The Birth of the Prison*, tr. Alan Sheridan (New York: Pantheon, 1977).

15. This has seemed to many of Foucault's ablest commentators to be the crucial message of *Discipline and Punish*. See, for instance, Nancy Armstrong, *Desire and Domestic Fiction* (New York: Oxford University Press, 1987), where "supervision" seems to constitute an activity much as affect does in affectivist accounts of literature. Thus, she describes the importance of "supervision" in legitimating women's activities: "Supervision presumably made all the difference between amusements that led to corruption and forms of leisure that occupied a woman constructively. The activities comprising her education could be considered educational only if they were supervised, and by the same token, virtually anything could be considered educational if it provided an occasion for supervision" (100).

16. Frances Ferguson, *Solitude and the Sublime: Romanticism and the Aesthetics of Individuation* (New York: Routledge, Chapman and Hall, 1992), esp. 1–36 and 62–96.

GEOFFREY GALT HARPHAM

Aesthetics and the Fundamentals of Modernity

The Ideology and Ecology of the Aesthetic

NO CONCEPT IS MORE fundamental to modernity than the aesthetic, that radiant globe of material objects and attitudes ideally independent of politics, rationality, economics, desire, religion, or ethics. For as Shaftesbury, Kant, Alexander Baumgarten, Friedrich Schiller, and their successors have elaborated it, the aesthetic gathers into itself and focuses norms and notions crucial to the self-description of an enlightened culture. These include the privilege of disinterested assessment; the autonomy of the artifact from historical, social, or economic forces; the uncoerced liberty of the judging subject; the universalizability of subjective responses; the human capacity to imagine and create objects, and indeed a "world," that are harmonious and whole; and even what might be called the destiny of freedom to actualize itself in the world. Interestingly, however, this defining concept is itself underdefined, for "the aesthetic" ambivalently refers both to particular kinds of objects and to the attitude appropriate to judging them. What renders the definition even less precise is that neither objects nor attitude can exist by themselves; each not only depends on the other but flourishes only in a certain kind of culture, a "modern" culture capable of sustaining a "disinterested" attention to things that have no utilitarian function, no necessary connection to meanings or concepts. One of the paradoxes of modernity is that modern cultures, for whom works of art are rigorously nonutilitarian, are in fact uniquely equipped to appreciate them; while premodern cultures, which invest what might be called "art objects" with numerous cultic, religious, or variously propagandistic ends, are, by the logic of modernity, manifestly unsuited for, even unworthy of them.

The aesthetic is thus—to an extent that remains to be assessed—an ideological creation, an attribute posited by modernity of itself. A brief *tour d'horizon* of modern ideologies confirms this point. The Anglo-American discourse of liberalism, for example, typically invokes the aesthetic in the course of defending the value of freedom against encroachments from metaphysics, theory, fixed values, universals of all sorts. Where Jeremy Bentham, Thomas Malthus, Herbert Spencer, and others envisioned a "science" of society, liberals followed J. S. Mill's argument that it fell to "art" to define the ends which science could then study.[1] An antiscientific aestheticism continues to define liberalism today. Michael Walzer begins his influential book *Spheres of Justice* with the premise that "distributive justice is not . . . an integrated science, but an art of differentiation."[2] For modern liberalism, "art" seems to represent a principle of humane inexactitude or unpredictability, one that not only allows for a certain speculative or intuitive component in analysis, but, by extension, constitutes a warrant for a practice of free self-determination unconstrained by the rules of rationality, utility, or social convention. Also traceable to Mill, this time to his conception of liberty as the cultivation of individual flourishing, even of "originality" or "eccentricity"—"the path that merely concerns [oneself]" —such a practice even informs projects as remote in spirit from Mill's enlightened utilitarianism as Nietzsche's self-forming Overman, the capitalist romance of the "self-made man," and the aestheticized *pratique de soi* advocated by Michel Foucault.[3]

Kant makes a powerful claim on liberal sympathies when he distinguishes between a public realm concerned with social organization and justice and a private realm in which the aesthetic is centered. Where and how to draw this distinction constitutes an ongoing debate within liberalism between, roughly, liberals and libertarians. What's wrong with Richard Rorty's (libertarian) position, according to Anthony Cascardi, is that it concentrates all its attention on the individual, sacrificing a crucial Kantian point, that aesthetic judgment, while based on private sensations of pleasure and pain, also lays the foundation for the formation of a community through an extension to everyone of individual judgments of taste. As Cascardi puts it, Kant's point is "that the aesthetic provides the means by which these realms may be made transparent to one another while their distinct identities are simultaneously preserved."[4] Cascardi especially wants to preserve, against Rorty's insistent privatization of aesthetics, a dialectic between the individual sensual experience and what Kant calls the "supersensible substrate of mankind," with its possibility for collective judgments.[5] Hence Cascardi's project for an "aesthetic liberalism" which "reflects an effort to grant the shaping power of art over our identity as individuals seeking at once to ground that identity in community and to distinguish it therefrom" (22). Debates within liberalism today typically "grant the shaping power of art," and often the shaping power of Kant as well. Even Jürgen Habermas, while wary of the libidinally disruptive experience of art and hostile to the Kantian categorical imperative, may still retain an unacknowledged allegiance to Kant. Habermas's "discourse ethics," according to Cascardi, covertly presumes a supersensible substrate of humanity in urging as an ideal the notion of distortion-free rational communication; and his normative speech community is, according to Terry Eagleton, simply "an updated version of Kant's community of aesthetic judgement."[6]

This community was first updated by Schiller, who, in *On the Aesthetic Education of Man,* extended the idea of the aesthetic from the subjective to the political, proposing an "aesthetic modulation of the psyche," an "aesthetic education" that would ultimately produce an "Aesthetic State."[7] Schiller's project has always excited and troubled leftist thinkers, many of whom, including Herbert Marcuse, Ernst Bloch, Theodor Adorno, and Frederic Jameson, have sought to return to the fountainhead, the fundament of modernity, the original ciphers of freedom, through the aesthetic. As Christopher Norris points out, aesthetics has long functioned on the left as a "secularised redemptive hermeneutic," holding out the promise that society could overcome its contradictions and theory could transform itself into a discourse responsive to art's always latent emancipatory potential.[8] Schiller, according to some in this tradition, represents an early progressive response to industrial alienation, a necessary political reworking of Kant that, according to Cascardi, actually "anticipates the diagnoses of modernity later put forward by Marx, Weber, and Lukács" (15).

But others are not so sure, either about Schiller or about the aesthetic. Terry Eagleton concludes his recent historical inquiry into *The Ideology of the Aesthetic* with a notably cautious endorsement of the aesthetic, which is, he suggests, to be distrusted whenever it posits pure, autonomous values, but prized when it insists upon a vital relation between bodily or material life and the universal level on which questions of reason and justice are raised. Any such endorsements actually seem to be wrung from recalcitrant material, for as Eagleton demonstrates, the aesthetic is dialectical virtually to the point of incoherence. While a "feminine" register of sensuous form dominates the originary work of Alexander Baumgarten, this pure spring is almost immediately fouled, first by Kant's "stark imperatives" and then by certain aspects of Schiller's worldly reinterpretation.[9] Eagleton applauds the Schillerian (and later, the Communist) politicization of the aesthetic but depreciates its corollary, the aestheticization of politics, which has had, he says, the effect of providing imaginary reconciliations to contradictions that remain unresolved in the real world. Even for the supposed beneficiaries, however, the aesthetic was not wholly beneficial. As Eagleton notes, the aesthetic provided the emergent middle class with "a superbly versatile model of their political aspirations, exemplifying new forms of autonomy and self-determination," and theorizing a new and mysterious circumstance in which values appeared to be floating free and bodily pleasures and drives were invested with fresh significance; but the aesthetic also signified a kind of internalized repression cognate with Gramscian "hegemony" (*IA,* 28).[10] In the end, as in the beginning, Eagleton cannot sustain a single attitude towards what he repeatedly calls this "markedly contradictory concept," and the book is both riveted and riven by paradox endlessly repeated. In analyses of Kant, Schiller, Hegel, Marx, Kierkegaard, Nietzsche, Freud, Benjamin, and Adorno ("two different Adornos"), Eagleton tracks the logic of "on the other hand" as it reinscribes itself, even in his own increasingly predictable argument(s) that while the aesthetic has functioned as a language consistent with political domination, it also, once upon a time, provided the most powerful available critique of bourgeois possessive individualism and appetitive egoism, and might, if it could return to its origin or essence, reclaim its destiny of imitating a defiantly independent *Lebenswelt.*

But that, as Eagleton himself demonstrates, is a big *if.* For his own laborious slogging through a mass of historico-philosophical corruption en route to an unspoiled, delightfully feminine, and corporeal origin is, as we have just begun to see, entirely typical of efforts both on the left and on the right to save the aesthetic from its own perversions. Just as Eagleton returns to Baumgarten as the source and regards Kant and others as the corruption, and just as Cascardi regards Kant as the author of a discourse sullied by pragmatism, still others return to Schiller as the fundament that subsequent thinkers have betrayed. The sense of corruption seems inescapable with a concept that, as Eagleton recognizes, can take "either a left or a right turn. The left turn: smash truth, cognition and morality, which are all just ideology, and live luxuriantly in the free, groundless play of your creative powers. The right turn . . . forget about theoretical analysis, cling to the sensuously particular, view society as a self-grounding organism" (*IA,* 368–369).

With respect to the right turn, Eagleton notes an "unnerving affinity," through a shared contempt for the utilitarian, between the aesthetic and the kind of cynical evil concentrated in "the upper echelons of fascist organizations" (*IA,* 412). Indeed, a great mass of evidence suggests that it is the right, not the left, that has found the idea of an aesthetic politics most attractive. What dismays those on the left is the conservative appeal not to the "free particulars" of the aesthetic but rather to its "transcendence," its erasure of history. When a canonical work of art is praised for containing "timeless and universal truths," or for being "as relevant today as it was when it was written, 830 years ago," or "appealing to everyone alike," one senses that the rhetoric of aesthetic praise itself occults or sublimates precisely those forces and factions that jostled that work, and not some other, into the canon in the first place. Such a hegemonic rhetoric, conservatives have discovered, can be applied to institutions, governments, authorities of all kinds. Many on the left suspect the aesthetic of being a double agent, accomplice to reaction, a mystified surrogate for political forces that operate within it in an attenuated or oblique way. The title of a recent article by the British Marxist Tony Bennett captures leftist distrust succinctly: "Really Useless 'Knowledge': A Political Critique of Aesthetics."[11]

As Bennett well knows, conservative theoreticians from Edmund Burke to Roger Scruton have argued for the usefulness of aesthetic knowledge as a way of recapturing a renewed social grace—or, Bennett might argue, of sheltering the world of privilege ("taste") from unwelcome political distractions, and the complacently self-sufficient subject from the claims of justice and the rigors of critical reflection. "In the sentiment of beauty," Scruton writes, "we feel the purposiveness and intelligibility of everything that surrounds us, while in the sentiment of the sublime we seem to see beyond the world, to something overwhelming and inexpressible in which it is somehow grounded."[12] The seductive power of the aesthetic actually intensifies as one moves farther and farther right. Fascism, according to a famous comment by Walter Benjamin in 1936, meant the aestheticization of politics; and others were quick to seize the hint, analyzing the link between aesthetics and politics as one explanation for the fascination of fascism, the way in which, in it, rational discourse was superseded by fantasy, myth, spectacle, and fetish.[13] Almost as if to illustrate what Eagleton describes as the contradictoriness of the aesthetic, Scruton and others on the right have established a "right" reading of Schiller's Aesthetic State as a vision of how society might look if it could overcome the baneful antinomies of secular rationalism, achieve the ordered perfection envisioned by poets and philosophers, and mime in social terms the sublime harmony achieved by poetry through the union of language and symbol, form and content, subject and object.

Strongly centralized governments seem to have a special genius for practicing politics as a form of art. In *On the Genealogy of Morals,* Nietzsche described the first politicians as "a conqueror and master race" whose "work is an instinctive creation and imposition of forms; they are the most involuntary, unconscious artists there are. . . . They do not know what guilt, responsibility, or consideration are . . . they exemplify that terrible artists' egoism that has the look of bronze and knows itself justified to all eternity."[14] Nietzsche may well have been thinking of the account by his teacher Jacob Burckhardt in *The Civilization of the Renaissance in Italy* of the Renaissance city-state as a "work of art" molded by the ruthlessly effective autocrat-warrior who, with little regard for concerns of morality or justice, ordered the state according to his own interests, making of the people a mere disciplined multitude. For Burckhardt, however, the state as a work of art was a calamity, stifling every possibility for a truly healthy culture.[15] Hitler himself seems to be anticipated in Nietzsche's words, and is portrayed in those terms more explicitly, if phantasmagorically, in Leni Riefenstahl's film *The Triumph of the Will,* in which he is shown descending from the clouds.[16] Such images may seem unworthy of serious philosophical consideration, but a comparable complex appears in Ernst Jünger's novel *Die Arbeiter* (The worker), which, according to recent work by Richard Wolin and Michael Zimmerman, exerted a powerful, and hardly unphilosophical, fascination on his most famous reader, Martin Heidegger.[17] The history of fascism compels a difficult recognition, that the violence of extreme reaction, racism, and even genocide represents not a total break with the Enlightenment tradition of modernity, but rather, as a political form instinct with the aesthetic, a recognizable variant within that tradition.

The vulnerability of the tradition to corruption through the aesthetic is demonstrated once again by postmodernism, which Norris has called "a wholesale version of aesthetic ideology" (*WWWP,* 24). Postmodernism can, perhaps, be considered the purest form of the aesthetic turned ideological, and perhaps not surprisingly, is a deeply fissured movement. Considering only the work of two of its most eminent apologists, Jean-François Lyotard and Jean Baudrillard, one can say that each side of the postmodern fissure realizes one of the possible ways of misreading the relations between the Kantian faculties. Describing himself as a Kantian "of the Third Critique," Lyotard seeks to stiffen the distinctions between theoretical reason, ethical understanding, and aesthetic judgment that are elaborated most decisively in the *Critique of Judgement,* where, Lyotard says, Kant finally "cures himself of the disease of knowledge and rules."[18] In his most widely known work, the early *The Postmodern Condition,* Lyotard claimed that the imperial violence of knowledge, in the forms of "metalanguages" and "metanarratives," could be resisted through art conceived as the site of a disruptively unique "event."[19] The postmodern artifact clears a space for innovation, for the "unforeseeable" or "impossible" move unrestrained by obligations to represent either the objective world or its own subjective nature. Lyotard's postmodernism departs, of course, quite radically from Kant's modernism, which posits a supersensible substrate of humanity, a space in which judgment can work its synthesizing analogies between the sublime and theoretical reason on the one hand and the beautiful and ethical understanding on the other. For Lyotard, the fact that judgment operates "without criteria" means precisely the opposite, that it cannot integrate or synthesize, and cannot therefore lay claim to worldly or theoretical knowledge. The best hope for resisting the "totalitarian" implications of the collapse of "phrase regimes" such as prescription and description is, he argues, to preserve the "abyss" between them. Thus what might seem a state of conceptual paralysis in which no movement between regimes is possible actually implies to Lyotard the prospect of human progress, of a move into the future enabled by the unaccountable aesthetic event.[20]

If for Lyotard the Kantian distinctions between the faculties must be purged of their universalizing tendencies and the lines between them drawn ever more sharply, for Jean Baudrillard culture has reached a stage in which the distinctions have been effaced by a postmodern practice of image-production that requires, and invokes, no original referent at all, existing only in the undecidable mode of "hyperreality." For Baudrillard, postmodernity has made it futile or impossible to distinguish between truth and true-seeming consensus judgments, "science" and "ideology," or representations and "simulacra." It is Baudrillard that Christopher Norris chiefly has in mind when he describes, and condemns, postmodernism as "a project of annulling all the terms and distinctions that Kant sought so strenuously to hold in place, and a consequent refusal to acknowledge any limits to the realm of imaginary representation" (*WWWP*, 24; see also 164–193).

What annoys those who, like Norris, see in these terms and distinctions a warrant for a politically progressive critique based on the ultimate accessibility of evidence, accurate representation, the probative powers of critique, and so forth, is postmodernism's ideological flaccidity. Especially in his more recent texts, Lyotard seems eager to avoid any positive program whatsoever, cultivating instead of a politics an ethics based almost exclusively on deferral, indeterminacy, or "hesitation." For those on the left, postmodernism is especially frustrating because it envelops without realizing Marxism, deploying Marxism's central categories through inversion: postmodernism stands for materiality without substance, totality without community, homogeneity without equality, economics without class, populism without humanity, dynamism without aspiration, and liberation without justice. For those on the right, postmodernism is equally offensive, representing uniformity without direction or purpose, collectivity without nationalism or racism, control without authority, passivity without faith. A "wholesale version of the aesthetic ideology," postmodernism seems ambivalently to detach itself from any ideology worthy of the name.[21] Perhaps because of its deeply inwrought aesthetic component, it takes a comparably ambivalent position with respect to the promises of Enlightenment rationality; for it is difficult to say whether postmodernism represents the culminating historical realization of the Englightenment tradition or its degradation.

What might be even harder to determine is how postmodernism can be the very flower of the "aesthetic ideology" when it had, not so many years earlier, been advertised as the "anti-aesthetic."[22] Has postmodernism recently gone to seed, or is the aesthetic to be distinguished from its own ideology? The term "aesthetic ideology" was coined by Paul de Man in essays written near the end of his life, when he showed a new interest in ideology critique. Aesthetics, de Man argued, was in Kant a "distinctive mode of understanding," one that had a clearly defined province and relative importance, preserved through what Norris calls the *"rigorous and principled insistence* that the faculties should maintain their internal system of differentiated powers and prerogatives, and not be tempted into various forms of illusory premature synthesis" of, for example, phenomenal perception and ethical categories or theoretical reason (*WWWP,* 18). De Man identifies a structural temptation in the aesthetic to the fusion and confusion of what Kant intended as an intricate network of differentiations between faculties, with the threatened result that form is simply taken for meaning, performance for cognition, perception for understanding—and, by natural-seeming extensions, aesthetic forms for the culture at large, and the culture at large for the state.

The stakes involved in these misprisions, these failures to respect boundaries, are high indeed. Ultimately, an imperial aesthetic—the "aesthetic ideology"—comes to substitute for those faculties it was intended to serve, with disastrous cognitive, political, and ethical consequences. Conceding that a comment in Joseph Goebbels's novel *Michael* to the effect that "politics are the plastic art of the state" is "a grievous misreading of Schiller's aesthetic state," de Man then adds that "the principle of this misreading does not essentially differ from the misreading which Schiller inflicted on his predecessor, namely Kant."[23] Fascism is a degenerate form of a degenerate form of Kant, succeeding by a highly effective suppression of the violence required to bring about its syntheses. Thus the aesthetic makes "claims on the shape and the limits of our freedoms" that are by no means merely theoretical.[24] According to Norris, de Man is here both describing and pleading guilty to a philosophical wrong turn that had informed his notorious wartime journalism for the Belgian collaborationist newspaper *Le Soir.* When, in the late '60s, de Man began to publish his major critical and theoretical essays, he devoted himself to tasks that, in effect, constituted a melancholy and penitentially rigorous critique of the "monadic" or "totalizing" figures characteristic of the aesthetic ideology, distinguishing, in his later work, between Kantian "critical hermeneutics" and the grievous misreading represented by Schillerian syntheses.

This account has, for many, the double virtue of establishing the worldliness of the later de Man and going some ways towards exculpating de Man from charges of personal immorality. And indeed it is striking how de Man routinely casts even the most technical-seeming issues in moral terms, particularly in terms of seduction. In an essay on "reception aesthetics" in *The Resistance to Theory,* de Man says, for example, that "the aesthetic is, by definition, a seductive notion that appeals to the pleasure principle"; and in "Phenomenality and Materiality in Kant," he comments that "morality and the aesthetic are both disinterested, but this disinterestedness becomes necessarily polluted in aesthetic representation [by] . . . positively valorized sensual experiences."[25] Norris reproduces this moralization of the aesthetic, if not the figure of sensory "pollution," when he describes de Man's sense of the aesthetic ideology as "a permanent temptation of thought, a desire . . . to conflate the two realms of phenomenal experience and conceptual understanding" (*WWWP,* 256). The history of literary thinking in particular gives ample reason for thinking the temptation to be permanent. For, as de Man and Norris point out, virtually all major schools of literary theory, such as formalism, reader-response criticism, reception theory, and, for that matter, any approach in which cognition, desire, and morality are fused or confused, succumbs to it. The list of the fallible includes not only T. S. Eliot but such mainstream scholars as H. R. Jauss, W. K. Wimsatt, M. H. Abrams, Earl Wasserman, Michael Riffaterre, Roman Jakobson—all of whom, no matter how rigorous their arguments or unimpeachable their scholarly rectitude, fall prey to the aesthetic ideology. In its ideological mutations, aesthetics yields a "knowledge" that is corrupt, but far from "useless."[26]

Against these temptations, de Man urges the ethical superiority of literature, whose rhetorical tropes and figures, irreducible to grammatical order, resist the seductions of aesthetic ideology, immersing the reader in the ways of unknowing by presenting a kind of meaning that simply cannot claim to be directly perceived.[27] The result is, as de Man tirelessly argued, a structural necessity of "misreading" that virtually defines the literariness of literature. It is, however, not immediately clear how this form of misreading, accurately reflecting the properties of literariness, differs from "grievous" misreadings such as Schiller's of Kant. More disquieting still is an internal difficulty. Rigorously argued, and argued on the very basis of rigor as against collapse, seduction, desire, de Man's distinction between literature and the aesthetic remains stubbornly counterintuitive, cutting across the grain of an ancient tradition in which even Kant participated, of considering literature, especially poetry, as the art of arts, the highest aspiration and purest instance of the aesthetic. De Man is not simply distinguishing between the essence and the rind of the aesthetic; he is claiming that what had always been considered the essence is in fact the rind.

As a consequence of his earnest efforts to warn against the seduction of the aesthetic, de Man has placed himself in a double dilemma. He has tried to critique the aesthetic by removing what is, on many accounts, its very heart; and he has, by casting the problem in political and moral terms, built back into the aesthetic the very energies he is trying to banish. We should not, however, be quick to accuse de Man of avoidable error, for as we have already seen, the effort to distinguish the fundament or essence of the aesthetic from some derivative or corrupt aspect of itself is a recurrent gesture. On one reading of this gesture, philosophers and critics have simply been extraordinarily subject to distraction or confusion. But on another, surely more powerful, reading, the aesthetic itself is, through a predisposition to sensory or ideological pollution, responsible for the misreadings that have plagued it, misreadings that both represent and re-present aesthetic over-determination. Positing in the first instance an illegitimate entanglement of objects and judgments, forms and concepts, the aesthetic cannot escape entanglement with its own others such as politics and morality, and is thus itself condemned to misreading as the only adequate principle of understanding.

Indeed, since Kantian "judgment" analogizes, and thus mediates, between sensory perception and both theoretical and ethical reason, it draws the boundaries between the faculties in dotted lines, so that "pollution" may be the very essence of judgment, an entailment of its "freedom." According to Gilles Deleuze, judgment is different in kind from theoretical or ethical reason, and has the quite distinctive function of providing the system of faculties with a basis in freedom. Whereas in the first two Critiques, either theoretical reason or speculative ethical understanding "legislates" over the other, in the instance of judgment described in the third Critique there is no dominance at all; the faculties enter into an unregulated yet harmonious accord. As Deleuze puts it, "The first two Critiques set out a relationship between the faculties which is determined by one of them; the last Critique uncovers a deeper free and indeterminate accord of the faculties as the condition of the possibility of every determinate relationship" (*KCP*, 68). Without the "free and indeterminate accord" articulated in the third Critique, the faculties would be frozen into postures of antagonism, much like those at some universities today; with such an accord, they can assume a variety of determinate relations. Thus the reason that Kant and his followers have to struggle to hold the distinctions between the faculties in place is that they do not hold themselves: unanchored by the freedom inscribed in reflective judgment, each term distinct from yet permeable to and realized in the others, the Kantian faculties invariably disappoint philosophers seeking rigorous distinctions, moralists seeking clean resistances, and aesthetes seeking art as such—those for whom "free and indeterminate" relations represent only incoherence, promiscuity, stain. Pre-corrupted, the faculties make but feeble protests against their own perversions.

Hence the bewildering spectacle of de Man trying to enlist Kant's aid in defending against a circumstance Kant regarded as benign, portraying as pollution what Kant defined as empowering complexity. Indeed, so significant are the differences between Kant and de Man that it may be doubted whether the latter's thought is "enlightened" at all. Certainly nothing like Kant's "motto of enlightenment"—"Have courage to use your *own* understanding!"—is to be found in de Man's work, which, on the contrary, typically denigrates any sense of individual cognitive success.[28] For de Man, a correct or adequate reading of a text cuts across the grain of the reader's desires, negating a narcissistic investment in the text. Nor does de Man anywhere celebrate human freedom, a mistaken enthusiasm for which, one may infer, could only produce misreading. De Man does not, in fact, seem greatly interested in progress in human institutions. Kant begins his answer to the question "What Is Englightenment?" by announcing that "*Enlightenment is man's emergence from his self-incurred immaturity,*" strongly implying that such an emergence is both timely and desirable—precisely the sort of buoyancy that de Man invariably calls "premature."[29] De Man's work occupies and seeks to prolong a moment of hesitation before the satisfying leap to achieved meaning, cultivating the obdurate theoretical problems that impede a passage from form to meaning, artwork to interpretation, rhetoric to questions of meaning and value, literature to the aesthetic. A Kantian pedigree might be claimed for the delay-inducing "misreading," for Kant insisted upon the purely subjective nature of judgment, its nonreliance upon any intrinsic qualities of the object being judged. But in Kant the autonomy of judgment from the thing in itself enables a direct appeal from the individual to the universal substrate of humanity; while in de Man, such appeals are not only premature but illusory, for the mind can claim to be disinterested only in the coldly technical apprehension of an anti-aesthetic "text."

In Kantian terms, then, de Man's work, with its dark forebodings of "prematurity," remains "immature" with respect to enlightenment. Norris, on the other hand, manifestly wishes to preserve the Enlightenment distinctions, and to move, after a decent interval to be sure, from the "distinctive mode of understanding" of the aesthetic to political argumentation. On the basis of the freedom inscribed in the aesthetic, Norris argues, one can not only criticize what is, but envision and depict what is not, or not yet.[30] The way to ensure the effectiveness of the critique is through the rigorous working out of distinctions, working through of arguments, close readings, interrogation of premises, etc., as guarantees against "the uncritical passage from art to the other dimensions of human experience (ethical, historical, political) [by which] the aesthetic ideology has left its disastrous imprint on the past hundred years of European life and thought" (*WWWP*, 22). But the question may be put to Norris: given that the passage must be made in order for freedom to be realized in the world, what, exactly, constitutes a "critical" as opposed to an "uncritical" passage, a "mature" as opposed to a "premature" synthesis? Mere delay in the passage cannot guarantee that the destination is not reached too soon; so how do we know if, in the honest effort to be enlightened, we have not in fact been fundamentalist? How can we specify the difference between the fundament of modernity and fundamentalism per se?

Negation

We seem to be approaching a maximum of theoretical confusion. I would argue, however, that we are also approaching the most definite and precise definition of the aesthetic that has yet been ventured—precisely *as* "theoretical confusion," as the undecidability between object and subject, freedom and the repressive law, critical and uncritical passages, grievous and necessary misreadings, even art and ideology.[31] While Eagleton remarks the contradictions of the concept of the aesthetic, he does not consider this more radical proposition, that the aesthetic represents "the concept" *as* contradiction. Wittgenstein seems more sensitive to this possibility when he asks, "Isn't the concept with blurred edges just what we want—especially in ethics and aesthetics?"[32] Want it or not, the blurred or contradictory concept is what we have "in ethics and aesthetics," for the reason that these categories, unlike, for example, the trivium and the quadrivium, or the categories of scholastic theology—categories that purported to represent real, if ideal, entities—designate kinds of mental representations whose common origin in mind guarantees a certain blurring. In the case of the aesthetic, blurring is achieved in manifold ways, from the projective act of judgment, through the permeation of faculties, on up to the large-scale delusions of ideology. On all levels, apparently crisp distinctions are blurred by misattribution, misprision, or misnaming.

The negative form of the agents of unclarity awakens a more general point, that the aesthetic is defined by negation. Recall Kant's description of judgment as not phenomenal perception, not theoretical reason, not speculative understanding, not desire, not utility, not politics—all the things judgment is "disinterested" in or "undetermined" by. The concept of the supersensible invoked by judgment has, Kant says, no peculiar realm of its own; it is "unbounded, but, also inaccessible" (*CJ,* 13). The judgment of taste is "based upon a concept," but one "from which nothing can be cognized in respect of the Object, because it is in itself undeterminable and useless for knowledge" (*CJ,* 208). Such judgments presuppose some *a priori* principle, "although that principle is neither a cognitive principle for understanding nor a practical principle for the will, and is thus in no way determinant *a priori*" (*CJ,* 32–33). Deriving from the free play of the faculties when raised to their highest powers of self-knowledge, the "unsought" or "undesigned" subjective purposiveness of the imagination cannot be discovered by reference to any set of preestablished rules. The act of judgment itself registers no intrinsic properties of the object, and even constitutes what John Sallis has called a "withdrawal from the object."[33] Responding to this pattern of insistences with his own distinctive rhetoric, Foucault asserts that, for Kant, enlightenment or *Aufklärung* "is neither a world era to which one belongs, nor an event whose signs are perceived, nor the dawning of an accomplishment. Kant defines *Aufklärung* in an almost entirely negative way, as an *Ausgang,* an 'exit,' a 'way out.'"[34] Lyotard describes the aesthetic as a strictly negative knowledge, a way out of positive determinations of all kinds, even a way out of knowledge as such: "The position of art," he writes, "is a denial of the position of discourse."[35]

In *Getting It Right: Language, Literature, and Ethics,* I sketched out the terms of a possible rapprochement between Kant and Freud in the area of ethics. Here, I want to suggest that, in the unconscious, Freud reinvented Kantian judgment. Of course, as Freud said, the unconscious knows no negation, but even this denial of negation is phrased in negative terms. Freud did not say, "The unconscious knows only positive terms," because the essential thing is not the unconscious itself but rather its relation to consciousness, a relation that is entirely negative. "The unconscious—what a strange word!" Lacan remarks. Yet "Freud didn't find a better one, and there's no need to go back on it. The disadvantage of this word is that it is negative, which allows one to assume anything at all in the world about it, plus everything else as well. Why not? To that which goes unnoticed, the word *everywhere* applies just as well as *nowhere.* . . . It is nonetheless a very precise thing."[36] Less precise, perhaps, than many thinkers, Lacan connects Kant and Freud, the aesthetic and the unconscious, the ethical and the psychoanalytic, through his devotion to such emblems of negation as the lost object, the algorithmic bar, the reality that cannot be spoken, the unsatisfiable desire. Disinterested in time, space, or reality in general, the Freudian unconscious replays the most salient features of Kantian judgment.

Indeed, on a number of occasions, Freud discusses "judgment," making it clear that this term, although vigorously conceived as "the intellectual action which decides the choice of motor action, which puts an end to the procrastination of thinking, and which leads over from thinking to acting," cannot bypass a certain "Kantian" or "reflective" basis in negation. For judging requires a degree of independence from repression and from the pleasure principle, and such independence is achieved only with "the creation of the symbol of negation," which enables repressed material to be admitted to consciousness and thus available for judgment, on the condition that it be denied.[37] If the implications of this account of judgment were permitted to rebound, we could then speculate that enlightened thought possesses something like an "unconscious" that retards a sturdy movement towards justice and morality, making all positive determinations seem premature, arrogant, ungrounded, unjust.

It might appear from this that the history of the aesthetic constitutes the chronicle of a formidable resistance to ideology. But in fact, the aesthetic seems to have hollowed out the ideologies that have appropriated it. The form of negation in liberalism is quite literal. In a famous essay in 1970, Isaiah Berlin gave the name of "negative liberty" to the fundamental liberal right of every individual to determine his or her own ends free from coercion or intrusion from the state apparatus, the right to assume the condition of the modern artifact: free, self-referring, autonomous.[38] The fascistic version of the aesthetic ideology suppresses negative liberty but promotes such forms of negative agency as restraint, discipline, passive beholding, irrationalist acceptance. Fascism might seem to invoke positive determinations, for as Philippe Lacoue-Labarthe and Jean-Luc Nancy point out, it is typically a mythology of identity; but "identity," especially racial or national identity, is constructed on the basis of what it is not—Semitic, Gypsy, Black, Swiss, Russian, Creole, and so forth, the misleadingly definite name (e.g., Aryan, "white," African-American) sublimating both external affinities and internal differences.[39] For its part, postmodernism encompasses both negative liberty, in the form of a resistance to what Lyotard calls hegemonic "metanarratives," and a detached acceptance of appearances. The indebtedness of postmodern theory to the third Critique is most strongly marked in its trademark phrases: judgment without criteria, images without originals, depthlessness, lack of affect. Marxist thought is most distinctively aesthetic in the negative, or dialectical, form of its arguments, in which, as Eagleton says of Adorno, "the reader has no sooner registered the one-sidedness of some proposition than the opposite is immediately proposed" (*IA*, 342). The dialectical tic is most evident, according to Tony Bennett, in the Marxist construction of aesthetics as not-science and not-ideology, so that literature's positivity "turns out to consist of a set of negatively defined relational attributes subjected to misleading ontologisation."[40] Occasional infatuations with Schiller notwithstanding, Marxism has often posed as the dialectical "opposite" of aesthetics; but

Marxism's own negative or dialectical construction of aesthetics raises the possibility that Marxism has borrowed its essence from the historically prior discourse of art. So despite a structural negativity that might seem to render the aesthetic an unreliable accomplice in any ideological project, the aesthetic has not only proven to be infinitely useful to such projects, but seems actually to have reformed them in its own non-image.

In order for the full significance of this curious fact to emerge, it must be generalized into the hypothesis that ideology itself has "aesthetic" elements. If, for example, ideology is considered simply to be "false consciousness," then it, too, is defined negatively. And if, moreover, ideology is constructed in the manner of Adorno as "an identity between concept and phenomenon"; or of Althusser, as "an imaginary relation to real conditions"; or of Eagleton, as "the value system that underlies our factual statements," then it draws even closer to the aesthetic, which, as we have seen, invariably begins by establishing some coimplication of subject and object. And if, following de Man, we understand ideology as "the confusion of linguistic with natural reality," we approach the aesthetic by the only slightly different route of misnaming.[41] The homologies between aesthetics and ideology help explain why, despite the fact that the aesthetic seems to offer a structural resistance to ideology, it also seems naturally or inevitably to assume ideological form. The aesthetic names both the perversion of ideology (inutility, ahistoricity, misnaming) and the inalienable essence of ideology itself, ideology in general. The appropriately dialectical conclusion is that ideology and the aesthetic constitute each other's negation, each other's misreading; both are real imaginative constructions that (somehow) effect a passage from the subject to the object, the sensory to the conceptual, the phenomenal to the moral or political. If the aesthetic is always already ideological, so, too, is ideology always already aesthetic.

The Gulf Wars

For a true measure of the stakes involved in this passage, we must, as de Man, Derrida, Norris, Habermas, Lyotard, and theoreticians without number have told us, return to Kant, attending to the following crucial passage at the beginning of the *Critique of Judgement,* in which Kant, discussing the "two kinds of concepts," those of nature and those of freedom, acknowledges that

> between the realm of the natural concept, as the sensible, and the realm of the concept of freedom, as the supersensible, there is a gulf fixed, so that it is not possible to pass from the former to the latter (by means of the theoretical employment of reason), just as if

they were so many separate worlds, the first of which is powerless to exercise influence on the second: still the latter is *meant* to influence the former—that is to say, the concept of freedom is meant to actualize in the sensible world the end proposed by its laws; and nature must consequently also be capable of being regarded in such a way that in the conformity of the law of its own form it at least harmonizes with the possibility of ends to be effectuated in it according to the laws of freedom. (*CJ*, 14)

Deeply influential even among those innocent of it, this passage posits a "gulf fixed" between the material or phenomenal world and our ideas about and idealizations of that world. It claims, moreover, that both "worlds" are entitled to very particular forms of autonomy, but that the supersensible realm of freedom is bound by an inner imperative to the goal of actualization, and not only actualization but the actualization of a particular end, born of freedom; and that the sensible world itself yearns towards such actualization, or at least is "capable of being regarded" as if it did. These positions represent nothing less than modernity in the grand style. But from the same premise, of a "gulf fixed" between the determined material world and the determining world of freedom, a number of anti-Enlightenment conclusions could also follow, so that, for example, a Nietzschean or postmodern gloss on the same passage would stress the incommensurability of mind and its objects, and the consequent helplessness of the intellect to achieve the worldly ends for which it appears to be destined; the arbitrariness of the dictates of Reason, which seek to enforce their program on a Nature powerless to reciprocate; the dogged resistance of Nature to freedom, its sullen enslavement to fundamentalisms of all kinds.

For virtually all participants, this gulf is the center of tension and attention, separating and linking sensory experience and judgment, private and public, particular and universal, sensible and supersensible, taste and reason, feeling and understanding. For some, the gulf is there to be conquered, overleaped, claimed; while for others, the existence of the gulf preserves a necessary separation. The Kantian passage, in short, establishes the terms of a "gulf war" between a first world, represented by the governing forces of reason, freedom, and the supersensible, and another world ruled by the forces of the natural and sensible. One surprising testament to the continuing vitality of the (in many ways) curiously antiquated thought of Kant is the fact that these terms apply, by a shoddy and corrupt allegory, to the recent Gulf War, as constructed almost overnight by the media and by the Bush Administration. The alignment of American-led coalition forces with "freedom" and "supersensible" idealism as against the armies of "interest"

—mercenaries, fanatics, and slaves—fielded by Saddam Hussein seems to many in the West perfectly appropriate. What might, if it had been articulated, have seemed less natural and certainly more debatable is the consequence that follows, explicitly in Kant and implicitly in American foreign policy: that the West is "*meant*" to govern Iraq, along with all the other territories on the far side of the gulf (a list that has included in recent times Chile, Cuba, Nicaragua, El Salvador, the Philippines, Libya, Panama, Vietnam, Laos, Saudi Arabia, Angola, and more), and that everything these countries do—their primitivism, their bizarre internecine cruelties, their fanaticism, their bigotry, their misogyny, their use of outlawed weapons, their sponsorship of terrorism, their ready embrace of genocidal war aims, even the ludicrously lurid corporeality of their official discourse—suggests that they are not only structurally amenable to such governance but require it for their own good.

This was the Gulf War the Bush administration wanted to fight, not a conflict between altogether different worlds, but rather an expanded form of riot control to preserve and stabilize a world already essentially modern. It was such a world that was projected by President Bush in a letter to Saddam Hussein dated January 9, 1991, one week before the "liberation of Kuwait" was to begin, a letter that began, "We stand today at the brink of war between Iraq and the world."[42] Almost like Alice stepping through the looking-glass, Iraq had departed from "the world," from the postcolonial "family of nations," by refusing the passive role of the "sensible," refusing to be either obediently postcolonial or post–Cold War. The invasion of Kuwait had toppled the old world order, whose boundaries had been drawn by the British, and deferred the realization of the "new world order" first announced in early September, 1990. As President Bush put the matter in an address to the nation and/or the world on the evening of the outbreak of war, it was to be "a new world order, a world where the rule of law, not the law of the jungle, governs the conduct of nations" (*GWR,* 313). With the collapse of the Second World, President Bush appeared determined both to relegate Iraq, an erstwhile junior partner in the First World, to the "jungle" of the Third World, and then to eliminate that World, so there would be simply one, resolutely modern and enlightened, world, in which fundamentalism and ethnocentrism would simply have vanished in the course of the inexorable evolutionary advance of *Homo sapiens* and the legitimate destiny of freedom, a world in which nature would submit to the rule of freedom as the law.[43]

The complex role of "freedom" in American policy, particularly in the Cold War and since, cannot be overestimated and must not be misconstrued. The American sense of freedom has, of course, been shaped by many hands, including Locke, Hobbes, Paine, Madison, Jefferson, Mill,

Stowe, Lincoln, Douglass, Wilson, Roosevelt, and others; but even granting historical and conceptual overdetermination, it is possible to isolate a distinctively Kantian strain, precisely because that strain runs beneath, or through, many of the others. In the instance of the Gulf War, freedom functioned in various ways. First, the invasion of Kuwait was treated not as the issue of an historical process but as a fresh and freestanding event that could be brought under no concept, made to serve no end (of the United States), a virtual Kantian artifact. Second, the invasion was deplored as a violation of the putative "freedom" of the Kuwaitis. And third, the invasion was held to inaugurate a fully warranted progression from tyranny towards the worldly realization, or rerealization, of freedom, in which the heroes were the liberal project pursuers of the West, seeking redemption from ancient syndromes, and the villains were so illiberal as to be virtually nonnarratable. The predominance of freedom as a rationale for policy also helps explain the war's most mystifying nonevent, the militarily odd decision not to pursue the remnants of the Iraqi military who were racing back to Baghdad after their defeat. A policy based on the freedom of Saudi Arabia or Kuwait could, with some ingenuity, or disingenuity, help explain the need for military intervention to an American public that has never believed in the worthiness of mere "interest" or "need." But despite a profound administration desire to see Saddam Hussein deposed, eliminated, removed, freedom could not sponsor an invasion of Iraq after the "liberation of Kuwait" had been accomplished. To everyone's amazement, the public rationale for the war—the freedom of Kuwait, rather than the overthrow of Hussein or even the destruction of his nuclear and chemical capacities— turns out to have been the functional rationale.

Freedom by itself is inadequate as a rationale for policy, and for what von Clausewitz calls its "continuation by other means," war, because while it seeks "actualization in the sensible world," it is powerless to specify positive ends: predicated on negation, it can be no more than the unconscious of policy. The proper telos of all cognition, according to Kant, is the exercise of practical reason, or ethics; and while judgment enables and points towards ethics, it cannot tell one how to behave. In order to be effective as action, freedom must suffer contradiction, must succumb to temptation, must be misread, perverted, corrupted, polluted with practical politics and worldly interest, so that it can acquire a countenance, or leave an enlightening trace in the pragmatics that it sponsors. Without such pollution, freedom, condemned to a virginal indeterminacy, is vulnerable to appropriation by precisely those interests least concerned with freedom, interests in need of a surrogate. Freedom unpolluted—or, more accurately, unrealized—is as indifferent to freedom as any fundamentalism.

The Gulf War provides eloquent testimony to the costs of purity. By failing to work out a positive program for peace, by deploying its armed forces with a wholly negative mission, first of "defense" and "security and stability in the region," and then of "the liberation of Kuwait," with the presumption that if obstructions were removed the peoples of the Gulf would naturally assume a free and indeterminate (i.e., pro-West) accord, the United States has succeeded in inflicting unpublicized but horrifying and militarily unnecessary misery on the Iraqi people, leaving them with less power in every sense than they had before the war; it has stalled, but also virtually guaranteed, imminent additional devastation to the Kurds, who thought they had been promised freedom in one sense and now find themselves free (i.e., cut loose) in quite another; it has redrawn boundaries that had been drawn in an utterly arbitrary way in the first place; and it has restored a politically regressive monarchy in Kuwait—all while strengthening Saddam Hussein's political position within Iraq.

In general, I am arguing that the ideological construction of the Gulf War betrays, in both senses of that term, the conceptual resources of Kant's critical philosophy. But I want, too, to assert that Hussein's Iraq has been portrayed in the West as a signal instance of what amounts to the "aesthetic ideology," its invasion of Kuwait an example of a premature or uncritical passage from one domain to another, or the seizure of power by those with no legitimate claim to it; while the West has depicted itself as the rightful executive of the laws of freedom that inform a properly enlightened aesthetic judgment, one that respected boundaries. Confused and destructive as it was, the Gulf War replayed in a different medium the intricate meditations of philosophers as they sought patiently to draw lines in the sand demarcating the realm of ideology from that of freedom. Constructed as an intra-aesthetic conflict between the pure form and its ideological corruption, the war confirmed Walter Benjamin's assertion that "All efforts to render politics aesthetic culminate in one thing: war."[44] Just as inevitable, I would argue, were the consequences of the fetishization of an inarticulate freedom, which, like Billy Budd, could only respond to challenge with violence. For the one-sided ferocity of the Gulf War represents not just the continuation of politics, nor even its failure, but also a powerlessness to specify or even to imagine positive political projects involving other nations because such projects conflict with a version of modernity founded in, and crippled by, freedom as an absolute, an inviolable dogma: People should be (because they are essentially) free. The rubble of Baghdad allegorizes—again, shoddily—Western rage at conceptual or ideological impotence, at its own incapacity to bring a nonmodern culture to acknowledge the superiority of the modern, the inability of smart bombs to impart enlightenment to their targets.

Such an inability implies another gulf, and another Gulf War which shadowed the first. While universal "freedom" named the justice of the American cause, it could not justify the inevitable loss of American lives because it could not be made coherent. To shepherd a rogue fragment of the world back into line so that the world could resume being what it already is, free, is not a cause Americans readily understand, much less would choose to die for. Only a palpable threat from some *other* "world," some danger to the American "way of life" or to "essential values," could make military intervention not just comprehensible but acceptable or necessary. A bridge had to be constructed, then, from freedom as a global value to freedom as a specifically American way of life. This transition was articulated with matchless efficiency by "Hollywood Huddleston, marine lance corporal" in a comment somehow obtained by President Bush and quoted in his January 16, 1991, speech: "Let's free these people so we can go home and be free again" (*GWR,* 314). The necessity for such a transition also drives what commentators called "the Hitler analogy" by which the Bush administration analogized from one genocidal despot seeking world domination to another. In geopolitical terms, the Hitler analogy suggests not so much a weak seam in the fabric of a free world as a more profound conflict between the self-proclaimed enlightened world and its other, a world that had rejected the primacy of the "laws of freedom" as it had rejected the colonial and neocolonial rulers who had imposed them, a world dogmatically unenlightened, seeking not to advance to new plateaus of reason but to return to some pure and sacred origin, a world that could not be brought to conceive itself as "meant to be governed" by laws external to their interests, a world that in all probability would concur with Theodor Adorno and Max Horkheimer's conception of enlightenment in general as "mass deception."[45]

Between these two gulfs—between the-modern-world-and-*its*-other, and the-modern-world-and-its-*other*—there is a gulf fixed, and the question is whether the laws of freedom, the laws implied in aesthetic judgment and realized in practical reason, are meant to govern the whole world or just the First World. If the world is not fundamentally modern or becoming-modern, if the earth contains several "worlds"—a prospect raised by Kant, as we have seen—then "freedom" will necessarily be subject to recoding as advantage. Thus, from the global point of view that modernity would claim for its own, the dominance of interest over shared values would make wars highly probable. Even more injurious to our sense of "national security," wars could not claim the kind of moral legitimacy and evolutionary sanction the United States has historically been eager to bestow on them. This Clausewitzian recognition might encourage a laudable principle of candor, for if war has no transcendental rationale, then policy makers might feel themselves obliged to articulate and justify the worldly means and ends attending the translation of "freedom" into a positive practical program. But such candor would itself imply that a diacritical and politicized freedom seeking its own advantage may, without self-betrayal, harden itself into belligerence, take up a shield, become a storm, binding, and perhaps strategically blinding, itself to interests for which it serves as surrogate. In coming to countenance, freedom, the fundament of cosmopolitan enlightenment, assumes—again, from the global point of view—the form of an ethnocentrism, a "law of the jungle." The very prestige that modernity accords to freedom as a mark of its own superiority to the jungle bespeaks a localism modernity claims to transcend. For it is only in a modern world, or in that fraction of the world conscious of its modernity, that freedom as such is an unquestionable good. But what the Gulf War—or, for that matter, any war—indicates is that modernity does not blanket the globe, and that, as a consequence, fundamental values clash in the form of fundamentalisms.

So while it might appear to be enlightened simply to assert that the globe contains many worlds, that values are variable and local rather than universal and constant, and that policy ought to reflect this simple fact, such an assertion does little to mitigate the threat of war. Moreover, in the present instance, the supposed beneficiary of such wise multicultural counsel does not appear to agree. Listen to Tariq Aziz, Iraq's Foreign Minister, speaking on January 9, 1991: "Concerning the new world order, or the international world order, I said I have no problem with that order. And we would love to be partners in that order. But that order has to be implemented justly, and in all cases, not using that order in a single manner, in a selective manner, impose it on a certain case . . . and neglect the other issues and not show sincerity and seriousness about implementing it on other issues" (*GWR,* 174). The complaint is not that the new world order is too disrespectful of difference but that it is too partial, too limited, too ethnocentric—in a word, insufficiently modern—to permit Iraq to join. The utterances of Aziz, and of Hussein himself, during the period before the war invoke precisely the same principles and values as those intoned by President Bush: peace, stability, security, defense, justice, common understanding, and liberty.[46] Iraq, it appears from the utterances of its officials, believes in enlightenment, in justice as fairness, in global citizenship as a humane and open conversation between equals. It really is a small world.

The universal acceptability of "freedom" and its collateral terms suggests both that the rhetoric, at least, of modernity may indeed have blanketed the globe, but also that this rhetoric is so empty as to accommodate any practices. The enlightenment-value, as it were, of "freedom" is precisely zero. Only in alloys with force or interest can freedom serve to promote modernity, and even then the application of principle to instance remains subject to the negations and misattributions that structure any act of judgment. It is difficult to know exactly how to feel about this fact as a general proposition. Nevertheless, two kinds of commitment recommend themselves to policy makers as ways of hedging some of the more extreme deformations that befall the cause of freedom. First, positive goals as well as negative liberties must be specified so that the relevant community can judge whether these goals would serve to advance freedom. The necessity of a determining "fundamentalist moment" that is at once the goal and the negation of freedom must be accepted, and accepted as non-tragic. Second, the value of freedom, and of modernity itself, must be recognized as subject to challenge from other fundamental principles, a challenge not necessarily resolvable by what Habermas calls "the unforced force of the better argument."

By themselves, of course, these commitments, even if adopted immediately and wholeheartedly by every human being on earth, do nothing to ensure peace. On the contrary, they presuppose an undecidability about which gulf we are or ought to be negotiating, or about whether the leader of the "free world" is by rights the leader of the whole world, or whether he is merely the head of one (unusually powerful) nation among many, a nation that, like some others, has chosen to call itself "free." And this undecidability implies that the gulf war may be as unwinnable in the political and military senses as it has proven to be in the philosophical.

Notes

1. J. S. Mill, *A System of Logic* (London and New York: Longmans, Green & Co., 1911), 65–66.

2. Michael Walzer, *Spheres of Justice* (New York: Basic Books, 1983), xv.

3. J. S. Mill, *On Liberty* (Harmondsworth: Penguin, 1984); Michel Foucault, *The Use of Pleasure*, vol. 2 of *The History of Sexuality,* trans. Robert Hurley (New York: Vintage, 1985).

4. Anthony Cascardi, "Aesthetic Liberalism: Kant and the Ethics of Modernity," *Revue Internationale de Philosophie* 45 (January 1991): 21. Further references are given in the text.

5. Immanuel Kant, *Critique of Judgement,* trans. James Creed Meredith (New York: Oxford University Press, 1928), 207–208. Further page references are given in the text to *CJ.*

6. See Cascardi, "Aesthetic Liberalism," 16–18; Eagleton, *The Ideology of the Aesthetic* (Oxford: Basil Blackwell, 1990), 405; further page references are given in the text to *IA*. Relevant texts of Jürgen Habermas include *The Philosophical Discourse of Modernity,* trans. Frederick Lawrence (Cambridge: MIT Press, 1987), 96ff.; "Philosophy as Stand-in and Interpreter," in *After Philosophy: End or Transformation?* ed. Kenneth Baynes, James Bohman, and Thomas

McCarthy (Cambridge: MIT Press 1987), 296–315; "Consciousness-Raising or Redemptive Criticism: The Contemporaneity of Walter Benjamin," in *Philosophical Profiles,* trans. Frederick Lawrence (Cambridge: MIT Press, 1983); and the recent *Moral Consciousness and Communicative Action* (Cambridge: MIT Press, 1990).

7. Friedrich Schiller, *On the Aesthetic Education of Man, in a Series of Letters,* ed. and trans. Elizabeth M. Wilkinson and L. A. Willoughby (Oxford: Clarendon Press, 1967), 163.

8. Christopher Norris, *What's Wrong with Postmodernism: Critical Theory and the Ends of Philosophy* (New York: Harvester Wheatsheaf, 1990), 17. Further page references are given in the text to *WWWP.*

9. Alexander Baumgarten, *Reflections on Poetry,* trans. K. Aschenbrenner and W. B. Holther (Berkeley: University of California Press, 1954). For a sharply critical discussion of Eagleton's "peculiar" discussion of the gender of aesthetics, see Christine Brooke-Rose, *Stories, Theories and Things* (Cambridge: Cambridge University Press, 1991), 275–283.

10. Eagleton's argument receives support from Meyer Abrams, who demonstrates that the eighteenth-century discourse of "taste" served a number of functions for the newly emergent bourgeoisie, none of them remarkable for their freedom from worldly concerns. Abrams notes the historically unprecedented emphasis on "the perceiver's stance" and "the contemplation model" of perception, an emphasis that foregrounded the "disinterested" (because affluent and leisured) connoisseur, as opposed to the classical emphasis on craft and production that had been so rich in the "concepts" and "ends" that Kant banished from the aesthetic. See Abrams, *Doing Things with Texts: Essays in Criticism and Critical Theory,* ed. Michael Fischer (New York: Norton, 1989), 139.

11. Tony Bennett, "Really Useless 'Knowledge': A Political Critique of Aesthetics," in *Outside Literature* (London and New York: Routledge, 1990), 143–166.

12. Roger Scruton, "Modern Philosophy and the Neglect of Aesthetics," *Times Literary Supplement,* 5 June 1987, 604, 616–617. See also Scruton, *Aesthetic Understanding* (London: Methuen, 1983).

13. Benjamin's comment occurs in "The Work of Art in the Age of Mechanical Reproduction," in *Illuminations,* ed. Hannah Arendt, trans. Harry Zohn (New York: Schocken Books, 1968), 241.

14. Friedrich Nietzsche, *On the Genealogy of Morals,* trans. Walter Kaufmann and R. J. Hollingdale, in *On the Genealogy of Morals and Ecce Homo,* ed. Walter Kaufmann (New York: Random House, 1969), 86–87.

15. Jacob Burckhardt, *The Civilization of the Renaissance in Italy,* 2 vols. (New York: Harper & Brothers, 1958), 1:22; see "The State as a Work of Art," 21–142 passim.

16. Mussolini, too, clearly felt that part of his mission was to "shape" the masses, who were "like wax in my hands." See Mussolini to Emil Ludwig in 1932, cited in Denis Mack Smith, "The Theory and Practice of Fascism," in *Fascism: An Anthology,* ed. Nathaniel Greene (New York: Crowell, 1968), 82.

17. Richard Wolin, *The Politics of Being: The Political Thought of Martin*

Heidegger (New York: Columbia University Press, 1990), 77–130; and Michael Zimmerman, *Heidegger's Encounter with Modernity: Technology, Politics, Art* (Bloomington: Indiana University Press, 1990), 46–93. For the aesthetic connection with German fascism, see Bill Kinser and Neil Kleinman's *The Dream That Was No More a Dream: A Search for Aesthetic Reality in Germany, 1890–1945* (New York: Harper and Row, 1969); also Walter Benjamin, "Theories of German Fascism: On the Collection of Essays *War and the Warrior,*" ed. Ernst Jünger, *New German Critique,* 17 (Spring, 1979), prefaced by Ansgar Hillach, "The Aesthetics of Politics: Walter Benjamin's 'Theories of German Fascism'"; and Alice Yeager Kaplan, *Reproductions of Banality: Fascism, Literature and French Intellectual Life* (Minneapolis: University of Minnesota Press, 1986). This material, and more, is intelligently surveyed in Martin Jay; "'The Aesthetic Ideology' as Ideology; Or What Does It Mean to Aestheticize Politics?" forthcoming in *Cultural Critique.*

18. Jean-François Lyotard, *Instructions païennes* (Paris: Galilee, 1977), 36. Quoted and translated in Bill Readings, *Introducing Lyotard: Art and Politics* (London and New York: Routledge, 1991), 106.

19. Jean-François Lyotard, *The Postmodern Condition: A Report on Knowledge,* trans. Geoff Bennington and Brian Massumi (Minneapolis: University of Minnesota Press, 1984).

20. This is especially true in the radical case of the sublime, for the sublime in Kant's formulation represents a limit to aesthetic gratification, since by definition no form can be adequate to the sense or feeling of the sublime. Thus the sublime checks the impulse to pass beyond aesthetic form to ideas of a supersensible character on ethics and politics. For a sympathetic and intelligent exposition of Lyotard, see Readings, *Introducing Lyotard,* 72–74. For critical readings, see Eagleton, *Ideology of the Aesthetic,* 395–401; and Norris, *What's Wrong with Postmodernism,* 7–15. Among a number of recent studies of Kant that focus on the sublime, albeit in very different ways, are Paul Crowther, *The Kantian Sublime: From Morality to Art* (Oxford: Clarendon Press, 1989); and John Sallis, *Spacings: Of Reason and Imagination in Texts of Kant, Fichte, Hegel* (Chicago: University of Chicago Press, 1987), esp. 82–131.

21. Eagleton constructs a "case for the defence of postmodernism" based on its iconoclasm, its demotic confounding of hierarchies, its subversions of closure, and its populism—then immediately follows with a case for the prosecution based on postmodernism's hedonism and "philistine anti-historicism," its erasure of truth, and its "blank, reified technologism" (*Ideology of the Aesthetic,* 373). For an influential discussion of the ideology of postmodernism, see also Fredric Jameson, *Postmodernism; Or, the Cultural Logic of Late Capitalism* (London: Verso, 1991).

22. See Hal Foster, ed., *The Anti-Aesthetic* (San Francisco: Bay Press, 1983).

23. Paul de Man, "Kant and Schiller," in *The Aesthetic Ideology,* ed. Andrzej Warminski (forthcoming). The quotation from Goebbels is taken from this unpublished MS, which is quoted in Martin Jay, "'Aesthetic Ideology.'" For a reading of Schiller sharply at odds with de Man's, see Joseph Chytry, *The Aes-*

thetic State: A Quest in Modern German Thought (Berkeley and Los Angeles: University of California Press, 1989). Chytry argues that Schiller "does not identify the moral with the aesthetic," but "fully recognizes the dangers of untrammeled aestheticism," which he sees as resulting from "an *inadequate* experience of beauty" (90).

24. Paul de Man, *The Rhetoric of Romanticism* (New York: Columbia University Press, 1984), 264.

25. Paul de Man, "Reading and History," in *The Resistance to Theory* (Minneapolis: University of Minnesota Press, 1986), 64; "Phenomenality and Materiality in Kant," in *Hermeneutics: Questions and Prospects,* ed. Gary Shapiro and Alan Sica (Amherst, Mass.: University of Massachusetts Press, 1984), 137–138. Gilles Deleuze argues forcefully, contra de Man's point, that morality for Kant is not disinterested: "*There is a single dangerous misunderstanding regarding the whole of practical Reason:* believing that Kantian morality remains indifferent to its own realization." See *Kant's Critical Philosophy: The Doctrine of the Faculties,* trans. Hugh Tomlinson and Barbara Habberjam (Minneapolis: University of Minnesota Press, 1984), 39. Further page references given in text to *KCP.*

26. For other discussions by de Man of the aesthetic ideology, see *Blindness and Insight: Essays in the Rhetoric of Contemporary Criticism* (Minneapolis: University of Minnesota Press, 1983), 187–190; *Resistance to Theory,* 3–26; *Rhetoric of Romanticism,* 263–290. See also Christopher Norris, *Paul de Man: Deconstruction and the Critique of the Aesthetic Ideology* (New York: Columbia University Press, 1988).

27. Paul de Man, *Allegories of Reading: Figural Language in Rousseau, Nietzsche, Rilke, and Proust* (New Haven: Yale University Press 1979), 17.

28. Immanuel Kant, "An Answer to the Question: 'What is Enlightenment?'" in *Kant: Political Writings,* ed. Hans Reiss, trans. H. B. Nisbet (Cambridge: Cambridge University Press, 1991), 54.

29. Kant, ibid.

30. See Christopher Norris, *Spinoza and the Origins of Modern Critical Theory* (Oxford: Basil Blackwell, 1991), 251–274.

31. Indeed, Eagleton notes the prominence of "confusion" in the discourse of aesthetics as early as Baumgarten. "'Confusion' here means not 'muddle' but 'fusion,'" Eagleton notes; "in their organic interpenetration, the elements of aesthetic representation resist that discrimination into discrete units which is characteristic of conceptual thought" (*Ideology of the Aesthetic,* 15).

32. Ludwig Wittgenstein, *Philosophical Investigations,* trans. G.E.M. Anscombe (New York: Macmillan, 1953), 77. For a discussion of ethical "blurring," see Geoffrey Galt Harpham, *Getting It Right: Language, Literature, and Ethics* (Chicago: University of Chicago Press, 1992), 18–38.

33. Sallis, *Spacings,* 86.

34. Michel Foucault, "What Is Enlightenment?" trans. Catherine Porter, in *The Foucault Reader,* ed. Paul Rabinow (New York: Pantheon, 1984), 34.

35. Jean-François Lyotard, *Discours, figure* (Paris: Klincksieck, 1971), 13. See Eagleton, *Ideology of the Aesthetic,* 344–365, on Theodor Adorno's aesthetics for an extended discussion of aesthetic negativity.

36. Jacques Lacan, *Television: A Challenge to the Psychoanalytic Establishment,* trans. Denis Hollier, Rosalind Kraus, Annette Michelson, ed. Joan Copjec (New York and London: Norton, 1990), 5.

37. Sigmund Freud, "Negation," in Philip Rieff, ed., *General Psychoanalytic Theory: Papers on Metapsychology* (New York: Macmillan, 1963), 216, 217.

38. Isaiah Berlin, "Two Kinds of Liberty," in *Four Essays on Liberty* (New York: Oxford University Press, 1970), 118–172. Berlin distinguishes between "negative liberty" and "positive liberty," a conception of the ideal that underlies "morally just public movements" and frequently takes coercive forms.

39. See Philippe Lacoue-Labarthe and Jean-Luc Nancy, "The Nazi Myth," trans. Brian Holmes, *Critical Inquiry* 16 (1990): 291–312. The authors analyze Nazism as a form of "combat" in which "it will be necessary to eliminate from [the world] the nonbeing or nontype par excellence, the Jew, as well as the nonbeing or lesser being of several other inferior or degenerate types, gypsies, for example" (311).

40. See Bennett, *Outside Literature,* 131–133. Nor is Kant the inventor of aesthetic negativity or aesthetic misnaming. The discourse of the beautiful, to which the discourse of the aesthetic is heir, shows the same symptoms. As Diderot remarked, Plato "shows us indeed what [beauty] is not, but tells us nothing at all about what it is." Denis Diderot, "The Beautiful," in *Aesthetic Theories: Studies in the Philosophy of Art,* ed. Karl Aschenbrenner and Arnold Isenberg (Englewood Cliffs N.J.: Prentice-Hall, 1965), 136. The circularity of many medieval and Renaissance meditations on beauty—was the object beautiful because pleasing, or pleasing because beautiful?—suggests an intractability that would be formalized as what I have been calling misattribution when, with Baumgarten and Kant, the discourse of the beautiful mutated into that of the aesthetic.

41. De Man, *Resistance to Theory,* 11.

42. Quoted in Micah L. Sifry and Christopher Cerf, eds., *The Gulf War Reader: History, Documents, Opinions* (New York: Random House, 1991), 178. Further page references are given in the text to *GWR.*

43. The position of Iraq with respect to the enumerated worlds is far from clear. For while most of the people lead "Third-World" lives, and while, for a time, Iraq had close relations with the Soviet Union, the ideology of Saddam Hussein's Baath party is, as Elie Kedourie notes, an amalgam of discredited Western ideas—the less moderate statements of Nietzsche, the racism of H. S. Chamberlain and Alfred Rosenberg, the concept of state socialism, and exclusive nationalism. See Kedourie, *Arab Political Memoirs and Other Studies* (London: Frank Cass, 1974).

44. Benjamin, *Illuminations,* 241.

45. Theodor Adorno and Max Horkheimer, *The Dialectic of Enlightenment,* trans. John Cumming (New York: Continuum Books, 1989).

46. All these terms are taken from the comments of Saddam Hussein in the now-famous conversation with U.S. Ambassador April Glaspie on July 25, 1990. See Sifry and Cerf, *Gulf War Reader,* 122–133.

III

Form, Disinterest, and Ideology

■ PETER BROOKS ■

Aesthetics and Ideology—What Happened to Poetics?

A CURIOUS HISTORY, that of American academic literary study in the 1980s. At just about the moment one thought the legacy of European structuralism and poststructuralism was becoming institutionalized in the American curriculum—and the American university was becoming the prime field for practices of textuality that in Europe remained confined to marginal fringes of the academy—a reversal was in fact underway, a reassertion of the the historical and ideological coordinates of literature. At the moment when the media discovered "deconstruction" and accused professors of turning from the evaluative and normative function of criticism, another kind of swerve was in fact taking place, one which would turn even many of the deconstructionists into practitioners of ideological and cultural critique. It was as if what appeared as the triumphal entry through the porticos of American academia of such structuralist demigods as Saussure, Jakobson, Lévi-Strauss, and Barthes, and such useful attendant priests as Todorov, Genette, Greimas, had prepared, not the cult of Derrida and de Man that we began to celebrate, but the masked arrival of the cult of Foucault. A certain Apollonian moment of criticism, best emblematized by Jonathan Culler's *Structuralist Poetics* (1975), was swiftly subverted by a Dionysian uprising which demonstrated that attempts to repress the referent only produced a more or less violent return of the repressed. The posthumous drawings and quarterings of Paul de Man provide an allegory of the situation and its treatment: History is waiting behind the arras, ready to smite if you have appeared to turn from it.

To understand the implications of this process, and the place of aesthetics in it, I need to back up for a moment. At a conference sponsored by *Partisan Review* at Boston University in 1979, I was engaged by Clement

Greenberg in a heated exchange in which he accused academic literary study of having abandoned what he saw as the primary function of criticism—judgments of value, discriminations between high and low cultural artifacts, principles of taste—in favor of sterile formalist descriptions, which precisely did not count as *criticism*. In reply to Greenberg, I urged that criticism had tasks other than the evaluative, that indeed judgments of value could often best wait until we had explored thoroughly the realms of textuality, and the relation of individual texts to generic expectations, the way they use and play against conventions, the way they relate to systems of meaning-making.[1] I was echoing positions articulated by (among others) Culler and, before him, Northrop Frye. In his "Polemical Introduction" to *Anatomy of Criticism* (1957), Frye asks what gives us confidence that our individual acts of exegesis and evaluation have any use. Isn't the enterprise of literary criticism a waste of time? Frye's answer was in general outline similar to that Culler would give, on different bases, in *Structuralist Poetics*: criticism needs an overall structural framework, articulating its grounds and identifying features of pertinence if the work of the individual critic is to be subsumed in a progressive continuing enterprise that is significant, that can be shared, taught, transmitted, and made the subject of an intelligible dialogue. Both Frye and Culler, in their different ways, claim that the study of literature needs to ground itself in the study of poetics, as precisely the grounds on which texts make sense, and can be made sense of. Culler's work represented the decisive contemporary version of poetics, in that it was founded on the linguistic model. Linguistics, in the wake of Ferdinand de Saussure, Roman Jakobson—and Claude Lévi-Strauss's application of it to anthropology—offered the most impressive formalization of a field of study and, since the material and manifestation of literature was inevitably linguistic, perhaps as well the truest insight into literariness.

In 1979, then, in argument with an influential practicing critic, I was urging that academic criticism at its best entertained close relations with poetics, which had a certain priority over aesthetics—understood here in the limited sense of the discrimination of the beautiful and significant in art—in the study of literature. To recast the issue: a fuller understanding of aesthetics has to include poetics as part of its domain, as the very grounding of any intelligible discussion of art. I held some form of the view succinctly expressed by the Danish linguist Louis Hjelmslev: "A priori it would seem to be a generally valid thesis that for every *process* there is a corresponding *system*, by which the process can be analyzed and described by means of a limited number of premises."[2] That is to say, one should generally try to work from specific textual instances to the general conditions and project of literature that they imply—and then back again, reinvesting in reading of the text what one has learned about its conditions of possibility and understanding. Such a concern with poetics was not necessarily incompatible with history—as I tried to suggest in my own books—since certain imaginative modes, their conventions and rules, are produced by certain historical contexts. Sharing the interests of what one might describe as the anthropological wing of literary structuralism, I also believed that this kind of study could lead one toward an understanding of humans as sign-making animals: literature was the most concerted and self-conscious instance of the effort of human consciousness to create meaning in its otherwise alien environment. In such a program of literary study, it was useful to be as wide-ranging and encompassing as possible in the vast domain of human fiction-making. The evaluative moment—discriminations of high from low, of more successful from less, of precious from cheap—was by no means unimportant, but it could wait: wait, precisely, on understanding, which risked narrowness and blindness if there were a premature closure to exploration of the field.

Poetics, I believed and still do believe, is the necessary grounding of aesthetics, and an important element in any productive construal of the notion of the aesthetic. What happened to poetics in the American university's teaching of literature is a vexed and interesting question. In lieu of an answer, I might cite my own experience with The Literature Major at Yale University—an undergraduate interdepartmental program in literature that came into existence in the early 1970s with a general bias toward structuralist poetics, offering courses that attempted, for instance, to look at narrative in a generalizing, "narratological" sort of way, superimposing different kinds of narrative in an effort to show their structural and dynamic constants as well as their verbal specificities. Early in the life of The Literature Major, I predicted that my interests in poetics and narratology might be outflanked, as it were, by a general semiotics, of the type best represented by Umberto Eco's *Theory of Semiotics* (Eco was indeed a visiting professor in the program), placing poetics and the study of literature in a larger science of signs. What happened was quite different: what came to take on a certain predominance in the program—though not to the exclusion of poetics, especially among those interested in narrative—was what I would call rhetorical reading. I use this term both in honor of the course created for the program by Paul de Man and Geoffrey Hartman, called "Reading and Rhetorical Structures," and because the more obvious label of "deconstruction" by now generates wildly irrelevant associations, and masks the kind of intense, laborious reading that students of de Man, Hartman, and of such other colleagues as J. Hillis Miller, Barbara Johnson, and Andrezj Warminski, were learning to perform.

It was in part on the basis of his experience in The Literature Major that Paul de Man once proposed replacing the Department of Comparative Literature by a "Department of Poetics, Rhetoric, and the History of Literature." I cite the proposed label because I think it well corresponded to what The Literature Major, and subsequently the Department of Comparative Literature, thought it was teaching—and to a large extent still does. Nonetheless, the place and the moment of poetics, at Yale and elsewhere, was precarious and perhaps evanescent. If exemplary deconstruction—in work of de Man and Jacques Derrida—arose from structuralism and phenomenology, as a critique of the notion of representation and an attempt to unlock and decenter any stable system of structure, in the hands of American student practitioners it too easily became simply another kind of textual exegesis, easy to learn and to use because American literary studies have long had an exegetical bias. For many American students, deconstruction was a brand of New Criticism in a new and more unconstrained form: a way of reading texts, without much context, in a kind of naked confrontation of reader and verbal art, in a "democratic" classroom practice where the individual's responses—what the individual made of the text—was the starting point for discussion.

That is, most American students have little background in either philosophy or formal poetics. They are used to construing texts, pretty much in the void. Once you teach them that there is a way of construing a text that does not assume that its rhetoric, structure, and argument work toward an organic unity—however complicated by irony or paradox—but may rather expose aporia, a fundamental disjuncture of apparent argument and rhetorical implication, they can quite easily produce "deconstructive readings" that have all the marks of professional accomplishment. With the difference, however, from the work of a de Man or a Derrida that there seems to be very little at stake in many of these readings—that there is no real interrogation of literature or language at work. Without a passage through either philosophy or poetics, deconstruction becomes one more exegetical practice to fill the classroom space, and the pages of the academic journals.

It is in this context that I wish to view the "New Historicist" turn of American criticism, its (re)invention of "Cultural Poetics"—Stephen Greenblatt is to be credited with both these labels, as well as with the best exemplification of what they can mean in practice. The way in which historical context and reference was bracketed, or simply ignored, in work both structuralist (though, as I mentioned, there was an "anthropological" orientation to some early structuralism, a concern with cultural systems, including their histories) and deconstructive (though Derrida has of course argued for the political significance of deconstruction) led to a corrective action, in the return of historical contextualization, placing literature in networks of other discourses, and other *dispositifs* of social power (I use a term of Michel Foucault's, since he has clearly been the major influence in the reorientation of criticism). So much was no doubt an inevitable and salutary correction within a system that had become skewed, and in any event the best structuralists, from Saussure on, never proposed that history be ignored, but rather bracketed in order to understand the synchronic logic of a system at a given moment.

But cultural poetics quickly gave birth to a subgenre of specifically ideological criticism, implicit of course in the Foucauldian exemplum, and influenced also by a return of Frankfurt School critical theory, by the British Marxist tradition running from Raymond Williams to Terry Eagleton, and by the unique, and uniquely sophisticated, American Marxism of Fredric Jameson. Here, for the first time since the 1930s, and in a vastly different form, we have an ideologization of the aesthetic: the claim that the critic can, and must, position him or herself as analyst and actor in an ideological drama, that not to do so is simply to be a bad-faith participant in hegemonic cultural practices. Let me cite as an example the final sentence of an essay (from the collective volume, *The New Historicism*) by Louis A. Montrose, entitled "Professing the Renaissance: The Poetics and Politics of Culture": "If, by the ways in which we choose to read Renaissance texts, we bring to our students and to ourselves a sense of our own historicity, an apprehension of our own positionings within ideology, then we are at the same time demonstrating the limited but nevertheless tangible possibility of contesting the regime of power and knowledge that at once sustains us and constrains us."[3] Montrose's is an intelligent essay, and in many ways typical of interesting new work on the Renaissance. And I don't disagree with his point, in that I believe the thoughtful, probing reading of texts is always subversive of received ways of thinking, since these resist and repress the uncomfortable insights brought by analysis. Nonetheless, the statement exudes a kind of self-importance and posturing that seems to me a sign of our current critical malaise. It is characterized by a kind of polysyllabic strutting and a rhetoric of virtue that seem to me to speak mainly of our bad conscience as academic literary critics.

For literary critics do suffer from bad conscience. They are infected by a continuing suspicion that they don't really have a valid subject to profess. They are, variously, poets, rhetoricians, poeticians, social critics *manqués*. Frye in his "Polemical Introduction" urged, "To defend the right of criticism to exist at all is to assume that criticism is a structure of thought and knowledge in its own right, with some measure of independence from the art it deals with."[4] Frye believed that one could demonstrate that the mental process involved in literary study "is as coherent and progressive as the study of science" (10–11); and Culler echoes these sentiments. But such a claim really applies only to poetics. And poetics, for all its importance, does not wholly satisfy. It doesn't satisfy because it necessarily formalizes and isolates the field of study, taking as its object the specificity of literature. If attending to the "literariness" of the literary solves our problems in one way, in another it only makes our malaise worse, since it isolates literature from human activity. The game of poetics comes to appear too mandarin, or too monkish.

Hence a critic like Montrose proposes that the "professor of literature" should be confronting problems of the following type:

> . . . the essential or historical bases upon which "literature" is to be distinguished from other discourses; the possible configurations of relationship between cultural practices and social, political and economic processes; the consequences of post-structuralist theories of textuality for the practice of an historical or materialist criticism; the means by which subjectivity is socially constituted and constrained; the processes by means of which ideologies are produced and sustained, and by which they may be contested; the patterns of consonance and contradiction among the values and interests of a given individual, as these are actualized in the shifting conjunctures of various subject positions—as, for example, intellectual worker, academic professional, and gendered domestic, social, political and economic agent. (19)

One senses that this is material to hide from the eyes of such as Lynne Cheney or Hilton Kramer or Dinesh D'Souza, or other recent critics of the academic humanities, since it so readily confirms their intemperate view that the academy has become a conspiracy of aging Sixties radicals made only slightly less dangerous by the fact that their prose can't shoot straight. The pretensions of literary criticism to public importance are matched by the refusal to speak any recognizably public language.

Montrose later in his essay summons us to a choice: "Critical research and teaching in the Humanities may be either a merely academic displacement or a genuine academic instantiation of oppositional social and political praxis" (26). The terms in which the choice is posed create a kind of academic melodrama, of the disempowered professorial wimp versus the macho resistance hero. Even if we want to align ourselves with the latter, and want to refuse definitively the notion of the critic as a genteel belated Victorian preaching sweetness and light, we may find that this version of the choice both plays into the hands of our enemies, and seriously undermines our ability to speak of literature with any particular qualifications for doing so. To put it another way: Montrose's choice seems to me not really a choice at all but a failed piece of analysis of the role of the professional student of literature, one that needs to be be subsumed and rethought in genuinely dialectical and historical terms.

Elements of the kind of reflection that I have in mind are provided by Terry Eagleton's ambitious book, *The Ideology of the Aesthetic*. The "aesthetic" here means of course not just discriminations of beauty but the domain of artistic creation and its reception. As Eagleton argues, the aesthetic plays a dominant role in modern thought in part

> because of a certain indeterminacy of definition which allows it to figure in a varied span of preoccupations: freedom and legality, spontaneity and necessity, self-determination, autonomy, particularity and universality, along with several others. My argument, broadly speaking, is that the category of the aesthetic assumes the importance it does in modern Europe because in speaking of art it speaks of these other matters too, which are at the heart of the middle class's struggle for political hegemony.[5]

From such premises, Eagleton is able to pursue a truly dialectical analysis of the place of the aesthetic as a domain at once liberating and repressive, creating images of community while mystifying their political realization. That is, while analyzing the ideological ends and needs that the bourgeoisie found in, and invested in, the category of the aesthetic, Eagleton respects and preserves its specificity as a category. He does not summon the critic to any facilely polarized choices in his or her practice. Indeed, he at least implicitly warns against the facile (and very American) assumption that academic and institutional politics have anything to do with the forging of a real politics of transformation.

Among the texts Eagleton discusses is Friedrich Schiller's *On the Aesthetic Education of Man* (1795), which remains in my view one of the most powerful and, for all its datedness, most persuasive arguments for the centrality of the aesthetic in culture and the need to make it a core concept in education. For Schiller, the aesthetic is what permits human beings to emerge from the purely physical while retaining the concrete and sensuous in their composition. It is the condition both of human freedom and of the well-regulated political state. The aesthetic provides the foundations of culture as an active, transformative medium in which people mutually civilize one another, and proclaim their necessary sphere of freedom from the state. Schiller's is an argument against egotism, against specialization, the fragmentation of human capacities and the mechanization of life. The aesthetic offers a hope of integration, an overcoming of alienation. Its core principle, the "play-drive" (*Spieltrieb*), is "directed toward annuling time within time, reconciling becoming with absolute being and change with identity."[6]

While it is obviously too idealist a proposal to meet the demands of modern capitalism and the modern state—not to mention the kinds of human misery that currently overwhelm us—and we have become skeptical about views of art as "reconciliation," Schiller's project nonetheless has a certain modernity because of its quasi-anthropological understanding of the *Spieltrieb* as a vital component of the human. Like the creation of sign-systems, the play of the aesthetic is one of humanity's basic accommodations in the world, permitting the illusion of a freedom from materiality. As Wallace Stevens would put it, in *Notes Toward a Supreme Fiction:*

> From this the poem springs: that we live in a place
> That is not our own and, much more, not ourselves
> And hard it is in spite of blazoned days.

As an argument that the aesthetic, and the serious kind of play that characterizes it, is a major component of the human that needs cultivation, nurture, Schiller's impassioned treatise continues to suggest a program for education. One cannot conceive of a true program of education that does not give a place to the aesthetic impulse as he defines it. The point seems obvious, but it bears repetition since the place accorded the *Spieltrieb* seems constantly threatened. And not only by utilitarian programs that would rationalize education according to the specialized needs in expertise of the modern state. Constantly trumping the aesthetic by the ideological and political—making the aesthetic simply a mask for the ideological—risks losing a sense of the functional role played by the aesthetic within human existence. Cultivating Schiller's play function involves a respect for the aesthetic—including a respect for poetics as a valid and important discipline—that the terms of an argument such as Montrose's simply short-circuit.

My argument is at bottom this: that it is all very well to teach as "an oppositional social and political praxis," and to ask students to consider "positionings within ideology," but that is not your first or your most important task in the classroom. Students are only too willing to short-circuit the aesthetic, and to perform any kind of reading, including the ideological, that you indicate to them. What is more difficult for them—and hence more necessary—is to slow up the work of interpretation, the attempt to turn the text into *some other* discourse or system, and to consider it as a manifestation of the conventions, constraints, and possibilities of literature. If I continue to believe, contra Greenberg, that aesthetic value judgments are not the first order of business in teaching literature, I now feel the need to assert that recognition of the aesthetic, as a constituted domain with its own grounds of meaning-making, is indispensable, and that as a consequence some deference to poetics is inevitable. Students need in their work on literature to encounter a moment of poetics—a moment in which they are forced to ask not only *what* the text means, but as well *how* it means, what its grounds as a meaning-making sign-system are, and how we as readers, through the competence we have gained by reading other texts, activate and deploy systems that allow us to detect or create meaning, and to rationalize and order meanings in categorical ways. As Geoffrey Hartman argued many years ago, the trouble with Anglo-American formalism is that it was never formalist enough.[7] The complaint remains valid even after the contributions of structuralist poetics: American pedagogical practice still tends to go right for the interpretive jugular. It does not sufficiently pause, and reflect, in the realm of poetics.

■   ■   ■

The demasking of ideology proposed by Montrose, and so many others, as the task of criticism points, I have suggested, to an uneasy conscience about our role as literary critics, a wish to have some leverage on the real affairs of the world. I think the resurgence of this kind of criticism at this moment has deeper, and more interesting, motivations than the one habitually proffered by the cultural Right, which sees overgrown sixties adolescents now come to power in the university. Jean-François Lyotard has noted that a prime characteristic of the postmodern condition is the decline of those "grand narratives" that sustained Western culture for decades, in particular the grand narrative of emancipation.[8] Literary studies—indeed the humanities in general—may be suffering from the decline of a grand narrative. This is not so much "emancipation"—though that was always part of the story proposed by the humanities, and certainly part of Schiller's aesthetic education—as something more like "redemption through culture." Charles Taylor in his important book, *Sources of the Self,* speaks eloquently of the force of "civic humanist thought" for those Victorians, such as Matthew Arnold, for whom the theory of culture was crucial, and who continued to be a major influence on our own concepts of culture and education at least until very recently. A key component of the public, civic notion of culture worked out by the Victorians was what Taylor calls "the Romantic ideal of self-completion through art."[9] The Victorians, that is, responded to the large historical movement toward secularization by investing culture—high culture—with the transcendent and redeeming force drained from religious belief. As Wallace Stevens put the extreme form of the case: "After one has abandoned a belief in God, poetry is the essence which takes its place as life's redemption."[10]

I doubt that there are many professors of literature today who would want to subscribe publicly to such a view. Not only the partisans of cultural critique but anyone who has registered the impact of the postmodern—of the post-Freudian, the post-Foucauldian, the postcolonialist—moment senses that both "self" and "poetry" have been deconstructed, to become simply nodes where certain codes intersect, in a mirage of inwardness and self-realization. We no longer have much confidence that we know what culture is for, what kind of self-realization it is supposed to promote. And we're fairly certain that to ask poetry to work redemption is to place on literary culture a burden that it cannot bear.

Yet our contemporary culture wars, including both the promotion of cultural-ideological critique and the right-wing response in defense of the Arnoldian view (in fact, an impoverished understanding of Arnold's much more complex and troubled vision), indicate that Taylor may be on target in calling the chapter of *Sources of the Self* which I have cited "Our Victorian Contemporaries." It's not clear that we have really been able to find new conceptual frameworks and new vocabularies for discussing our relation to culture, and the relation of culture—including education—to daily life and to the state. The public passions aroused by such cultural incidents as exhibiting Robert Mapplethorpe's photographs, assessing Paul de Man's collaborationist past, or the explanatory placards in "The West as America" show at the National Gallery all indicate that we continue to play out in debates over the definition and the uses of culture issues of a quasi-theological kind that matter enormously to us. The National Endowments for the Arts and for the Humanities in the post–Cold War moment may have come to house more ideologues than the Pentagon. More than politics in the usual acceptation, it is cultural politics that absorb much of our anxiety about values. And if this demonstrates that culture is indeed a realm of ideological debate, it nonetheless confirms that culture, including the aesthetic, is a constituted realm that cannot simply be reduced to ideology. The positions taken by ideological literary critics like Montrose appear to reject the Victorian valuation of the aesthetic but perhaps in a deeper sense confirm it. Such discomfort with traditions of scholarship and interpretation, such a "strong stake," as Montrose puts it with an echo of Pierre Bourdieu, "in making their own discursive practice a direct intervention in the process of ideological reproduction" (22), indicate that the aesthetic still is very much at issue among those who want to expose it as part of a nefarious hegemonic practice. To place the study of literature in the context of "cultural studies," as is sometimes currently proposed, will be a mistake if thereby the specificity of the aesthetic domain is lost.

A different way to make my point would be to say that professors of literature—of the humanities in general—have no choice but to work within inherited traditions, since the notion of "tradition" is absolutely central to any humanistic work, and indeed one of the defining characteristics that set the humanities apart from the natural and even the social sciences. The humanities are predicated on the preservation and transmission of texts and artifacts of the past. Scholarship in the humanities cannot free itself from tradition without becoming autistic. Teaching the humanities involves submerging one's individual personality into something larger, into a cultural tradition which one speaks through, and allows to speak through oneself. The humanist is always a bit like what Keats in his famous definition of "negative capability" calls the "chameleon poet." The "poetical character," says Keats, "has no self—it is every thing and nothing—it has no character. . . . What shocks the virtuous philosopher, delights the camelion Poet. A poet is the most unpoetical of any thing in existence; because he has no identity—he is continually in for—and filling some other Body."[11] The same is true for the teacher of literature, who is forever taking up and enacting other individualities, setting his voice in dialogue with others. And the chorus of those other voices echoing from the past is precisely cultural tradition. It is the force and presence of something larger than ourselves that we must listen to in order to make our own utterances richer, more comprehensive, more attuned to the complexities and contradictions of dialogue. Respect for tradition means an awareness that you speak with words and concepts that have been used by others before you, that they are not yours alone, but come freighted with prior implications, that your originality is always tempered by the weight of an otherness.

The obvious move at this point in my argument is to cite T. S. Eliot in "Tradition and the Individual Talent," and I shall not resist it, though I risk the accretion of associations more reactionary than I intend. (But then, Eliot's criticism is not so unproblematically reactionary as many now assume.) Eliot writes of the poet: "What happens is a continual surrender of himself as he is at the moment to something which is more valuable. The progress of an artist is a continual self-sacrifice, a continual extinction of personality."[12] What Eliot says of the poet is perforce true of the critic, who needs to surrender his or her personality to something larger, to culture. The critic needs to speak in his or her own voice, to be sure, but it's a voice of a persona that does not simply coincide with the living person: it is the voice of a persona shaped by culture, a product of what Barthes called the *déjà-lu,* the intersection of traditions (virtually another way to say poetics), the echo-chamber of voices from the past. The critic and teacher is always something of a ventriloquist, projecting and dramatizing voices from the cultural tradition, while trying to situate the personal voice in dialogue with them.

A recent trend toward the personalization of criticism, indeed toward the cult of the critic's personality, seems to me regrettable, a kind of academic version of the postmodern replacement of personhood by celebrity—as if one did not really exist until celebrated in *People* magazine. We have come to understand—as one of the lessons of modern ethnology—that knowledge is situated, that the observer is part of the observed, the storyteller part of the story. The "we" of a genteel academic tradition generalized at the expense of repressions and exclusions needed to be exploded; the critic needed to assume his or her place in the field of knowing. But I find there is currently a tendency to fall into the assumption that the critical personality can and should flaunt its idiosyncrasies without submitting to the test of that otherness which is culture—without undergoing the discipline of listening to the voices of cultural traditions before, and at the same time as, one speaks in one's own voice. Forgetting that they are only chameleon poets, critics end up speaking as if they were virtuous philosophers. There is a considerable rhetoric of virtue in Montrose's essay, for instance, and it is not untypical. There is indeed often a measure of moral arrogance in the critical stance that derives, *grosso modo,* from Foucault, who often gives the impression that we, as analysts, know better—better than the deluded discourses we are unmasking, better than the poor old Renaissance, or better, especially, than the benighted, repressed, neurotic, oppressive nineteenth century. Virtuous philosophizing really undoes the work of situating knowledge, and knower in relation to it. It tacitly assumes a place of privilege—within contemporary American academia, of all places—from which it proffers its discourse.

The respect for tradition that seems to me so necessary a part of criticism can lead, and has led, to a certain conservative, even fundamentalist position, which asserts that respect for the past means not tampering with it, allowing it to "speak for itself," conferring upon it the "intellectual authority" that is otherwise so lacking in contemporary life and discourse. Proponents of an education based on "intellectual authority" (William J. Bennett's phrase) appeal to a canonical sense of tradition: an inherited body of knowledge—itself embodying certain transcendent "values"—which has assumed fixed form and should be preserved and transmitted, by teachers and scholars, with fidelity and reverence.[13] This view ignores the fact that the canon as we know it, in our great books courses, anthologies, and polemics, is historically contingent, an historical culture formation, based on readings, interpretations, discriminations performed by people and cultural institutions in historical time. More generally, and still more seriously, such a notion of tradition denies and represses the fact that traditions not only shape individual interpretations but are themselves the product of interpretations. The appeal to tradition as a grounds that allows you to evaluate individual interpretations—and to rule some out of court—can never be more than partially convincing since tradition itself is the product of other interpretations, and thus itself a very uncertain grounding. The scholars and teachers largely responsible for new thinking in the humanities over the past two or three decades have made us acutely aware that traditions are really constructions, and that our interpretive and constructive work both continues and modifies the tradition. To say this is of course to undermine any unproblematic notion of intellectual authority: to ask where traditions came from, who formed them, what interests they have served, whether they are the *right* traditions for future work. The interpretive disciplines can have no traditions unless they construct them, in an act that always matches piety toward the past with betrayal of it, since it remakes the past in the present, giving it a shape that makes contemporary sense, so that it can be handed on to the future.

Stanley Cavell has recently suggested that there is an "internal relation" of tradition to treason: handing something on is also handing something over, in an act of translation that is always also one of subversion.[14] Here lies the exhilaration as well as the discomfort of professing literature. And for me the uncertain relation of tradition to treason suggests that the critic needs a certain humility, a certain awareness that one does not speak ex cathedra, but from a very uncomfortable and unstable and indeed slippery ground. The ground permits one to make "interventions" in "the process of ideological reproduction," of course. But such interventions risk being merely personal, merely virtuous philosophizing, merely the arrogance of claiming to know better, if they are not tempered by passage through the *askesis* of poetics and reading. One cannot claim to speak for the text until one has attempted to let the text speak through oneself.

When Geoffrey Hartman complained that Anglo-American formalism was never formalist enough, he may—in a very different critical context from that we know at present—have meant something similar. The critic needs the self-imposition of the formalist *askesis* because this alone can assure the critic that the act of interpretation has been submitted to an otherness, that it is not simply an assimilation of the object of study. The realm of the aesthetic needs to be respected, by an imperative that is nearly ethical. It's not that the aesthetic is the realm of a secular scripture, that poetry has taken the place of a failed theodicy, that critics are celebrants at the high altar of a cult of beauty isolated from history and politics. It is rather that personality must be tempered by the discipline of the impersonal that comes in the creation of form. "Form" in this sense is really an extension of language, which is itself impersonal in the same way. The human subject comes to being in language, as a system that preexists the individual locutor, that is transsubjective. To believe that we possess the language when we speak is an illusion. To understand that it possesses and defines us—that it is a formal system in which and through which we speak—is a necessary condition of subjectivity.

This leads me to a final point. The need to submit the individual critical talent to the discipline of form, to respect for the aesthetic, ought to be accompanied by acknowledgment of the formal discipline of a common language. In my view, this should be a more public language than that most often spoken in the academy. The construction of cultural traditions, the modification of accepted interpretations, the creative transmission of the past, need to enter the space of public dialogue. I am aware of how difficult this is—of how little the organs and media of public debate think they need or want informed academic discourse, of how trivial, distorted, and bad-faith have been most of the public discussions of intellectual issues produced by the academy. Nonetheless, scholars need to try to go public with their ideas, and they can do so only when they are willing and able to speak a public language. My worst fear for the humanities of the future is that they will allow themselves to become privatized, marginalized, trivialized, content with debates within closed compartments, and with internecine struggles. Humanists sometimes seem to match a certain arrogance of their critical pronouncements with excessive diffidence in the public sphere, accepting marginal status in the republic, and sometimes even in the university. They need to keep in mind that, whatever their critics may assert, they do speak of essential issues of value, by way of others' recorded struggles to say how life should be lived.

A. Bartlett Giamatti—when, as president of Yale University, he inaugurated the Whitney Humanities Center in 1981—quoted the rhetorician Quintilian on the orator, whom Quintilian (citing Cicero) calls "a good man, skilled in speaking." Giamatti commented:

> Quintilian gives a potent model for the humanist, one who connects private and public life through a rhetorical act that is skillful because it is first wise, effective because first it is ethical. In that ancient vision of the civic being, so fresh today, language is the ligature binding private moral concerns and the shapely civic life. The humanist is whoever understands that linkage and strives, at every moment, to strengthen its meaning for our common good.[15]

Noble words. To live up to them requires constant attention to that "ligature" of language, studying how we can do justice to the place of the aesthetic within the public, civic realm.

Notes

1. My talk and the exchange with Greenberg are printed in *Partisan Review* 47, no. 3 (1980), 409–414 and 422–423.

2. Louis Hjelmslev, *Prolegomena to a Theory of Language,* cited by Jonathan Culler, *Structuralist Poetics* (Ithaca: Cornell University Press, 1975), 7.

3. Louis A. Montrose, "Professing the Renaissance: The Poetics and Politics of Culture," in *The New Historicism,* ed. H. Aram Veeser (New York and London: Routledge, 1989), 31.

4. Northrop Frye, *Anatomy of Criticism* (Princeton: Princeton University Press, 1957), 5.

5. Terry Eagleton, *The Ideology of the Aesthetic* (Oxford: Basil Blackwell, 1990), 3.

6. Friedrich Schiller, *On the Aesthetic Education of Man* (*Über die ästhetische Erziehung des Menschen*), trans. Elizabeth M. Wilkinson and L. A. Willoughby (Oxford: Clarendon Press, 1967), 97.

7. Geoffrey Hartman, "Beyond Formalism," in *Beyond Formalism* (New Haven: Yale University Press, 1970), 42.

8. See Jean-François Lyotard, *La condition postmoderne* (Paris: Editions de Minuit, 1985).

9. Charles Taylor, *Sources of the Self* (Cambridge: Harvard University Press, 1989), 418, 409.

10. Wallace Stevens, *Opus Posthumous* (New York: Vintage, 1990), 185.

11. John Keats to Richard Woodhouse, 27 October 1818, in *English Romantic Writers,* ed. David Perkins (New York: Harcourt Brace Jovanovich, 1967), 1220.

12. T. S. Eliot, "Tradition and the Individual Talent," in *The Sacred Wood* (London: Methuen, 1920), 52–53.

13. See William J. Bennett, *To Reclaim a Legacy,* reprinted in *The Chronicle of Higher Education,* 28 November 1981, 20.

14. Stanley Cavell, "In the Meantime," *Yale Journal of Criticism* 5, no. 2 (1992), 229.

15. A. Bartlett Giamatti, "Introductory Remarks," *On the Occasion of the Inauguration of the Whitney Humanities Center, Yale University, February 4, 1981* (New Haven: Yale University Printing Service, 1981).

■ MARIA DIBATTISTA ■

"Sabbath Eyes"
Ideology and the Writer's Gaze

WHEN VIRGINIA WOOLF set out to patrol the contested literary ground of the thirties in her influential essay "The Leaning Tower," she provided this image to keep us "steady in our path": "A writer is a person who sits at a desk and keeps his eyes fixed, as intently as he can, upon a certain object."[1] There is nothing socially exalted or spiritually commanding about this figure, yet Woolf endows it with an almost talismanic power to guide her through the ideological minefield of thirties culture. It is not difficult to surmise why this should be so. The writer's undistracted, disinterested gaze epitomizes for Woolf the aesthetic disposition toward the world. Such impartiality ought to ensure him safe conduct, an expectation connected with her feeling that the writer is a figure in the world but somehow never directly in its midst. These feelings, of course, are all the more remarkable, and perhaps a little foolhardy, since they are avowed and defended at the historical moment when the writer's distance from immanent worldly concerns seemed increasingly untenable.

Indeed the very sedateness of Woolf's image may strike us as escapist. Without expecting her to respond to the cataclysm of modern history with the same urgent outrage of Picasso's *Guernica,* we might be baffled by the reassuring familiarity evoked by her genre picture: the writer ensconced in a hushed interior, rapt in his vision, a still point in the turning world. The world, of course, was not turning in 1940, it was convulsed. If we seek a scenic image to convey what it felt like to be a writer displaced by the upheavals of class struggle and world war, we should do better to ponder Cyril Connolly's abject picture of the writer "in the dilapidation of wartime, [occupying] a corner even more dilapidated, sitting with his begging bowl in the shadow of the volcano."[2] Woolf's depiction, by contrast, seems devised to locate a zone of quietness in which the artist may work, sequestered and, to the degree possible, insulated from the "bark of the guns and the bray of the gramophones" that assaulted Woolf's ears in *Three Guineas,* disturbing her ability to heed "the voices of the poets, answering each other, assuring us of a unity that rubs out divisions as if they were chalkmarks only."[3] In opposing the dialogic and harmonizing voices of the poets to the discord of embattled ideologies, Woolf dramatizes a fundamental difference between the way art and ideology represent, and impose themselves upon, the world. The figure of the writer at his desk absorbed in contemplation is not just a convenient image to localize this opposition; by the thirties and forties it had become the object of contestation itself. How to interpret this image, how to defend the writer's separate peace against the clamor of contending ideologies is the burden of Woolf's essay, and of mine.

Woolf's image of the writer gazing fixedly reminds us that the aesthetic originates, biologically and etymologically, in *aesthesis,* in the perceptions of the sensitized body. The aesthetic, to adopt Terry Eagleton's bracing formulation, comprises "nothing less than the whole of our sensate life together—the business of affections and aversions, of how the world strikes the body on its sensory surfaces, of what takes root in the gaze and the guts and all that arises from our most banal, biological insertion into the world."[4] Eagleton's metaphors of insertion and insemination suggest that the aesthetic gestates in a place set apart, yet paradoxically deep within, the common life. Nothing can take root which is not sheltered from the surface agitations of the world. What takes root in the gaze takes root in the core of the mind where sensations germinate into intensities of human response: affections and aversions. Woolf herself believed that creative perception was highly, that is deeply, unconscious. The "work done by unconsciousness," she speculated, is accomplished when the "under-mind works at top speed while the upper-mind drowses" (134). It is work that cannot be initiated, much less completed until there is "a rest, a chance to turn aside and look at something different." Only after this pause from conscious, directed thought can "the thing in itself, the thing the writer wants to write about," appear at once simplified and composed. To designate the "unconscious" work of aesthetic perception, as Eagleton does, as a business, is to risk either the illogic of a mixed metaphor or the efficient but demoralizing consolidation of psychological with economic activity, by which the things of the mind, "things in themselves," will be delivered over to the contingencies and self-interestedness of the marketplace.

It is, on the contrary, ideology which is "business-like" in distributing the affections and mobilizing aversions on its own behalf. James Agee was reacting against this affinity when, in the "keyword" list appended to *Now*

Let Us Praise Famous Men, he placed ideology between escapism and business.[5] Although ideology shares with the aesthetic a Greek ancestry, deriving from "idein," to see, what ideology "sees," as Agee suggests, is determined by both escapist (that is utopian, wish-fullfilling) fantasy and the executive ambitions of thought. The reputation of ideology as a reserve of inept and brutal thought-administrators dates to Napoleon, who attributed "all the misfortunes which have befallen our beautiful France" to Enlightenment ideologues and their abstract doctrines. Ideology is thus construed to be the misfortune of Beauty, be it the beauty of objects or of nations. But it is also, in the sense generally accorded it by Marx and Engels, the misfortune of enlightened, progressive politics, since ideology, like the camera obscura, inverts the world and its material determinations so that "men and their circumstances appear upside down."[6] Raymond Williams, in his entry on ideology in *Keywords,* prefers a "more neutral sense of ideology" as "the set of ideas which arise from a given set of material interests." Ideology as a mode of genuine, as opposed to false consciousness, acknowledges and advances its own interests to social hegemony. Eager for results, it is not content to contemplate, but most actively works to realize its vision of "a unity that rubs out divisions as if they were chalkmarks only." However one regards the work of ideology—as the legitimate business of politics or as a delusional enterprise—one should not confuse or conflate it with the work of writing. Herself a skilled propagandist of strong political convictions, Woolf remains adamant that to *be* a writer means precisely to "think of things in themselves" rather than to work at "influencing the world to higher ends."

Woolf's refusal to justify the work of art by linking it *directly* to the work of world-reformation, startling now, was more so then. The compelling, well-nigh irresistible ethos of thirties literary culture enjoined the serious writer to "go over" to the progressive side of the class conflict. The writer who remained uncommitted not only lost the chance to influence the world to better ends, but, as Edward Upward warned, forfeited any possibility "to write a good book or tell the truth about reality."[7] Woolf was of a different persuasion. She never accepted as categorical the ideological imperative to declare one's allegiance in the momentous battles which would decide the fate of "the great principles of Justice and Equality and Liberty."[8] Though these were her principles, Woolf would not concede that such imperatives should drive the writer from his desk or determine what he writes when he returns to it. For the writer to align his vision with ideological horizons, however noble, even needful, is to risk being something else, somewhere else.

The greatest risk is that the writer will be deported to the realm of the topical. Woolf admits in *Three Guineas* that great art can serve the political purposes of the present, and indeed offers a reading of Sophocles' *Antigone* as antifascist propaganda: Antigone is the type of Mrs. Pankhurst, imprisoned in Holloway, or of Frau Pommer, the wife of a Prussian mines official at Essen "arrested and . . . tried on a charge of insulting and slandering the State and the Nazi movement." Creon, exacting blind obedience "in little things and great," is a type for Hitler and Mussolini. Yet these characters, transported to the new mise-en-scène history has prepared for them, refuse to remain permanently in the domain of social relevance. The times may find "it easy to squeeze these characters into up-to-date dress," but it will also discover that "it is impossible to keep them there. They suggest too much; when the curtain falls we sympathize, it may be noted, even with Creon himself." Propagandists and ideological critics may denounce literature precisely on the grounds that it produces such undesirable identifications. That Creon can be contemplated with the same impartial gaze as Antigone suggests "that Sophocles . . . uses freely all the faculties that can be possessed by a writer; and suggests, therefore, that if we use art to propagate political opinions, we must force the artist to clip and cabin his gift to do us a cheap and passing service. Literature will suffer the same mutilation that the mule has suffered; and there will be no more horses" (170). Propaganda, employed in the cheap and passing service of politics, is the *timely* art; it propagates nothing beyond its present moment and so can at best aspire to the period piece. Literature refuses to restrict its means, discipline its thoughts, limit its sympathies. It is thus more *expensive* to the mind, which must use all of its resources and work all its faculties, but its achievements are less "dated" and more enduring, since literature never mulishly services the present, but gallops over and beyond it.

A deep suspicion currently attaches to the distinction Woolf upholds between the fecundity of literature and the sterility of ideology, between the aesthetic as a self-perpetuating tradition and ideology as "a cheap and passing service" to the imperious present. In the most general instance, it is a suspicion directed against modernity itself as the triumph of aesthetic, at the expense of social, enlightenment. Raymond Williams frets in his *Keywords*, whose first entry, indeed, is "aesthetic," that the history of the word is "an element in the divided modern consciousness of *art* and *society*: a reference beyond social use and social valuation which, like one special meaning of *culture*, is intended to express a human dimension which the dominant version of *society* appears to exclude."[9] Eagleton also contends, in his probing, if selective history of these issues in *The Ideology of the Aesthetic*, that the moment of dissociation—of sensibility, of human disciplines—is "the moment of modernity." Art in the modern era becomes autonomous, no longer obligated to address, much less solve, questions of ethical import, social value, and political consequence. The price it must pay for its self-regulated existence, however, is the gradual atrophy and expiration of its social powers. Eagleton dramatizes the empty freedom of modern art by hazarding "the rather exaggerated formulation that aesthetics is born at the moment of art's effective demise as a political force, flourishes on the corpse of its social relevance."[10] Modern art is the severed limb of the body politic, disconnected from the common life.

Yet even were we to realize a society in which the "three mighty regions of the cognitive, the ethico-political and the libidinal-aesthetic" might reconverge in the undivided consciousness of a redeemed mankind, we might still have reason to suspect, even indict, the writer's gaze on psychoanalytic grounds. The very term "gaze" has attained the questionable status of being at once keyword and shibboleth. As an aesthetic gesture, the gaze barely retains its traditional association with the still hush of visual wonderment: the dreamy look or the rapt contemplation which once was a sanctioned way to apprehend the imposing reality of the world. The gaze no longer suggests an imaginative relation to reality, but its subjugation by the controlling look of the dominators. If the eyes fix themselves on a certain object, it is to immobilize it so that the gaze can work its dark magic, project its own fantasies, enact its own desires upon it. The gaze replicates a patriarchal ideology of domination by condemning its object to the passive, feminine position where its separate identity can have no meaning except as an uncanny reminder and fetishistic defense against the threat of castration.

Freud, whose investigations into infantile sexuality provide the groundwork for the indictment of the gaze, reached other, competing conclusions. In *Three Essays on Sexuality,* in which he first proposes the term "sublimate," Freud speculated that scopophilia (pleasure in looking) serves the interest of natural selection rather than personal or social hegemony. Visual impressions, he asserted, "remain the most frequent pathway along which libidinal excitation is aroused." But there are interesting turns, appealing diversions along this frequent pathway that conduct to more disinterested, "higher" aims: "It is usual for most normal people to linger to some extent over the intermediate sexual aim of a looking that has a sexual tinge to it; indeed, this offers them a possibility of directing some proportion of their libido on to higher artistic aims."[11] Scopophilia offers the possibility of that libidinal sublimation that takes root in the gaze; in other words, the aesthetic.

More directly to our purposes in determining the provenance of the writer's gaze, Freud was struck by the complementariness of scopophilia and epistemophilia as component instincts. The love of looking, he observed, first manifests itself as companion to sexual curiosity, the origin of the love of human researches. A look becomes more properly speaking a *perception* (from *percipere,* to take hold of, from *capere,* to take) when it achieves this more sublimated form. The aesthetic not only looks at its object, but takes something from it, a knowledge of it, perhaps, or perhaps merely a feeling, a sentiment, without making any direct claims, or performing any actual violence, upon it.[12] One question posed by Woolf's essay, and indeed by this volume of essays, is how the aesthetic takes hold of its objects and whether its grasp differs from the more determined embrace of ideology. Is the aesthetic in the grip of libidinal and ideological compulsions to which it necessarily blinds itself? Is there, as Woolf insinuated, an unconscious power that can relax the firm hold of ideology, a power of temporary self-oblivion that prevents the writer from taking his own interest to be identical with the interests, indeed the value, of things in themselves? Can the writer's interests ever be wholly, or even partially, disinterested? Alfred North Whitehead once proposed that the Quaker word "concern" might stand to express and monitor the self-interested, affective component in human perception. "Concernedness," he affirmed, "is the essence of perception."[13] What, then, are the concerns that animate the affective, aroused body that gazes fixedly on its object and how are we to determine and evaluate the ends of these concerns?

Keenly ideological critics, looking at the writer as if in a glass darkly (very darkly), see only their own concerns, that is, see only the looming shadows of ideology. They remind us that the writer does not gaze on his object through a transparent pane, but through the prism of class interests, political sentiments, social sympathies. The writer's gaze is complicit with the Injustice of the world and thus can never be free of its guilt. Even the most detached observation may abet the work of the oppressors in subtly according to things as they are the indomitability of things that will continue to be. The writer's gaze enacts and perpetuates the original sin of the aesthetic, for what takes root in the gaze begins in the "innocent" pleasure of looking but may succumb to the sinister blandishments and sadistic thrills of an investigative, controlling voyeurism, which finds its social form in the surveillant gaze of Jeremy Bentham's Panopticon and the telescreens of *1984.* From the guilt rooted in the gaze, there may no deliverance except through the uncompromising injunction of Saint Mark: If thine eye offend thee, pluck it out.

Less drastic measures, however, may allow us to recuperate the gaze for social as well as aesthetic good. Such a rehabilitation would entail the painstaking but necessary work of discriminating among the special properties and various tasks (both for good and evil) of the eye. In the sexual and social domain alone we might begin to distinguish among the different looks that characterize the human response, from the infant's first sightings of the Mother to the formative moment when it both sees and misrecognizes itself in the complex refractions of the "mirror phase"; the furtive glimpses and flirtatious glances excited by sexual curiosity (for Freud the origin of our sense of beauty); the adolescent's *averted* glance or sullen stare, eyeing the world through the riot of hormones and locked in the rebellion against elder generations; the *insulting* look of indifference, even contempt, peculiar to the *disappointed* eye. In the personal as well as public domain, the eye's refusal to focus on the other may be more alienating and injurious than the offending gaze.

Then we might more be more meticulous in identifying the social significance of those *glaring* looks that are not stages in our psychic development nor expressions of our affections and aversions, but intimidations of the will to power seeking dominion through the eye. Such discriminations became acts of cultural criticism in the work of Theodor Adorno who warned, for example, of "the fixed, inspecting, hypnotic and hypnotized stare that is common to all the leaders of horror." Adorno traced the social contagion of such stares from the "appraising look of the manager asking an interview candidate to sit down, and illuminating his face in such a way as to divide it pitilessly into bright, utilizable parts, and dark, disreputable areas of incompetence," to its last brutally efficient refinement in the "medical examination to decide between capacity for work and liquidation."[14] To the indurate administrative stare we might compare and contrast the technological equivalent of the surveillant gaze, quick to pick up any deviations from the prescribed regime: the scan. In the scanning look, at once hurried and indifferent, the eye aspires to the efficiency of computerized intelligences in gathering, sorting, or merging information, but becomes too impatient to linger over surfaces, probe their depths, excavate their rich interiors.

Of the clairvoyant powers of the eye we have lost the habit, perhaps even the nerve, to speak. Still, who forgets, once encountered, F. Scott Fitzgerald's sign for the transcendental gaze, the gigantic, dilated eyes of Dr. T. J. Eckleburg, whose brooding oversight of the valley of ashes could symbolize at once the Superego sternly reproving the libidinal indulgences —and their waste products—of postwar society, the omniscient novelist of traditional fiction become dour and academic, or the uncanny visage of an ever-watchful, all-judging God. But in all these "gazes," there is no freedom or pretense of disinterestedness. The relation between the gaze and its chosen object is determined by sexual compulsion, or by the ideological will to power over the innermost recesses of the mind, or by the categorical imperative of a moral law not of human making.

In a world in which God is thought to be absent or dead, that is, in the world of modernity, only the aesthetic gaze, indifferent to everything but what is before its fascinated eyes, discloses things in their troubling reality, in the justice and injustice of their existence. Such a vindication of the ideologically "indifferent" gaze may strike some as an ingenious paradox, a self-serving contradiction in terms, or simply a lame apology for Woolf's daring to exempt the writer from the urgent work of reforming the world, where Injustice prevails. Yet Adorno, in his postwar reflections on damaged life, *Minima Moralia,* was equally, if not *more* insistent that only the gaze indifferent to all but its chosen object does *ultimate* justice to what exists:

> No gaze attains beauty that is not accompanied by indifference, indeed almost by contempt, for all that lies outside the object contemplated. And it is only infatuation, the unjust disregard for the claims of every existing thing, that does justice to what exists. In so far as the existent is accepted, in its one-sidedness, for what it is, its one-sidedness is comprehended as its being, and reconciled. The eyes that lose themselves to the one and only beauty are sabbath eyes. They save in their object something of the calm of its day of creation.[15]

Adorno, like Woolf, would steady us in our path by advising us to linger with the particular, rather than rushing off to "influence the world to higher ends." What passes beyond the particular "without having first entirely lost itself," advises Adorno, "what proceeds to judge without having first been guilty of the injustice of contemplation, loses itself at last in emptiness." Adorno makes the writer's *unconcern* with all that lies, awaiting criticism and correction, beyond the particulars that fascinate him the basis of his canonization of the gaze in sabbath eyes. Adorno admits, as does Woolf, that the writer's sabbath eyes will be "startled from [their] rapture." He admits too that truth resides in "the just overall view that makes its own the universal injustice that lies in exchangeability and substitution." In Adorno's formulation we observe not a desperate paradox, but a dialectical reversal in which the aesthetic may be seen to rejoin and redeem its ideological components and counterparts. It is the aesthetic that makes Injustice its own, acknowledges it, and so attains to that self-awareness that distinguishes the false consciousness from the true, the "just overall view" from the partial, self-indemnifying one. If thine eye offend thee, pluck it out, but, as Adorno instructs us, nothing that does not suffer the worldly indifference, the arrant injustice of the gaze, can hope to be delivered unto truth.

■   ■   ■

The writer's visionary composure, then, attests to a deep absorption in the *reality,* not the power or utility, of things. It attests, too, to the conviction that the writer must regard what exists before he can attain a "just overall view" in which things will be seen as they are and as they might become in a redeemed existence. Such a belief lies behind Woolf's reluctance to respond in kind to the urgent solicitations or brash provocations of ideology, intent on transforming the general state, not contemplating the unique particulars, of things as they are. This belief, however, is advanced at a time when sustained contemplation of the events and the evils convulsing the world became itself a source of disturbance. How justify the writer's contemplative stillness when contemporary events cried out, as they did in the thirties, for action rather than vision, or, at the very least, for a vision that defined the terms of conscionable action? This is the anguished predicament voiced by Stephen Spender in the foreword to his 1939 volume of poetry, *The Still Centre* (a title that concedes high modernist sympathies). Spender describes the historical pressures that infiltrated the writer's working space, distressing as well as distracting his imagination: "The violence of the times we are living in, the necessity of sweeping and general and immediate action, tend to dwarf the experience of the individual, and make his immediate environment and occupation perhaps something that he is even ashamed of."[16] Spender seems to lurk within, rather than proudly occupy, his artistic preserve. He is haunted by the spectacle of violence outside its confines, and feels a creeping sense of shame in "deliberately [turning] back to a kind of writing that is more personal."[17] The writer at his desk feels the dark angel of History hovering at his back, casting a dark shadow on the objects of his gaze.

Next to Spender's chiaroscuro portrait of the writer defensively shading his eyes from the blinding glare of current and public events, Woolf's image may appear a mere silhouette, too slender to attract, much less sustain our attention. Woolf candidly admits to the initial thinness of her representation: "What do we see," she asks, "—only a person who sits with a pen in his hand in front of a sheet of paper." Yet we should not be in haste to dismiss this figure as blandly generic or shockingly disregardful of the "material" conditions of writing at a time when the very survival of literature and of democratic culture was in doubt. Spender himself came to appreciate how Woolf elaborates the "apparently simple image of a writer sitting in a chair at his desk" to unfold a complex and dense symbolism "of the writer's high calling, expressed in terms of the simple machinery of his trade, scarcely altering through the ages, and joining him to past writers."[18]

Spender further noted the special place within this complex symbolism of the hand holding the pen, through whose veins "there flows the blood which is the whole life of the literary tradition joining the writer, sitting at his desk, with Shakespeare." Spender might have noted that Woolf was not eccentric in her quasi-mystical feeling for the pen in hand as an image of the artist's unalienated labor, the point at which tradition and the individual talent may be said—even seen—to communicate. Walter Benjamin attributes a similar aura to the expressive body of the storyteller, whose imagination works through and with the associated faculties of hand and eye. Benjamin invokes Paul Valéry's testimony that artistic observation can attain a mystical depth such that "the objects on which it falls lose their names" and become part of a new reality that derives its "existence and value exclusively from a certain accord of the soul, the eye, and the hand of someone who was born to perceive them and evoke them in his own inner self." "With these words," concludes Benjamin, "soul, eye, and hand are brought into connection. Interacting with one another, they determine a practice."[19]

This is the practice uniting physical with spiritual grace that Yeats saw manifest in "the old nonchalance of the hand." The hand impresses the form that the eye beholds, but what the eye beholds, as Valery reminds us, is not what everyone beholds, but what the artist is born—fated—to perceive and evoke in his own inner self. The artist touched by such grace is both technically and spiritually equipped to fashion "the raw material of experience, his own and that of others, in a solid, useful and unique way." The authority of this spiritual practice is finally what justifies Benjamin's otherwise perplexing definition of the storyteller as "the figure in which the righteous man encounters himself."[20] In the extravagant mysticism of this image, Benjamin recovers for us the lost unity and fullness of a tradition in which vision, creation, and divination are one. In such a tradition, all things are eligible for consecration by sabbath eyes. With the decline in the belief in the artist's distinct place at the apex of "the hierarchy of the world of created things," with the ideological assault on the artist's right to exist anywhere above or apart, the coordinated faculties of hand, eye and soul become disassociated, their powers atrophy, and the voice of and for righteousness dissolves to a whisper, easily drowned out by the blare of gramophones and loudspeakers.

What it would mean to exist in a society from which even the memory of individual, righteous response has been liquidated is what George Orwell imagines in *1984*. Winston Smith, the last man and, so *1984* suggests, the final victim of an ideologically fanatic regime, experiences the extinction of writing as both an individual practice and a shared tradition. In the totalitarian society of Ingsoc, writing, in Woolf's and Benjamin's sense, is a criminal activity. One is proscribed from directing one's gaze at any object other than the omnipresent telescreen, to which Winston Smith surrenders his imagination, and his life, at the narrative's (if not the novel's) close. In this end we see the eclipse of the novel's more promising beginning, a beginning that, like Woolf's, locates creative will in the image of a writer at his desk. Smith, ensconced in a small alcove that eludes the searching gaze, at once surveillant and hypnotic, of the telescreen, inaugurates the novel's "plot" of resurgent, rebellious individualism simply by removing himself from public sight and fixing his gaze on the objects, no longer as familiar or as available as they once were, of the writer's trade:

> The pen was an archaic instrument, seldom used even for signatures, and he had procured one, furtively and with some difficulty, simply because of a feeling that the beautiful creamy paper deserved to be written on with a real nib instead of being scratched with an ink pencil. Actually he was not used to writing by hand. Apart from short notes, it was usual to dictate everything into the speakwrite, which was of course impossible for his present purpose.[21]

We would be wrong to read into Winston's connoisseurship the last gasp of commodity fetishism, although it would be right to stress the purely aesthetic considerations that determine his choice of paper and taste in pens. It is surely no surprise that the aesthetic emotion could only survive in an ideological regime as an *antiquarian* feeling for pen and paper. These relics (contraband in the official culture of Ingsoc) are Smith's only connection to a vanished culture in which the physical act of writing was endowed with an aura of unalienated labor. The technology of speakwrite obliterates the neurological connection between mind and hand, thought and the tools of its material embodiment. Winston's relationship to the traditional implements of pen and paper is further determined by his chosen form of personal expression: a diary written in the fragmented, free-associational mode of experimental modernism. In a society where all life is subsumed into social mechanism, subjectivity becomes the outlaw, and the innovative techniques of modernism become, in Orwell's projection of the ironies history unfailingly produces, the rhetoric of a retrograde and criminalized individualism.

In this regard, the detail that tells us most about the precarious ideological position of the writer is that he is—and must remain—seated. The writer, that is, does not, like the politician or the orator, "stand up." He forgoes, in his role as writer, the posture of advocacy and the pleasures, as well as the powers and dangers, of direct address: he stands up for nothing, even if the results are worthy (like "influencing the world to higher ends"). The chair, in this analysis, thus becomes a very important part of the writer's outfit, one which no writer willingly relinquishes, since it furnishes him, not only with physical support and a measure of protection (if Winston were to stand up, he would be "discovered" and betrayed), but with his angle of vision, "his attitude toward his model." "It is a fact, not a theory," Woolf contends, "that all writers from Chaucer to the present day, with so few exceptions that one hand can count them, have sat upon the same kind of chair—a raised chair. They have all come from the middle class; they have had good, at least expensive educations. They have all been raised above the mass of people upon a tower of stucco—that is their middle class birth; and of gold—that is their expensive education." By a deft act of symbolic enlargement, the chair has been raised, then expanded until it encompasses the space it occupies—a tower, the site ordained for the writer-seer, keeping watch over a less farseeing humanity.

With this architectural figure, Woolf completes her picture of the writer and discloses the ideological foundation and romantic ancestry of modern writing. The writer at his desk descends from a line of romantic tower-dwellers. His genotype, as Edmund Wilson showed, is the visionary isolato, elevated above the demoralizing economic cares, vexing social worries and spirit-rending historical conflicts of life lived far below.[22] The tower he inherits, whether of ivory or stucco, encompasses antithetical perspectives: it is an isolated refuge from the stormy unsettlements of life, and often mimics the decor, as well as plunders the symbolism, of hermetic laboratory or monastic cell; yet from its height the eye may behold the sweeping prospects of history or entertain transcendental imaginings. The tower, as Northrop Frye has more systematically observed, accommodates the imaginative man in his *penseroso* phase, and also marks what Frye calls "the point of epiphany" at which the "undisplaced apocalyptic world and the cyclical world of nature come into alignment."[23]

As one would expect from the author of *To the Lighthouse,* Woolf regards the tower, and indeed is concerned with its preservation, primarily as an epiphanic site, yet she readily exposes its ideological foundation in class privilege:

> All through the nineteenth century, down to August 1914, that tower was a steady tower. The writer was scarcely conscious either of his high station or his limited vision. Many of them had sympathy, great sympathy, with other classes; they wished to help the working class to enjoy the advantages of the tower class; but they did not wish to destroy the tower, or to descend from it—rather make it accessible to all. (138)

It is essential to writing, Woolf had argued in her famous meditation on women and fiction, to have a room of one's own and five hundred pounds a year. It is essential to *great* writing to have a room with an expansive view, one more likely to be enjoyed from the top of a tower than from a tenement window. But in 1914 the tower began to lean. Woolf neither eagerly anticipates nor calmly abides the time when it will topple altogether. A writer, she simply looks intently at the tower class, fixing her gaze on the moment when it is "stung into self-consciousness, into class-consciousness, into the consciousness of things changing, of things falling, of death perhaps about to come" (147).

This is what she sees: the tower class whose ideological supports began to buckle could not continue as "writers" because "they had nothing settled to look at; nothing peaceful to remember; nothing certain to come" (147). The world appears to them "not altogether up-side down, but slanting, sidelong." Inevitable distortions of outlook ensue. They cannot, as their secure forbears could, look any class directly in the face, but can only look "up, or down, or sidelong." They experience a kind of social vertigo in looking down from their high, yet oddly unsettled station, followed by self-pity that such discomfort is their primary social emotion. Finally, anger sets in against the very society that supports them. Neither capable of defending, nor inclined to descend from their tower, they nevertheless displayed a surprising power which, Woolf granted, "if literature continues, may prove to be of great value in the future. They were great egotists" (148).

We might suspect Woolf of sarcasm here, since, beginning with her private condemnation of "the damned egotistical self that ruins Joyce and Richardson in my mind" and her public denunciation of the egotistical patriarchs in A Room of One's Own, egotism was for Woolf the imperious, destructive emotion that aborted any creative effort of will or imagination, a view, as Valentine Cunningham has amply documented, widely held by both literary and social critics of the day.[24] But the sardonic is not Woolf's customary tone, and she never feigns respect for a quality she cannot admire. She actually defends the great egotists of the post-1914 generation, noting that if they have proved "incapable of giving us great poems, great plays, great novels" they nonetheless wrote about themselves "honestly, therefore creatively. They told the unpleasant truths, not only the flattering truths." In this particular they are in fact judged superior to the writers of the nineteenth century, who, nurtured by peace and prosperity, "never told that kind of truth," and thus, like Thackeray or Dickens, so often wrote, for all their individual genius, about "dolls and puppets, not about full-grown men and women" (148). The egotists' creative legacy, Woolf speculates, will be in converting autobiography from a mode of self-invention (even self-mythification) into a discourse of self-appraisal.

I want to test this theory as Woolf implies a writer might, indeed *should* test it, that is, by keeping my eyes fixed on a certain object—Christopher Isherwood, one of the most thorough yet elusive self-chroniclers of the Leaning Tower generation. In his autobiographical fictions of the thirties, *Lions and Shadows* and *Berlin Stories,* we can judge whether Woolf was right in attributing to the thirties generation an honesty that would be of great value to the continuing life of literature in laying the foundations of a new moral realism.

▪ ▪ ▪

Isherwood, let it be noted, is a curious kind of egotist. His representation of the things of this world—objects, people in their different relations, personal and public events—reflects his cultural tastes and political dispositions, but seldom his sexual longings and only on crisis occasions his artistic ego. The ideological foundations of his oddly reticent egotism are exposed in *Lions and Shadows,* Isherwood's retrospective, fictionalized account of how he came into his artistic estate as member of the richly provided tower class just at the historical moment when that tower began to lean. Like Woolf, Isherwood sees 1914 as a divide between two literary epochs. It is a divide emotionally marked by "a feeling of shame that we hadn't been old enough to take part in the European War."[25] For Isherwood, and presumably for his generation, the traumatic legacy of the Great War took the form of "the Test" that would never come, and would be failed if it did. Art was for Isherwood a way of placing himself "apart and above 'the Test,' because the Test was something for the common herd." He adopts the persona of "austere ascetic, cut off from the outside world, in voluntary exile, a recluse." The General Strike of 1925 would reawaken his public conscience, but primarily in the negative form of an unmitigated loathing for his class, "so sure of themselves, so confident they were right, so grandly indifferent to the strikers' case." Trapped in a tower crumbling beneath him, Isherwood can only "shudder with fear and hatred," all the while hating himself for remaining fixed in place (140).

To such personal and imaginative dejection we might ascribe the emergence of the aesthetic that directs his social investigations in *The Berlin Stories.* We find this aesthetic articulated in the passage on which Isherwood's repute may largely be said to rest, the single paragraph from the "Berlin Diary (August 1930)" that opens *Goodbye to Berlin*:

> I am a camera with its shutter open, quite passive, recording, not thinking. Recording the man shaving at the window opposite and the woman in the kimono washing her hair. Some day, all this will have to be developed, carefully printed, fixed.[26]

The writer at his desk is here figured as a permanently dilated camera eye, passively recording the external world in "shots" of unflinching because unreactive realism. He devotes himself to capturing the instantaneous gesture, behavior or mood, abandoning all deep researches into character or social milieu.

The ideological passivity and moral neutrality implicit in this figure is a function of the writer's isolation: "I am in a foreign city, alone, far from home." The camera does have a "point of view," then, the point of view of a stranger whose choice of subjects is neither as passive nor as random as

Isherwood's syntax implies. The man and woman who attract the camera-eye are preparing for the routine intimacies from which the foreigner is excluded. They have places to go, and business, commercial or erotic, to attend to. From the depths of the dark streets against which these figures are highlighted, the camera also records the sounds "so piercing, so insistent, so despairingly human" in whose reverberations ("lascivious and private and sad") Isherwood hears the echo of his own isolation magnified. Isherwood's estrangement from the round of common life, though a sign here of his status as outsider, remains the objective condition of art: it confers and establishes distance at the very instant of emotional identification and need. We recall here Woolf's similar understanding that the writer is a person in the world (here the city of Berlin), but never directly in its midst.

The camera, then, is not a figure for the mechanical eye, but the complete sensory apparatus of the coordinated aesthetic body: eye, ear, the hand that clicks the shutter, and all the internal, spiritual sensors that register the tremors, however faint, that anticipate the seismic upheavals of a city on the verge of economic and political collapse. Isherwood further makes it clear that the reality captured by the still shots of the camera cannot be "developed" anywhere. The writer needs a darkroom, sequestered from the light and noise of common day, in his case the writing-table in his room at Frau Schroeder's, which emits the weird aura of a vulgarian's reliquary: "Here, at the writing-table, I am confronted by a phalanx of metal objects—a pair of candlesticks shaped like entwined serpents, an ashtray from which emerges the head of a crocodile, a paper-knife copied from a Florentine dagger, a brass dolphin holding on the end of its tail a small broken clock. What becomes of such things? How could they ever be destroyed?" (2). When Isherwood sits down at his writing-desk, he is confronted with the clutter, not the order, of things. These uncanny objects, in which neither form nor function is distinctly, much less beautifully articulated, "stand like an uncompromising statement of . . . Capital and Society, Religion and Sex." Here we might reverse Eagleton's formulation and say that what Isherwood confronts at his writing desk is social relevance flourishing on the corpse of art. These objects, which lack the formal dignity of artifacts, exhaust their function as ideological expressions, as pure denotations of Capital and Society, Religion and Sex.

Art itself is commissioned as weaponry in the battle of ideologies, as Isherwood discovers when he visits a communist clubhouse where young "pathfinders" are inducted into the true faith. The art whose ideological contamination he laments is especially dear to him, because it is his art, the art of the photograph: "They showed me dozens of photographs of boys, all taken with the camera tilted upwards, from beneath, so that they look like epic giants, in profile against enormous clouds" (198). The "War-spirit" that infused his dreamy adolescence in the twenties culminates in these bloated fantasy images, images fashioned by other hands to recruit *yet another* generation of heroic youth to meet "the Test." These images are accompanied by a text notable for "a curious underlying note of hysteria, as though the actions described were part of a religious or erotic ritual." Sex and Religion are fused to engender ideological rapture. With the production of this image, the ideological invasion and usurpation of the writer's sanctuary becomes complete. The writing desk has become "a kind of altar" to the savage idols of ideology.

Isherwood responds to these desecrations, as writers of his Leaning Tower generation did, with a determined act of creative egotism. Against the modest claim that he is a vigilant, but purely reactive observer—"I am a camera"—he risks the superb pride of the declaration "I am Berlin." Thus in the diary entry describing the hard, bitter winter of 1932–1933, Berlin is contemplated as a body of reality whose inner structure conforms, achingly, to Isherwood's own: "Berlin is a skeleton which aches in the cold: it is my own skeleton aching. I feel in my bones the sharp ache of the frost in the girders of the overhead railway, in the ironwork of balconies, in bridges, tramlines, lamp-standards, latrines. The iron throbs and shrinks, the stone and the bricks ache dully, the plaster is numb" (186). No longer encapsulated within the tower, Isherwood's sensitized body becomes the agonized site of that writing against yet within the cold that begins with the snowfall of Joyce's "The Dead" and by Orwell's *1984* has become the permanent climate of modernity. Subduing all natural reflexes to recoil, his body expands so that Berlin might be given human definition, and not contract and dwindle, as it is in danger of doing, "to a small black dot, scarcely larger than hundreds of other dots, isolated and hard to find, on the enormous European map" (186).

The eye hypnotized and fascinated by that small black dot can also see itself. On the brink of departure, taking one last stroll through the city, Isherwood recalls the men and women he has met, whose fates, though unknown in their particulars, are certain in their generalities: prison or death. In thus recalling to himself the fate of the Lost, he is shocked to encounter his own reflection, caught in the unseemly expression of a smile:[27]

> I catch sight of my face in the mirror of a shop, and am shocked to see that I am smiling. You can't help smiling, in such beautiful weather. The trams are going up and down the Kleiststrasse, just as usual. They, and the people on the pavement, and the teacosy dome of the Nollendorfplatz station have an air of curious familiarity, of striking resemblance to something one remembers as normal and pleasant in the past—like a very good photograph.

> No. Even now I can't altogether believe that any of this has really happened. . . (207)

What explains that smile, suffused with the aura of normalcy "a very good photograph" can evoke, when the streets are Hitler's? Isherwood's weird smile I imagine to resemble Chaplin's pained grin in the last shot of *City Lights,* a grotesque blend of hopeful sentiment and horrified enlightenment that attends the moment when the storyteller finally encounters himself. It is an encounter long deferred, but not fatally delayed. His smile is the disassociated response that splits reality into two fields—the ideological and the aesthetic—along the fault lines of personal affections (the memories of friends either dead or lost) and primary sensations (the warmth of the sun, so incongruous given the endless ideological winters and cold wars of modern history, or the white heat of political pogroms). In the enigma of that inappropriate yet humanly irresistible smile, Isherwood captures the estrangement between art and society at the moment of its impending divorce, the moment the aesthetic body, with its affections and aversions, sensations and perceptions, recoils from history in horrified disbelief.

Isherwood's disavowal of History, like Woolf's refusal to allow literature to be conscripted into ideological campaigns, should not be construed as an aesthetic alibi. Such responses register a more difficult and complex attitude toward the writer at his desk as a seer divided between the obligation to reflect, and the hope to remake, the world. Literature is not a safety zone, neutral zone, or dead zone, but a force field where what takes root in the gaze can germinate into creative or critical counterresponse. Woolf herself professed the belief that literature "is no one's private ground; literature is common ground" (154), adding that there are no barriers, no wars there. It is common ground because anyone might find their way there for themselves. But they can only stay there *by* themselves. Whether the writer looks upon human life from afar or from on high, ultimately he remains alone before his object.

Trotsky understood the relation between literature and revolution to depend precisely on the sufferance, indeed the cultivation of the writer's subjective vision of things as they are. In his "Manifesto: Towards a Free Revolutionary Art," he asserts that the artist "cannot serve the struggle for freedom unless he subjectively assimilates its social content, unless he feels in his very nerves its meaning and drama and freely seeks to give his own inner world incarnation in his art." They also serve, then, who occupy the inner world where the drama of freedom makes itself felt aesthetically, that is in the very nerves and root of the gaze. The writer who remains at his desk and remains true to what he sees remains faithful to the ideology of revolution, which is the ideology of "ultimate free expression":

In the present period of the death agony of capitalism, democratic as well as fascist, the artist sees himself threatened with the loss of his right to live and continue working. He sees all avenues of communication choked with the debris of capitalist collapse. Only naturally, he turns to the Stalinist organizations which hold out the possibility of escaping from his isolation. But if he is to avoid complete demoralization, *he cannot remain there,* because of the impossibility of delivering his own message. . . . He must understand that his place is *elsewhere,* not among those who betray the cause of the revolution and mankind, but among those who with unshaken fidelity bear witness to the revolution, among those who, for this reason, are alone able to bring it to fruition, and along with it the ultimate free expression of all forms of human genius. [Emphasis mine][28]

Neither the work of art nor of revolution can be brought to fruition if the writer is not free to remain apart, contemplating and reinventing the recalcitrant, fugitive reality of the world. We shall know that reality, Woolf assures us, by its fruits, for whatever reality touches, "it fixes and makes permanent." It is the "business" of the writer "to find [this reality] and collect it and communicate it to the rest of us." Both the aesthetic and social "concerns" of the writer dictate that he remain "at enmity with unreality." Both literature and society are better served when the writer remains in his enviable estate in the presence of this reality, free to describe how the world looks when "it is bared of its covering and given an intenser life."[29]

No wonder, then, that Woolf trusts to this image of the writer riveting his gaze on the objects of human life to steady us in our path as we bridge the gulf "between the dying world and the world that is struggling to be born" (151). Within that fixed gaze, the abiding reality of things in themselves is not only held sacred. It is secured.

Notes

1. Virginia Woolf, "The Leaning Tower," in *The Moment and Other Essays* (New York and London: Harcourt, Brace, 1948), 128. Further references to this essay will be noted in the text.

2. Cyril Connolly, "Writers and Society, 1940–43" in *The Condemned Playground* (London: Hogarth Press, 1985), 260.

3. Virginia Woolf, *Three Guineas* (New York: Harcourt Brace and World, 1966), 143.

4. Terry Eagleton, *The Ideology of the Aesthetic* (London: Basil Blackwell, 1990), 13.

5. James Agee, *Now Let Us Praise Famous Men* (Boston: Houghton

Mifflin, 1988), 456–457. Escapism is preceded in the list by "mysticism, intellectual, and emotional outlet"; business is followed by "big business, big operator, layout, setup, pushover" (this last term initiating a new theme elaborating the "business" of thought in a series which begins with "scientist" and extends to "sponsor"). The list itself is intended to collect the terms "a careful man will be watchful of, and by whose use and inflection he may take clear measurement of the nature, and the stature, and the causes, and the timbre, of the enemy."

6. Both of these entries are cited in Raymond Williams, *Keywords* (New York: Oxford University Press, 1976), 127.

7. Cited by Valentine Cunningham as he compiles and analyzes recurrent instances of "Going Over" as a "key metaphor" for writers of the thirties. The term encapsulated, as he notes, "the widespread feeling among '30s authors of being travellers, on the road, making some literary or metaphoric journey (or both), of being involved in a pilgrimage to socialism and Moscow, it might be, or to Christ and the Church." See his *British Writers of the Thirties* (Oxford: Oxford University Press, 1989), 211.

8. Woolf, *Three Guineas,* 143.

9. Williams, *Keywords,* 28.

10. Eagleton, *The Ideology of the Aesthetic,* 368.

11. *Three Essays on Sexuality,* vol. 7 of *The Standard Edition of the Complete Psychological Works of Sigmund Freud,* ed. James Strachey (London: Hogarth Press, 1975), 156–157.

12. Laura Mulvey laid the groundwork for the ideological critique of the gaze in cinematic representation with her influential "Visual Pleasure and Narrative Cinema," *Screen* 16 (Autumn 1975): 6–18. She has since reconsidered and departed from her position and is currently investigating the ideological *uses* of the gaze as an investigative, contestatory, educative power in her work on Orson Welles, "Citizen Kane at 50," forthcoming from the British Film Institute.

13. Alfred North Whitehead, *Adventures of Ideas* (New York: Mentor, 1955), 182.

14. Theodor Adorno, *Minima Moralia* (London: Unwin Brothers, 1978), 131.

15. Ibid., 76.

16. Stephen Spender, *The Still Centre* (London: Faber & Faber, 1939), 10–11.

17. For a shrewd reading of this volume as a deliberate retreat from the public world, signalling the end of Spender's "uneasy alliance with communism" and the collapse of his belief that poetry *can* make something happen, see Samuel Hynes, *The Auden Generation* (Princeton: Princeton University Press, 1978), 365–367.

18. Stephen Spender, *World Within World* (New York: Harcourt, Brace and Company, 1951), 143. Spender goes on to explain how his view of the relation of politics and art divided him from Woolf. "She felt," he relates, "that though we were aware of the calamitous condition of the world, we reacted to it with our intellects and wills, before we had experienced it fully through our sensibility." Spender then tells us how he might have responded to Woolf's crit-

icism: "I might have replied—though I did not—that, often passing Edith Cavell's monument near Charing Cross, with its inscription of *Patriotism is not enough,* I reflected that I would like to have *Sensibility is not enough* engraved on my tombstone."

19. Walter Benjamin, "The Storyteller," in *Illuminations* (New York: Schocken Books, 1977), 108.

20. Ibid., 109.

21. George Orwell, *1984* (New York: Signet, 1981), 9–10.

22. See Edmund Wilson, *Axel's Castle* (New York: Charles Scribner's Sons, 1931), especially the introductory chapter.

23. Northrop Frye, *Anatomy of Criticism* (Princeton: Princeton University Press, 1957), 203.

24. Cunningham rightly observes that "the '30s make a kind of apotheosis of Romanticist individualism in a literature of self-regard that got fuelled by the new psychology and philosophy and the mass of great writers—Conrad, James, Lawrence, Proust, Joyce, Woolf, T. S. Eliot, to name no others—attendant in their train. This is a period when . . . autobiography, the published letter and diary, the self-declarative title with *I* in it, the eagerly egotistic self-explanation ('Why *I* Write'), flourish as never before" (*British Writers,* 214). Cunningham goes on to record the growing critical "contempt for this egocentricity," but mistakenly, I believe, reads Woolf's own comments as a pure "gibe" at the thirties poets. See *British Writers,* especially 214–221.

25. Christopher Isherwood, *Lions and Shadows* (New York: New Directions, 1977), 55.

26. Christopher Isherwood, *Goodbye to Berlin,* in *Berlin Stories* (New York: New Directions, 1963), 1.

27. *The Lost,* Isherwood tells us in his 1954 preface to the work, was his initial title for the book, one that reflected his first idea of treating his Berlin adventures in the melodramatic manner of Balzac. "I stretched it to mean not only The Astray and The Doomed—referring tragically to the political events in Germany and our epoch—but also 'The Lost' in quotation marks—referring satirically to those individuals whom respectable society shuns in horror: an Arthur Norris, a von Pregnitz, a Sally Bowles" (Ibid., v). The mixed mode—half tragedy, half satire—is symptomatic of Isherwood's complex historical and moral tonalities.

28. Leon Trotsky, "Towards a Free Revolutionary Art," in *Leon Trotsky on Literature and Art* (New York: Pathfinders, 1970), 120.

29. Woolf, *A Room of One's Own* (New York: Harcourt Brace, 1957), 114.

■ SUSAN J. WOLFSON ■

"Romantic Ideology" and the Values of Aesthetic Form

If the varieties of formalism have insisted that value (where they have admitted it) is the product of a certain play of significations, they have
tended to isolate that process from the material matrix within which
[old-style] historicism, in however idealist a form, has tried to place it.
— *Terry Eagleton, "Marxism and Aesthetic Value"*[1]

Ideology against Aesthetic Form

ALTHOUGH THIS ESSAY will contest both the *if* and the (implied) *then* of its
epigraph, it will begin in a similar syntax. If the 1970s was the decade during which the aesthetics of formalist close reading were being challenged by
the practices of deconstructive close reading, an important essay of the
same decade, Terry Eagleton's "Marxism and Aesthetic Value," sought to
bracket the whole issue of the literary, in whatever manner of reading, and
to call for its "re-situat[ion] within the field of general cultural production"
(166). In this and other negotiations of "aesthetic value" through the
methods and aims of Marxist critique, formalist criticism suffered a sharp
devaluation—an appropriate and inevitable response, implied Eagleton, to
its own "reductive operations" (166). This was also the fate of formalism in
studies of Romanticism, especially in new-historical perspectives. Formalist criticism, we were told, not only needed an ideological critique but was a
method that isolated itself from such concerns; the entire issue of literary
form merited attention only insofar as it could be shown to collaborate with
class-interested mystification. Specific events of poetic form were thus subsumed by a general view of literature as an "ideological formation," and

any "specialized analyses"—"stylistic," "rhetorical," "formal"—were entertained only insofar as their approaches could, indeed "must," find "their *raison d'être* in the socio-historical ground"; so the introduction to Jerome McGann's interventionist, and subsequently influential critique, *The Romantic Ideology,* put it.[2] The operation that mattered was to show how "social forms" shape "forms of consciousness," "forms of thought," and "forms (or 'structures') of feeling," all working in behalf of an uncriticized "ideological form."[3]

This submission of aesthetic forms to ideological form emerged in Romantic studies in no small part in response to powerful readings, by an earlier generation, of its poetry as a psychologically centered discourse that was "political" only in terms of idealized constructions cast beyond their specific sociohistorical movement.[4] These apparent escapes from history, along with the insularity of their literary maps, are what McGann means by "The Romantic Ideology": this phrase denotes a discursive strategy that is "everywhere marked by extreme forms of displacement and poetic conceptualization whereby the actual human issues with which the poetry is concerned are resituated in a variety of idealized localities" (so he writes on page 1 of *The Romantic Ideology*). This is what joins poetry to ideology, for "poetry, including Romantic poetry, 'reflects'—and reflects upon—those individual and social forms of human life which are available to the artist's observation, and which are themselves a part of his process of observation" (12). The self-consciousness of this process and its representation in aesthetic complexity, while long esteemed in criticism of Romantic poetry, are for McGann a dangerous illusion: not only do these aspects imply Romanticism's power to examine and explore "its own illusions and the arguments it makes for them," they also absorb readers in an "illusion" that they "can benefit from [such works] by turning this experiential and *aesthetic* level of understanding into a self-conscious and critical one" (13, his emphasis). For criticism to wrestle free of—indeed, McGann urges, "escape" from—the seductive weavings of aesthetic complexity, it must guard against the trap that Romanticism has set, its intent (in Wordsworth's words) to create the taste by which it is to be enjoyed.[5] For when "forms of thought enter our consciousness as forms (or 'structures') of feeling," McGann cautions (adding that this "is what takes place through poetry and art"), they "threaten to reify as ideology in the secondary environment of criticism" (13). Our defense requires us both to resist the romance of aesthetic forms and to "expose" their "dramas of displacement and idealization" (1). Elaborating the strategy of exposure, Marjorie Levinson emphasizes the privileged role of criticism in this defense, its charge to perform what is, in effect, a *decreation* of the taste by which a work asks to be enjoyed. Criticism must "take up a position within but not *of* the ideology [the work] seems to articulate" and in this position refuse seduction: "To read this way is to split the atom of Romantic symbolism and organicism . . . to set image *against* idea, form *against* content, process *against* product, in the hope that we may thus compel a tired organic apparition to reveal its fabulous fusions."[6]

Although (as Romanticism itself knew) resistance to uncriticized prescriptions is invigorating, no project of critical inquiry, I want to argue, gains much by blunting its instruments of reading. To suspect formal complexities merely as a threat to ideological clarity or to reduce such articulations to dubious events of tired apparition and fabulous fusion is to court unproductive simpliffications of the way aesthetics and ideology interact.[7] My aim in this essay is not to urge a nostalgic, retrograde return to the mid-century critical procedures that reject attention to sociohistorical contexts. But I do wish to retain the chief contribution of formalist criticism (particularly in the second half of our century) to literary study—namely, its subtle attention to aesthetic structures—in order to challenge and complicate the accounts given in some influential "ideological" critiques about what such attentions can or cannot show in our post-New-Critical age.[8] To refresh the value of close reading, we need to see poetic form in shapes other than those described by the so-called "Romantic Ideology" of wholeness, coherence, and insularity, and we need to see how poetic form in these other shapes can be involved in processes of ideological critique—how, in fact, attention to aesthetic formation in its particularities, densities, and complexities can be generated out of the very criticism that has emerged in antithesis to it.[9]

That these issues are being debated in analyses of formalist experimentation in modernism and postmodernism as well (as other essays in this volume show) does not so much define these later movements as bold interventions into a complacent tradition as suggest how such issues always come into play in self-consciously "modern" movements, including Romanticism. Romanticism is an important phase in this question, because it is the discourse in which the contested term "organic form" was so forcefully and pervasively articulated as to become virtually equated with it. As Levinson and McGann may have already suggested, Romanticism has emerged as a key site for waging the ideological critique of formalism: both "isms" have been charged with mobilizing aesthetics in order to recast sociohistorical contradiction and resolve ideological conflict, and in this respect, both have seemed the all-too-visible patrons of "insular" New Criticism.[10] In order to review this account, we need to loosen the grip of the equations to which recent critical narrative have habituated us, and we need to give fuller attention to how events of form in Romantic poetry (not just its themes and rallying cries) may sponsor rather than suppress ideological critique. If, in the practices of Romanticism, these critiques do not

achieve overall theoretical coherence, their energies, in both critical and poetic texts, often enact the motions of later ideological criticism. It is not always the case that the fractures and fissuring in the poetic forms of
Romanticism merely betray the historical contradictions that the structure
of poetic argument occludes. It is sometimes the case that a dislocation or
disruption of habitual forms of representation actively points the way to
ideological critique.

To test this proposition, it is necessary to develop a reading of how, in
various and specific ways, the forms of Romantic poetry operate. I will
focus primarily on the formal actions of some political poems that William
Blake published in the 1780s in which events of form—rhyme, wordplay,
syntax, and the play of the poetic line—participate in and help shape a critical view of revolutionary warfare particularly relevant to this decade. For a
coda, I will turn to a later decade of Romanticism, one more directly but
also more desperately engaged with progressive political reform, and suggest how some formal events in Percy Bysshe Shelley's political poetry reflect critically on the very conception of poetics as symbolic politics.

Beyond "Organic Form"

If it seems banal to recall a fact that New Criticism has helped us forget, that
Romanticism had a political content and context and, in many respects, a
political impetus, it may also seem a desperate defense of Romantic poetics
to suggest that its *formalist* poetics were similarly motivated. For there is no
use denying that the critiques of Romanticism's idealizing poetics were
forcefully provoked by Romanticism's own pronouncements. Most often
cited is Coleridge's celebration of "organic form" over the "mechanical regularity" of "pre-determined form" and his alignment of this aesthetic principle with natural process: poetic form is "innate," taking shape as "it
develops itself from within. . . . [S]uch is the Life, such the form."[11] From
this effacement of the "constructedness" of poetic form (its representation
as transparent, natural, and accidental), the dominant view of Romantic
form evolved. For nineteenth-century readers such as Matthew Arnold and
Charles Kingsley, the very idea of "Romantic form" was oxymoronic and
its consequences unfortunate. Not only did the theoretical alliance of art
with nature misunderstand both provenances, they argued, but it guaranteed the intellectual failure of poetry.[12] In this century, New-Critical formalism revived the Coleridgean notions of intrinsic organization on behalf
of its own aesthetics of poetic structure, while the countermovement of
Marxist and new-historicist critique read the same discourse of "organic"
structure as an aesthetic complicity with class-interested strategies of
smoothing over historical conflict and contradictions with claims of natural

and innate organization.[13] Whatever the sympathies, "organic form" was made synonymous with Romanticism in general and its poetics of form in particular.

While the notion of aesthetic form as a self-contained unity—claiming universality by attributing its principles of development to nature rather than to history and culture—has been rightly identified as a particular *aesthetic* ideology, it has been more problematically designated as "*The* Romantic Ideology." In such terms, Romanticism is charged with privileging its poetic discourse, "unlike non-aesthetic utterance," to offer its social evaluations "to the reader *under the sign of completion.*" This sign, contends McGann (whose voice and italics these are), "is what formalists recognized as their object of study." He urges us instead to see both the "experience of finality and completion" and the representation of "the poem as transhistorical" as functions of a specific discourse given to claims of "historical totality": "Its integral form is the sign of this seeming knowledge—and it persuades its reader that such a totality is not just a poetic illusion, but a truth."[14] Eagleton's critique of Romantic organicism has a similar target. In "the privilege accorded by the Romantics to the 'creative imagination,'" he contends,

> the literary work itself comes to be seen as a mysterious organic unity, in contrast to the fragmented individualism of the capitalist marketplace: it is "spontaneous" rather than rationally calculated, creative rather than mechanical. . . . At the centre of aesthetic theory at the turn of the eighteenth century is the semi-mystical doctrine of the symbol. For Romanticism, indeed, the symbol becomes the panacea for all problems. Within it, a whole set of conflicts which were felt to be insoluble in ordinary life . . . could be magically resolved.[15]

The anti-Romantic bias of this narrative may be due to Eagleton's having based it on an analysis of post-Romantic fiction, whose forms of displacement he sees complicit with the emergence of "organicist" social theory: both claim the "spontaneous unity of natural life-forms, and more generally . . . denote symmetrically integrated systems characterised by the harmonious interdependence of their component elements."[16]

Although Eagleton's analogy is compelling, what is problematic is the uncritical equation of poetic form with coherence, finality, and completion, and a sense therefore of its categorical immunity to the ideological conflicts discovered and contemplated by the historicist critic. Tested against the density and specificity of the texts themselves, "The Romantic Ideology" seems to me to be chiefly a *theorist's* ideology, a construction (however brilliant) by those wanting to reserve for scholarly and theoretical critique the alertness they deny to the writers they study. Donald Wesling offers a more productive approach to the whole rhetoric of "organic form," I think, when he suggests that in poetic theory and practice alike, it operated as "a calculated overstatement of a literal impossibility," a "hyperbole" deployed as a necessary "rationale for innovation in the patterning of poetic language."[17] If this hyperbole constitutes "the primary myth of post-Romantic poetics" (2), what invigorates the poetics of Romanticism itself is a simultaneously involved indulgence and critical testing of this myth.

The degree to which the historical situation of Romanticism affected its formalist poetics is not something that can be decided by assertion, but needs to be tested by reading textual events in the context of historical and political concerns. We need to reexamine the overcredited claim that Romantic poetic theory collaborated in leaving "unproblematized as aesthetic, formal and natural" the construction of its "poetic discourse," and that exemplary texts such as the Preface to *Lyrical Ballads* show how "at a stroke, all the specific forms of enunciation that make poetry poetry rendered accidental" and "dismissed."[18] The Preface itself is quite undecided on the question, in fact, entertaining competing ideas of poetic formalism: some of its statements credit accounts of the "Romantic Ideology"; some mobilize form, as an event and signifying practice, in behalf of social critique; and still others resort to form to shore up certain notions of class and aesthetic differences. And in larger terms, Wordsworth is very attentive to the signifying value of form itself in the volume's experimental poetics. Part of the rhetorical boldness of this project is its overt refusal of traditional contracts about poetic form. In a vocabulary keyed to the lexicon, Wordsworth states his terms directly at the start of his Preface: if "it is supposed, that by the act of writing in verse an Author makes a *formal* engagement that he will gratify certain known habits of association," the subversion he has undertaken "to *perform*," he flatly states, will seem aberrant.[19]

While his agrarian myth has its own illusions about the foundations of poetic form (in "rural occupations . . . the passions of men are incorporated with the beautiful and permanent forms of nature" [*LB*, 245]), Wordsworth's commitment to it entailed certain decisions that he knew would be provocative. Charles James Fox, for instance, complained about seeing the same measure used for the shepherd tales of *Michael* and *The Brothers* as for the poet's own lyric meditations: "I am no great friend to blank verse for subjects which are to be treated with simplicity," he grumbled.[20] But the effect was calculated: Wordsworth had originally tried *Michael* as a ballad, a "low" form, but then decided to democratize blank verse.[21] This is a move that reverses Eagleton's polarities: far from obscuring the artifice of poetic form, Wordsworth motivates it to confront and reform certain codes in the institution of literature, and to challenge, thereby, an implied class claim.

This is not to say that all of Wordsworth's formalism is democratic: he speaks of the language of his poems as "purified" of the "real defects of common speech" (*LB,* 245), and he keeps tripping over the patent formalism of submitting such speech to "metrical arrangement."[22] Yet in these various and sometimes contradictory gestures, Wordsworth shows a Romantic poetics alert to what is at stake in defining an aesthetic discourse and in using its enactment in poetic forms to comment on larger social and cultural forms.

Wordsworth's decisions about poetic form reflected and participated, in their own way, in a politics of the aesthetic being promoted in some liberal journals toward the end of the eighteenth century. *"Is Verse essential to Poetry?"* asked the title of an essay in *The Monthly Magazine* in 1796, and stayed to answer, "Whatever is the natural and proper expression of any conception or feeling in metre or rhyme, is its natural and proper expression in prose."[23] The question is infused with political significance: it is only the elitist class politics of certain poets, the essay suggests, that account for the "exclusive appropriation of the term *poetry,* to verse" (453). Possessing "arrogant assumption," this "ambitious race," "not satisfied with holding the almost undisputed possession of the first division in the ranks of literary merit, have . . . conjured up a wall of separation between themselves and other writers. Fancying the inhabitants of this consecrated inclosure a privileged order, they have been accustomed to look down, with a kind of senatorial haughtiness, upon the prose-men, who inhabit the common of letters, as a vulgar, plebeian herd" (453). The "monopoly" of verse over the domain of poetry is not only an "arbitrary" sign of privilege in the "republic of letters," the essay contends, but ultimately a dispensable one (453). Having cited metrical composition as the ally of a dubiously "consecrated inclosure," the essay proceeds to undermine the "solid foundation" of meter's value as both a distinguishing mark and the agent of poetry's "privileged order." The strategy is to expose the self-subverting irony of the terms of privilege, by converting class distinction into generic constriction, revealing its protective inclosure as imprisonment: verse "confin[es] the productions of the muses within the enclosure of measured lines" (453) and poetry is falsely "confin[ed] within the narrow inclosure of metre" (455). The analogy to class politics is not casual, for in the 1790s, the privileged orders, alarmed by the Revolution abroad and reverberations at home, were retrenching and shoring up their vulnerable privileges. The term *inclosure* is particularly charged, for this decade was also witnessing an acceleration in the enclosure of open fields and common lands, acts of definition and discrimination that at once served the interests of landowners and produced wide-scale misery in the dispossessed "plebeian herd."[24]

The political implications of aesthetic choices urged by the *Monthly's* essay virtually design the map of poetic form in William Hazlitt's lecture, in 1818, "On the Living Poets." He famously allied "the Lake school of poetry"—indeed attributed its very "origin"—to the French Revolution. Not only did radical politics parallel Laker aesthetics, Hazlitt argued, they were complicit. A change in poetry "went hand in hand" with "the change in politics," the one as "complete, and to many persons as startling," as the other: "According to the prevailing notions, all was to be natural and new. Nothing that was established was to be tolerated. . . . [K]ings and queens were dethroned from their rank and station in legitimate tragedy or epic poetry, as they were decapitated elsewhere; rhyme was looked upon as a relic of the feudal system, and regular metre was abolished along with regular government."[25] Publicly presented in 1818, this extravagant satire was calculated in part to embarrass the decidedly more conservative political evolution of Wordsworth and Coleridge. But the retrospect is not just a local barb; it is a register of how formal practices, in both Revolutionary and Regency England, evoked a symbolic politics. Hazlitt's narrative reminds us, moreover, that in the historical moment of Romanticism not only could form signify politically, but that the possible mystifications of organic form were less an issue than the legible drama of new forms resisting and replacing the old. Such discussions provide important clues to the ideological contexts for Blake's formalist poetics in the 1780s, a decade emerging from the American Revolution on the one side, and leading to the French Revolution (and its English reverberations) on the other.

Blake's Politics in Rhyme and Blank Verse

Having announced his decisive move "beyond formalism," Geoffrey Hartman later found himself with a lingering addiction, and the first reason he gave was his inability to discover a "method to distinguish clearly what is formal and what is not."[26] To read poetry in the sensitive register that Hartman had developed was to discover and rediscover how much the effort at such distinction could be baffled by a semantics of form. Blake, for one, sensed a productive resource in this semantics, even a potential for ideological critique. To show how this works, as well as to renew a case for the need for close attention to the play of aesthetic form in any assessment of the ideological work of literary aesthetics, I turn to the rhymes of "Gwin, King of Norway," a politically tuned ballad Blake printed in 1783 in *Poetical Sketches*.[27] The dramatic situation concerns a peasant uprising in medieval Europe, an event Blake bends into a social text rhetorically tuned to what McGann calls a "double perspectivism"—that is, "two dialectically functioning historical frames of reference . . . the frame of the poem's plot or 'story'" and "the frame of the poem's narrating voice."[28] In Blake's ballad, the former is medieval northern Europe and the latter England in the 1780s, a decade in which the empire was suffering erosions of royal power and prestige at home, being weakened abroad by rebellions and then full-scale war with America, and drawn into new conflicts with its long-standing enemies, Spain and especially France. In "Gwin," Blake puts both his story and the ballad form in this dialectical perspectivism. To write the historical frame, he draws on the traditional status of the ballad as cultural language rather than individual voice; for the rhetorical present, he involves his reader in the recent emergence of the *literary* ballad by exploiting the resources of poetic form to advance a critique of the military ideology of his own age.

The ballad opens as a caution to "Kings" about the consequences of tyranny, epitomized in Gwin, oppressor of the "nations of the North," and then moves into its central drama, the uprising led by "Gordred the giant," who slays Gwin in battle. David Erdman is right about the content: the ballad reflects an "intense, even propagandistic abhorrence of war-making kings," the recoil spelled as much by the compound adjective as by "kings": the way such tyrants unleash fury and slaughter not just in their own war-making but in the actions they provoke and may compel in others.[29] Not only Blake's content but also his formalist poetics imprint this abhorrence as well, deploying their resources to convey the contamination that Erdman names. This imprint registers almost immediately in the way parallel images begin to involve the same words. The tyrannical "Nobles" who "feed upon the hungry poor" (5–6), produce a counterimage of revolt in the poor, who, "furious as wolves" (27), become "lions' whelps, roaring abroad, / Seeking their nightly food" (19–20). A verbal parallel limns the legacy of noble arrogance: "let ten thousand lives / Pay for the tyrant's head" (31–32), these "numerous sons of blood" shout as they roll "like tempests black" (17–18) to meet Gwin and "his host as black as night" (55). *Black* covers both sides. This reproduction of violence also operates subverbally in the way Blake exploits puns latent in the name *Gordred*. The alarm sounded by Gwin's watchmen, "Arouse thyself! the nations black, / Like clouds, come rolling o'er!" (35–36) bears the phonic latency of "rolling gore," a flood led by Gordred and rhymed aptly in this stanza with its mighty provocation, "Gwin . . . of Nore" (34). This latency soon erupts as "fields of gore" (46), and echoes in the report that "Earth smokes with blood, and groans, and shakes, / To drink her children's gore" (73–74). Allied with *blood,* in fact, *Gordred* releases not only *gore,* but "Gore-dread" and its nearly redundant cause, *gored red*—the second word distilled in the image of the battle's "red fev'rous night" (84).

In this phonic and semantic field, the gore-rhyme *war,* as word and event, impends with near inevitability. And once it sounds in Blake's verse

(62), the duplication of violence emerges as the dominant trope: "The armies stand, like balances / Held in th'Almighty's hand" (66). That "th' Almighty" is named only in a device of simile (and with an internal pun on military "might") depletes the moral theology of this war; indeed, the poem's unsimilized theology is an undiscriminating "god of war . . . drunk with blood" (93), the war-gore that unites the sons of Gordred and of Nore in forces that are made to seem part of the indifferent violence of nature:

> And now the raging armies rush'd,
> Like warring mighty seas;
> The heavens are shook with roaring war,
> The dust ascends the skies!
>
> (69–72)

As sound and action, "warring" subtends "roaring war" with a cognitive punning that exploits the phonic resonance, and from stanza to stanza keeps alliance with "gore":

> Earth smokes with blood, and groans, and shakes,
> To drink her children's gore,
> A sea of blood; nor can the eye
> See to the trembling shore!
>
> (73–76)

In a *sea* that, punningly, lets the eye *see* only blood, distinction of foe and foe is overwhelmed:

> And on the verge of this wild sea
> Famine and death doth cry;
> The cries of women and of babes.
> Over the field doth fly.
>
> (77–80)

> Now death is sick, and riven men
> Labour and toil for life;
> Steed rolls on steed, and shield on shield,
> Sunk in this sea of strife!
>
> (89–92)

"By the time Gordred cleaves Gwin's skull," remarks Robert Gleckner, "the social and political 'meaning' of that victory has paled to insignificance —even irrelevance. . . . Visionary history inheres in the 'vale of death' and the 'river Dorman' as the loco-descriptive symbols of the universal battle's 'sea of blood.'"[30]

This common fate is also communicated by the structure of Blake's similes. Before this rhetoric achieves the summary formulation of "The armies stand, like balances / Held in th'Almighty's hand" (66), Blake uses it to suggest an affective, if not a moral, balance. In the figures of Gordred's "sons of blood" advancing "Like rushing mighty floods" and "Like clouds come rolling o'er" (24, 36) and of Gwin's troops, "Like clouds around him roll'd" (60), the same vehicle serves, reinforced by the same stanzaic position as last line. Over the course of the ballad and battle, Blake manipulates this parallelism into a semantic trope. First, and again with the force of syntactic repetition, he encompasses both armies not even with the same but with one common simile, intensified by a redoubling of tenor and vehicle: "And now the raging armies rush'd, / Like warring mighty seas." Tenors and vehicles merge: the armies rush and rage like seas which themselves are imaged at war. This intensified comparison then yields to a stark metaphor: the battlefield is not just "like" a sea which is itself a battlefield, but sea and battlefield conflate: "A sea of blood," a "wild sea," a "sea of strife" (75, 77, 92). This transformation is completed as the metaphor is finally, and literally, overwhelmed by its vehicle, "sea," which emerges in the ballad's final stanza as a universal force, obliterating distinction between tenor and vehicle and, with this erasure, between the armies themselves:

> The river Dorman roll'd their blood
> Into the northern sea;
> Who mourn'd his sons, and overwhelm'd
> The pleasant south country.
>
> (113–116)

The "human forces actually become what they formerly were merely like," observes Vincent de Luca; "they are enveloped in the element and annihilated by it."[31] This envelopment is more haunting for the way the stanza's weak rhymes release another chord, in which the words *Dorman, northern, mourn'd* absorb and eerily reverberate the sounds of *war, gore, Nore,* and *Gordred.* Blake's poetics of rhyme and related parallelisms do not imply the moral or political equivalence of oppressors and desperate subjects; but they do suggest how extreme political imbalances will press toward equalizing parallels, if only, but massively, in the mutual annihilation of violent action.

The critical commentary advanced by this poetics of rhyme is complemented in *Poetical Sketches* by an equally pointed semantics of blank verse, a form already, and powerfully, politicized by Milton's defense of the measure in *Paradise Lost*. Flouting the decorum of heroic couplets to write "*English* Heroic Verse without Rime," Milton troped his choice as liberal political action: "ancient liberty recover'd to Heroic Poem from the troublesome and modern bondage of Riming" that can act only by "vexation, hindrance, and constraint."[32] In Blake's age, this motion was seconded by Lord Kames, who summoned a similar discourse of "liberty": "Our verse is extremely cramped by rhyme; and the peculiar advantage of blank verse is, that it is at liberty to attend the imagination in its boldest flights."[33] Even Dr. Johnson, not a fan of blank verse, always made an exception for the power of Milton's "versification, free . . . from the distresses of rhyme"; the connection with a national poetics of liberalism is more evident in his life of Young, where he is happy to praise those "Who nobly durst, in rhyme-unfetter'd verse, / With British freedom sing a British song."[34] On the other side of the question, however, there is a politics of restraint, represented by Dryden's insistence that one of the "advantages which Rhyme has over Blanck Verse" is that it "Bounds and Circumscribes" an "Imagination" that might otherwise run "Wild and Lawless."[35] It is suggestive of the political valence borne by these formal signals that the radical Joseph Priestley felt the importance in the 1770s of contesting Milton's defense by using a language of impending political offense: "The liberty of drawing on the sense from one blank verse to another hath been greatly abused."[36]

Energized by the revolutions in America and France that were alarming conservatives all over Europe as an apocalypse of wild and lawless forces, Blake raised the stakes, launching a revolutionary poetics in *Milton* (1804) that outdid Milton, by expressing heroic contempt for any "tame high finisher of . . . paltry Rhymes; or paltry Harmonies" (plate 41, 9–10). The sneer at paltry harmonies gives no quarter to blank verse, and the parodic headnote of *Jerusalem* "To the Public" calls it bondage, a prescription by the literary institution that can only hinder the "true Orator":

> I consider'd a Monotonous Cadence like that used by Milton & Shakspeare & all writers of English Blank Verse, derived from the modern bondage of Rhyming; to be a necessary and indispensible part of Verse. But I soon found that in the mouth of a true Orator such monotony was not only awkward, but as much a bondage as rhyme itself. . . . Poetry Fetter'd, Fetters the Human Race! Nations are Destroy'd, or flourish, in proportion [to] their Poetry!
> (plate 3)

This test has become a favorite reference for poets concerned with "how radical innovative poetic styles can have political meanings."[37] On its basis, Blake is celebrated as the "first one to decisively link it all," proclaiming "a liberation through–& *from*—the poem, as an instrument of vision & of a new politics of revolution."[38]

Before launching this new line, however, Blake was more directly involved in the politics of blank verse—resisting the conservativism of Dryden but not uncritical of the cant of liberty summoned in defenses of the measure. We see this in the way "King Edward the Third" manipulates its verse forms into a political critique similar to that of "Gwin," this time focusing on English ideology of empire. A composition largely of dramatic blank verse, "King Edward" summons this form in part to evoke the Shakespearean stage of English wars with France, a reference strengthened by Blake's situation of his own scenes—Crécy before the battle of 1346—to predate and prefigure Shakespeare's histories. And both these eras, as history, return (as we shall see) to Blake's century via particular linguistic signs, ones that provoke awareness of the perpetuation of the same antagonisms in contemporary British tensions with France. The trajectory of this history, extending from Edward's reign to Blake's present, defines the sketch's political perspectivism. Edward the Third generates his line in English history, Henry the Fifth and Sixth, even as their Shakespearean characters engender Blake's; and all these royal and dramatic precedents resonate in Blake's decade in the conduct of George the Third.[39]

The history implied by these repetitions bears on a crucial formal aspect of this sketch, its prelusiveness. Blake's text presents six related "scenes": invocations, conversations, debates, and a "war song," all in the hours before the battle. His stopping short of the battle and its British victory does not, as is usually supposed, write a "fragment." Nowhere does he call "King Edward" such; nor is there any typographical sign to denote an unfinished piece.[40] The fragmentary state is a formal determination, not a symptom of an incomplete venture: although Blake's readers know that the English prevailed at Crécy, as they would, in another cycle of history, at Harfleur and Agincourt under Edward's descendant, Henry V, Blake's refusal to signal these outcomes (either as action or prophecy) functions semantically as a refusal of the ideological satisfactions that such conclusions might supply. Rather than sketch a plot to sustain nationalist propaganda, Blake diverts his reader's attention into various critical perspectives on the motivations and self-interests that impel its history of military adventurism.

This critical perspective on ideological formation correlates with the other form of this sketch, blank verse. If in Miltonic legacy, this measure signifies "ancient liberty" recovered from the bondage of inculcated practice, in "King Edward," Blake performs another turn by leaguing the apparent freedom of the line with a motivated rhetoric, a recurring imperialist cant of "Liberty." The way the design of the line tropes the orderings of self-interest that underwrite English claims is the subtle contradiction in Edward's opening exhortation to his subjects:

> O thou, to whose fury the nations are
> But as dust!
> . . . .

Let Liberty, the charter'd right of Englishmen,
Won by our fathers in many a glorious field,
Enerve my soldiers; let Liberty
Blaze in each countenance, and fire the battle.
The enemy fight in chains, invisible chains, but heavy;
Their minds are fetter'd; then how can they be free,
While, like the mounting flame,
We spring to battle o'er the floods of death!
And these fair youths, the flow'r of England
Venturing their lives in my most righteous cause,
O sheathe their hearts with triple steel, that they
May emulate their fathers' virtues,
And thou, my son, be strong; thou fightest for a crown. . . .
(SC. 1, 1–21)

This rhetoric convinces Mark Schorer that the whole sketch is "an extended defense of war and national interests" and Northrop Frye that it is "simply 'Rule Britannia' in blank verse."[41] Its cant is indeed blatant: we hear it again as the King exhorts "just revenge for those / Brave Lords, who fell beneath the bloody axe at Paris" (1.43–45) and proclaims "our right to France" (3.72), and again, as the Bishop, in a business council at home, refers to English merchants as "sovereigns / Of the sea" and claims this as a Heaven-given "right" (2.78–80). Yet Blake's very multiplication of this rhetoric in several venues makes its transparent motivation as much an issue as its claims.

As a *poetic* rhetoric, moreover, its formalism is subtly subversive. Predicting the cry of *Jerusalem*, "Poetry Fetter'd, Fetters the Human Race!" Blake motivates the fettered poetry of "King Edward the Third." Despite the "natural" cadence, the visible form of the line sets the claims of liberty at odds with the poetics of liberty and its not-quite-invisible chain of special interests. Blake's formalism, mingling manipulative eloquence in the pulse-quickening form of verse, is both politicized and rhetoricized: by exposing the formal design in Edward's language of liberty, he implies similar designs in other languages, including those of history and national ideology. And he intensifies this critical regard with a semantics of rhyme in the midst of this blank verse, the chime of *Liberty-enemy-heavy-free* (1.11–14). Edward's own rhetoric links the middle words to the "fetter'd" minds of France and the first and last to England; but in Blake's verse, one chord joins them all. The phonics signify what the sketch exposes at large: British minds, fettered by political and moral cant, are less free than they imagine. The chain includes even Edward's blithe description of "Liberty" as a "charter'd" English "right" (1.9). The claim, unironic for him, would chime for a reader in the 1780s with emerging critiques of the tyranny veiled in ideologies of "charter'd" rights.[42]

Blake's formalist critique of chartering forecasts the staging of patent economic self-interest in scene 2. As King Edward exhorts his army, his son at home, the Duke of Clarence, celebrates the swirling activity of chartered English business, imagining that from abroad, his father

> sees commerce fly round
> With his white wings, and sees his golden London,
> And her silver Thames, throng'd with shining spires
> And corded ships; her merchants buzzing round
> Like summer bees, and all the golden cities
> In his land, overflowing with honey.
>
> (2.9–14)

Frye finds the "most puzzling feature" of these lines and the sketch as a whole to be the frank admission "that economic ambitions are the cause of the war. Industry, commerce, agriculture, manufacture and trade are the gods directing the conflict"—gods sufficiently "worthy of worship" that "there seems to be no use looking for irony." Erdman finds any irony at best "hidden."[43] But irony presses forth in the next scene when the Prince's minstrel, Sir John Chandos, reacting to his patron's claim of the "genuine spirit of Liberty" within every "genuine Englishman" (3.189–190), observes,

> Teach man to think he's a free agent,
> Give but a slave his liberty, he'll shake
> Off sloth, and build himself a hut, and hedge
> A spot of ground; this he'll defend; 'tis his
> By right of nature.
>
> (3.195–199)

The coercive force of this instruction has exactly to do with the ironic disparity of form and content: of instructing the illusion of freedom; of harnessing liberty to the interests of royal power; of disguising these interests as a "right of nature." The uncertain blend of liberal idealism and pragmatic sense in the voice of Sir John acquires a more sinister ring in the rhetoric of the King's rejoinder, "O Liberty, how glorious art thou! / I see thee hov'ring o'er my army . . . I see thee / Lead them on to battle"(3.204–207), where liberty itself is conscripted to "my" army and a war to secure English commercial hegemony.[44] To underscore the shifty illusions of liberty, Blake bends the formalist poetics of his verse into an insistently critical mirror of the ruling powers, for instance when the Prince announces,

> my blood, like a springtide,
> Does rise so high, to overflow all bounds
> Of moderation; while Reason, in his
> Frail bark, can see no shore or bound for vast
> Ambition.
>
> (3.234–238)

Blake's enjambment here displays the disease of ambition: if the suspension of *vast* at the end of the line romantically tropes blank space as a visual pun for the unbounded field that the Prince imagines for the enterprises of ambition, the weakness of *bounds* in syntax and sensibility makes an opposite point about this costly intemperance.

An important shift in the poetics of form occurs in scene 4. After sixteen lines, the sketch seemingly sets aside the aesthetics of historical verse drama for prose—specifically, a dialogue between Sir Thomas Dagworth and the Blake-informed voice of "William his Man" in which the mobilization of military enterprise by ambition receives its sharpest commentary. Yet if this shift implies a turn from the rhetoric and aesthetics of illusion to the discourse of frank critique, such semantics are complicated by the return of the artist in this scene: we hear that Chandos has composed a "war-song" that has so pleased his Prince (who has an affection for the genre) that he has "made [him] a 'squire"—a reward sufficient to inspire another such song from Chandos "about all us that are to die, that we may be remembered in Old England" (4.44–50). Scene 6, the last, is the unmediated script of the minstrel performing this war-song. A composition in blank pentameter stanzas, it displays what has always been the implicit, if unacknowledged, artificiality of the line. With this patent formation of stanzas and song, Blake's sketch concludes by presenting the formalization of war into poetry—and reflexively, implying that national "history" too is an aesthetic formation.

In the aesthetics of desire borne by this "war-song," *war* is, significantly, the only rhyme, a sounding intensified by its status within the *Sketches* as a repetition: the opening line, "O sons of Trojan Brutus, cloath'd in war," chiming with "Heated with war" and then "covered with gore" (6.10–11), repeats the key rhymes of "Gwin." The repetition is enhanced by a host of other verbal and imagistic repetitions whose cumulative effect is to make the line of Brutus in England seem merely one more warpath. Again we hear of "thunder," of "rolling dark clouds," of a "sickly darkness," of the "wrath and fury" of "wild men, / Naked and roaring like lions," of "savage monsters rushing like roaring fire," of "red lightning . . . furious storms" and a "molten raging sea" (6.2–31). Even as the song advances a vision of eventual prosperity, its language bears marks of this past violence: the promise that "plenty shall bring forth, / Cities shall sing, and vales in rich *array* / Shall laugh, whose fruitful laps bend down with fullness," refigures "the firm *array* of battle" (6.46–48, 25, emphasis mine; cf. 6.13); the prospect of "Cities" recalls the city in ashes that produced Trojan Brutus; and the summary icon of Liberty bears the legacy of violence recorded in the singer's opening stanzas:

> "Liberty shall stand upon the cliffs of Albion,
> "Casting her blue eyes over the green ocean;
> "Or, tow'ring, stand upon the roaring waves,
> "Stretching her mighty spear o'er distant lands;
> "While with her eagle wings, she covereth
> "Fair Albion's shore, and all her families."
>
> (6.55–60)

Everything here is a repetition: Liberty's blue eyes cast back a genetic history of "eyes" that "glare against the stormy fires / Heated with war"; the roaring waves of her domain evoke the memory of the "roaring" armies of the invading fathers (6.22, 26, 27); and the iconography of the mighty spear, its imperial(ist) thrust, and the eagle, reinscribe the "spears" of the fathers and their spoil of "mighty dead" (6.34–35), as well as the aggressive "empire"-building that has them roaming "Like eagles for the prey" (6.42–45). There is an even further, ultimately more potent, range of repetition: in a sketch that opened with the King's manipulative rhetoric of Liberty, the same language is replayed, now fully contextualized in the history of violence that it sustains and perpetuates.

Poetical Sketches expands this formalist critique by displaying the line in a visionary mode that discloses repetition, both conceptual and verbal. Following "King Edward the Third" is the sonnet-like "Prologue . . . of King Edward the Fourth." Blake's grim joke is that Edward the Fourth is not Edward the Third's son (who predeceased his father by a year) but a king born almost a century after the battle of Crécy. The thwarted succession is scarcely felt, however, for the term of continuity between the two sketches is a perpetual, irremediable English thirst for war, reaching not just across generations but across centuries. The "Prologue" gives this language a succinct, ritualistic form, in which repetitions not only echo previous sketches and war literature, but suggest the frustrating repetitions of history itself:

> O For a voice like thunder, and tongue
> To drown the throat of war!—When the senses
> Are shaken, and the soul is driven to madness,
> Who can stand? When the souls of the oppressed
> Fight in the troubled air that rages, who can stand?

When the whirlwind of fury comes from the
Throne of God, when the frowns of his countenance
Drive the nations together, who can stand?
When Sin claps his broad wings over the battle,
And sails rejoicing in the flood of Death;
When souls are torn to everlasting fire,
And fiends of Hell rejoice upon the slain,
O who can stand? O who hath caused this?   [13]
O who can answer at the throne of God?
The Kings and Nobles of the Land have done it!
Hear it not, Heaven, thy Ministers have done it!

The echo of the opening chorus of *Henry V*—a text that precedes Blake's and a hero whose reign occurs between that of the two Edwards—amplifies the indictment: the allusion to Shakespeare's (ostensibly) nationalistic history, again with France as enemy, is yet one more parody of the enthusiasms that mobilize military slaughter. The repetition is that of history itself, summarized in the sketch's emphatic structuring by syntactic and verbal repetitions: "When . . . who can stand?" The stunning modulation of this formula in line 13, in which the issue of resistance turns into an interrogation of agency—"O who hath caused this?"—yields a pair of declamations in which political agents, "Kings and Nobles," and Heaven's Ministers are indicted together. The equivalence is crucial. Erdman, hearing a "warning" only to the "Kings and Nobles" to "look out for the wrath of God and the people," is troubled by the "inconsistent theology" that at once seems sarcastically to worry about the fate of Kings and Nobles should God hear of their deeds, and to suggest, in the image of the fury descending from the "Throne of God," that God himself is a responsible agent of war.[45] Yet, as in "Gwin," apparent inconsistency has a basic critical point: in a theological register, God's Ministers are revealed as complicit with earth's rulers; in a political register, earth's rulers are shown to justify themselves in the rhetoric of divine ministry. Blake uses the couplet function of final lines in this slightly expanded sonnet for a repetition that exceeds even the semantic linkage implied by rhyme.

A Coda on Shelleyan Aesthetics and Politics

What has to be said in relation to the historical moment of Blake's *Poetical Sketches* is that their politics of form were enacted largely on a coterie stage, and so could not claim much by way of actual political agency, except in the prophetic imagining of future readers earned by future fame. The problem of actual audience was also the self-created plight of the other Romantic poet celebrated for his political radicalism, Shelley, its most blatant example being the daring, unpublishable oratory of *The Mask of Anarchy, Written on the Occasion of the Massacre at Manchester.*[46] It may be, as Ronald Tetreault contends, that this poem is rhetorically heightened by its internal, fantasized oration to the "Men of England" (the 226 lines of 147–372 comprising the last sixty percent of *The Mask*); it is everywhere animated in its dazzling variety of modes—commendatory direct address, question and answer, and variations on the imperative mood, including the jussive, the hortative, and the optative.[47] But this display notwithstanding, the poem's larger rhetoric is that of dream vision, and its larger historical context includes the fact that it was not published to those whom it addresses—an event that, whatever Shelley's fantasy, could not have been unanticipated, given the Crown's eagerness to prosecute for libel and heresy.[48] There is no better description of this doubleness than Thomas Edward's: "*The Mask of Anarchy* is a case of a public poem with revolutionary intentions having to face and cope with the fact that its generating consciousness, the poet's mind, is in no position to do more than write a poem"; its political issues are converted into "rhetorical and symbolic 'properties' in a moral drama whose relation to the actual public case grows increasingly tenuous."[49]

Although this circumstance is elided by champions of Shelley's politics, the fact is that between the production of the poem and its popular reading is a gap in which abides the poet as *un*acknowledged legislator— Shelley's uncertain negotiation of the promise of aesthetic agency and his own circumstances as dreamer in Italy and unpublished poet in England.[50] This gap is not just an unlucky product of state repression, but is in some ways courted by the poem itself as it converts politics to aesthetic spectacle and finally leaves its spectacle as a figment in the mind of the sleeping poet. Internally, these poetics register multiple tensions between content and form—the fantastic allegorical parade of abuses tagged with their English enactors ("I met Murder on the way— / He had a mask like Castlereagh" [5–6], etc.) that serves Shelley as a language of political critique; the seemingly effortless victory over Anarchy by Hope; and the advent of an epipsychic oratory, an address to the "Men of England" that Shelley can represent only fantastically. Without working out all these ambivalent registers of poetic form in the politics of *The Mask*, I'd like to concentrate on three key moments: the opening frame of dream vision; the emergence of its epipsychic oration; and the poetics of its conclusion.

■   ■   ■

The opening is problematic enough, not only in the visionary situation of the poet's political thinking but also in the workings of his verse. *The Mask* begins, "As I lay asleep in Italy / There came a voice from over the Sea." The news (the voice from over the Sea) of the massacre enters the poet's consciousness in a dream state. This voice-infused dormancy will be allegorized as a prerevolutionary ground of social actions in stanzas that frame the oratory to the "Men of England": "Rise like Lions after slumber . . . Shake your chains to Earth like dew / Which in sleep had fallen on you" (151–153; 368–370). But *The Mask*'s other frame, unreturned-to and repressed by this one, is that of the poet's own, unaltered slumber—a figure of self-imposed alienation from the world he would influence and of the estrangement of writing from its social events:

> As I lay asleep in Italy
> There came a voice from over the Sea,
> And with great power it forth led me
> To walk in the visions of Poesy.
>
> (1–4)

Poetic form may sustain the passion of *The Mask's* internal epipsychic oratory, but in this opening verse it bears a semantic function contrary to such energy. The origin of its hypnotic and nearly claustrophobic single rhyme is not the first end-word, but "as*leep*" (itself oozing suggestively out of the initial *As I*). The quadruple end-rhyme is a dreamy extension of *sleep* into its site in *Italy*; the *Sea* across which lies England; the poet's sign of self, *me*; and the field of action, *Poesy*. Poesy, moreover, is not securely located in this syntax: the *of* situates it both as the agent of privileged visions and as a product of vision itself. It is a reflection of the perplexed figurative logic of Shelley's political poetics that this latter, specular status is not fully distinguishable from that of the masquerade that soon appears.

   The Mask never really unmasks this origin. The initiating verbal form, "*As* I lay asleep," turns out to imprint a syntax that binds the dream of political oratory, whose "words of joy and fear arose"

> *As if* their Own indignant Earth
>
> .   .   .   .
>
> Had turned every drop of blood
> By which her face had been bedewed
> To an accent unwithstood,—
> *As if* her heart had cried aloud:
>
> 'Men of England, heirs of Glory . . .
>
> (138–147, my italics)

Echoing the initial *As* the conducts the poem to its visions of Poesy, these syntaxes of *As if* have the reflexive effect of restraining the political agency of the oratory to a dream. Indeed, its words, arising by inexplicable agency and borne by fantastic illusion, work with supernatural power to transform the chains of tyrannical law into so much dew.

This dreamy shimmer is a tension that both sustains the poem's idealism and exposes the ideological bind of political poetics, and it persists in the poem's most critical formalist maneuver, its suppression of its initiating frame. That *The Mask* sheds its dream frame and remains in the rhetoric of its fantasized speech suggests the imaginative investment that Shelley has in casting himself into this epipsychic oratory. It has become a fully imagined, substitute reality. At the same time, our awareness of the sleight of hand in this formalist suppression reveals an aesthetic ideology that is as delimited as it is motivated by its challenge to political ideology. Shelley's transformation of the poem into an aesthetic oration in the verse form of a popular ballad enacts the problematic of poetic form and politics—whether aesthetic action can become a political event, or can only expose its substitute nature; whether symbolic politics are political or merely symbolic. The fact that the dream frame is not reinscribed at the close of *The Mask* does not resolve the question; it is a formalism that aggravates it. Its dropping away attempts to release the fantasy oration into a potentially wider circulation, implying that a political action has emerged from visionary poesy, that the dream song has scripted a voice for the "Men of England." If the frame were to return, it would expose the oration as an unreal event—a wish and a dream, a fantasy wrought by the visions of Poesy—at the very moment that Shelley wants to insist on its political potency.[51]

A sonnet written later in the same year, *England in 1819,* continues the visionary indictment of Peterloo, this time by pointed image rather than direct name. Like *The Mask,* it is strained by a gap between composition and reception, and between fantasy and action—but with a sense of craft suggesting that these very strains are now cannily managed figures of their dilemma; Shelley didn't kid himself about the prospect of publication, yet the conscious cancellation of an immediate audience puts him in the peculiar position of writing a political poem whose main interest seems to be that of self-arousal.[52] It is under this tension that we have to assess the sonnet's most dramatic (and most admired) event of form: the drive of its syntax toward a predicate that seems to trope, in a kind of symbolic poetics, the action it describes.

> An old, mad, blind, despised, and dying King;
> Princes, the dregs of their dull race, who flow
> Through public scorn,—mud from a muddy spring;
> Rulers who neither see nor feel nor know,
> But leechlike to their fainting country cling
> Till they drop, blind in blood, without a blow.

> A people starved and stabbed in th'untilled field;
> An army, whom liberticide and prey
> Makes as a two-edged sword to all who wield;
> Golden and sanguine laws which tempt and slay;
> Religion Christless, Godless—a book sealed;
> A senate, Time's worst statute, unrepealed—
> Are graves from which a glorious Phantom may
> Burst, to illumine our tempestuous day.

But arousal it is. With impressive skill, Shelley·defies the formal patterns of both the Shakespearean and Italian sonnet, increasing the syntactic pressure of his list of ills and grievances toward the predicate, which finally emerges in line 13 with "Are graves." And even the form of this final, but hardly Shakespearean, couplet falls to the momentum of a syntax whose energy concentrates on "Burst," all but submerging the pattern of the rhyme.

Yet as forceful as this play against formal prescription is, it registers with uncertain effect. For some readers, such as Stuart Curran, the form is as revolutionary as the statement: "the sudden enjambment of the final couplet, with its ambiguous modal auxiliary—'may'—throw[s] the accumulated weight of the single-sentence catalog onto the active, explosive verb so long awaited. . . . Shelley pivots his poem on a syntactic potentiality—'may'—that yields to the bursting of its formal bonds in a movement parallel to the revolutionary explosion that will invert the anti-forms repressing contemporary society. The form symbolically consumes itself, as surely as does the society it catalogs."[53] While for Curran the rhetorical function of *may* takes precedence over its ambiguous mode, for other readers it is this mode that matters most. To F. R. Leavis, the final couplet is a "pathetic weakness" of both form and statement: this is a politics (as in *The Mask*) governed by a Phantom of miraculous agency, undercut by "an oddly ironical stress [that] results from the rime position" of *may*.[54] Timothy Webb feels this effect, too, but evaluates it differently, finding the tentativeness of *may* tough-minded: "Shelley's intellectual honesty prevents him from even believing wholeheartedly in such an incarnation: the rhyme scheme insists that we underline the improbability of this redemption by stressing the word *may*. . . . A mere escapist would not have allowed that ironical and limiting stress on *may*. Surely the point is that Shelley's sense of evil is too strong rather than too weak?"[55]

What these divergent readings show us at the deepest level of significance, however, is that the question Webb poses rhetorically is one that the sonnet allows to be genuine and genuinely unresolvable. Paul de Man has described such events as a deconstructive contest between semiology and rhetoric, in which "the same grammatical pattern engenders two meanings that are mutually exclusive."[56] It is no overstatement to say that Shelley's sonnet stakes the force of its predicate—both its conceptual and, more specifically, political force—on a simultaneous reading of the sonnet's form and its grammar. In the register of form, *may* signifies both as a weak rhyme overridden by enjambment, and lending force, thereby, to *Burst;* in the register of grammar, *may* designates a merely tentative hope. Curran argues for the former, in effect a signifying form, and Webb and Leavis reverse his emphasis, seeing weak rhyme conveying, for better or for worse, weak confidence. There is, moreover, a semantic indeterminacy in the two incompatible senses of *may.* If it means "perhaps," it is tentative, whether optimistically or skeptically, in the way that Leavis and Webb recognize. But if it means "is enabled," or even "is empowered to," then it is energized in the way that Curran suggests: the accumulating catalogue of oppression by which *may* is preceded is the enabling ground for revolution.[57]

The multiple array of signals bristling in this climactic couplet—fantasy, hesitation, faint hope, affirmative prophesy—make the question ultimately undecidable, and the real work for the reader is to sense the how poetic form keeps the possibilities in tension. Even Shelley's letter to Leigh Hunt pivots interestingly on the point: "I do not expect you to publish it, but you may show it to whom you please," he wrote to him.[58] Publication would provoke two audiences, the oppressed for whom the sonnet articulates political grievance and the oppressors for whom the sonnet articulates a political threat. The compromise action of giving it to Hunt with no demands, but with a calculated overload on *may,* places the agency of finding an audience on him: he may (with permission) show it; he may (as a possibility of his choice and discretion) determine its readers.

In writing poetry about politics from a point of disengagement—whether Shelley's masked fantasies in Italy about current events in England, or Blake's effort to tune the play of poetic form to the energies of political critique as he writes about England's past—both Romantics may court accusations of bad faith, attempts to play out as aesthetic complexity what remain contradictions in historical and political existence. Yet their engagement with poetic form shows how at certain historical moments literary imagination can work powerfully at the intersection of aesthetics and ideology. If this intersection does not constitute the fully material matrix demanded by today's ideological critiques, it does complicate accounts of Romanticism that would position it as the repression or evasion of critique. And beyond that, it makes a good case for how aesthetic form not only reflects received ideological forms but also reveals the complex and frequently critical careers of ideology in the specifics of writing—careers in which the instabilities of aesthetic performance against ideological script play a role as important for understanding politics as for understanding poetry.[59]

Notes

1. Terry Eagleton, "Marxism and Aesthetic Ideology," in *Criticism and Ideology: A Study in Marxist Literary Theory* (1976; London: Verso, 1978), 166; citations hereafter appear parenthetically.

2. Jerome McGann, *The Romantic Ideology: A Critical Investigation* (Chicago: University of Chicago Press, 1983), 3, his italics; citations hereafter appear parenthetically.

3. Jerome McGann, "Keats and the Historical Method in Literary Criticism," in *The Beauty of Inflections: Literary Investigations in Historical Method and Theory* (Oxford: Clarendon Press, 1988), 12–14; originally published in 1979.

4. These readings were advanced most influentially by M. H. Abrams in *Natural Supernaturalism: Tradition and Revolution in Romantic Literature* (New York: Norton, 1971) and Harold Bloom in "The Internalization of Quest Romance" in *The Ringers in the Tower: Studies in Romantic Tradition* (Chicago: University of Chicago Press, 1971), 13–35 (originally published in 1968), as well as in his monographs *The Anxiety of Influence: A Theory of Poetry* (New York: Oxford University Press, 1973) and *A Map of Misreading* (Oxford: Oxford University Press, 1975). In these studies of psychological agon, "form" is not a question of poetic form (indeed, Bloom cheers assaults on "the impasse of Formalism" [*Anxiety*, 12]), but of how "one poet helps to form another" (5); the critical act that "one poet performs upon another" is not to be read in the text itself but in the "relationship *between* texts" (*Map*, 3, Bloom's italics).

5. For those who don't know Wordsworth's credo (from *Essay, Supplementary to the Preface* [to the *Poems* of 1815]), it is worth quoting in full: "If there be one conclusion more forcibly pressed upon us than another by . . . the fortunes and fate of poetical Works, it is this—that every author, as far as he is great and at the same time *original,* has had the task of *creating* the taste by which he is to be enjoyed: so has it been, so will it continue to be. . . . for what is peculiarly his own, he will be called upon to clear and often to shape his own road:—he will be in the condition of Hannibal among the Alps" (*The Prose Works of William Wordsworth,* ed. W. J. B. Owen and Jane Worthington Smyser, 3 vols. [Oxford: Clarendon Press, 1974], 3:80, Wordsworth's italics). The seductiveness of his forms of thought has to do not just with their originality, but with the forcefulness of their conception, which amounts, in Wordsworth's summary metaphor, to imperial incursion.

6. Marjorie Levinson, *Wordsworth's Great Period Poems: Four Essays* (Cambridge: Cambridge University Press, 1986), 9–10, her emphases.

7. I review some aspects of "the Romantic ideology"—in terms having to do more with rhetorical process than form—in "Questioning 'The Romantic Ideology,'" *Revue Internationale de Philosophie* 44 (1990): 429–447. For similar

critiques, see Peter J. Manning's trenchant "Placing Poor Susan: Wordsworth and the New Historicism," in *Reading Romantics: Texts and Contexts* (New York: Oxford University Press, 1990), 300–320 (originally published in 1987), and David Simpson's tactful quarrel with McGann in *Wordsworth's Historical Imagination: The Poetry of Displacement* (New York: Methuen, 1987), 14ff.

8. "Close reading," as a practice of attention, need not be complicit with the methods and agenda of the New Criticism in which its skills were first exercised and refined. In the dominant mode of New Criticism, though there were interesting tensions and exceptions, close reading sought to explicate the complex achievement of an aesthetic unity that was not referable to "extrinsic" frames of reference. One of the more problematic results of the move beyond New Criticism, I think, has been an ideological suspicion of textual complexity and a consequent alienation of how the actions of texts elude and resist the critical arguments imposed upon them.

9. In this respect, I indicate my agreement with Derek Attridge's desire, in his essay for this volume, for an account of literary form "that does not fall into the dualisms of the aesthetic tradition," such as "the opposition of form and content, which sets formal properties apart from any connection the work has to ethical, historical, and social issues."

10. I'm paraphrasing the representative analysis of Eagleton's "Ideology and Literary Form" (*Criticism and Ideology*, 102–161): the question for him is one of discerning how literary form in general deploys its "devices" to resolve "ideological conflicts" (129), how its processes recast "historical contradiction into ideologically resolvable form" (114) or, failing this, are ruptured from within by the pressure of ideological contradiction.

11. S. T. Coleridge, *Lectures 1808–1819 On Literature*, ed. R. A. Foakes, 2 vols. (Princeton: Princeton University Press, 1987), 1:495.

12. Arnold implied a lapse when he opposed the Romantic expression of sensibility, with its "source in a great movement of feeling, not in a movement of mind," to the poetics of "high seriousness," demonstrated by "the noble and profound application of ideas to life . . . under the conditions immutably fixed by the laws of poetic beauty and poetic truth" ("The Function of Criticism at the Present Time" [1864], in *The Complete Prose Words of Matthew Arnold*, ed. R. H. Super, 11 vols. [Ann Arbor: University of Michigan Press, 1973], 3:264; Preface to *Poems of Wordsworth* [London: Macmillan, 1879], xiv–xv). The language of law suggests a formalism regarded not just as technique but as a whole mode of behavior in the domain of true poetic power. In this perspective, even Arnold's praise of Wordsworth is tacitly qualified by a sense of its artlessness: The "accident . . . of inspiration, is of peculiar importance. It might seem that Nature not only gave him the matter for his poem, but wrote his poem for him. He has no style. . . . Nature herself seems . . . to take the pen out of his hand, and to write for him with her own bare, sheer, penetrating power" (Preface to *Poems*, xxii, xxiv). Kingsley went further, reading Romantic poetics as an antiformalism complicit with intellectual and moral failure: A "poetry of doubt, even a sceptical poetry, in its true sense, can never possess clear and sound form, even organic form at all. How can you put into form that thought which is by its

very nature formless?" ("Alexander Smith and Alexander Pope," *Fraser's Magazine* 48 [Oct. 1853]: 460).

13. The Coleridgean legacy registers, for instance, in Cleanth Brooks's case for "the structure of a poem as an organism" (*The Well Wrought Urn: Studies in the Structure of Poetry* [1947; New York: Harcourt Brace Jovanovich, 1975], 218) and in Elizabeth Nitchie's assertion: "Surely form itself is good only if it is organically unified with content" ("Form in Romantic Poetry," in *The Major English Romantic Poets: A Symposium in Reappraisal,* ed. Clarence D. Thorpe, Carlos Baker, and Bennett Weaver [Carbondale: Southern Illinois University Press, 1957], 4). R. S. Crane articulates the principle of aesthetic agency in this project: in attempting to account for the way form operates in actual poetic composition (as opposed to theory), he complains that there is "nowhere present in [the critical languages of his contemporaries] any means for dealing precisely and particularly with . . . the forming principle or immediate shaping cause of structure in individual poems" (*The Languages of Criticism and the Structure of Poetry* [Toronto: University of Toronto Press, 1953], 140).

14. McGann, "Keats and the Historical Method," 22–23.

15. Terry Eagleton, *Literary Theory: An Introduction* (Minneapolis: University of Minneapolis Press, 1983), 19–20, 21.

16. Eagleton, "Ideology and Literary Form," in *Criticism and Ideology,* 103–104. In Romantic studies, this critique of organicism has been applied by David Simpson (who has written alertly about slippery interactions of irony and authority in poetic practice in *Irony and Authority in Romantic Poetry* [London: Macmillan, 1979]). He proposes that Coleridge's theory of organic form evolved as a "discursive response to the material basis of culture and political life in early nineteenth-century England," one marked by the contentiousness of "wars, civil rights trial, food riots, radical and reform movement." Organic aesthetics is thus not only a compensation; it is a tactical opposition to mechanic form's display of "the signs of its own construction" and "the details of its own coming into being." And this opposition is one that cooperates, in a kind of Burkean sense, with privilege-protecting political ideologies given to representing "a contrived or constructed paradigm" as "innate" and to disguising "human agency as spontaneous evolution" ("Coleridge on Wordsworth and the Form of Poetry," in *Coleridge's Theory of Imagination Today,* ed. Christine Gallant [New York: AMS Press, 1989], 214, 215, 216).

17. Donald Wesling, *The Chances of Rhyme: Device and Modernity* (Berkeley: University of California Press, 1980), 2.

18. This representative view of Romantic ideology is voiced by Antony Easthope, *Poetry as Discourse* (London: Methuen, 1983), 23, 123. The first phrase is drawn from a general announcement of his alignment with projects to make "available for interrogation" what is "conventionally left unproblematized" (23); "enunciation" refers to a view of a poem's discourse as a "'speech event,' the act of uttering these words in language" (42). "English bourgeois poetic tradition," he contends, "can be defined precisely as a regime of representation aiming to disavow enunciation so as to promote . . . the effect of an individual voice 'really' speaking by concealing the way it is produced as

an effect" (46); he claims both that Romantic theory "is founded on precisely [its] misrecognition" of "any activity of means of representation in producing" what it represents and that the Preface is emblematic of a poetry that "means to *efface* enunciation altogether . . . to be so wholly transparent to experience that it is virtually identical to it" (125, his emphasis).

19. Preface to *Lyrical Ballads* (1800), in *Lyrical Ballads: Wordsworth and Coleridge. The Text of the 1798 Edition with the Additional 1800 Poems and the Prefaces,* ed. R. L. Brett and A. R. Jones (1965; London: Methuen, 1986), 243–244, my italics; hereafter, this edition is cited parenthetically with the abbreviation *LB.*

20. Fox is quoted in Stephen Maxfield Parrish, *The Art of the "Lyrical Ballads"* (Cambridge: Harvard University Press, 1973), 183.

21. The common attitude toward the ballad is given by the *Encyclopedia Britannica* of 1797: this is a poetic form "adapted to the capacity of the lower class of people." I owe this reference to Michael Mason's introduction to his edition of *Lyrical Ballads* (London: Longman, 1992), 9.

22. I give fuller attention to the problematic formalism of meter, in the Preface and in other texts, in "Romanticism and the Measures of Meter," *Eighteenth-Century Life* 16, no. 3 (November 1992): 162–180.

23. *"The Enquirer. No. VI. Question: Is Verse essential to Poetry?" Monthly Magazine* 2 (July 1796), 455; cited hereafter parenthetically. Owen and Smyser cite and quote briefly from this essay in the commentary on the Preface to *Lyrical Ballads* and identify the author as William Enfield (Wordsworth, *Prose Works,* 1:173–174).

24. In the last four decades, almost two and a half million acres were enclosed (Kenneth MacLean, *Agrarian Age: A Background for Wordsworth* [1950; Hamden, Conn.: Archon, 1970], 14). For statistics as well as a discussion of the controversy, especially of the impact of enclosure on the unpropertied laborer, see 12–26.

25. William Hazlitt, "On the Living Poets," Lecture 8 of *Lectures on the English Poets* (1818), in *The Complete Works of William Hazlitt,* ed. P. P. Howe, 21 vols. (London and Toronto: J.M. Dent and Sons, 1930–1934), 5:161–162.

26. Geoffrey Hartman, *The Fate of Reading and Other Essays* (Chicago: University of Chicago Press, 1975), vii. He is referring, of course, to his *Beyond Formalism: Literary Essays 1958–1970* (New Haven: Yale University Press, 1970).

27. Quotations of Blake are from *The Complete Poetry and Prose of William Blake,* ed. David V. Erdman (Garden City, N.Y.: Anchor Doubleday, 1982); references in the text are to the line numbers unless otherwise specified.

28. McGann applies these terms to a brilliant reading of *Don Juan* ("The Book of Byron and the Book of a World," in *The Beauty of Inflections,* 266).

29. David Erdman, *Blake: Prophet against Empire* (Princeton: Princeton University Press, 1954), 18.

30. Robert Gleckner, *Blake's "Poetical Sketches"* (Baltimore: Johns Hopkins University Press, 1982), 119. See also William Keach's brief but trenchant analysis of how "Gwin" and "King Edward the Third" focus attention on the images of violence that animate Blake's representation of revolutionary energy

as a collective social conflict ("Blake, Violence, and Visionary Politics," in *Representing the French Revolution: Literature, Historiography, and Art,* ed. James A. W. Heffernan [Hanover: University Press of New England, 1992]: 24–40; see esp. 26–28).

31. Vincent Arthur de Luca, *Words of Eternity: Blake and the Poetics of the Sublime* (Princeton: Princeton University Press, 1991), 77.

32. John Milton, *Complete Poems and Major Prose,* ed. Merrit Y. Hughes (New York: Odyssey, 1957), 4.

33. *Elements of Criticism by Henry Home, Lord Kames,* ed. Abraham Mills (New York: Mason Bros., 1857), 316.

34. Samuel Johnson, "Milton," *Lives of the English Poets* (1783), ed. George Birbeck Hill, 3 vols. (Oxford: Clarendon Press, 1905), 1:139; and "Young," 3:377; the verse is Johnson's quoting of Thomson's politically charged praise of Philips in *Autumn* as "the second" after Milton to use blank verse in this noble fashion.

35. John Dryden, "To the Right Honourable Roger Earl of Orrery" (dedicatory epistle to *The Rival Ladies,* 1664), in *The Works of John Dryden,* vol. 8, *Plays,* ed. John Harrington Smith and Dougald MacMillan (Berkeley and Los Angeles: University of California Press, 1967), 101.

36. Joseph Priestley, *A Course of Lectures on Oratory and Criticism* (London: J. Johnson, 1777), 305.

37. Charles Bernstein, ed., *The Politics of Poetic Form: Poetry and Public Policy* (New York: Roof, 1990), vii.

38. Jerome Rothenberg, "Ethnopoetics & Politics / The Politics of Ethnopoetics," in ibid., 2.

39. See Erdman, *Prophet against Empire,* 3–19.

40. Because the event is left in suspense, readers tend to judge this sketch "unfinished" and call it a "fragment": see Henry Crabb Robinson's initial remark of this kind from 1811 (G.E. Gentley, Jr., ed., *William Blake: The Critical Heritage* [London and Boston: Routledge and Kegan Paul, 1975], 163), followed, among others, by Margaret Ruth Lowery, *Windows of the Morning: A Critical Study of William Blake's "Poetical Sketches," 1783* (New Haven: Yale University Press, 1940), 112); Erdman, *Prophet against Empire,* 18, 56, 63–64, 83; Harold Bloom's notes in *The Complete Poetry and Prose of William Blake* (969), and Robert Gleckner, *Blake's "Poetical Sketches,"* 96. For an illuminating critique of the "reception protocols" involved in the construction of the genre of the fragment, both in publication and reading, see Marjorie Levinson, *The Romantic Fragment Poem: A Critique of a Form* (Chapel Hill: University of North Carolina Press, 1986), especially the first two chapters.

41. Mark Schorer, *William Blake: The Politics of Vision* (1946; New York: Random House, 1959), 165; Northrop Frye, *Fearful Symmetry: A Study of William Blake* (1947; Princeton: Princeton University Press, 1969), 180.

42. During the 1780s, the language of "chartering" was focusing ever sharper critical discussion. By the time *The Rights of Man* appeared in 1792, Paine was insisting that "it is a perversion of terms to say that a charter gives rights. It operates by a contrary effect, that of taking rights away. Rights are

inherently in all the inhabitants; but charters, by annulling those rights in the majority, leave the rights, by exclusion, in the hands of a few. . . . [T]he only persons on whom they operate, are the persons whom they exclude" (*The Rights of Man*, in *Two Classics of the French Revolution* [New York: Anchor Doubleday, 1973], 458). Even Paine's opponent, Burke, was noting the "fallacious and sophisticated" perversion of the rhetoric of "chartered rights," distinguishing public instruments such as the Magna Carta from the charters awarded to commercial interests: "*Magna Charta* is a Charter to restrain power, and to destroy monopoly: the East India Charter is a Charter to establish monopoly, and to create power. Political power and commercial monopoly are *not* the rights of men. . . . These Chartered Rights . . . suspend the natural rights of mankind." Paine's condemnation is noted by Erdman (*Prophet against Empire*, 276–277), and Burke's remarks, from a document of 1784 abstracting his speech on the East India Bill, are cited by Heather Glen (*Vision and Disenchantment: Blake's "Songs" and Wordsworth's "Lyrical Ballads"* [Cambridge: Cambridge University Press, 1983], 382 n. 62). In the next decade, Blake's *Songs of Experience* will comment bitterly on London's "charter'd" streets and "charter'd Thames," a discourse he tacitly evokes in a sketch that follows "King Edward"—"Prologue to King John"—which retroactively applies one more irony to Edward's sophistries by naming the king who provoked *the* English charter, the Magna Carta, whose purpose was to protect citizens against royal tyranny.

43. Frye, *Fearful Symmetry*, 180; Erdman, *Prophet against Empire*, 69. This perception notwithstanding, Erdman does say that "Blake's early intellectual growth is in part the story of his learning to see the larger web of commerce and war within which 'peace' was often mere hallucination" (4).

44. David Simpson observes that by the turn of the century such arguments were being made on behalf of the political expedient of repressing unrest. Arthur Young, for example, backed off from his early support of enclosure, in recognition that if a man is allowed to "love his country the better even for a pig" (that is, given land enough to keep a pig), he will feel that he "has a stake in the country," and therefore will be "never prompt to riot in times of sedition" (*Wordsworth's Historical Imagination: The Poetry of Displacement* [London: Methuen, 1987], 78; Young is also cited in MacLean, *Agrarian Age*, 23). Simpson notes *The Anti-Jacobean's* support for this idea: ownership "tends to connect more firmly the links of the social chain; and to encrease that attachment to *home*, which is the source of much individual comfort and of infinite public good" (3 [1799]: 458–459; in *Historical Imagination*, 78).

45. Erdman, *Prophet against Empire*, 16, 29.

46. The "Peterloo Massacre," a term parodying the celebrated English victory at Waterloo, refers to a savage, sabre-wielding attack by drunken local yeomanry and the regular cavalry on an orderly, nonviolent demonstration of between eighty and one hundred thousand men, women, and children in St. Peter's Field, near Manchester, on 16 August 1819; they had gathered to urge parliamentary reform, specifically greater representation for the Manchester working-class population. The militia killed about a dozen people and brutally

wounded hundreds more. Although it is unclear how much the London Home Office urged this suppression in advance in order to quash the reform movement, or just found it convenient, with the Prince Regent, to congratulate the militia after the fact, the narrative to which Shelley reacted was the one conveyed by the left-wing and radical press. Quotations of Shelley's poetry follow *Shelley's Poetry and Prose,* ed. Donald H. Reiman and Sharon B. Powers (New York: Norton, 1977).

47. Ronald Tetreault, *The Poetry of Life: Shelley and Literary Form* (Toronto: University of Toronto Press, 1987), 205–206. Most critical commentary describes and celebrates *The Mask* as a poem of powerful, radical public address. Stephen C. Behrendt goes so far as to see it addressing several audiences: the oppressed (with encouragement, instruction, and inspiration), the aristocracy (with warning and instruction), and the liberal, enlightened readers of *The Examiner* (with a sense of social urgency about the project of reform); *Shelley and His Audiences* (Lincoln: University of Nebraska Press, 1989), 199–202.

48. Shelley drafted the poem as soon as he heard about the massacre in a letter from Peacock in early September; on the twenty-third, he sent a copy to Leigh Hunt, his friend and editor of the reformist journal, *The Examiner;* Hunt, nervous about the renewal of oppressive libel and sedition laws, did not publish the poem until after the passage of the Reform Bill in 1832, when, of course, its hotter rhetoric could be read with historical distance and its cooler rhetoric as sensibly prophetic of the means by which (some shallow) reforms had been won. That the poem was not publishable in 1819 or any time soon thereafter is quite frankly conceded by Mary Shelley in her edition (1839): "Shelley loved the People. . . . He believed that a clash between the two classes of society was inevitable, and he eagerly ranged himself on the people's side. He had an idea of publishing a series of poems adapted expressly to commemorate their circumstances and wrongs. He wrote a few; but, in those days of prosecution for libel, they could not be printed" ("Note on Poems of 1819," *The Poetical Works of Percy Bysshe Shelley,* ed. Mrs. Shelley, 4 vols. [London: Edward Moxon, 1839], 3:205–207).

49. Thomas Edwards, *Imagination and Power: A Study of Poetry on Public Themes* (New York: Oxford University Press, 1971), 160, 168.

50. Michael Henry Scrivener ignores this gap, deciding that the question of Shelley's self-imposed distance bears only on the poem's idiom of "symbolic reference," which he still wants to see as politically potent: a "proposal for massive nonviolent resistance" would "push the reform movement leftwards," even at the risk of revolution (*Radical Shelley: The Philosophical Anarchism and Utopian Thought of Percy Bysshe Shelley* [Princeton: Princeton University Press, 1982], 208, 198). Richard Holmes calls *The Mask* "the greatest poem of political protest ever written in English" (*Shelly: The Pursuit* [1974; New York: Viking Penguin, 1987], 532); and to Paul Foot it is "one of the great political protest poems of all time" (*Shelley's Revolutionary Year: The Peterloo Writings of the Poet Shelley* [London: Redwords, 1990], 15).

51. My thinking about the ideological function of the unclosed frame has

been helped by Richard A. Burt's analysis of a similar phenomenon in *The Taming of the Shrew*, "Charisma, Coercion, and Comic Form in *The Taming of the Shrew*," *Criticism* 26 (1984): 295–311.

52. See his letter to Leigh Hunt, 23 December 1819, in *Letters of Percy Bysshe Shelley*, ed. Frederick L. Jones, 2 vols. (Oxford: Clarendon Press, 1964), 2:167. The sonnet was published much later than *The Mask of Anarchy*, for the first time (two decades after its composition) in Mary Shelley's edition of 1839.

53. Stuart Curran, *Poetic Form and British Romanticism* (New York: Oxford University Press, 1986), 55.

54. F.R. Leavis, *Revaluation: Tradition and Development in English Poetry* (1936; New York: George R. Steward, 1947), 228.

55. Timothy Webb, *Shelley: A Voice Not Understood* (Atlantic Highlands, N.J.: Humanities Press International, 1977), 107–108.

56. Paul de Man, "Seminology and Rhetoric," in *Allegories of Reading: Figural Language in Rousseau, Nietzsche, Rilke, and Proust* (New Haven: Yale University Press, 1979), 9.

57. And McGann does not comment on poetic form, although on the level of grammatical mood he discerns a sad ambivalence. For him, if *may* "hopes for a future promise, a glimpse of some far goal in time," its "subjunctive" is "deeply . . . allied to [a] sense of hoplessness" and, in this aspect, "the consciousness out of which Shelley's greatest works were created" (*Romantic Ideology*, 112–113).

58. *Letters of Percy Bysshe Shelley*, 2:167.

59. I tender my habitual, but no less grateful, thanks to Ronald Levao for alert, helpful, and sympathetic attention to this essay; I also thank William Keach for his careful reading and generous conversation.

■ WILLIAM KEACH ■

"Words Are Things"

Romantic Ideology and the Matter of Poetic Language

CURRENT CRITIQUES OF THE aesthetic bear more sharply on Romanticism than on any other period of cultural history. The discourse of the "aesthetic" that culminates in Germany in the formulations of Kant, Schiller, and Hegel, and that finds its closest English counterpart in the efforts of Wordsworth, Coleridge, and Shelley to define the "poetic," laid the foundations of an "ideology" (in Marx's and Engel's—not in Destutt de Tracy's or Napoleon's—sense of the term) that is now under intense critical pressure. The most telling pressure has come from historicist and materialist directions—from Jerome McGann, John Barrell, David Simpson, Jon Klancher, Marjorie Levinson, Anne Janowitz, Clifford Siskin, and, as part of a much broader analytical agenda, from Terry Eagleton. But poststructuralism, as Christopher Norris has shown, has had its own reasons for needing to deconstruct the pre-Romantic and Romantic sources of the aesthetic.[1] Paul de Man's late essays on "Phenomenality and Materiality in Kant" and "Aesthetic Formalization: Kleist's *Über das Marionettentheater*" offer revealing and influential accounts of aesthetic ideology's seductive entrapments.[2]

There is no reason in my view to try to protect Romantic ideologies of the aesthetic or the poetic from these critiques, for the simple reason that such critiques are, with varying degrees of accuracy, correct. But there is every reason to hold onto the "aesthetic" and the "poetic" as historically specific conceptualizations of great value, as urgent and contradictory discourses in which the effort to value formal design—or accident—in the work and play of cultural production generates problems that haven't been fully resolved in our own attempts to escape from ideology into "theory" or "science."

There may even be a strange kind of testimony to the prevailing pertinence of Romantic articulations of the aesthetic in the fact that historical materialists and poststructuralists have sometimes found themselves in surprising agreement about the problem, and the problematic, of the aesthetic. Eagleton is "glad to observe a certain unexpected convergence" between his own and de Man's "demystification of the idea of the aesthetic," and—despite his dismay at de Man's "unremitting hostility to the practice of political emancipation"—he is "in entire agreement" with the argument that "aesthetic ideology, by repressing the contingent, aporetic relation which holds between the spheres of language and the real, naturalizes or phenomenalizes the former, and is thus in danger of converting the accidents of meaning to organic natural process in the characteristic manner of ideological thought."[3] De Man, for his part, focuses in the two essays I've cited on the question of "materiality" (or "materialism") and the aesthetic to a degree that seems surprising from the perspective of most of his earlier work. This focus, along with his insistence that "the aesthetic . . . is primarily a social and political model" and his (unelaborated) emphasis on "*historical* modes of language power," brings his analysis closer to the concerns characteristic of the tradition in which Eagleton stands than one would have thought possible.[4]

What such unexpected convergences indicate, I think, is that in its founding historical moment, the ideology of the aesthetic poses questions about the cultural valuing of formal articulation that neither poststructuralism nor Marxism, with their opposed assumptions about history and about social and discursive totality and determination, have been able definitively to answer. The Marxist critique, with its point of departure in *The German Ideology,* has been powerfully effective in exposing the idealizations and mystifications of Romantic ideologies of the aesthetic. We have been able to see how ideas of the aesthetic developed as responses to historically specific contradictions within bourgeois capitalist culture in its moment of emergent dominance; how Romantic ideologies of the aesthetic and of the poetic characteristically idealize a union or integration of opposed, alienated modes of experience (as in the Romantic symbol) and suspend or bracket the kind of practical activity that inevitably threatens such idealizations (as in the Kantian judgment of taste). The Marxist critical tradition has been less successful, however, in generating an alternative positive account of our responses to form. Formalism, and the aspects of art and literature that constitute its focus, have been relentlessly critiqued under the categories of reification, commodification, and fetish. Or, less often, they have been recognized as legitimate if limited manifestations of cultural activity, as in

Trotsky's repeated acknowledgment in *Literature and Revolution* of a "law of art." But Marxism has as yet given us only glimpses—in the work of the Bakhtin circle, in Jameson's *Marxism and Form,* in Tony Bennett's *Formalism and Marxism*—of an adequate materialist understanding of formal values. The current task, as I see it, is to understand how critically to rethink and affirm the materiality of formal articulation in art and literature—not just in an imagined socialist future, but in cultural situations that remorselessly reify, commodify, fetishize such articulation. This is a version, of course, of what the Romantics themselves had to do, in economic and social circumstances that crucially anticipate our own. We have something to learn by returning to the old sites of Romantic contradiction and resistance with a sense of sympathetic or perhaps rueful self-recognition, rather than of triumphant or cynical superiority. What we will find there are efforts to validate as well as to escape from the materiality of form in artistic representation—in the instances I want to explore here, efforts to come to terms with that aspect of language that makes it a part of material reality and that gets foregrounded rather than denied in literary form and style.

This essay traces questions of material form and aesthetic ideology as they appear in English Romantic understandings of poetic language. The sign or signature of these questions in most of the texts I'll be looking at is the claim that "words are things"—a claim that in shifting and conflicting ways will take us from affirmations and interrogations of the material efficacy of the Romantic symbol to confrontations with the marketing and consumption of literary texts—with the transformation of poems into commodities. As I've just indicated, my argument is guided by a belief that current demystifications of the aesthetic reveal a good deal about our own unfinished critical work as well as about the limitations and inconsistencies of Romantic ideology.

▪   ▪   ▪

In an often-quoted letter of 22 September 1800, Coleridge said to William Godwin:

> I wish you to write a book on the power of words, and the processes by which human feelings form affinities with them—in short, I wish you to *philosophize* Horn Tooke's System, and to solve the great Questions—whether there be reason to hold, that an action bearing all the *semblance* of pre-designing Consciousness may yet be simply organic, & whether a *series* of such actions are possible—and close on the heels of this question would follow the

old "Is Logic the *Essence* of Thinking?" in other words—Is *Thinking* impossible without arbitrary signs? &—how far is the word "arbitrary" a misnomer? Are not words &c parts & germinations of the Plant? And what is the Law of their Growth?—In something of this order I would endeavor to destroy the old antithesis of *Words & Things,* elevating, as it were, words into Things, & living Things too.[5]

Byron also, at various moments in his life as a writer, denies "the old antithesis," but his ways of doing so are, if not antithetical to, mainly at odds with the emphasis of Coleridge's "elevating" endeavor. Most famously in canto 3 of *Don Juan,* the narrator observes that poets "in these times" are all said to be "such liars," reflecting on the performance of a court poet whose situation is remarkably made to connect Robert Southey's career with Byron's own:

> But words are things, and a small drop of ink,
>   Falling like dew, upon a thought, produces
> That which makes thousands, perhaps millions, think. . . .
>   (3, st. 88)[6]

For Byron, the power of words as things comes not from any transcendent coalescing of verbal signs with natural objects perceived through the impassioned imagination, but rather—as Kurt Heinzelman so impressively shows—from a complexly practical grasp, at once ambitious and anxious, of printing and publishing. *Don Juan* is "overtly—even self-consciously—conscious of its own status as a commodity," Heinzelman observes; "The Byron of the *Don Juan* period not only accepts income from his work but is acutely aware that 'Byron' is both a political and a saleable 'thing.'"[7] The socioeconomic and political perspectives on words-as-things opened up by Heinzelman need to be extended—and they need to be linked to questions about linguistic representation such as those posed in Coleridge's letter to Godwin. In the lines from canto 3 of *Don Juan,* the way in which "ink" gets formally taken up into its rhyming partner "think" is, as Sheila Emerson suggests, emblematic of the productive material force Byron attributes to the recognition that "words are things."[8] Such argumentative rhyming calls attention to its own phonetic and graphic materiality as one of the means by which the passage "produces" the responses Byron imagines.

The issues raised divergently by Coleridge and Byron belong to fundamental debates in eighteenth- and early nineteenth-century thinking about language. They also, of course, engage a wide range of recent theoretical work. Michel Foucault never explicitly addresses the claim that "words are things" in *Les mots et les choses,* but his version of the old belief in a radical "break" between classical and Romantic attitudes to language offers one possible model for understanding why Coleridge in his way, and Byron in his, want to "destroy the old antithesis of *Words & Things.*" If the Enlightenment really held, as Foucault says, that words provide a spontaneous and transparent representational "table" or "grid for the knowledge of things," and if "at the beginning of the nineteenth century, [words] rediscovered their ancient, enigmatic density" and withdrew from representation into their own immanent order, then Coleridge and Byron might be read as articulating their own awareness of such an epistemic crisis.[9] I trust it is clear from my summary of the Foucauldian position that I don't find it historically or conceptually convincing. I want to introduce it here, though, because it's an influential and relevant account of shifting relations between words and things that needs to be worked through, and because it contains local insights that may prove helpful in thinking about the questions I'm pursuing. Foucault points out, for instance, that already in the *Port-Royal Logic* and in Condillac we find a recognition that the verbal sign "in order to function, must be simultaneously an insertion in that which it signifies and also distinct from it."[10] This is an important insight, and I'll return to it later. As for Foucault's general position on these matters, he is most persuasive when he says, in *The Archaeology of Knowledge,* that " 'Words and things' is the entirely serious title of a problem," of the ironically revealed "task" of "no longer treating discourses as groups of signs . . . but as practices that systematically form the objects of which they speak."[11]

Further poststructuralist help in thinking about words-as-things might be sought, and sporadically found, in Lacan's doctrine of what he variously calls the "autonomy," "supremacy," or "materiality of the signifier," and especially in such Marxist efforts to enlist Lacan in the quest for a materialist theory of language as Rosalind Coward and John Ellis's *Language and Materialism* and Michel Pecheux's *Language, Semantics, and Ideology.* But the trouble with the Lacanian doctrine and its Marxist appropriations is that in isolating the physical (phonetic or graphic) aspect of the verbal sign from the larger manifold and changing semiotic entity of which it is by definition a part, we may end up with a conceptually weak and ultimately trivializing kind of materialist stance. Fredric Jameson objects to efforts to ground a "genuinely materialistic view" of language in "the Lancanian notion of a 'material signifier' " by arguing that "Marxism is . . . not a mechanical but a historical materialism: it does not assert the primacy of matter so much as it insists on an ultimate determination by the mode of production."[12] Derek Attridge cites this passage from *The Political Unconscious* in support of his own more focused and pertinent argument that an "account of 'poetic' language as involving a heightened awareness of the production of meaning by language is . . . more amenable to a materialist philosophical (and political) position than an emphasis on the material signifier alone."[13] The curious phonetic and graphic connection of "ink" to "think" in Byron's rhyme is powerfully provoking not because of any "supremacy" or "autonomy" established by the physical properties of the signifiers themselves, but because the rhyming connection is a key part of a productive relationship between two signs that are themselves part of the way in which the entire passage generates its social, economic, and political meanings.

To see what's theoretically at stake in Romantic assertions that words are things, it's helpful to look back past Coleridge and remind ourselves of just how insistent Enlightenment philosophy had been in driving words and things apart. We tend to remember Thomas Sprat's ideal of a "close, naked, natural" scientific prose that would deliver "so many *things, almost in an equal number of words,*"[14] and Jonathan Swift's wonderful parodic satire of this ideal in the Academy of Lagado's "Scheme for entirely abolishing all Words whatsoever" by refusing any representation of things at all.[15] But behind both Sprat's ideal and Swift's parody is the philosophical recognition, misleadingly downplayed by Foucault, that words are related to things not directly and transparently, but indirectly and arbitrarily. "*Words in their primary or immediate Signification,*" writes Locke in book 3 of the *Essay Concerning Human Understanding,* "*stand for nothing but the Ideas in the Mind of him that uses them,* how imperfectly soever, or carelessly, those *Ideas* are collected from the Things, which they are supposed to represent" (3.2.2).[16] Words are primarily the signs of ideas, and only secondarily of things: Locke's clear implication is that even if our ideas were perfectly and carefully derived from things, the primary signifying relation between word and idea could carry no guarantee of transparency and stability. Swift's satire hardly touches this aspect of Locke's position, which may best be summarized in his skeptical formulation of the "double Conformity" concept in book 2 of the *Essay:* "Men are so forward to suppose, that the abstract *Ideas* they have in their Minds, are such, as agree to the Things existing with them, to which they are referr'd; and are the same also, to which the Names they give them, do by the Use and Propriety of that Language belong. For without this *double Conformity* of the *Ideas,* they find, they should both think amiss of Things in themselves, and talk of them unintelligibly to others" (2.32.8).

It is commonplace to read Romantic endeavors such as Coleridge's "to destroy the old antithesis of *Words & Things*" as projects (once regarded as triumphs, now more often as mystifications) to overcome the gaps and slippages acknowledged in Locke's analysis of "double Conformity." Less common are recognitions of the degree to which recent deconstructions of the Romantic symbol (like de Man's) are anticipated in Enlightenment thinking itself. From this perspective, the assertion that "words are things" may be read as a truculent, truncated defiance of Lockean semiotics. But this reading doesn't really take in the force of Byron's version of the claim, with its concern for words as material text and as commodity. For this, we need to go back and connect what Locke says about the "Propriety" of language with what he says about "property," and work forward through Adam Smith and David Ricardo until we can reimagine historically what kind of status as an economic "thing" early nineteenth-century writers could attribute to a text, to a literary "thing" made out of language. Heinzelman has begun this process, and without in any sense claiming to have achieved a comparable further movement of socioeconomic and linguistic integration, I want very briefly to suggest extensions in the direction of Romantic thinking about language. One way of beginning to pose the problem in Lockean terms might be to set the commitment to "Natural Law" on which his analysis of property is grounded against the consistently conventionalist and institutionalist assumptions of his analysis of language, and to ask: If the "right" or "title" to property derives from the appropriation and transformation of nature by human labor for human use, what "right" or "title" to property can derive from work on and in language, which for Locke originates not in any "natural connexion" but in "arbitrary imposition?" Is language inherently enough like money to place any property made from it outside the range of Locke's labor theory of value? In Locke's theory, we recall, it is "the *invention of Money,* and the tacit agreement of Men to put a value on it, introduced (by Consent)," that disrupts the natural constrains on the accumulation of property, and thus its allegedly self-governing social function.[17]

▪   ▪   ▪

I'll come back to some of these questions in a direct way when I come back to Byron. For the moment, I want to pursue more indirect linguistic directions by working my way further inside Coleridge's view of words-as-things, and now also Wordsworth's. Perhaps the best known of all Romantic claims that "words are things" is the one Wordsworth makes in his 1800 note to "The Thorn." The specific occasion for the claim is his defense of "repetition and apparent tautology" in the language of "The Thorn" and of other poems in *Lyrical Ballads,* on the ground that in attempting "to communicate impassioned feelings" a "speaker will cling to the same words, or words of the same character."[18] "There are also various other reasons why repetition and apparent tautology are frequent beauties of the highest kind," Wordsworth continues: "Among the chief of these reasons is the interest which the mind attaches to words, not only as symbols of the passion, but as *things,* active and efficient, which are of themselves part of the passion." Frances Ferguson says in commenting on Wordsworth's note that it "puts into question the primacy of the symbol in literary language."[19] But in fact Wordsworth's setting not words-as-signs but words-as-"symbols" in opposition to words-as-"things" disguises the way in which he offers, under this latter category, a compressed version of "symbol" as Coleridge famously defines it in *The Statesman's Manual*: "A symbol . . . always partakes of the reality which it renders intelligible; and while it enunciates the whole, abides itself as a living part in that unity of which it is the representative."[20] In this sense "symbols" are "things" for Coleridge, and his definition shares with Wordsworth's note a Romantic rewriting of that recognition that Foucault locates in Enlightenment theory: the verbal sign "must be simultaneously an insertion in that which it signifies and also distinct from it." For Wordsworth more emphatically than for Coleridge, what makes words take on the force of things is passion. Behind the theoretical claim of Wordsworth's note we should hear and feel the force of all those moments in his writing when "things," under the pressure of passion, come movingly, hauntingly to life—and when other people are loved, valued, and mourned as "things":

> A motion and a spirit, that impels
> All thinking things, all object of all thought,
> And rolls through all things
> ("Tintern Abbey," 100–102)[21]

> ye who pore
> On the dead letter, miss the spirit of things. . . .
> (1850 *Prelude*, 8.296–297)

> As a huge stone is sometimes seen to lie
> Couched on the bald top of an eminence;
> Wonder to all who do the same espy,
> By what means it could thither come, and whence;
> So that it seems a thing endued with sense. . .
> ("Resolution and Independence," 57–61)

> No mate, no comrade Lucy knew;
> She dwelt on a wide moore,
> —The sweetest thing that ever grew
> Beside a human door!
> ("Lucy Gray," 5–8)

> She seemed a thing that could not feel
> The touch of earthly years.
> ("A Slumber Did My Spirit Seal," 3–4)

Contextualized in this way, Wordsworth's sense of words-as-things seems to recede from any obvious emphasis on the materiality of language. And of course "things" recurrently lose their materiality in Wordsworth. The childhood moment recollected in the Fenwick note to the "Intimations Ode" is paradigmatic in this regard: "I was often unable to think of external things as having external existence, and I communed with all that I saw as something not apart from, but inherent in, my own immaterial nature" (*Poetical Works* 4:463). This relation to things is predominant throughout Wordsworth's writing—so that when the thorn itself in the first stanza of that poem is seen as "a wretched thing forlorn" (9), we connect it retrospectively with "our mortal Nature" and its capacity to "tremble like a guilty thing surprised" ("Intimations Ode," 146–147). Words are things for Wordsworth when things are spirits, or ghosts.

Nowhere are the complications in Wordsworth's attitude towards words-as-things more apparent than in what he says about books-as-things in book 5 of *The Prelude*. At the beginning of this book, thoughts about the materialization of spirit in printed words produce generalized elegiac lamentations:

> thou also, man! hast wrought,
> For commerce of thy nature with herself,
> Things that aspire to unconquerable life;
> And yet we feel—we cannot choose but feel—
> That they must perish.
> (5.18–22)

Books for Wordsworth are preeminently "things that aspire," and the contradictoriness of that perception compels him to ask

> why hath not the Mind
> Some element to stamp her image on
> In nature somewhat nearer to her own?
> (5.45–47)

The word "stamp" here is one of many indications in book 5 of the material concreteness of Wordsworth's anxiety about books as objects. Even a volume of Shakespeare or Milton, when "held . . . in my hand," seems but a "poor earthly casket of immortal verse" (5.163–164). This figure of the book as tomb or sepulcher haunts even such moments of recollected pleasure as the memory of the "little yellow, canvas-covered book" of Arabian tales, since Wordsworth's regarding it as "but a block hewn from a mighty quarry" links it to tombstones, his favorite image for writing that is at once more permanently materialized than a book and more at home with matters of the spirit, with "a promise scarcely earthly" (5.460–468). The ostensible resolution of these broodings on the material word as a matter of life and death resides in appeals to "Nature," when he affirms for example, "This verse is dedicate to Nature's self, / And things that teach as Nature teaches" (15.230–231). Yet at the end of book 5, the realm of things that words come to inhabit is again undeniably sepulchral:

> Visionary power
> Attends the motions of the viewless winds,
> Embodied in the mystery of words:
> There, darkness makes abode, and all the host
> Of shadowy things work endless changes. . . .
>
> (5.595–598)

As embodiments of thought or spirit, in becoming "things" words for Wordsworth enter a realm of frail mortality and perishable materiality that is the precondition of their passing over into "visionary power."

Wordsworth agrees with Coleridge that words may become "living things"—"active and efficient," as he says in the note to "The Thorn"—but for him this means that they also become mortal, perishable things. The way Wordsworth differs from Coleridge is accentuated by a passage from one of Coleridge's notebooks: "The focal word has acquired a *feeling* of *reality*—it heats and burns, makes itself be felt. If we do not grasp it, it seems to grasp us, as with a hand of flesh and blood, and completely counterfeits an immediate presence, an intuitive knowledge."[22] Here words are not so much reified as personified. And despite Coleridge's self-consciousness about the rhetorical figure ("seems to grasp us, as with a hand," "counterfeits"), the emphasis is on words themselves, not on writer or reader, as active agents. In the note to "The Thorn," Wordsworth characteristically balances such an awareness of words-as-living-things against his recognition of "the interest which the mind attaches to words." That "the mind" here may refer to the poet, to the dramatized fictive speaker, or to the reader is consistent with Heinzelman's argument that Wordsworth ideally sees writer and reader engaged in an act of "reciprocal labor," though I would want to argue that the reciprocity is less a matter of stable cooperation than of power struggle—of "mutual domination" and "interchangeable supremacy," to adopt Wordsworth's language for the interaction between mind and nature in the final book of *The Prelude* (14.78–86).[23] Most conspicuous in Wordsworth and Coleridge are the curious ways in which words-as-things testify not to language as a material process or product, but to the mind's privileged work in giving life to all things, including words.

In Coleridge we can see a concerted effort to counter materialist accounts that identify words as things as well as Lockean accounts that insist on their discrepancy. (It has to be acknowledged that by the end of the eighteenth century Locke's position had been interpreted along increasingly sensationalist—and in that limited sense materialist—lines.) Coleridge was fascinated, as James McKusick has shown, with Horne Tooke's etymological derivation of *think* from *thing,* on the model of the Latin noun *res* and its dubious derivative, the verb *reor,* "I think, I imagine."[24] According to Horne Tooke, "*Res,* a thing, gives us *Reor,* i.e. I am *thing-ed.* . . . [W]here we now say, I *think,* the antient expression was—*Me thinketh,* i.e. *me thing-eth, It Thingeth me.*"[25] In an 1806 notebook entry Coleridge cribs Horne Tooke's speculative etymology and, with an almost malicious self-delight, inverts it, as McKusick says, "to support the idealist position that things are generated by thought and have no logical priority to consciousness":[26]

> Reo = reor probably an obsolete Latin word, and res the second person singular of the Present Indicative—If so, it is the Iliad of Spinozo-Kantian, Kanto-Fichtian, Fichto-Schellingian Revival of Plato-Plotino-Proclian Idealism in a Nutshell *from* a Lilliput Hazel. Res = thou art thinking. —Even so our "Thing": id est, thinking or think'd. Think, Thank, Tank = Reservoir of what has been *thinged.* (*Notebooks* 2, #2784; Jan. 1806)[27]

That Coleridge and Tooke are both in the dark as to the most likely etymological origins of *thing* (it comes from Old English and Old Norse sociopolitical words meaning "meeting" or "public assembly") is less interesting here than the divergent efforts they both make to coerce *things* to their respective ideological and philosophical perspectives. Coleridge deploys his *think–thing* etymology recurrently in later notebook entries, for instance in 1809: "Words as distinguished from mere pulses of Air in the auditory nerve must correspond to thoughts, and thoughts is but the verb-substantive Participle Preterite of *Thing.* . . . [A] thing acts on me but not on me as purely passive, which is the case in all *affection,* affectus, but res agit in coagentum—in the first, I am *thinged,* in the latter I thing or think" (*Notebooks* 3, #3587; July–Sept. 1809). Coleridge understandably bypasses that aspect of words that might identify their thing-ness as pure phonetic signifier ("mere pulses of Air in the auditory nerve"), but instead of going on to inquire into the production of linguistic meaning as a material social process, he identifies words-as-things with an originary perceptual activity in the mind. His inversion of Tooke's false etymology has again become an algorithm for idealist epistemological play.

Coleridge was philosophically interested in puns; and in an 1810 note-book entry that mentions "my intended Essay in defence of Punning," he appears to be on the point of devoting sustained attention to the phonetic, if not the graphic or economic, materiality of language. Again, though, his concern with words-as-things veers off in another direction—this time in a direction signaled by one "Mʳ Whiter of Clare Hall," who attempted to show, Coleridge says, "that words are not mere symbols of things & thoughts, but themselves things—and that any harmony in the things sym-bolized will perforce be presented to us more easily as well as with addi-tional beauty by a correspondent harmony of the Symbols with each other" (*Notebooks* 3, #3762; 1810). This is more than a familiar-sounding specula-tion on verbal mimesis. Coleridge is inspired here by Walter Whiter's *Ety-mologicon Magnum or Universal Etymological Dictionary* (1800) and its introductory argument that phonetic patterns, even when they don't imi-tate properties of things as in onomatopoeia, still correspond to the order-ing of things in nature. Whiter inspires Coleridge's notion that words become things because they correspond to them, not according to older Adamic or Cratylean theories of linguistic mimesis, but according to prin-ciples of harmony simultaneously and congruently at work in the physical world and in language. Words are things in this sense because they operate according to principles of order that also govern things, principles that ulti-mately derive from the structure of the creative mind. It is as if the rules governing the deep structures of language in the Chomskyan sense were transformations of the laws of physics. Words-as-things thus get swept up in the grand theoretical project of the Coleridgean Logos: the infinite mind of God externalizes or embodies itself in a created natural world that is the text of divine utterance, capable of being read by the finite human mind with its imperfect linguistic resources. As Coleridge promises his infant son in "Frost at Midnight":

> so shalt thou see and hear
> The lovely shapes and sounds intelligible
> Of that eternal language, which thy God
> Utters, who from enternity doth teach
> Himself in all, and all things in himself.
> (58–62)[28]

Things are the words of God; God's words are things. This is not what the Byron of *Don Juan* 3 has in mind.

To say that Coleridge's position on words-as-things resembles in sev-eral respects the Renaissance order of things as characterized by Foucault is to recognize one of the ways in which nineteenth-century thinking about language looks backwards rather than forwards. In American writing

Ralph Waldo Emerson continues and amplifies the Coleridgean vision, with some additional help from Swedenborg, when he says in *Nature* that "The use of the outer creation [is] to give us language for the beings and changes of the inward creation. . . . It is not words only that are emblematic; it is things which are emblematic."[29] Though the roots of this conception of language—in opposition to the Lockean emphasis on language as a humanly constructed system of arbitrary signs—are essentially theological, it has in spite of itself led to rich speculation on the power of material things as constituents of or constraints on verbal meaning.

A remarkable late experiment in the Coleridgean-Emersonian vein is Kenneth Burke's quirkily insightful essay, first published in the 1962 number of *Anthropological Linguistics* and collected in *Language as Symbolic Action,* called "What Are The Signs of What? A Theory of 'Entitlement.'" "What might be discovered," Burke asks, "if we tried inverting [the customary view that 'words are the signs of things'], and upholding instead the proposition 'that things are the signs of words'?"[30] What Burke discovers is the way in which "things of the world become material exemplars of the values which the tribal idiom has placed upon them." There are, as Burke is aware, curious logical difficulties with the "inversion" he entertains, particularly with what happens to the phrase "signs of" (things can be thought of as "signs of" words only if they are already discursive constructs). Still, his analysis of how things or "thing-situations" may come to function as abbreviations or summaries of verbal expressions can help us understand an important aspect of social figuration in Romantic writing. It can help us grasp the force of that late remark by the conservative Coleridge in *Table Talk* that ironically anticipates, as Heinzelman observes in quoting it, Marx's ideas of alienation and human reification: "It is not uncommon for 100,000 *operatives* (mark this word, for words *in this sense* are things) to be out of employment at once in the cotton districts, and, thrown upon parochial relief, to be dependent upon hard-hearted task-masters for food."[31] The word "operatives" has become a thing because the workers to whom it was applied in early industrialized Britain are treated as things, as mechanical functions. In Burke's terms, these workers stand as signs, "material exemplars," of the social relations implicit in the "tribal idiom" of early nineteenth-century capitalism.

▪ ▪ ▪

In Coleridge and Wordsworth the belief that words are, or may become, things reveals contradictory ways of linking the political and the linguistic in their ideologies of the poetic—linkages that idealize but also expose the limits of English "nature" and English national culture as independent sources of value. The links we've just been looking at can also provide useful points of departure for exploring very different relations of words to things in Blake and Shelley, differences that have inevitably to do with distinctively Blakean and Shelleyan forms of the connection between visionary idealism and radical politics. Within the constraints of this essay, however, I need to postpone such exploration and return, as promised, to Byron.

"I have not loved the world, nor the world me,—/ But let us part fair foes" Byron wrote in that summer of 1816, when Mary Shelley was conceiving in words her monstrous "living thing" and Percy Shelley speculating in the verse of *Mont Blanc* on how "the everlasting universe of things flows through the mind." Byron continues,

> I do believe,
> Though I have found them not, that there may be
> Words which are things . . .
> (*Childe Harold* 3, st. 114)

This is the most striking occasion in Byron's writing when the claim that "words are things" fails him; it's telling that it comes in a text where the relation of words to things is made so much a matter of isolated psychic expression and projection into nature, rather than of pragmatic social and cultural efficacy. These lines near the end of *Childe Harold* 3 echo, of course, the climactic anticlimax of the storm on the Lake of Geneva seventeen stanzas earlier, and specifically Byron's professed inability to "throw / Soul, heart, mind, passions, feelings . . . into *one* word, / And that one word were Lightning" (3, st. 97). The only "thing" fit to be identified with Byron's "word" at this moment is lightning, and Byron makes high drama of the fact that his words here can only name and refer to, not become, that thing. But as the Byron of *Don Juan* 3 realizes, written and printed words become things in senses unintended by their author, unacknowledged by the words themselves. In John Murray's 1832–1833 ottavo edition of *The Works of Lord Byron,* an engraved facsimile of the manuscript of stanza 92 of *Childe Harold* 3, where the Alpine thunder and lightning is said to give "every mountain . . . a tongue," is offered to the purchasers of this edition "as dashed off by Lord Byron, in June, 1816, during one of his evening excursions on the Lake of Geneva." The facsimile appears not in volume 8, which contains the text of *Childe Harold,* but at the beginning of volume 9, along with engraved scenes of Petrarch's tomb and of Seville, as an artifact whose value no longer depends on its original poetic context. We are directed by the editor, Thomas Moore, to look back at volume 8 for Sir Walter Scott's praise of this "thunder-storm . . . described in verse almost as vivid as its lightnings." Scott's "almost" indicates that he accepts Byron's claim not to have found "one word" that was "Lightning." Yet Byron's words about lightning have become a thing with a cultural and economic life of its own.

Prior to the momentary and strategic demurral at the end of *Childe Harold* 3, Byron twice invokes "words are things" as a maxim he approves of in contexts that are overtly political and social. On 16 November 1813, he writes in his journal about attending a performance of *Antony and Cleopatra* the previous night with Monk Lewis. Byron is clearly, though somewhat defensively, partial to Antony: "Why do they abuse him for cutting off that poltroon Cicero's head? Did not Tully tell Brutus it was a pity to have spared Antony? and did he not speak the Phillippics? and are not '*words*[s] *things?*' and such '*words*' very pestilent '*things*' too? If he had had a hundred heads, they deserved (from Antony) a rostrum (his way stuck up there) apiece—though, after all, he might as well have pardoned him, for the credit of the thing."[32] A year after he had made his own first parliamentary speech opposing the Frame-Breaking Bill in the House of Lords, Byron is obviously fascinated with political oratory that is "performative" and "illocutionary" (to use J.L. Austin's terms): Cicero's accusations against Antony, Antony's potential pardon and actual order of execution—these are classic instances of words as acts, deeds, "things" of state. Subsequent references to Madame de Staël (who "*talks* folios") and Sheridan (whose talk kept Byron, Rogers, and Moore entertained "without one yawn from six till one in the morning") link this journal entry to a letter to Rogers dated 27 February [1814(?)]. The occasion is Byron's making an excuse for not attending one of Madame de Staël's soirées: "I believe that I need not add one [an excuse] for not accepting Mr. Sheridan's invitation on Wednesday, which I fancy both you and I understand in the same sense:—with him the saying of Mirabeau, that '*words* are *things*,' is not to be taken literally" *Letters and Journals* 4:74). Byron liked Sheridan and had admired his famous Parliamentary speeches—but "Poor dear Sherry!" had become a drunken parody of the great orator. The maxim Byron associates with Cicero and Mirabeau is pathetically deflated in the joke he shares with the impeccably self-possessed Rogers: even Sheridan's dinner invitations are no longer to be treated as real things.

I've paused over these early instances of Byron's thinking of words as things because their emphasis on speech contrasts so pointedly with the emphasis on writing in canto 3 of *Don Juan*. The attitude towards language in this canto implicates both the predatory mercantilism of Lambro's piracy and the sumptuous, fetishized materiality of the feast indulged in by Juan

and Haidée while Lambro is away. On his way home, we learn in stanza 15,
Lambro

> had chain'd
> His prisoners, dividing them like chapters
> In number'd lots; they all had cuffs and collars,
> And averaged each from ten to a hundred dollars.

Lambro is "a man who seldom used a word / Too much," we are told, preferring instead to move men "with the sword": the odd way in which *word*
gets taken up into *sword* in this stanza and yet rhymes with it only to the eye,
not to the ear, bears a diacritical relation to the *ink/think* rhyme in *Don Juan*
3, st. 88 (and to *Childe Harold* 3, st. 97, where *word* also gets taken up into
sword but to quite different effect). The imagery of language and writing
carries over, in a different key, into the lush decoration of the hall where
Haidée's feast has been laid. The room is hung with demask tapestries, and
above these

> The upper border, richly wrought, display'd,
>   Embroider'd delicately o'er with blue,
> Soft Persian sentences, in lilac letters,
> From poets, or the moralists their betters.
>
> These oriental writings on the wall,
>   Quite common in those countries, are a kind
> Of monitors adapted to recall,
>   Like skulls at Memphian banquets, to the mind
> The words which shook Belshazzar in his hall,
>   And took his kingdom from him. . . .
>
> (Don Juan 3, st. 64–65)

These lines critically anticipate the lyric "The isles of Greece" sung by
Lambro's minstrel, and the narrator's comment on it, "But words are
things." In the hall's embroidered border, words are literally, opulently
materialized; at first the physical qualities of the "soft Persian sentences" appear to make any semantic content beside the point. But whether he reads
Persian or not, Byron knows that such "oriental writings" may pronounce
a death-sentence on the very sensuousness they embody—as in the account
of Belshazzar's feast in the book of Daniel, to which Bryon alludes: "They
drank wine, and praised the gods of gold, and of silver, of brass, of iron, of
wood, and of stone. In the same hour came forth fingers of a man's hand,
and wrote over against the candlestick upon the plaster of the wall of the
king's palace . . . Then the king's countenance was changed, and his
thoughts troubled him" (Dan. 5:4–6).

The stanzas that precede the performance of Lambro's minstrel should alert us to troubling strains in the "but words are things" passage that follow it. So should the reference to Cadmus in the minstrel's song itself: "You have the letters Cadmus gave—/Think ye he meant them for a slave?" ("The Isles of Greece," st. 10). Writing and luxurious consumption, writing and moral warning, writing and political decay: all these connections inform the lines following "But words are things." Here are the key stanzas:

> But words are things, and a small drop of ink,
>   Falling like dew, upon a thought, produces
> That which makes thousands, perhaps millions, think;
>   'Tis strange, the shortest letter which man uses
> Instead of speech, may form a lasting link
>   Of ages; to what straits old Time reduces
> Frail man, when paper—even a rag like this,
> Survives himself, his tomb, and all that's his.
>
> And when his bones are dust, his grave a blank,
>   His station, generation, even his nation,
> Become a thing, or nothing, save to rank
>   In chronological commemoration,
> Some dull MS oblivion long has sank,
>   Or Grave stone found in a barrack's station
> In digging the foundation of a closet,
> May turn his name up, as a rare deposit.
>   (*Don Juan* 3, st. 88–89)

When Byron wrote *Don Juan* 3, hundreds of thousands of copies of his words had been reproduced and sold; for more than two years he had foregone his earlier disdain for authors who wrote to make a living and—to cover the costs of indulgences that Balshazzar would have enjoyed—had accepted payments from the publisher he was making rich. If ever a writer appreciated the force of words-as-things in the full social, cultural, commercial meaning of this phrase, it was the Byron of *Don Juan* 3. And if he is astonished by the power of "ink" to make "thousands, perhaps millions, think," he is also appalled by the economic dispersal of his own thinking, his own identity, on material terms over which he has no control. In ways that connect him with the soldiers in the War Cantos whose identities are reduced to "three lines of a despatch" or citation in "a *bulletin*" (7, st. 20–21), Byron has no choice but to consign what Walter Benjamin would call his "aura" to "a rag like this," like *Don Juan,* and to the interests of those who will read him and write about him.

It is the aristocratic and enormously popular Lord Byron who, at the very moment when he is about to earn profits from his writing, articulates a more developed awareness of the reification of words than any of his contemporaries. This awareness permeates much of Byron's later work and continues to evolve in ways that carry complex political implications. Jerome Christensen has used Marcel Mauss's analysis of gifts-as-things to link the public and commercial appropriation of Byron's writing with other appropriations of his social identity: "Lord Byron bestows gifts . . . he gives because he is obliged by the thing given him, his title, which compels his return and in turn makes him a compelling thing."[33] This strikingly glosses the movement from "words are things" to the writer as "thing" in *Don Juan* 3, st. 88–89. Though the writer in these stanzas is imagined to be dead, the possibility that the living poet's very self and voice will be reified—transformed by publishers, booksellers, bookbuyers into a fetishized commodity—is a real threat. The social character of Byron's poetry can survive the impositions of market forces only for readers who recognize, as he did, its inevitable vulnerability to them.

▪ ▪ ▪

Terry Eagleton invites us to understand "the aesthetic as a kind of incipient materialism."[34] Just what kind or kinds of incipient or covert materialism the romantic "poetic" may contain is what this essay has tried to suggest. There is, of course, much more to do: we need a more comprehensive materialist analysis of Romantic philosophies of language and of Romantic poetic style, for one thing, to complement the excellent recent work on early nineteenth-century literary commodification and reception. But even the highly selective movement we've just followed from Coleridge and Wordsworth to the Byron of *Don Juan* clarifies the importance for romantic literary culture of Eagleton's describing the commodity, in his chapter on "The Marxist Sublime," as a "grisly caricature of the authentic [aesthetic] artefact."[35] And it may help us respond more resourcefully to the force of the remark from W.J.T. Mitchell's *Iconology* which Eagleton quotes: "The terms that Marx uses to characterise the commodity are drawn from the lexicon of Romantic aesthetics and hermeneutics."[36] This "lexicon" is immersed in an ideology of imaginative transcendence which Marx enables us to suspect and resist. But Marx's own indebtedness to the Romantic tradition with which he broke should remind us that the work of suspecting and resisting the ideology of the aesthetic begins, however partially and contradictorily, in Romanticism itself.

Notes

1. Christopher Norris, *Deconstruction and the Interests of Theory* (Leicester: Leicester University Press, 1988).

2. Paul de Man, "Phenomenality and Materiality in Kant," in *Hermeneutics: Questions and Prospects,* ed. Gary Shapiro and Alan Sica (Amherst: University of Massachusetts Press, 1984), 121–144; "Aesthetic Formalization" appears in Paul de Man, *The Rhetoric of Romanticism* (New York: Columbia University Press, 1984), 263–290.

3. Terry Eagleton, *The Ideology of the Aesthetic* (Oxford: Basil Blackwell, 1990), 10. Eagleton ends his comment on de Man by quoting the following "remarkable flash of prescience" from Gramsci's *Prison Notebooks:* "It could be asserted that Freud is the last of the Ideologues, and that de Man is also an 'ideologue'." It is part of Eagleton's joke here to let the reader figure out that Gramsci is referring to Henri de Man, Paul de Man's uncle, whose *Au-delà du Marxisme* Gramsci frequently criticizes; see Antonio Gramsci, *Selections from the Prison Notebooks,* ed. Quintin Hoare and Geoffrey Nowell-Smith (New York: International Publishers, 1971), 375–377.

4. De Man, *Rhetoric of Romanticism,* 264; for "*historical* modes of language power," see the end of "Anthropomorphism and Trope in Lyric," in ibid., 262.

5. *The Collected Letters of Samuel Taylor Coleridge,* ed. Earl Leslie Griggs, 6 vols. (Oxford: Clarendon Press, 1956–1971), 1:352.

6. All quotations of Byron's poetry are from George Gordon, Lord Byron, *The Complete Poetical Words,* ed. Jerome J. McGann, 5 vols. (Oxford: Clarendon Press, 1980–1986). What I say about Byron here is indebted to L. E. Marshall's "*Words* are *things:* Byron and the Prophetic Efficacy of Language," *Studies in English Literature* 25 (1985): 801–822.

7. Kurt Heinzelman, "Byron's Poetry of Politics: The Economic Basis of the 'Poetical Character,'" *Texas Studies in Language and Literature* 23 (1981): 361–388. For an excellent analysis of Keats's connection to some of the questions raised in this essay, see Heinzelman's "Self-Interest and the Politics of Composition in Keats's *Isabella,*" *ELH* 55 (1988), 159–193, and (on both Byron and Keats) Sonia Hofkosh, "The Writer's Ravishment: Women and the Romantic Author—The Example of Byron," in *Romanticism and Feminism,* ed. Anne K. Mellor (Bloomington: Indiana University Press, 1988). 93–114.

8. Sheila Emerson, "Byron's 'One Word': The Language of Self-Expression in *Childe Harold* III," *Studies in Romanticism* 20 (1981): 363–382.

9. Michel Foucault, *The Order of Things: An Archaeology of the Human Sciences* (New York: Random House, 1970), 238–242.

10. Ibid., 61.

11. Michel Foucault, *The Archaeology of Knowledge,* trans. A. M. Sheridan Smith (London: Tavistock, 1972), 49.

12. Fredric Jameson, *The Political Unconscious: Narrative as a Socially Symbolic Act* (Ithaca: Cornell University Press, 1981), 45.

13. Derek Attridge, *Peculiar Language: Literature as Difference from the Renaissance to James Joyce* (Ithaca: Cornell University Press, 1988), 154 n. 34. Attridge's entire chapter on "Literature as Imitation: Jakobson, Joyce, and the Art of Onomatopoeia" is pertinent to the semiotic dimension of my argument.

14. Thomas Sprat, *History of the Royal Society,* ed. Jackson I. Cope and Harold Whitmore Jones (St. Louis: Washington University Press, 1959), 27.

15. Jonathan Swift, *Gulliver's Travels,* ed. Herbert Davis (1726; Oxford: Basil Blackwell, 1959), 185.

16. All quotations from John Locke, *Essay Concerning Human Understanding,* are from Peter H. Nidditch's edition (Oxford: Clarendon Press, 1975); subsequent citations are, like this one, given parenthetically in the text.

17. John Locke, *Two Treatises of Government,* ed. Peter Laslett (Cambridge: Cambridge University Press, 1970), 292–293; see also 299–301.

18. William Wordsworth, *Lyrical Ballads: The Text of the 1798 Edition with the Additional 1800 Poems,* ed. R. L. Brett and A. R. Jones (London: Methuen, 1963), 283. Wordsworth's extended note on "The Thorn" first appeared in the 1800 edition of *Lyrical Ballads.*

19. Frances Ferguson, *Wordsworth: Language as Counter-Spirit* (New Haven: Yale University Press, 1977), 14.

20. *Lay Sermons,* ed. R. J. White, vol. 6 in *The Collected Works of Samuel Taylor Coleridge* (Princeton: Princeton University Press, 1972), 30.

21. All quotations, except for *The Prelude,* are from *The Poetical Works of William Wordsworth,* ed. Ernest de Selincourt and Helen Darbishire, 5 vols. (Oxford: Clarendon Press, 1940–1949). *The Prelude* is quoted from the Norton Critical Edition of the 1800, 1805, and 1850 texts, ed. M. H. Abrams, Stephen Gill, and Jonathan Wordsworth (New York: Norton, 1979).

22. From a notebook entry in MS. Egerton 2801, f. 145, quoted in *Inquiring Spirit: A Coleridge Reader,* ed. Kathleen Coburn (London: Routledge and Kegan Paul, 1951), 101.

23. Kurt Heinzelman, *The Economics of the Imagination* (Amherst: University of Massachusetts Press, 1980), 200.

24. James McKusick, *Coleridge's Philosophy of Language* (New Haven: Yale University Press, 1986), 48.

25. Horne Tooke, *The Diversions of Purley* (London, 1786–1805; rpt. Menston, England: Scolar Press, 1968), 2:405–406.

26. McKusick, *Coleridge's Philosophy of Language,* 48.

27. *The Notebooks of Samuel Taylor Coleridge,* ed. Kathleen Coburn (New York: Bollingen Foundation and Pantheon Books, 1961).

28. *The Complete Poetical Works of Samuel Taylor Coleridge,* ed. Ernest Hartley Coleridge, 2 vols. (Oxford: Clarendon Press, 1912).

29. Ralph Waldo Emerson, *Essays and Lectures,* ed. Joel Porte (New York: The Library of America, 1983), 20–21.

30. Kenneth Burke, *Language as Symbolic Action: Essays on Life, Literature, and Method* (Berkeley: University of California Press, 1966), 360–361.

31. Quoted in Heinzelman, *Economics of the Imagination,* 300 n. 40.

32. *Byron's Letters and Journals,* ed. Leslie A. Marchand (Cambridge: Har-

vard University Press, 1976–1982), 3:207. All subsequent quotations are from this edition and are cited parenthetically in the text.

33. Jerome Christensen, "Theorizing Byron's Practice: The Performance of Lordship and the Poet's Career," *Studies in Romanticism* 27 (1988); 487.

34. Eagleton, *Ideology of the Aesthetic,* 196.

35. Ibid., 208.

36. W.J.T. Mitchell, *Iconology* (Chicago: University of Chicago Press, 1986), 188.

IV

Liberatory Aesthetics

■ DEREK ATTRIDGE ■

Literary Form and the Demands of Politics

Otherness in J. M. Coetzee's *Age of Iron*

> The consequence is that they reject beauty and harmony and produce a
> mere chronicle of the "iron age."
>
> —*Georg Lukács*

DURING RECENT DECADES, there have been few places in which the writing
and reading of literature has been more tested by political exigencies and
expectations than the Republic of South Africa. The demand that the production and judgment of literature be governed by its immediate effectiveness in the struggle for change (or against change) has been immensely
powerful, and has given rise to a suspicion of anything appearing hermetic,
self-referential, formally inventive, or otherwise distant from the canons
and procedures of the realist tradition.[1] Despite the problems inherent in
the assumptions that literature can and should serve preexisting political
ends and that there is no space for other kinds of work alongside the popular
and overtly political, it seems to me that the challenge which such a situation directs at "elite art" and its claims cannot be ignored. Lessons learned in
South Africa have often proved valuable elsewhere, and the predicament
literature finds itself in there has implications which extend to writing and
reading in less politically fraught contexts.

The author who represents the best-known and most striking example
of the tension between innovative writing and political demands in contemporary South Africa is J. M. Coetzee.[2] From his first published fiction,
Dusklands (1974), to his sixth and most recent at the time of writing, *Age
of Iron* (1990), he has engaged with the political issues that have rent, and

continue to rend, his native country, most obviously colonialism and its legacy of racial, sexual, and economic oppression.[3] In the same series of works, he has used a variety of formal devices that disrupt the realistic surface of the writing, reminding the reader forcibly of the conventionality of the fictional text and inhibiting any straightforward drawing of moral or political conclusions. As a result, readers with strong convictions have sometimes found his novels insufficiently engaged with the contingencies of the South African situation, while Coetzee's own comments on his fiction and on the responsibility of the novelist have, if anything, added fuel to the fire.[4] However, these doubts about the novels' political efficacy, and the unusual demands which they make on the reader, have not prevented them from becoming internationally one of the most highly regarded contemporary fictional oeuvres in English, and though one must always be suspicious of the reasons for rapid canonization—it's possible that, despite Coetzee's efforts at defamiliarization, his novels are being read as reinforcements of entrenched ideologies, and it's obvious that the rapid accumulation of academic criticism is partly a function of the splendid opportunities they offer for interpretative and theoretical commentary—there is plenty of evidence that a large number of readers around the world find in his writing a peculiar power and urgency.[5]

It seems likely, therefore, that the formal singularity of Coetzee's works is an important part of their effectiveness as literature; what I wish to argue here is that this effectiveness is not separate from the importance these works have in the ethico-political realm, but rather that it constitutes that importance. Furthermore, I believe that this importance is considerable. Coetzee's handling of formal properties is bound up with the capacity of his work to engage with—to stage, confront, apprehend, explore—*otherness,* and in this engagement it broaches the most fundamental and widely significant issues involved in any consideration of ethics and politics.[6] I also believe that what happens in Coetzee's work, and in responses to it, is only a more dramatic version of the processes involved in all literary uses of the formal properties and potentialities of language.

The issue of otherness and its political ramifications is, of course, particularly acute in colonial and postcolonial writing, and has been much discussed. However, the link between this question and the formal practices of literature—and in particular the practices we label "modernist," of which Coetzee may be taken as a late exemplar—has not been given a great deal of consideration.[7] The reason for this is obvious: the category of form is closely associated with a tradition of literary (and more generally, artistic) commentary we can call "aestheticism" (recognizing that the term covers a wide variety of works and theories). And aestheticism—with modernism often adduced as a major example—is regarded as being defined precisely by the avoidance of political responsibility, by the vaunting of an artistic autonomy that has little interest in modes of otherness in cultural and political life. Yet the importance of form to literature needs no demonstrating; it is at the heart of every writer's practice, and any account of literature's difference from other textual activities and products—however guarded or problematized—must involve some version of it.

What is needed, in order to bring the issue back to the center of discussion, is an account of form—or rather of some of the properties of writing that have elicited this term—that does not fall into the dualisms of the aesthetic tradition. In particular, the opposition of form and content, which sets formal properties apart from any connection the work has to ethical, historical, and social issues, produces a highly reductive account of the operation of these properties. One familiar version of this tradition is the Romantic notion of "organic form" which, while arguing for the possibility of a perfect fit between form and content that would render them inseparable, nevertheless relies on a prior theoretical separation between them. Most claims for the importance of form in literature operate on this model, and it is very difficult to verbalize a positive response to the formal features of a work without using some version of the scheme whereby sound echoes sense, form enacts meaning. But unless we can rescue literary discourse from these oppositions, form will continue to be treated as something of an embarrassment to be encountered, and if possible evaded, on the way to a consideration of semantic, and thus historical, political, and ideological, matters. [8]

Without having the space to develop this suggestion very far (though in due course I shall attempt to exemplify some of its implications in Coetzee's writing), I want to propose as an initial step that we think of the literary text not as an object possessing a meaning or meanings but as an *act of signification*. [9] I leave open the double reference of this phrase—to an act of writing and an act of reading—because I wish to emphasize that both are productive of the text as literature. The act of reading is clearly a response to the act of writing, but the notion of "response" here is a complex one, since it is not merely a matter of an act calling forth a wholly secondary and subsidiary reaction, but of a reenactment that makes the "original" act happen, and happen differently with each such response.

In my choice of terms I am taking advantage of some of the language's polysemic potential. The multiple significance of the term "act" is highly apt, since the act of a literary work can be thought of as a deed, the imitation of a deed, and the record of a deed. The double function of "writing" and "reading" as verbs and nouns is useful, too, since they allow us to retain in the nominal use—"writing" as a physical object and "a reading" as a commentary—a sense of the acts that produced them, and in a way never cease to produce them. In the reading of the writing that is literature, one might say, meaning is both *formed* and *performed*; language functions, as it always does, to bring meaning into existence, but not as some kind of free-standing conceptual matter. Meaning remains inseparable from the language that constitutes it, and it cannot be carried away by the reader for use elsewhere.

In order for a literary work to take place, the act of reading must be responsive to its *uniqueness*. This is hardly a new or controversial assertion, but what is less easy to grasp is that such uniqueness exists not in opposition to some notion of generality but arises as a *product* of generality. The literary work is constituted, that is, not by an inviolable core but by the singular putting into play—while also testing and transforming—the set of shared codes and conventions that make up the institution of literature and the wider cultural formation of which it is part. Hence it is a uniqueness derived not from an unchanging essence but from a capacity to be endlessly transformed while remaining identifiable—within the institutional norms—as what it is. Therefore, a response which might be called "responsible," that would simultaneously reenact and bring into being the work *as literature* and not as something else, and as *this* work of literature and not another one, would be a response that takes into account as fully as possible, by restaging them, the work's own performances—of, for example, referentiality, metaphoricity, intentionality, and what we might call ethicity. A necessary condition for such a response would be careful attention to the work of reference, metaphor, intention, and ethics (prerequisites for the responsible reading of any text, as one relates it to its numerous contexts, past and present), since only through such attention can the work's staging of these relations be apprehended and shared. But this is not a sufficient condition: to go no further would be to treat the text as history, reportage, confession, sermon, or some other type of nonliterary discourse. To read the text as literature is to experience those modes as processes, not pathways to a final goal of self-sufficient meaning. Let me quickly add that this does not involve a reassertion of the traditional boundaries between literature and its textual others; on the contrary, it is to render those boundaries porous and problematic, since the "literariness" of *any* text would be the degree to which it is open to such a staging of the primary functions of language and discourse.

What I am trying to counter is a common view (implicit if not explicit) of the literary work as a static, self-sufficient, formal entity which, while it may be the product of historical processes and the occasion for various interpretations across time, is itself a fixed linguistic structure without a temporal or performative dimension—or, at most, a simple linear one derived from the necessary sequentiality of reading.[10] This view is usually attended by a sense of reverence for the formal object that is the literary text, whereas

I am arguing for an engagement with the text that recognizes, and capital-izes on, its potential for reinterpretation, for grafting into new contexts, for fission and fusion. At the same time, I do not want to suggest that literari-ness is merely a bogus category foisted on an undifferentiated body of texts by a certain ideology; there seems to me to be a real difference between a text that exists as an object to be interpreted (whose raison d'être *is* that final interpretation) and one which exists only in an act that unites a reading and a writing, between the presentation of truth and the performance or produc-tion (which is also a kind of suspension) of truth. That the same text may be both of these is not, as I see it, a major problem.[11]

What difference does this way of conceiving of literature make to our understanding of form? The properties which have gone under that name—sound-patterns, rhythm, syntactic variation, metaphorical elaboration, narrative construction, and so on—are precisely what call forth the performative response I have been describing.[12] The text's references—to history, to shared codes, to psychological states—in themselves invite only a referential reading; its moral pronouncements invite only a behavioral—or perhaps spiritual—response; its encoding of intention invites only a biographical reading; and so on. But when the language in which these rela-tions to the extratextual are established is significantly organized, when it has salient qualities which are not exhausted by these functions, we can say that they are being performed, that every reference outwards is also, and in the same gesture, a reference inwards, that every metaphor is also a staging of metaphoricity, every embodied intention an enactment of intentionality.

If the literary work exists as a unique act, then, that uniqueness is con-stituted by its form, understood as its singular performance of linguistic and cultural norms. But in this sense *form is always already meaning*; as an act of signification a literary work is meaning in motion, and there is no mo-ment, not even a theoretical one, at which it is possible to isolate a purely formal property—at least not without turning the literary text into some-thing else. The sounds or shapes of the text are *meaningful* sounds and shapes, and it is as such that they participate in the literary act.[13] The effect of this mobilization of meaning by formal properties is that it can never close down on a represented world, can never become solely the reflection of or pointer to a set of existents outside language. The question of meaning and reference is kept alive as a question; referentiality is enacted—but not simply endorsed—in every literary act. The literary text thus has available to it all the resources of meaningful language—it can prove, describe, evoke, cajole, move, warn, persuade, promise, or narrate in the most con-crete and convincing manner possible—without suffering the limitations imposed on purely instrumental language by the purposes which it must serve.[14] (The need to generate pleasure is perhaps the one requirement that remains, and this is a pleasure generated precisely by the performative—or, more accurately, performing and performed—dimension of literature that I am describing.) Literary form therefore produces (in conjunction, of course, with the assumptions and conventions of the literary institution which govern reading) a suspension of linguistic instrumentality, which we can think of as *blocking* the aesthetic urge to separate form from content and to assign content alone to the domain of ethics and politics.

Acts of literature do not operate directly upon the political realm; when literary works are politically effective in this direct way— *The Mask of Anarchy* or *The Ragged-Trousered Philanthropists,* for example—it is not their literariness that is crucial but some other quality or qualities (such as rhetorical or argumentative effectiveness, vividness of description, or modeling of utopian projects), and even then the effects have no predictable relation to the aims or nature of the work. But literature can act powerfully to hold the political and the ethical up for scrutiny by means of its power of suspension, momentarily dissociating them from their usual pressing context, performing the ethical decision and the political gesture. [15] It can do this only in a unique text, whose uniqueness is not some essential and transhistorical core but its singular staging, by means of its mobile signifying forms, of the manifold capacities of language; and this staging, we must remember, happens only through repeated acts of reading (or reading/writing) whereby the uniqueness is reenacted differently with each repetition.

In its blocking of both the aesthetic and the instrumental, the literary text fails to answer to our habitual needs in processing language; it thus estranges itself, presents itself as other, puts us under a certain obligation (to attend scrupulously, to suspend as far as we can our usual assumptions and practices, to translate the text into our terms only in the harsh awareness of the betrayal that this involves). [16] To respond fully to literature is to be responsively aware of that otherness, in the unique form that the text gives it, and of the demands it makes upon us. [17] Let me make it clear once more that "otherness" here is neither a mystical ideality nor an inviolable materiality, neither a Platonic Form nor a Kantian *Ding an sich.* The other—insofar as we can apprehend it at all—*is* the familiar, strangely lit, refracted, self-distanced. In literature it emerges, as I have been arguing, in the process of self-distancing and self-division achieved by the suspension and playing-out of our dominant linguistic and cultural relations. It is, in each text, a *singular* process; otherness cannot be generalized—which would mean that it could be coded, carried away, replicated—but must be staged *as* uniqueness, as untranscendable contingency.

To be sure, we cannot but read in terms of our own expectations and schemata; but it is this that makes the obligation to the other limitless, not subject to the rational procedures of interpretation and critical evaluation that necessarily remain the bread-and-butter activities in any reading. There is thus an ethical dimension to any act of literary signification, and there is also a sense in which the formally innovative text, the one that most estranges itself from the reader, makes the strongest ethical demand.[18] But of course ethics concerns persons and not texts, and this may sound like a rather cheap metaphorical point; if, however, the literary text is an act of signification (which is to say human signification), the demands it makes— to respect its otherness, to respond to its uniqueness, to avoid reducing it to the familiar and the utilitarian even while attempting to understand it— may be ethical in a fundamental, nonmetaphorical sense. Formal innovation (of the sort that matters in literature) is innovation in meaning, and is therefore a kind of ethical testing and experiment. Indeed, ethics may be the wrong word, implying as it does a philosophical conceptualization which the demands of otherness disturb.[19] Whatever else the "modernist" text may be doing (and all literary texts function as a number of things besides literature), it is, through its form, which is to say through its staging of human meanings and intentions, a challenge that goes to the heart of the ethico-political.

▪　▪　▪

Otherness, then, is at stake in every literary text, and in a particularly conspicuous way in the text that disrupts the illusions of linguistic immediacy and instrumentality. Among these texts are some in which the other is thematized as a central moral and political issue, and in these texts the capacity of formal techniques to stage otherness can be exploited with particular force and relevance. J. M. Coetzee's novels are cases in point. They can be read as a continued, strenuous enterprise in figuring alterity, a project which is at once highly local in its engagement with the urgent political and social problems of South Africa and widely pertinent in its posing of the question of otherness and its relation to language, culture, and knowledge. Figures of alterity recur in these novels, usually as subordinate third-world individuals or groups perceived from the point of view of a dominant, first-world culture (though one whose claim to any kind of "firstness" is frequently put in question). Instances are the Vietnamese "enemy" and the native South Africans in the two novellas of *Dusklands;* the farm servants in *In the Heart of the Country;* the barbarians, and in particular the barbarian girl, in *Waiting for the Barbarians;* Friday in *Foe;* and Vercueil in *Age of Iron. (Life & Times of Michael K* is an interesting case, since the main figure of alterity in this novel is also the individual whose inner life is presented in detail.)

The task Coetzee has set himself is to convey the resistance of these figures to the discourses of the dominant culture (the culture, that is, which has conditioned the author, the kind of reader which the novels are likely to find, and the genre of the novel itself) and at the same time to find a discursive means of representing the claims they make upon us. Such claims, however, are not to be understood in traditional humanist, Enlightenment, or Romantic terms: it's not a question (only) of sympathy for a suffering fellow human being, or of the equal rights of all persons, or of the inscrutable mystery of the unique individual. The demands these figures make upon the culture which excludes them are also demands made upon all these discourses, which thereby come under pressure to abandon their universalizing pretensions and to recognize their historical origins and contingent existence. The novel can succeed in making these claims felt only if its representational methods convey with sufficient force and richness that alterity, an alterity that impinges upon us not by initiating a dialogue—something that is ruled out in advance—but by interrupting or disturbing the discursive patterns in which we are at home. And my hypothesis is that it is thanks to his allegiance to certain aspects of the tradition of formal experimentation we associate with modernism that Coetzee succeeds in doing this to the remarkable extent that he does.

I shall have to limit most of the remaining discussion to one of Coetzee's novels—though with the reminder that it cannot serve simply as an *example*, exemplarity being a property that is put in question by the uniqueness of each literary act.[20] I choose *Age of Iron*, partly because, as a recent work, it has suffered less the domestication of a critical reception (and one of the problems of this topic, or course, is that traditionally the task of criticism and pedagogy has been to *reduce* otherness in the texts it reads—especially in modernist texts). The other reason is that, being less obviously innovative in its formal devices and choice of subject-matter than the earlier novels, its forceful presentation of otherness is more open to explanation in terms of the canons of realism; what I wish to argue is that even in this novel, formal, "modernist" devices play a crucial role, and that without them its political importance would be greatly diminished. If I were looking for the Coetzee novel with the most striking devices of self-reflexiveness and challenges to the reader, I would have chosen *Foe;* in that novel the otherness of the text is entirely evident, though I should add that this does not mean that the relation between textual and thematic otherness is entirely transparent.[21]

These are the opening paragraphs of *Age of Iron,* which broach the question of alterity from the outset:[22]

> There is an alley down the side of the garage, you may remember it, you and your friends would sometimes play there.

Now it is a dead place, waste, without use, where windblown leaves pile up and rot.

Yesterday, at the end of this alley, I came upon a house of carton boxes and plastic sheeting and a man curled up inside, a man I recognized from the streets: tall, thin, with a weathered skin and long, carious fangs, wearing a baggy gray suit and a hat with a sagging brim. He had the hat on now, sleeping with the brim folded under his ear. A derelict, one of the derelicts who hang around the parking lots on Mill Street, cadging money from shoppers, drinking under the overpass, eating out of refuse cans. One of the homeless for whom August, month of rains, is the worst month. Asleep in his box, his legs stretched out like a marionette's, his jaw agape. An unsavory smell about him: urine, sweet wine, moldy clothing, and something else too. Unclean.

For a while I stood staring down on him, staring and smelling. A visitor, visiting himself on me on this of all days. (3–4)

The initial and overriding reaction that most readers have to this narrated encounter is probably similar to the one they would have to an encounter with a mysterious and disturbing stranger recounted in a realist novel or even in a vividly written piece of historical reportage; the sense of otherness is derived from the immediacy of the writing, prompting identification with the speaker, and from the graphic, disturbing description of the figure encountered. It's an experience calculated to stir the memories and consciences of the novel's affluent first-world readers. But already there is something else at work, unsettling this mode of identificatory, and somewhat guilty, reading; the slightly self-conscious literariness of the style ("his jaw agape," "visiting himself"), the rhetorical repetitions ("derelict . . . derelicts"; "month . . . month"; "staring . . .staring", "visitor . . . visiting"), the unidentified but very specific second person ("you may remember it"), the gaps in motivation (what has prompted this visit? or this account of it?), the self-ironizing tone ("a visitor").

The stranger (who is familiar in his strangeness—"a man I recognized from the streets") is both concretely present as a specific individual, who smells and wears a baggy suit, and at the same time an echo from across a long cultural history: the visitant, the annunciator, the holy fool, the *arrivant* ("this of all days," we quickly discover, is the day on which the speaker has been told that her cancer is terminal—furnishing an explanation for the visit at a different interpretative level.)[23] As we move through this paragraph, performing its singular disposition of words, motifs, allusions, enacting its largely paratactic and often verbless sequences, we respond not only to a vividly reported encounter with an alien and somewhat threatening individual, but also to an unsettling textual experience, enthralling in its very capacity to disquiet, that challenges generic preconceptions and refuses to accede to our interpretive desires for recognizable narrative procedures (which now include canonized modernist procedures, such as those of Beckett and Kafka, who are often echoed in Coetzee's work). We are both invited to give this first-person text, with its deictics and its direct address, the emotional and axiological investment of an autobiographical account and at the same time are kept at a distance, made to feel that the very status and function of autobiography are being put in question. An array of meanings—not all consistent with one another—are powerfully evoked, put in play, projected toward the future (of our reading, and of the created characters). The text's otherness is not a reflection or enactment of the otherness of the man in the cardboard house, as if the two alterities could be separated and then shown to be matched; the act of writing is an act of producing otherness, and our reading is a way of activating that otherness, familiar in its strangeness, uncannily homely.

The speaker (or rather writer, since we soon learn that we are reading a letter, of a rather strange sort) is a Mrs. Curren, a retired classics teacher living alone in Cape Town, and her words are addressed to her closest relative, a daughter now living in the United States. (We may note in passing that a little knowledge about the author produces a further sense of textual estrangement, as we measure the distance between a man in his middle age and an elderly woman). As the days pass, the visitor (whose name is as uncertain as his past and his race, but whom Mrs. Curren comes to call Vercueil) draws closer and closer to her, yet his estranging otherness remains undiminished—one might even say it is heightened by the increasing physical intimacy between the two.[24] The novel, too, remains elusive, in spite of the readerly involvement it invites; it never conforms to the expected patterns of, say, the political documentary or the allegorical tale, though it functions effectively as both of these mutually contradictory genres. Its epistolary status is undermined by the absence of any of the markers of a real letter, culminating in a final sentence that is beyond all letter-writing. And the language remains highly deliberate and self-aware, consciously fashioned out of the culture's inheritance rather than pretending to immediacy and originality; as a professor of classics Mrs. Curren stands for the whole Western inheritance from Greece and Rome, its ethical and political language rendered suspect even as it forms itself into telling moral apothegms.

The otherness which makes demands on us as we read this novel is not an otherness simply *outside* language or discourse; it is an otherness brought into being by language, it is what two thousand years of continuously evolving discourse has excluded—and thus constituted—as other. Not *its* other, which would, as an opposite, still be part of its system; but heterogeneous, unassimilable, and unacknowledged unless it imposes itself upon the prevailing discourse, as Vercueil does, or unless a fissure is created in that discourse through which it can make itself felt, as happens in Coetzee's writing. Modernism's foregrounding of language and other discursive and generic codes through its formal strategies is not merely a self-reflexive diversion but a recognition (whatever its writers may have thought they were doing) that literature's distinctive power and potential ethical force resides in a testing and unsettling of deeply held assumptions of transparency, instrumentality, and direct referentiality, in part because this taking to the limits opens a space for the apprehension of the otherness which those assumptions had silently excluded. Since it is language that has played a major role in producing (and simultaneously occluding) the other, it is in language—language aware of its ideological effects, alert to its own capacity to impose silence as it speaks—that the force of the other can be most strongly represented. The effect is one that I would want to describe as textual otherness: a verbal artefact that estranges as it entices, that foregrounds the Symbolic as it exploits the Imaginary, that both speaks and says that it cannot speak.

▪ ▪ ▪

Before I continue my discussion of *Age of Iron,* I would like to test and clarify my argument by making two brief comparative forays. A figure of otherness with many affinities to Vercueil is Melville's Bartleby: a visitant who, although in this case hired in regular fashion, soon challenges the norms of the office and of conventional fictional characterization to become an inexplicable, irreducible presence, making his home where he has no right of domicile, evincing—without any use of force—a powerful independence of mind. Moreover, what produces for the reader the strongest sensation of otherness is not the narrator's entirely understandable astonishment and rage at Bartleby's unexplained behavior, but his moments of acceptance and longer periods of tolerance, for which Christian charity does not adequately acccount.

To give just one example, when the narrator visits his chambers on a Sunday morning he finds his key obstructed; in what follows, the most potent strangeness lies in the *absence* of antagonism and confrontation:

> Quite surprised, I called out, when to my consternation a key was turned from within, and, thrusting his lean visage at me, and holding the door ajar, the apparition of Bartleby appeared, in his shirt

sleeves, and otherwise in a strangely tattered deshabille, saying quietly that he was sorry, but he was deeply engaged just then, and—preferred not admitting me at present. In a brief word or two, he moreover added, that perhaps I had better walk around the block two or three times, and by that time he would probably have concluded his affairs.

Now, the utterly unsurmised appearance of Bartleby, tenanting my law chambers of a Sunday morning, with his cadaverously gentlemanly *nonchalance,* yet withal firm and self-possessed, had such a strange effect upon me that incontinently I slunk away from my own door and did as desired. But not without sundry twinges of impotent rebellion against the mild effrontery of this unaccountable scrivener. Indeed, it was his wonderful mildness, chiefly, which not only disarmed me but unmanned me, as it were. For I consider that one, for the time, is sort of unmanned when he tranquilly permits his hired clerk to dictate to him and order him away from his own premises.[25]

Like *Age of Iron,* the text stages the question of responsibility to and for the other, and though in this case the narrator finally shirks that responsibility, there is a hint of what a fuller acknowledgment of it might mean in his reaction to Bartleby's death in prison. It could be argued, therefore, that Melville subverts the prevailing conventions of narrative—through his introduction of a character whose acts cannot be accounted for by those conventions—in a protomodernist manner that resembles Coetzee's manipulation of the codes of fiction. Nevertheless, it is important to recognize the differences between these two works as deployments of the materials of fictional narrative. Melville achieves his effect by laboriously building up in rich detail a conventional narrator, group of characters, and setting before threatening the whole edifice by introducing the uncanny *arrivant* (who, by contrast, is only sparsely described), and provides a conclusion which, however open-ended, appears to reassert the threatened conventions by providing a psychological and narrative key: the Dead Letter Office in which Bartleby is said to have worked. Our reading therefore tends to veer between two alternatives, the naturalizing and the allegorizing (or perhaps settles on one). Mrs. Curren's letter is itself, perhaps, a dead letter, gone astray before it even reaches the post office, and it is certainly a letter from the dead. Instead of an attempt to construct a familiar world into which the other erupts as a character, the writing is estranging from the start, enacting more inescapably the otherness that constitutes the literary. Rather than oscillating between naturalization and allegorization, the novel stages both these modes of writing and reading simultaneously and undecidably.

The second comparison I want to make takes us to a description of an encounter with otherness in an avowedly nonliterary text contemporaneous with *Age of Iron*, Rian Malan's *My Traitor's Heart*, an Afrikaner's autobiographical account of the workings of apartheid. In this passage, the author recounts a drive across the Cape Flats at night with a friend, tense with the knowledge that cars have recently been stoned by the wretchedly poor black inhabitants of the area.

> Halfway across the flats, the headlights picked out a strange apparition at the roadside. From the corner of my eye, it looked like a giant water boatman, skating down the shoulder of the freeway in the dark. I twisted around for a second look and saw a crippled black man flying along on a single roller skate, his thin, useless legs drifting beneath a wasplike torso. His elongated crutches were sweeping back and forth like oars, and he was literally rowing toward Cape Town.
>
> The instant we passed him, Jill spoke sharply. "You're not going to stop," she said. I didn't really want to. In fact, I'd have preferred to pretend we hadn't seen him at all, but now that she'd mentioned him, I felt obliged to act. So I braked and pulled off the freeway. [26]

Reluctantly, they pick up the cripple, who sits between them and chatters loudly in Xhosa—which they don't understand—as they drive to a point well short of his destination and drop him again, still gripped by fear.

Malan's description, read as a piece of autobiographical reportage, works powerfully to evoke an experience of otherness generated by a particular sociopolitical system; its energies are devoted to painting a shocking picture and securing the emotional identification of the reader, rather than bringing forward the question of the representation of otherness, which would only interfere with that primary purpose. But even if this passage were encountered in a fictional text, where the reader would be more inclined to introduce such questions, I suspect that such power as it would have—it would, of course, lose the forcefulness that it gets from the thought that "this really happened"—would come from the striking nature of the events and objects described. The formal properties of the language, that is to say, are subjugated to the function of representation. The human image is powerful, but the experience of encountering it is not enacted in language that stages otherness through a process of formal estrangement. Compared with the slow accumulation of information as we take in, with Mrs. Curren, the odd yet familiar figure of the derelict in her back yard, Malan's presentation of the experience is obvious and inert. First the effect is summed up—"a strange apparition"; then it is described in hallucinatory terms as a giant insect; and finally a "second look" produces an explanation, a bizarre one, it is true, but one grounded in reality. Here too a bald summary—"a crippled black man"—precedes a more elaborate description, with no self-distancing in the language. The confusion of the literal and the figurative—the fantastic water boatman is "skating" rather than rowing, whereas the real skater is "literally rowing"—seems to have no function, and remains a distraction. As a result, there is little sense of the magnitude of the demands made by the other in the ethical situation; the cripple becomes a focus for the antagonism between the author and his lover, and the political point of the episode—the fear of liberal whites when confronted by the reality of black lives—remains a trivially local one, with no ethical challenge.

▪ ▪ ▪

Vercueil is not the only figure of alterity in *Age of Iron*. At the same time as we follow the story of his strange intimacy with the increasingly ill Mrs. Curren, we witness her growing awareness that her black servant and family are not as easily known as she once thought. It is a story of violence in the townships, police brutality, and children caught up prematurely in the deadly battle to put an end to apartheid and all its works. It could have been the basis of a powerful novel. But such a novel, even in Coetzee's spare and focussed prose, would have functioned primarily as fictionalized history, as a vivid account of what "really happened" and as a call to put a stop to such events. *Age of Iron* is that, as *Cry the Beloved Country* or *To Every Birth Its Blood* are, but it is the juxtaposition of that function with the differently disturbing narrative of Vercueil's and Mrs. Curren's relationship (or relationship without a relation, as Levinas might say) that constitutes the uniqueness of its signifying act. Mrs. Curren's realization of the otherness of her servants is a shock to her liberal principles and classical education; but this lack of understanding is primarily a forceful demonstration of the need for political action to transform social relations, whereas the incomprehensibility of Vercueil marks an insistence that a rationalistic and instrumental view of politics is not enough for the achievement of a genuine transformation. We might say that morality, as commonly understood, is based on the familiar—known and thoroughly internalized codes, expectations, and goals, enforced by a variety of institutions—and that politics, insofar as it is a moral enterprise, is equally within this domain. But the demands of otherness, of an ethics that exceeds all moral codes and unsettles all institutions, require a politics that constantly reinvents itself, alert at every moment to the exclusions that its programs and pronouncements necessarily entail.

Hence the significance of the conflict on the subject of Vercueil between Mrs. Curren and Florence, her maid, who is caught up directly in the violent political struggle of the townships:

> "This man lives here. It is his home."
> Florence's nostrils flared.
> "He lives here," said Florence, "but he is rubbish.
> He is good for nothing." . . .
> "He is not a rubbish person," I said, lowering my voice, speaking to Florence alone. "There are no rubbish people. We are all people together." (47)

It must emphasized once more that the novel does not simply endorse Mrs. Curren's liberal truisms, and she herself comes to question them forcefully during the course of the novel.[27] But her platitude is the only verbal defense she has against the political rationality that dismisses some human beings as worthless, and which she feels an obligation—whose source remains obscure and inexpressible—to resist. It is in her actions towards Vercueil that she manifests a responsibility for the other that exceeds all instrumentalism, and the odd silence about her motivation (in what is a long monologue of self-revelation) testifies again to the impossibility of accounting for such an ethical response in the language of liberal humanism she has at her disposal. We are left with an awareness that respect for and openness to the other, which implies a readiness for self-reinterpretation of the kind Mrs. Curren goes through during the course of the novel, is a difficult, unprogrammable, but absolutely necessary part of the refashioning of a society.

These are not scenes from a novel whose moral efficacy lies primarily in its realistic depiction of human crises, nor in its risky but suggestive allegorizing (the dying Mrs. Curren as the cancerous social body of South Africa; Vercueil as the angel of death, alterity in its most absolute manifestation). Both these modes work forcefully even while they constantly undermine one another as interpretative models—this is an example of form as the dance of meanings—but they are also *self*-undermining. The account of Mrs. Curren's visit to the burning township strains to achieve the power of a Conradian description of human brutality and the lucid dreadfulness of a Dantean infernal vision, but it is accompanied by her own sense that she is hopelessly out of place there—which is also a sense that such descriptions, vitally important as they are in the arousal of international indignation, do not probe the ethical sources of the inflicted suffering to which they bear testimony. (It is significant that Vercueil, with the utmost brusqueness, refuses to accompany her.) And the allegorical narrative is presented as Mrs. Curren's own literary self-indulgence (she terms Vercueil "the messenger" in one of the quotations above, and there are many such moments), thus depriving it of final authorial endorsement, and reminding us that allegorical readings of this kind entail an abstraction away from the concrete details which must be absolutely central to any ethical act. So the text resists our commonest habits of reading, and especially our familiar ways of finding moral support and justification in literature, to confront us with the difficulty, and at the same time the necessity, of a just response to alterity, of trust in the other, of openness to the future. And it does this by mobilizing the resources of language in a way that subjects us to the always contingent and unpredictable demands of otherness.

▪ ▪ ▪

Literature, I have claimed, is born from, or in, an act of reading an act of writing. Any such event involves an apprehension of the other, of the otherness of the other, through its holding open of the gates that the usual processing of language keeps firmly shut. There are numerous practices by means of which this openness may be achieved, and the history of literature could be written as a history of these techniques. Modernism, as I've been using the terms, refers to one set of such practices, one which proved to be resistant enough to habits of reductive reading to bring about significant shifts in critical and pedagogic method in this century—though too often these have ended up as reductive tools anyway. The danger that I see in current modes of cultural and historical criticism, immensely valuable as they are, is that unless handled with extreme subtlety and responsibility they can miss precisely what it is that literature *as literature* has contributed, and has to contribute, to our political and ethical thinking—and acting. This is not to deny the significant effect that literary texts have had in thematizing historical issues, in forming and changing ideology, in popularizing worthy— or unworthy—causes, in providing education and information. But it is to assert that the *literary,* in spite of, or rather because of, the difficulties of categorization and definition it presents, is also worth our continuing attention.

Notes

I would like to thank Rosemary Jolly, Benita Parry, and George Levine, whose astute comments on earlier versions of this essay have been invaluable, and audiences at Harvard University and The University of Pennsylvania, whose questions after talks on this topic were probing and constructive.

1. See Karen Press's discussion of these pressures in contemporary South Africa ("Building a National Culture in South Africa," in *Rendering Things Visible: Essays on South African Literary Culture,* ed. Martin Trump [Athens: Ohio

University Press, 1990], 22–40). Press argues in favor of the construction of a "national culture" which allows for the intrinsic unpredictability of art, and against calls for a "people's culture" serving a specific political program; but since the only art she considers acceptable is art that identifies itself with a Marxist approach (a "historical materialist understanding of society" [36]), the important question of unpredictability is approached under rather severe restraints.

2. That it should be a member of South Africa's privileged white group who occupies this position is, or course, not fortuitous; given their upbringing, education, and cultural situation, such writers are more likely to feel the need, and possess the means, to engage with recent literary (and critical) developments in Europe and North America. It should be added that the most interesting and politically responsible of internationally successful white novelists—I am thinking in particular of Coetzee, Nadine Gordimer, and Breyten Breytenbach —show an acute consciousness of the limits imposed upon them by their position in South African society.

3. Coetzee's novels are: *Dusklands* (Johannesburg: Ravan Press, 1974; London: Secker & Warburg, 1982; New York: Viking, 1985); *In the Heart of the Country* (London: Secker & Warburg, 1977; New York: Harper and Row, 1977 [as *From the Heart of the Country*]; Johannesburg: Ravan Press, 1978); *Waiting for the Barbarians* (London: Secker & Warburg, 1980; New York: Viking, 1980; Johannesburg: Ravan Press, 1981); *Life and Times of Michael K* (London: Secker & Warburg, 1983; Johannesburg: Ravan Press, 1983; New York: Viking, 1984); *Foe* (London: Secker & Warburg, 1986; Johannesburg: Ravan Press, 1986; New York: Viking, 1987); *Age of Iron* (New York: Random House, 1990; London: Secker & Warburg, 1990).

4. His most inflammatory comments on this subject were made in an address given in Cape Town in 1987, subsequently published as "The Novel Today" (*Upstream* 6, no. 1 [1988] 2–5), in which he observed that "in times of intense ideological pressure like the present, when the space in which the novel and history normally coexist like two cows on the same pasture, each minding its own business, is squeezed to almost nothing, the novel, it seems to me, has only two options, supplementarity or rivalry"—and advocated the position of rivalry (3). The debate surrounding Coetzee's fiction and its relation to South African politics is sketched in the opening chapters of Susan VanZanten Gallagher's *A Story of South Africa: J.M. Coetzee's Fiction in Context* (Cambridge: Harvard University Press, 1991) and of David Attwell's *J.M. Coetzee: South Africa and the Politics of Writing* (Berkeley: University of California Press, and Cape Town: David Philip, 1993). Like his book, Attwell's essay "The Problem of History in the Fiction of J.M. Coetzee" (in Trump, *Rendering Things Visible*, 94–133) is a valuable discussion of the questions of realism and referentiality in relation to Coetzee's work. Perhaps the best-known critique of the political implications of Coetzee's fiction is Nadine Gordimer's review of *Michael K*, "The Idea of Gardening," *New York Review of Books* 2 Feb. 1984, 3, 6.

5. The relation of Coetzee's fiction to the canon and the processes of

canon-formation is a complex one; I have broached some of the issues in "Oppressive Silence: J. M. Coetzee's *Foe* and the Politics of the Canon,*" in *Decolonizing Tradition: New Views of Twentieth-Century "British" Literature,* ed. Karen Lawrence (Urbana: University of Illinois Press, 1991), 212–238.

6. I am not attempting in this essay to make a distinction between ethics and politics, but am treating the political as one domain of the ethical; for a fuller discussion of this interrelatedness see my essay, "Trusting the Other: Ethics and Politics in Coetzee's *Age of Iron,*" in the forthcoming *South Atlantic Quarterly* special issue on Coetzee, edited by Michael Valdez Moses. Coetzee himself, however, contrasts the two terms in *Doubling the Point: Essays and Interviews,* ed. David Attwell (Cambridge: Harvard University Press, 1992); see, for instance, pp. 200 and 337–338, where the political is more narrowly associated with mass action and the use of violence.

7. One interesting exception is Neil Lazarus's discussion of contemporary white South African writers, "Modernism and Modernity: T. W. Adorno and Contemporary White South African Literature," *Cultural Critique* 5 (Winter 1986–7): 131–155. But the view of modernism which Lazarus takes from Adorno is not one that valorizes an opening onto otherness; for instance, his categorization of Coetzee's writing as modernist rather than postmodernist is based on its being "*ethically* saturated, . . .*humanistic* in its critique of the established order, . . .concerned to *represent* reality, and . . . *rationalistic*" (148; author's emphases). The modernism with which I am aligning Coetzee involves a questioning of just these qualities, at least as self-evident values (even "ethical" is problematized, as we shall see).

8. This argument has implications for the other arts too, of course, but they are not to be discovered by a simple process of extrapolation. I should make it clear that I am assuming that literature is not a transhistorical and transcultural category but an institution and a practice with historical and geographical determinants and limits.

9. I hope in the future to be able to elaborate upon the somewhat gnomic account of literature put forward in the following paragraphs. It derives in part from, and points towards a development of, various discussions by Jacques Derrida of literature; see, in particular "Signature Event Context," in *Limited Inc,* ed. Gerald Graff (Evanston: Northwestern University Press, 1988), 1–23, and, in *Acts of Literature,* ed. Derek Attridge (New York: Routledge, 1992), "This Strange Institution Called Literature" (33–75), "Ulysses Gramophone: Hear Say Yes in Joyce" (253–309), and the extracts from "Psyche: Invention of the Other" (310–343) and *Signsponge* (344–369). My introduction to *Acts of Literature* (1–29) also includes some consideration of these topics. My debts to Derrida's discussions of the literary work and the institution of literature will be evident throughout this essay; I have not documented them point by point.

10. This hypostatization of the work—usually the poem—as a voice moving steadily from the moment of the beginning to the moment of the conclusion is, to borrow Derrida's terms, a phonocentric representation which overlooks the importance of the *writtenness* of literature; it remains idealized and, in a sense, static. The more overtly static, spatialized view of the literary work as

object that I am describing also fails to take account of writing in Derrida's sense, of the work as act, staging, or performance.

11. A large part of the inspiration for current views of literature as an illusory cultural category produced entirely by ideological operations comes from Michel Foucault, and it is interesting to see him struggling with this issue in a 1975 interview: having answered "I don't know" to the question whether literature is defined by criteria internal to the texts, and explained that his interest is only in how nonliterary texts enter the field of the literary, he valorizes the writing of Bataille, Blanchot, and Klossowski for its ability to put philosophy in question ("The Functions of Literature," in *Michel Foucault: Politics, Philosophy, Culture,* ed. Lawrence D. Kritzman [New York: Routledge, 1988], 307–313). Derrida, who values literature for the same ability, is more certain that "potentiality is not hidden in the text like an intrinsic property" but that *within* a given context, certain literary texts have potentialities which are "richer and denser" ("This Strange Institution Called Literature," in *Acts of Literature,* 46–47). Since our apprehension of a text is always contextualized, as Stanley Fish has demonstrated eloquently in a number of essays, the question of an absolute "intrinsic" difference between literary and nonliterary texts does not arise.

12. I have discussed one type of literary signification that stages the coming into being of meaning in "Literature as Imitation: Jakobson, Joyce, and the Art of Onomatopoeia," chapter 5 of *Peculiar Language: Literature as Difference from the Renaissance to James Joyce* (Ithaca: Cornell University Press, 1988).

13. I am using "meaning" as a blanket term here, and a longer exposition would have to consider some of the different notions that it comprises, including referentiality, emotion, acts of promising, persuading, warning, etc.

14. This may sound like an echo of Kant's *Zweckmässigkeit ohne Zweck,* and it may seem that we are squarely back in the heartlands of the aesthetic tradition. However, the continuation of my argument is an attempt to show that far from being the self-contained manifestation of purposefulness without purpose, literature has the potential to function powerfully as an ethical force (without being yoked to a preexisting purpose).

15. A sense of the connection in Derrida's thought between something like form as I am describing it and the realm of the ethico-political can be gained from the following comments in "This Strange Institution Called Literature":

> A work laden with obvious and canonical "metaphysical" theses can, in the operation of its writing, have more powerful "deconstructive" effects than a text proclaiming itself radically revolutionary without in any way affecting the norms or modes of traditional writing. For instance, some works which are highly "phallocentric" in their semantics, their intended meaning, even their theses, can produce paradoxical effects, paradoxically antiphallocentric through the audacity of a writing which in fact disturbs the order or the logic of phallocentrism. (Derrida, *Acts,* 50)

16. In different ways, both Russian Formalism and Brechtian theory depict the importance of literature in terms of effects produced by a kind of self-estrangement arising from formal processes; both have had a significant influence on my argument (and so, I suspect, has Tony Bennett's *Formalism and Marxism* [London: Methuen, 1979], first read a dozen years ago). A longer

account, in both cases, would have to look closely at what precisely the alienating effects are claimed to *reveal* about the world. Heidegger's valorization of poetry, too, has connections with what I am proposing, though it also moves too quickly to a revelatory function.

17. My privileging of otherness as a way of apprehending the demands of literature and the responsibilities of the reader owes a great deal to the work of Levinas. The Other as that which exceeds all totalization, and as that for which I am responsible, is a continuing motif in Levinas's writing, including his major works *Totality and Infinity: An Essay on Exteriority,* trans. Alphonso Lingis (Pittsburgh: Duquesne University Press, 1969) and *Otherwise than Being or Beyond Essence,* trans. Alphonso Lingis (The Hague: Martinus Nijhoff, 1981). For shorter treatments, see "Time and the Other" (37–58), "Ethics as First Philosophy" (75–87), and "Substitution" (88–125), all in *The Levinas Reader,* ed. Sean Hand (Oxford: Basil Blackwell, 1989); and the interviews in *Ethics and Infinity,* trans. Richard A. Cohen (Pittsburgh: Duquesne University Press, 1985). I should add that my appropriation of Levinas's thought is extremely selective, and also that his own discussions of literature and art do not go in the same direction as mine—see, for instance, his critical comments on "poetic activity" as a beguiling rhythm in need of disruption in *Totality and Infinity* (203), and the essays on art in *The Levinas Reader.* My argument comes closer to the suggestion made by Robert Bernasconi and Simon Critchley in their editorial introduction to *Re-Reading Levinas* (Bloomington: Indiana University Press, 1991) that there might be a Levinasian hermeneutics which "would perhaps be defined by its readiness for re-reading because it would have no interest in distilling the content of a text into a 'said'" (xi).

18. This may sound like a devaluation of the realist tradition, but it is a critique only of a certain way of reading that tradition—a reading, it is true, which realist authors often invited, but not one that is inevitable. To respond in full responsibility to the act of a realist work is to respond to its unique staging of meaning, and therefore to its otherness. It could even be said that the realist work is more, not less, demanding than the modernist work, in that its otherness is often disguised, and requires an even more scrupulous responsiveness.

19. It is for this reason that Derrida, following Heidegger, tends to avoid the term "ethics"; as he explains in a transcribed commentary, "It is not as a sign of protest against morality that I don't use the word 'ethics,' but this word is heavily loaded with a history, with a historical determination; it seems to me that one has to begin by tracing the genealogy of an ethical discourse before settling into it" (Jacques Derrida and Pierre-Jean Labarrière, *Altérités* [Paris: Osiris, 1986], 70). Derrida goes on to speak of a responsibility that is not intrinsically ethical, but which makes demands in a manner that is even more imperious.

20. See Jacques Derrida, *The Other Heading: Reflections on Today's Europe* (Bloomington: Indiana University Press, 1992), and the introduction, entitled "For Example," by Michael B. Naas (vii–lix).

21. I have discussed some of these demands, in connection with the question of otherness, in "Oppressive Silence." See also Gayatri Chakravorty

Spivak's discussion of the "absolutely other" in "Theory in the Margin: Coetzee's *Foe* Reading Defoe's *Crusoe/Roxana*," in *Consequences of Theory,* ed. Jonathan Arac and Barbara Johnson (Baltimore: Johns Hopkins University Press, 1991), 154–180.

22. Since my argument concerns the operations and effects of the novel through its entire length, the discussion of a single passage can do little more than point to these larger-scale matters. It is not intended to be a "close reading" in the traditional sense.

23. On the *arrivant,* see the contribution by Derrida to the forthcoming proceedings of the 1992 Colloque de Cerisy on *Le passage des frontières: autour du travail de Jacques Derrida.*

24. We learn the man's name when Mrs. Curren tells Florence, "'His name is Mr. Vercueil. . . . Vercueil, Verkuil, Verskuil. That's what he says. I have never come across such a name before'" (37). Benita Parry, who writes perceptively on the importance of names in the novel, points out the link to the Afrikaans word "verskuil," "concealment or masking of the self" ("Thanatophany for South Africa: Death With/out Transfiguration," *Southern African Review of Books,* Jan/Feb 1991, 11). To know the other's name is to reduce his or her otherness, and Coetzee's fiction repeatedly presents us with nameless characters—the barbarian girl, the medical officer in *Michael K*—or characters whose names are in one way or other problematic—Michael K himself (who is consistently called "Michaels" by the medical officer), Friday, the real names of Mrs. Curren's servant Florence and her family.

25. Herman Melville, *"Bartleby" and "Benito Cereno"* (New York: Dover, 1990), 16.

26. Rian Malan, *My Traitor's Heart: A South African Exile Returns to Face His Country, His Tribe, and His Conscience* (New York: Random House, 1990), 178–179.

27. I have no space to go into the question of Mrs. Curren's otherness, though I have already suggested in commenting on the opening paragraphs that her language estranges even as it encourages identification. She writes from the position of the other as a woman in a patriarchal society, as a liberal in a society dominated by a conservative, if not fascist, ideology, as a classicist in a culture that has forgotten much of its past, and—most profoundly and problematically, as a human being approaching death. All of these give her a kind of authority to address the other and the question of the other, but it is an authority whose sources remain obscure and troubled. I have devoted more attention to her values, and the challenges they receive from the radical youths of the township, in "Trusting the Other."

REGENIA GAGNIER

A Critique of Practical Aesthetics

THIS ESSAY WILL ATTEMPT to reclaim the value of practical aesthetics. By practical aesthetics I mean aesthetics both as practiced in works of art and literature and as qualified by Kant's distinction between "practical" and "pure," where the practical relates to an ethical disposition or "habitus." Although such value was theorized in the eighteenth century by aesthetic philosophers like Kant and Friedrich Schiller, and was assumed by Marxist aesthetics in the European tradition of the last century and a half, it comes as a surprise to recent decades of students, for whom aesthetics is a limiting category, a tool of hegemony, either dividing the people by hierarchies of taste or operating in practice as a subtle tool of control (as in aesthetic applications of Foucault's *Discipline and Punish*).[1] In reviving an occluded tradition of critical and progressive aesthetics, I shall not deny the force of these recent critiques.

From Kant on, modern aesthetics was seldom about the beautiful object alone (formalism) but rather about the relation between the receptive subject and the object. For Kant, the relationship was one of disciplined freedom, specifically the "free play" of imagination synthesizing one's perceptions of the beautiful object and one's store of concepts. This free play is a symbol of the morally good, in which one acts according to duty (autonomously) rather than uncontrolled desire (heteronomously), freely rather than according to necessity. Thus for Kant the beautiful provided a sensuous, perceptual "symbol" of the moral law that could only be apprehended abstractly or intellectually.

Recent critics have persuaded us that the history of aesthetics has been complicitous with the negative aspects of the Enlightenment and modernity: claims for freedom and autonomy have masked practices of domination and exploitation. Too many crimes have been committed in the name of that universal Reason that Kant relied upon to clarify one's duty. One turns rather from Kant's positive notion of freedom to Hume's more accessible, but negative, notion of freedom—to fulfill my desires without your foot on my back ("universally allowed to belong to every one who is not a prisoner and in chains").[2] Practical aesthetics offers two relevant focuses here: its emphasis on sensuous human activity and the quality of daily life (what Marx called *praxis*), and its often submerged, and often self-contradictory, demands for freedom. As the last couple of decades have reconsidered literary and art history from a critical perspective, progressive critics can now see what is in fact that history's dual function, both oppressive and liberatory (as Marx described the historical bourgeoisie).

The argument for the duality of the aesthetic goes like this. The aesthetic has been a site of state power since the rise of modernity, whose social organization depends less upon external constraints and visible exercises of authority than upon an ideological model of self-regulating and self-determining subjectivity. Modern society cultivated a new form of human subjectivity that inscribed the law in itself rather than in an external authority. Instead of relying on the coercive powers of absolutism, bourgeois society relocated the power of the state within the subject herself, within the region of perception, sensation, sensuous material life (sometimes called "sensibility"). Like the modern notion of the aesthetic artifact, the modern bourgeois subject was "autonomous," that is, self-regulating.[3]

On the other hand, the state was now in danger of the subject's subjective revolt, which it had authorized even while it sought to control it. A new kind of subject—individualist, sensuous, passionate—posed a potential challenge to the status quo. When art is—and it is not always—something more than cultural capital, this challenge is more apparent in works of art and literature than in works of philosophy per se, which deal more exclusively with the cognitive.

There is a third function of the aesthetic. In releasing (or confining) each subject to his or her own private space, the aesthetic can also dissolve social bonds. It can also serve as a means of individual escape, the trivial version of art for art's sake.

Thus I want to discriminate between three practical—that is, actual historical—functions of the aesthetic: the self-regulation of the bourgeois subject (which has been strongly emphasized in recent histories of the novel); the individualist, passionate revolt (which I shall claim for one tendency of Victorian aesthetics and some of our "liberation aesthetics" today); and the escapist belief that *only* art can make one free, because society never will (a position I shall associate with decadents of all epochs). The first has been the concern of structuralist, poststructuralist, and Foucauldian students of power, control, and self-regulation. It is not my main concern here. In what follows I shall provide two historical narratives that illustrate the distinction between practical aesthetes and decadents, showing how aesthetics can be a liberating project and how that project can be derailed. I distinguish between aesthetes and decadents by the aesthete's ability to cope with her own and others' freedom and the decadent's fear of the freedom of others. I shall conclude with a section on practical aesthetics today.

The Aesthetes: Art as a Transformation of Daily Life

Three of the greatest aesthetes of nineteenth-century Britain were also great social critics: John Ruskin, William Morris, and Oscar Wilde. Their critiques of industrial capitalism and mass society, and the influence of their teachings on each other, the British Labour Party, the welfare state, Indian nationalism, modern ecological and gay rights movements, and European socialism are well known. Ruskin was not only an authoritative art critic and prose stylist, but throughout his work and especially in *Unto This Last* (1860) he attacked the basic assumptions of the dominant social science of his day, political economy, including its assumptions concerning wealth, value, the laws of the market, and "economic man." He attacked the division of labor, the competitive wage system, and the arms race as a source of economic growth; and he proposed the foundations of social justice in a paternalistic welfare state. Morris, a poet, novelist, master designer and craftsperson, was also a political propagandist and agitator. And Wilde, the most popular aesthetic figure of the fin de siècle, insisted in "The Soul of Man Under Socialism" (1891) that a healthy material base and equality of opportunity for all were the *preconditions* of liberal democratic society. He further queried whether the mass media might not be its death. Each of them called himself a socialist (Morris, of course, most consistently), although Ruskin's brand was Tory paternalist, Morris's was Marxist, and Wilde's tended toward anarchism, or what I call an anarchocynicalism.[4] More important than such labels, though, was the centrality to each one's aesthetic of different kinds of freedom: Ruskin desired a world free from poverty; Morris, a world free from hierarchy, or the fixed hierarchy of the class system; and Wilde, a world free from the oppression of conventional thought and behavior, or what is now called conventional "lifestyle." Unlike the monumentally abstract eighteenth-century science of perception and sense called aesthetics, for the Victorians aesthetics was the realm of daily life and its vicissitudes. The Hegelian philosopher of aesthetics, Bernard Bosanquet, made this point at the end of the century when he saw Moris's unalienated worker as the objective correlative of Kant's Genius, Schiller's play-impulse, and Hegel's Ideal (*History of Aesthetic,* 1892).

My example of Ruskin's critique of daily life in England is his section contrasting the "Two Boyhoods" from the fifth volume (1860) of his defense of J. M. W. Turner, *Modern Painters.* (I note only in passing the practical nature of *Modern Painters,* a defense of the work of a contemporary.) In "Two Boyhoods" Ruskin constrasts the Venice of Giorgione (1477–1510) with the England of Turner (1775–1851). He begins with a(n idealized) description of social order and physical beauty, the (romanticized) Venice of the quattrocento, whose beauty is premised on its justice:

> A wonderful piece of world. Rather, itself a world. It lay along the face of the waters, no larger, as its captains saw it from their masts at evening, than a bar of sunset that could not pass away: but for its power, it must have seemed to them as if they were sailing in the expanse of heaven, and this a great planet, whose orient edge widened through ether. A world from which all ignoble care and petty thoughts were banished, with all the common and poor elements of life. . . . Such was Giorgione's school.[5]

He then turns to Turner's school, Covent Garden, and makes the quintessential Ruskinian aesthetic statement, the reduction of aesthetics to material base: "With such circumstances round him in youth, let us note what necessary effects followed upon the boy['s art]." His impoverished childhood resulted in Turner's "notable endurance of dirt . . . and all the soilings and strains of every common labour"; his "understanding of and regard for the poor . . . and of the poor in direct relations with the rich"; and his discrediting of a religion "not to be either obeyed, or combated, by an ignorant, yet clear-sighted youth, only to be scorned" (146–150). Turner saw beauty neither in the works or souls of humankind nor in God, but only, by contrast, in the solitude of Nature. In the Yorkshire hills, he found

> freedom at last. Dead-wall, dark railing, fenced field, gated garden, all passed away like the dream of a prisoner. . . . Those pale, poverty-struck, or cruel faces;—that multitudinous, marred humanity—are not the only things God has made. Here is something He has made which no one has marred. Pride of purple rocks, and river pools of blue, and tender wilderness of glittering trees, and misty lights of evening on immeasurable hills. (150)

Yet Turner is not an escapist nature painter, nor does Ruskin praise him for his representations of the green and pleasant land. The typical Turner painting was a wash of light—the beauty of the physical earth—now exposing the piteous failures of humankind. Ruskin attributes these failures first to the European drive for conquest and domination.

The European death of the nineteenth century was of another range and power [than that depicted by Salvator or Durer]: more terrible a thousand-fold in its merely physical grasp and grief; more terrible, incalculably, in its mystery and shame. What were the robber's casual pang, or the range of the flying skirmish, compared to the work of the axe, and the sword, and the famine, which was done during [Turner's] youth on all the hills and plains of the Christian earth, from Moscow to Gibraltar? He was eighteen years old when Napoleon came down on Arcola. Look on the map of Europe and count the blood-stains on it, between Arcola and Waterloo. (152)

In his condemnation of empire, Ruskin alludes to Turner's projected epic poem on the decline and fall of naval powers, and to Turner's own verses accompanying his *Slavers Throwing Overboard the Dead and Dying—Typhon Coming On* (1840). In the painting and verses, Turner extends his censure of the slave trade to the global market in general.

After slavery and imperialism, Ruskin turns to "the English practice" of exploitation, as embodied in the domestic casualties of the Industrial Revolution: "The life trampled out in the slime of the street, crushed to dust amidst the roaring of the wheel, tossed countlessly away into howling winter wind along five hundred leagues of rock-fanged shore. Or, worst of all, rotted down to forgotten graves through years of ignorant patience, and vain seeking for help from man, for hope in God—infirm, imperfect yearning, as of motherless infants starving at the dawn" (152). This was what Turner painted, Nature casting its blinding light on human misery of human making: "Light over all the world. Full shone now its awful globe, one pallid charnel-house,—a ball strewn bright with human ashes, glaring in poised sway beneath the sun, all blinding-white with death from pole to pole—death, not of myriads of poor bodies only, but of will, and mercy, and conscience; death, not once inflicted on the flesh, but daily fastening on the spirit" (153).

One can find the same rich sympathy regarding human need, human suffering, and human memory in Morris's utopian novel *News from Nowhere* (1890), in which the virtues of an economically just, sexually liberated, and ecologically preserved utopia pale, for generation after generation of readers, before the psychological splendor of the one character from the pre-utopian past—a character with memory—William Guest. An old man, Guest is one of the few in utopia conscious of the unbearable temporality of the body; his bafflement and pain in the new world order characteristically remain Morris's (and most readers') imaginative center. If, according to the customary dialectic of utopian fiction, the idyllic nature of the utopia only throws into relief the deficiencies of the present the author is criticizing, William Guest's complex relationship to memory (the hell that Victorian society was) and desire (the vision of what it could be) cannot help but make the callow young utopians look thin. Even Pater, generally taken to be an apolitical writer, introduced Morris's and Pre-Raphaelite poetry in general as "the desire of beauty quickened by the sense of death."[6] The essay "Aesthetic Poetry," which Pater withheld from publication until 1889, formed the basis of his aesthetic manifesto the "Conclusion" to *Studies in the History of the Renaissance* (1873) and its notorious materialism.

In his critical writing, Morris differed from Ruskin in that he found the class system—today called "functionally interdependent juxtapositions"—more detrimental to society than poverty: "I went to Iceland and I learned one lesson there, thoroughly I hope, that the most grinding poverty is a trifling evil compared with the inequality of classes," a notion that put him fundamentally at odds with the political economists, who, with the exception of Mill, equated growth with production rather than distribution of wealth.[7] In "Art Under Plutocracy," a lecture Morris delivered in 1883 (Ruskin chaired the session), he denied the autonomy of art, claiming first that "art should be a help and solace to the daily life of all men" (57), and he extended art's arena "beyond those matters which are consciously works of art . . . to the aspect of all the externals of our life" (58). In "How We Live and How We Might Live" (1884), Morris says that after competition between nations, capital, and classes has ceased (that is, under socialism), humankind will be free to determine its genuine needs. He anticipates that the first demand will be for the body, for good health, of which, he says, the "vast proportion of people in civilization scarcely even know what it means" (148). This good health extends to liberatory sensuous experience: "To rejoice in satisfying the due bodily appetites of a human animal without fear of degradation or sense of wrong-doing. . . . I claim it in the teeth of those terrible doctrines of asceticism, which, born of the despair of the oppressed and degraded, have been for so many ages used as instruments for the continuance of that oppression and degradation" (148). The second demand will be for education: "Opportunity, that is, to have my share of whatever knowledge there is in the world according to my capacity or bent of mind, historical or scientific; and also to have my share of skill of hand which is about in the world, either in the industrial handicrafts or in the fine arts. . . . I claim to be taught, if I can be taught, more than one craft to exercise for the benefit of the community" (150). Morris then claims the right to reject certain kinds of work, those Ruskin had called "destructive" (e.g., war) and "nugatory" (e.g., jewel-cutting): "I won't submit to be dressed up in red and marched off to shoot at my French or German or Arab friend in a quarrel that I don't understand; I will rebel sooner than do that. Nor will I submit to waste my time and energies in making some trifling toy which I know only a fool can desire; I will rebel sooner than do that" (151–152). With the advent of useful and freely chosen labor "would come the time for the new birth of art, so much talked of, so long deferred; people could not help showing their mirth and pleasure in their work, and would be always wishing to express it in a tangible and more or less enduring form, and the workshop would once more be a school of art, whose influence no one could escape from" (153). Morris concludes with the demand "that the mutual surroundings of my life should be pleasant, generous, and beautiful" (153), blaming urban squalor, overcrowding, disease, and industrial pollution not, as in political economy, on natural scarcity and human over-population, but rather on exploitation and the desire for profit.

Wilde's contribution to liberatory aesthetics has lived longer than Ruskin's and Morris's, appearing most often, though not exclusively, to-day as toleration of thought and "lifestyle" in gay studies or Queer Nation. Just as the artwork under aestheticism was autonomous, had to be true to its own organic development, to the laws of its own form, so Wilde insisted in *The Portrait of Mr. W. H.*, "The Soul of Man Under Socialism," "The Critic as Artist," and elsewhere that human individuals had unique temperaments and tastes that should be allowed to flourish according to the laws of their own being; and his fictional work, both novel and short stories, typically consisted of thought experiments on the social limits of this aesthetic auton-omy. Yet unlike later proponents of the life-as-art thesis, like Foucault in his last years, who wanted "to live life with the freedom of art," Wilde was sufficiently like his teachers Ruskin and Morris to insist upon initial distrib-utive justice as a precondition of genuine individual development and social utility.[8] That is, he refused to entertain the idea of an opposition—often endorsed by political economists—between liberty and equality. His work "The Soul of Man" is a lasting monument to the project of socialism pre-cisely because it is both socialist *and* individualist.

Some years ago I contrasted Wilde's socially-oriented aestheticism with the properly decadent aestheticism of Joris-Karl Huysmans's Des Esseintes in *A Rebours* (1884). I said that if Des Esseintes was solitary, neu-rotic, reactive against the bourgeoisie he despises, formally monologic, and concerned with perversion, Wilde was public, erotic, active, formally dia-logic, and concerned with the inversion of middle-class language and life.[9] Des Esseintes buried himself in a fortress, made a fortress of himself against others, and consumed the exotica of the world outside the West. In "The Decay of Lying" (1891), Wilde debunked both the connoisseur's practice of accumulation and the ethnographer's of objectification, saying, "The actual people who live in Japan are not unlike the general run of English people; that is to say, they are extremely commonplace, and have nothing curious or extraordinary about them. In fact the whole of Japan is a pure invention." The goal of the positive Victorian aesthetics I have been discussing was not to objectify others as art, but to provide the conditions that would allow oneself and others to live with the freedom of art.

The Decadents: Art as Escape from Others

The difference between aestheticism as presented by Ruskin, Morris, and Wilde and the English Decadence can be illustrated from the psychology of progressivism. Anyone who has moved in progressive or Leftist circles— and here I include feminist circles—has witnessed the demoralizing case of the wannabe progressive who is incapable of operating in conditions of uncertainty, risk, or vulnerability; incapable of living without authoritarian or hierarchical structures; incapable, in short, of living with change. Since risk, vulnerability, and instability are the inevitable conditions of progressivism, this psychological incapacity, no matter how fervent the conscious commitment, throws the wannabe Leftist perpetually into contradiction between her emotional needs and her abstract desires. Due to the nature of nurture as we have known it, some people are psychologically incapable of living with freedom.

This psychological contradiction is the secret of the Decadence. Unlike Morris and Wilde, who at least attempted to live life with the freedom of art, who risked social position, exposed themselves to emotional instability, recognized their interdependence with others, and promoted—even precipitated—change, the Decadents *desired* freedom (from bourgeois constraints, conventions, etc.), but they *required* control, stability, and distance from others. This contradiction leads to the hysterical and outrageous quality of the writing of a Huysmans, Bram Stoker, Joseph Conrad, or Frederick Rolfe, which after imaginatively exploring the horizons of desire always culminates in recuperative and repressive closure. Feminist theorists from Simone de Beauvoir to Carol Gilligan and Nancy Chodorow through Jessica Benjamin have often described the personality with hard boundaries, the emotional inability to expose oneself to the risk of others, which has been associated, rather parochially perhaps, with the masculine need to differentiate the male self from the socially devalued mother. In the broad social arena—the *society* with hard boundaries, the modern militarized nation-state—the fear of undifferentiation manifests itself as fear of engulfment by the mass, of external invasion by barbarian hordes. The antidote to this social undifferentiation is to maintain hierarchy, a social space in which everyone knows her place and all social relations are predetermined. The personality or state with hard boundaries seeks immunization against contamination and an illusory autonomy from other personalities and states. It does not seek change, but "scientifically" calculates "fair" exchanges. It sees risk in terms of sacrifice. In its hardest form, it is the psychological condition of military hierarchy and conservatism; in its unconscious and contradictory form, it is the psychological condition of decadents, for whom art is the *only* space—a tiny, safe space—of freedom.

I shall take as my example Frederick Rolfe's *Desire and Pursuit of the Whole: A Romance of Modern Venice* (1909). Appropriated as a cult work in the 1960's, the novel has again lapsed out of fashion except among aficionados of gay history. The subject of desire and pursuit is Nicholas Crabbe, an English expatriate and writer barely surviving in Venice. Like his namesake, he is hard on the outside but inwardly soft; the whole he desires and pursues is the Love of Plato's parable. The requirements of the beloved who will be Crabbe's other half are absolute loyalty, fidelity, and the physical attributes of a young Venetian sailor, all of which he finds in a sixteen-year-old female earthquake victim named Ermenegilda. Soft on the outside but inwardly hard, Ermenegilda is adopted by Crabbe as his gondolier, dressed and addressed as a boy (now called "Zildo"), and devoted to sharing Crabbe's fate in his adopted city. Having obliterated her sex—except in rare and poignant moments when Crabbe stumbles upon vestigial traces of her femininity, for example a rag doll concealed in their pupparin—Crabbe and the narrator fervently establish Zildo and Crabbe's perfect sympathy (meaning, a contemporary reader will quickly note, Zildo's sympathy with Crabbe, whom he/she always addresses as Master).

Their perfect sympathy is contrasted with Crabbe's uncompromising lack of sympathy with all of his compatriots, whether at home or in Venice. The imaginative investment inspiring half of the text is the fantasy of perfect love with Zildo; that driving the other half—and it is equally impassioned—is a typically Decadent hatred of bourgeois English life: its materialism and spiritual shallowness, its lack of imagination and lack of appreciation of the "natural aristocrat" (e.g., Crabbe), its vulgar and tedious heterosexual domesticity. The objects of Crabbe's prolonged and eloquent vituperation are scarcely veiled associates of Rolfe. W. H. Auden, who wrote the foreword to the only edition still in print, described Crabbe/Rolfe as the quintessential paranoid. I quote at length because the portrait could be of any number of fictive and real characters in the European Decadence.

> A paranoid goes through life with the assumption: "I am so extraordinary a person that others are bound to treat me as a unique

end, never as a means." Accordingly, when others treat him as a means or are just indifferent, he cannot believe this and has to interpret their conduct as malignant; they are treating him as an end, but in a negative way; they are trying to destroy him.

The "normal" person knows that, as a matter of fact, in most of our relations most of the time, we are doing no more than make use of each other, as a rule with mutual consent, as a means to pleasure, intellectual stimulus, etc., but keeps up the convention, both with himself and other, that we love and are loved for "ourselves alone," a fiction which is probably wise, for not only would social life be unbearable without it, but also the possibilities of genuine agape which, rare and delicate as they may be, do exist, would wither without its protective encouragement.

But it is a salutary experience also that, every now and then, we should have it stripped from us and that is what the paranoid does. His inordinate demand that we love him very much and his accusation when we do not that we hate him very much compel us to realise that we very rarely love or hate anybody; on the contrary, we can only stand each other in small doses without getting bored. The paranoid is the epitome of the bore. Crabbe was mistaken in thinking that the British colony in Venice hated him, but he was quite correct in thinking that they would be highly relieved to hear that he was dead.

Any paranoid is a nuisance, but a penniless one is a torment. The average person, if he has enough money in his pockets to be comfortable, will feel an obligation to help an acquaintance in a financial jam such as being unable to pay a hotel bill, but he hopes that will be the end of the matter and he certainly does not expect it to be taken too personally. Personally, however, is just how the paranoid takes it; he will never leave a benefactor alone because, to him, the important thing is not his hotel bill but the interest another has shown in him by paying it; consequently, he will soon create another crisis as a test and continue until the wretched benefactor can bear no more and the inevitable explosion occurs.[10]

We see that the loyal and true Zildo is merely a fantasy-reaction against the "betrayals" of the perfidious English, whom Rolfe/Crabbe never ceases to test and who never fail to fail the test.

To go somewhat beyond Auden's commonsensical ethos of self-interest, it takes a Crabbe to show us how very little most of us adhere to Kant's categorical imperative to treat others as ends in themselves rather than means to our own profit, pleasure, stimulation, comfort, etc. It takes a

Crabbe to show us that while we use others we are nonetheless resentful when they take our use of them *personally*—as if it were our purpose to use them rather than simply our purpose to be profit-maximizing, pleasured, stimulated, comforted and so forth. Those who are exploited for our gain only imagine that we have harbored malice aforethought. This precisely describes the resentment business communities feel when they are confronted with an exploited labor market's demands for justice.

In the end, the beauty and charity of Venice and Zildo are the background to Crabbe's abuse/neglegence at the hands of his compatriots. Since they will not justly give him his due, he starves to death. Rolfe depicts the homeless (in Italian, "without-roof") Crabbe wandering all night in the Field of Mars, dying of exposure in the public spaces of gorgeous Venice, composing his magnum opus *Towards Aristocracy*. Even the title is an oblique and decadent reference to the properly aesthetic and socialist poem by Edward Carpenter, *Towards Democracy* (1883), reminding us of the intertextuality of Decadence and Aestheticism. Carpenter, one of the more out homosexuals in nineteenth-century England, and one of the most genuinely democratic and progressive writers of the age, is the perfect foil to Crabbe/Rolfe, who, as Auden partially says, must in the long run love a girl rather than a seventeen-year-old boy because boys were historically autonomous pursuers of self-interest and not realistically capable of absolute and life-long devotion to middle-aged men with no money. They did not, like historical (and aristocratic) girls, "choose" to serve and then find that in their service was their "perfect freedom." (This explains the social and narratological bases of the conclusion, in which Zildo is gendered as female; whereas through most of the text, and as Rolfe's realistic object of desire, she is male.) Indeed the "out" and open lovingness of an Edward Carpenter is the perfect contrast to the love-as-domination of the repressed Rolfe.

For most readers from Auden to the present, the troubling aspect of Crabbe's martyrdom at the hands of the treacherous but banal English is Crabbe/Rolfe himself. Although perspicacious about the faults of the English, Crabbe/Rolfe is utterly blind to his own. Although he often praises Venetian charity, he is incapable either of accepting it himself or of getting a job, insisting always on his "right" to his own expropriated property. Obliterating Zildo's femininity, he never ceases to remind the reader of his own "abnormally masculine" physique and temperament. What Crabbe sees is a failure of nobility on the part of *everyone* but himself and Zildo, and what he demands from *everyone,* despite his ardent religiosity—Rolfe tried hard to enter holy orders and, failing that, deceptively used his initials *Fr.* to signify "Father"—is the repentance that should be the Lord's. Seeing himself as a rebel of heroic, even sublime, proportions, he bears all the marks of the most conservative Englishness: love of hierarchy and of ritual for its own sake, obsession with private property (including the Beloved), general inflexibility, and a deluded self-sufficiency. While he protests that he wants (comm)unity (the desire and pursuit of the whole), the novel chronicles the assertion of his autonomy—as an artist, an expatriate, and a lover: his boundaries, like the crab's, are armored, impermeable.

Wilde told a story about love called "The Teacher of Wisdom." In it, a holy man seeks for the perfect knowledge of God, of God as an object to be known by him. At the end of his life he has failed to know enough. When he gives up the search, he receives by this sacrifice the perfect love of God, or the gift of himself as a subject of God's love. Given Rolfe's rigid need to know and control the other, the only way the relation of self to other can be resolved with mutuality is to be magical, romantic. The fantastic Zildo reappears as a deus/dea ex machina, as, in fact, the principle of justice (but, as we shall see, a particular kind of justice). Finding Crabbe dead from starvation and exposure (or the negligence of others), Zildo now repays his first sacrifice with one greater: she gives him her blood, proclaiming, "you get back what you give." As he had saved her from the earthquake, so she now saves him. At this moment, and for the first time, Crabbe and the narrator call her "she" rather than "he," and the desire and pursuit of the whole is crowned and rewarded by heterosexual love. Thus not risk, nor generosity, nor change (the values of the earlier, socialist aesthetes) rule Rolfe's world, but the firm principle of exact exchange: you get back what you give, measure for measure. Moreover, you get back what you give in symmetrical gender relations, the male and the female, the hard and the soft. The formal disparity between the Venetian romance of the marvelous Zildo and the satirical realism of English finance at home and abroad also indicates the autonomy of the aesthetic that Ruskin, Morris, and Wilde had repudiated: only art (the dreamy boy-girl Zildo) can save Crabbe; for Rolfe, art is an escape from, not a transformation of, daily life.

While Ruskin, Morris, and Wilde wrote for freedom, equality, and toleration, the Decadents may be characterized by their fear of the freedom of others: of women (like New Woman literature and late-Victorian Gothic, which expresses the fear of undifferentiation from female or feminized bodies of various morphologies); of racial others (the "heart of darkness" literature of the British recoiling from their own projections on Asia, Africa, and Latin America); of working-class others (the East End poverty and "naturalist" literature that thrived in the 1890's); national others (the literature of expatriatism, whether in Venice, Mexico, or New Zealand). Indeed, the most salient characteristic of the Decadence to surface in recent criticism is English writers' abjection—their fear of loss of boundaries—and their recuperative attempts to fortify the rigid boundaries of the self and British society against the barbarians at the gates. (Both the U.S. and England have gone through cycles of such Decadence, the most recent signified by irrational fears of "multiculturalism" and "diversity," the struggle over educational policy taking up where immigration policy leaves off.)[11] Since this decadent fear of the freedom of others is a dominant strain in canonical Western literature in the twentieth century and should be familiar to students of European and American modernism, here it need only be said that it effectively terminated the liberatory aesthetics of the Victorian socialist aesthetes.

Practical Aesthetics Today

However one estimates the romance of Zildo or the realism of Rolfe's quarrels with recalcitrant publishers, one aspect of Rolfe's novel indubitably resonates with the concerns of practical aesthetics. Auden refers to Rolfe's artistically embodied love for Venice. Yet Rolfe's love for Venice is uniquely powerful because it is a passion for the city on the part of a man with no other home, a homeless, indeed a starving, man. This part of the novel is also true: Rolfe was for long periods homeless and hungry. He writes the sufferings of those who sleep on the streets; who watch helplessly the disintegration of their clothes, beginning with underwear; who experiencing mental and physical agony and loneliness contrive "to present to the world a face offensive, disdainful, utterly unapproachable" (281). He chronicles how the homeless live by bread alone, until they can stomach only a handful of water, taken surreptitiously at night from a public lavatory. He tells what it is like to die alone, outside. Yet just beyond this vale of tears there is always the daily life of tranquil Venice, described in the prose with reverent detail. The destitute Crabbe

> slowly paced along cypress-avenues, between the graves of little children with blue or white standards and the graves of adults marked by more sombre memorials. All around him were patricians bringing sheaves of painted candles and gorgeous garlands of orchids and everlastings, or plebians on their knees grubbing up weeds and tracing pathetic designs with cheap chrysanthemums and farthing night-lights. Here, were a baker's boy and a telegraph-messenger, repainting their father's grave-post with a tin of black and a bottle of gold. There, were a half a dozen ribald venal dishonest licentious young gondolieri, quiet and alone on their wicked knees round the grave of a comrade. (281–282)

I conclude the historical part of this essay with these two images—of human vulnerability and our consequent interdependence, as figured here in the homely pieties of daily life (images that Auden himself would associate with Italy in his hymn to the unheroic but tolerant life of the senses, "In Praise of Limestone"). Human vulnerability and our consequent interdependence remain central to practical aesthetics. In a culture that values scientistic desires for neutrality, practical aesthetics is about the quality of daily life, sensuous human experience. The passionate *care* that Ruskin and Morris felt for the mass and that Wilde, in his defense of speech, felt for the inarticulate, the silent, and the censored must oppose the self-proclaimed "scientific" distance from normativity. Practical aesthetics also provides a glimmering of another principle of justice than the rational one of exact exchange or "you get back what you give." The definition of justice as "exact exchange," of equal rewards for equal contributions, had always been the promise of capitalism as theorized by political economy. Yet because of its never-level playing fields, brutal expansionism, and exploitative profits, it has never fulfilled its promise. The problem of homelessness, whether its cause be pride, or profligacy, or genuine incapacity, calls forth, on the other hand, the only principle of justice that *is* just in a world in which people are born unequal or into unequal circumstances: to each according to her needs, from each according to her abilities.

The fact/value distinction that has subordinated literature and art to sciences like economics in the past century in the Euro-American community does not survive in times of crisis, which require both memory and desire, trained abilities and creative imagination. In Latin America, art has set itself a more urgent task than in the contemporary United States. From March through August of 1980 the government of Nicaragua waged the National Literacy Campaign that began the process of teaching campesinos to read and write, encouraging them "to emerge from their isolation and learn something of the world, to help them relate to their neighbors" (in the interior of Nicaragua farms are often very far apart).[12] The Campaign, which reduced illiteracy from 60 percent to 13 percent, was supported by national poetry workshops founded to "create the conditions for all the people's civic participation," and Daniel Ortega's cabinet included four established poets.[13] In his manifesto of art and politics "In Defense of the Word" (1983), the Uruguayan writer Eduardo Galeano describes what it is like to write for (on behalf of) illiterates, beginning with the observation that "the abyss"—a term familiar to students of the nineteenth century as referring to the social distance between the rich and poor—is even greater in Latin America than in North America and the methods necessary to maintain it even more bloody.[14] For Galeano, art must awaken consciousness and expose ideological lies:

> I think that a primordial function of Latin American literature
> today is the rescue of the word, frequently used and abused with

impunity for the purpose of hampering and betraying communication. "Freedom" in my country is the name of a jail for political prisoners, and "democracy" forms part of the title of various regimes of terror; the word "love" defines the relationship of a man with his automobile, and "revolution" is understood to describe what a new detergent can do in your kitchen; "glory" is something that a certain smooth soap produces in its user, and "happiness" is a sensation experienced while eating hot dogs. "A peaceful country" means, in many countries of Latin America, "a well-kept cemetery." . . . By writing it is possible to offer, in spite of persecution and censorship, the testimony of our time and our people—for now and for later. One may write as if to say: "We are here, we were here; we are thus, we were thus." In Latin America a literature is taking shape and acquiring strength, a literature that does not lull its readers to sleep, but rather awakens them; that does not propose to bury our dead, but to immortalize them; that refuses to stir the ashes but rather attempts to light the fire. (193)

We don't have to go to Latin America to understand the importance of such practical aesthetics. Adrienne Rich concludes "Blood, Bread, and Poetry: The Location of the Poet" (1984) with what it means to write for illiterates in the United States: "I write in full knowledge . . . that I live in a technologically advanced country where 40 percent of the people can barely read and 20 percent are functionally illiterate."[15] In Britain, practical aesthetics' modernist goals dressed in new, postmodern forms appear in the aesthetics of new urban movements. In a chapter called "Diaspora, Utopia and the Critique of Capitalism" in his *There Ain't No Black in the Union Jack* (1987), Paul Gilroy describes the "three core themes of black expressive culture":

> 1. A critique of . . . work, the labour process and the division of labour under capitalism.
> 2. A critique of the state revolving around a plea for the disassociation of law from domination. . . .
> 3. A passionate belief in the importance of history and the historical process . . . as an antidote to the suppression of historical and temporal perception under late capitalism.[16]

Although they derive from different sources, these core themes are consistent with the projects of the Victorian aesthetes, as are the new social movements' refusal (according to Gilroy) of the mediation of the established political system, the centrality they accord to the needs of the body, and their utopian insistence upon the *immediate* satisfaction of all needs. When

Gilroy introduces Rudolph Bahro's "elements of a utopian vision which combines a critique of productivism with an ethical dimension and some explicit concern with the necessary realization of individual autonomy" (234)—elements which Gilroy finds echoed in the contemporary aesthetics of black Britain—one can see the lineaments of a historical trajectory of liberatory aesthetics whose current proponents no longer occlude the history of slavery and racism but to the contrary self-consciously reveal it in the expressive culture of the diaspora. Gilroy, among others, has shown that Victorian aesthetics were inculpated in the history of racism; and this essay began by acknowledging the dual force of the aesthetic—how the names of enlightenment and liberation have been lent to obfuscation and domination: race and gender have become the critical cases. Yet precisely because of the knowledge that informs these critiques, liberatory aesthetics may be even more liberatory today. Whether in Morris or Gilroy, the aesthetic demand is for good health, physical pleasure, one's share of knowledge and skill of hand, meaningful labor, a beautiful and bountiful earth.

Furthermore, these demands are no more "utopian"—in the sense of being "no place"—than the science of economics itself. First, economics reduces human psychology to one crude motivation of acquisitiveness. Although nods are made to the "ceteris paribus" clause, "other conditions" are rarely taken into account. Second, economics imagines (or "models") macroscopic economic relations as if they were strategic interactions among profit-maximizing individuals (rather than, like Marx and Weber, seeing contingent socioeconomic arrangements as fundamental in the construction of *different kinds* of human psychology and interaction). Finally, economics universalizes its reductive psychology and hypothetical sociology, its "ideal types"—in Weber's sense of "one-sided accentuations of one or more points of view"—of a specific historical and geographical social arrangement, as scientific laws. "Rational economic man," who, faced with an array of goods and services, dispassionately weighs his various possibilities for satisfaction and chooses the one that maximizes a utility function, and capitalism itself, which promises every man and woman the just fruits of our labor and abstinence, are themselves utopian. For all the political use they are put to, economic rationality and capitalism as just exchange cannot be found empirically anywhere in reality.[17]

The "demands" of practical aesthetics may be met by responses like this: "A request . . . gains nothing in legitimacy by virtue of being based on the hardship of an unmet need. Rights do not flow from hardship, but from the fact that the alleviation of hardship improves the system's performance. The needs of the most underprivileged should not be used as a system regulator as a matter of principle: since the means of satisfying them is already known, their actual satisfaction will not improve the system's performance, but only increases its expenditures."[18] This is Jean-François Lyotard's account of a systems-theoretic approach to social welfare. Practical aesthetics would reject its fundamental definitions, as Ruskin rejected those of its ancestral science, classical political economy. For example, one might say that the economy (the "system") does not equal "growth" or GNP; "growth" is not its priority; the measure of the system's "performance" must be gauged in terms of actual benefits to citizens—and *which* citizens are included and excluded must be specified; efficiency and performance must have some reference to the experiences of daily life, and so on.

We should not abandon the hope of providing for all a more aesthetic, a freer, life. As educators, this means, in part, that we should engage in dialogue with other disciplines whose perspectives are both insufficient in our view and more powerful than our own. Traditional humanists clamor that we in culture studies are being colonized by the social sciences, but the reverse is the goal: many cultural critics feel the need to show the scientists —"social" and "hard"—the tools of accountability, self-criticism, and value.

Just one example of the need to integrate practical aesthetics into other disciplines that may not know they need it is a course at Stanford called Peace Studies. Developed during the Vietnam War, the Peace Studies Program had subsided by the Gulf War into a branch of International Relations, a field directed by political scientists and economists. During the Gulf War, a special course, generously funded and widely publicized, was devised with guest lecturers from the sciences and social sciences. Pursuing the themes of peace as (1) the absence of war or (2) positive wellbeing, the topics included Augustinian and neo-Catholic "just war" theory, the economics of "defense," and game theory, all of which distanced students from the experience of war (and of peace). In this distancing effect, the course imitated the media representation of the Gulf War itself, with its high-tech "Nintendo" airstrike strategies. The way a student translated it to me was that the course provided a "value-free introduction to war and peace." (Think about it: a value-free introduction to war and peace.) Although every existing national literature arguably includes a literature devoted to war, its goals, and its effects upon daily life, and although these literatures of war offer students unique perspectives, neither cultural critics nor literary texts appeared at any time in the Peace Studies course. On the other hand, Peace Studies students who also took the English Department's graduate and undergraduate courses on the literature of war found critical perspectives; victims' voices; the unequal composition of the military and differential benefits of personnel depending upon age, sex, race, and sexual orientation;[19] and the "aesthetic," or concrete and differentiated, experiences of war in China, Palestine, and Latin America as well as in Europe and

North America, through the eyes of women and children as well as men. Students learned, through several autobiographies, how Jews lived and died in the Second World War, and they also learned, through auto-biographical fiction, how twenty million Chinese died.

We who do practical aesthetics are critical: we see in sensuous daily experience symbols of the morally good; we see in the admittedly constrained creativity and freedom of art both positive and negative possibilities for human—and not just human—life. We rarely make monistic claims for The Good, The True, or The Beautiful, but if we are not cowards we do insist that we know when we are confronted with evil, with lies, and with ugliness. Whatever the Good society may be, pain and poverty, as Wilde said in "The Soul of Man under Socialism," are bad. However much intellectuals argue about the status of Truth, a government that justifies or ignores pain and poverty lies. To be sure, now as in the nineteenth century, practical aesthetics is not the only source of criticism of pain, poverty, and disinformation, but grounded in sense and committed to expression it is perhaps uniquely suited for wide access. This access has little to do with universal taste but much to do with the universal conditions for human life: nurturance, food, shelter, language. Just as these are limits upon human nature or possibility, so they are also the bases of human society, the source of our interdependence, which we may acknowledge with motives for freedom and justice or with manipulations of power. Rational economic man insisted upon his abstract autonomy, his competitive struggle against all others. In relation to him, aesthetics has traditionally been feminized, placed in the secondary, devalued position. Practical aesthetics is about the ultimate value, and quality, of our interdependence.

Notes

1. For the first approach, see Pierre Bourdieu, *Distinction: A Critique of the Judgment of Taste* (Cambridge: Harvard University Press, 1984); Stanley Fish, *Doing What Comes Naturally* (Durham, N.C.: Duke University Press, 1989); and Barbara Herrnstein Smith, *Contingencies of Value: Alternative Perspectives for Critical Theory* (Cambridge: Harvard University Press, 1988). Among the Foucauldian approaches are Nancy Armstrong, *Desire and Domestic Fiction* (New York: Oxford University Press, 1987) and D. A. Miller, *The Novel and the Police* (Berkeley: University of California Press, 1988).

2. David Hume, *An Inquiry Concerning Human Understanding* (Indianapolis: Hackett, 1981), 63.

3. For an extended discussion of the duality of the aesthetic, see Terry Eagleton, *The Ideology of the Aesthetic* (Oxford: Basil Blackwell, 1990), 1–30, 366–417.

4. Whether Morris was a libertarian Marxist or a communist anarchist

with strong leanings toward Marxism, or whether Wilde was more influenced by Kropotkin or Chuang-tze are issues hotly debated by the Blessed and on which I myself hold some rather strong views. Since this article, however, is for a general audience, I can only refer the reader to such specialist volumes as Florence Boos and Carole Silver's collection *Socialism and the Literary Artistry of William Morris* (Columbia: University of Missouri Press, 1990). For Wilde, see my *Idylls of the Marketplace: Oscar Wilde and the Victorian Public* (Stanford: Stanford University Press, 1986), 29–34, 215 nn. 24–27 and my introduction to *Critical Essays on Oscar Wilde* (New York: G. K. Hall, 1991). 7–9.

5. John Ruskin, *Unto This Last and Other Writings* (London: Penguin, 1985), 144–145. Further references are given in the text.

6. *Selected Writings of Walter Pater,* ed. Harold Bloom (New York: Signet, 1974), 195.

7. *Political Writings of William Morris,* ed. A. L. Morton (New York: International Publishers, 1973), 17. Further references are given in the text.

8. For a comparative discussion of Foucault and Wilde's aestheticism, see Gagnier, *Critical Essays on Oscar Wilde,* 8–9.

9. Gagnier, *Idylls,* 5.

10. Frederick Rolfe [Baron Corvo], *The Desire and Pursuit of the Whole* (New York: Da Capo Press, 1986) vi–vii. Further references to the novel are given in the text.

11. Donna Haraway discusses the history of American decadence in terms of fear of others in *Primate Visions* (New York: Routledge, 1989). See especially chap. 3, "Teddy Bear Patriarchy," 26–58.

12. *Envio* (Managua) 17 (November, 1982): 14–15.

13. Interviews with various ministers, television documentary. *A Young Revolution,* PBS, 1990.

14. Eduardo Galeano, "In Defense of the Word," in *Days and Nights of Love and War* (New York: Monthly Review Press, 1983), 181–194.

15. Adrienne Rich, *Blood, Bread, and Poetry: Selected Prose, 1979–1985* (New York: Norton, 1986), 174.

16. Paul Gilroy, "*There Ain't No Black in the Union Jack*": *The Cultural Politics of Race and Nation* (Chicago: University of Chicago Press, 1991), 199.

17. For the idea of economics as methodologically utopian, see Max Weber, "Objectivity and Understanding in Economics," in *The Philosophy of Economics,* ed. Daniel M. Hausman (Cambridge: Cambridge University Press, 1984), 99–112.

18. Jean-François Lyotard, *The Postmodern Condition* (Minneapolis: University of Minnesota Press, 1984), 63.

19. It is perhaps most surprising that the social-scientific Peace Studies course did not deal with such primary sociological matter as the composition of the military; but, according to the course organizer, the course was not about the sociology of war but rather about different theoretical models of peace.

■ CHERYL A. WALL ■

On Freedom and the Will to Adorn

Debating Aesthetics and/as Ideology in African American Literature

The will to adorn is the second most notable characteristic in Negro expression. Perhaps his idea of ornament does not attempt to meet conventional standards, but it satisfies the soul of its creator. . . .

Whatever the Negro does of his own volition he embellishes. His religious service is for the greater part excellent prose poetry. Both prayers and sermons are tooled and polished until they are true works of art. The supplication is forgotten in the frenzy of creation. The prayer of the white man is considered humorous in its bleakness. The beauty of the Old Testament does not exceed that of a Negro prayer.

—*Zora Neale Hurston*[1]

In absence of fixed and nourishing forms of culture, the Negro has a folklore which embodies the memories and hopes of his struggles. Not yet caught in paint or stone and as yet but feebly depicted in the poem and novel, the Negroes' most powerful images of hope and longing for freedom still remain in the fluid state of living speech. . . . Negro folklore remains the Negro writer's most powerful weapon, a weapon which he must sharpen for the hard battles looming ahead, battles which will test a people's faith in themselves.

—*Richard Wright*[2]

Whatever she planted grew as if by magic, and her fame as a grower of flowers spread over three counties. Because of her creativity with flowers, even my memories of poverty are seen through a screen of blooms—sunflowers, petunias, roses, dahlias, forsythia, spirea, delphiniums, verbena . . . and on and on.

—*Alice Walker*[3]

IN 1934 ZORA NEALE HURSTON published an essay, "Characteristics of Negro Expression," which set forth the aesthetic principles she believed undergirded African American oral performance, music, and dance. First among them was the heightened sense of drama that marked every phase of black life. "Everything is acted out," she asserted. "There is an impromptu ceremony always ready for every hour of life. No little moment passes unadorned."[4] This concept of ritualized improvisation was reflected in casual conversations, customs of courtship, and worship practices. Its complement was the "will to adorn," which was expressed both through the form of the ceremonies and their linguistic content.

Drawing on her notes and transcriptions from years of ethnographic field work, Hurston enumerated the contributions African Americans had made to the English language; she listed examples of the distinctive metaphors and similes, double descriptives, and verbal nouns. Then in one of the most detailed descriptions of the essay, she connected the linguistic practices with the world view which produced them as she described a room she had observed in Mobile, Alabama. Furnished with an overstuffed mohair living room suite, an imitation mahogany bed, a chifforobe, and a console victrola, the room was papered with Sunday supplements of the local newspaper, Seven calendars and three wall pockets, one decorated with a lace doily, were hung along the walls. For Hurston, no gesture was more telling than the lace doily adorning the wall hanging: a decoration of a decoration. In her interpretation, it conveyed that "there can never be enough of beauty, let alone too much" (178). Despite, or perhaps because of, the fact that the gesture, like the prayer extolled in the passage I have chosen as an epigraph, did not conform to "conventional standards," they both exemplified Hurston's assertion that the expression of beauty, whether through action or words, was a cardinal principle of African American vernacular culture.

Surveying the same body of oral expression—though appalled by the material culture in which it was embedded—Richard Wright saw and heard not the will to adorn, but the will to be free. In "Blueprint for Negro Literature," published in 1937, Wright maintained that Negro folklore contained "in a measure that puts to shame more deliberate forms of expression the collective sense of the Negro's life in America."[5] He argued, moreover, that black writers ought to tap the "racial wisdom" distilled through what he later designated "The Forms of Things Unknown."[6]

Given the subversive content and political implications of this wisdom, which Wright designated "nationalist," its expressions were necessarily veiled. Consequently, and perhaps against our expectations, Wright privileged private discourse over the culture's public social dramas with which

Hurston was more concerned. Indeed, he rendered the public private when he extolled the "blues, spirituals, and folk tales recounted from mouth to mouth, the whispered words of a black mother to her black daughter on the ways of men, the confidential wisdom of a black father to his black son, the swapping of sex experiences on street corners from boy to boy in the deepest vernacular, [and] work songs sung under blazing suns" (6). For Wright the conception of these expressions as private suggested both the sense that whatever happened in the African American community, behind the veil in terms of Du Bois's famous metaphor, was necessarily private—the white world was the public sphere—and the sense that blacks could only communicate the anger and rage which their oppression provoked furtively and in language too coded to be understood by those outside the race.

From the perspective of a half century, it might seem most notable that in essays published only three years apart, Zora Neale Hurston and Richard Wright concluded that oral lore could and should be the "generative source" of African American literature.[7] Wright states so explicitly when he claims folklore as the black writer's "most powerful weapon." Although Hurston does not discuss formal fiction and drama in the context of her ethnographic writing, she adheres to the principle of ritualized improvisation throughout her literary work. In the case of each writer, his or her own fiction has provided the best textual evidence for these conclusions.

Whatever the similarity between their conclusions, the more vivid and certainly profound differences in their conceptions have gained critical currency. If for Wright the "folk" culture is defined by absence, for Hurston it is an overflowing presence. Wright's metaphors encode physical constriction, while Hurston's convey psychological and spiritual expansiveness. Where he sees provisions of bare sustenance, she sees a banquet of verbal riches. In one telling contrast, the prayers which to her signified beauty were to Wright evidence of the lamentable fact that for millions of African Americans their only guide to personal dignity as well as their only sense of the world outside themselves came through "the archaic morphology of Christian salvation" (6). Hurston was quick to observe that the "Negro is not a Christian really," and to leave it at that.

The definitions of culture on which their analyses depended were fundamentally at odds. For Wright, the forms of culture had already been fixed, and blacks were shut out of them. While he urged writers to recognize the value in life as the folk lived it, he saw in that recognition the emergence of "a new culture in the shell of the old." The writers' larger mission was to make people realize a meaning in their suffering: for at the moment they began to do so, Wright predicted, "the civilization that engenders that suffering is doomed" (8). To achieve their mission, writers had to develop a perspective on the world, a sense of the interconnectedness of the suffering and hopes of black Americans and other oppressed people. Marxism provided one source for that perspective as well as a means, ultimately, to transcend the nationalist consciousness that was the legacy of Jim Crow.

For Hurston cultural forms were not fixed. African American folklore, she averred, "is not a thing of the past. It is still in the making" (180). Her analysis was much more concerned with the process of cultural production than with its products. Consequently, she valorized adaptability, variety, and dynamic suggestion as foundational principles of black expressive forms from speech to music to dance. In their forced encounter with Western culture, Hurston argued, Africans in America had seized the Europeans' language and remade it so compellingly that European Americans changed their way of speaking.[8] African American music and dance had likewise transformed the national culture in the 1920s.

The arena for struggle and resistance which Hurston defines is cultural. Rather than awaiting writers and intellectuals to lead it, as Wright described, Hurston maintained that the struggle had long since been joined. The intellectual's role was to analyze the ways in which the culture of the "Negro farthest down" had pervaded the national culture. It was to devise, in other words, a deconstructive practice to refigure and reinterpret the centrality of the margin. To do so meant rejecting "conventional standards," which obscured black people's cultural contributions. One needed instead to formulate alternate standards which would, for example, validate the jook as, "musically speaking," the most important place in America.[9] Hurston did not comment on the fact that Southern jooks, like all other public places in the United States South, were segregated.

In the longstanding debate over the relation between aesthetics and ideology in black literature, African Americanist critics have deployed the contrasting positions of Hurston and Wright with their respective emphases on beauty as a cultural value and on the priority of political struggle. That debate mirrors the current controversy in the interpretive communities which occasions this volume. Critics of what was once known as the mainstream have been forced to acknowledge the ideologies at work in the construction of even the "masterpieces" of English and American literature and to confront the concurrent loss of "enduring" criteria by which to assign aesthetic value. Their situation is an inversion of that facing critics of African American literature.

From its beginnings in the United States, black writing has been defined as having *only* an ideological importance. Houston Baker argued in a 1972 essay that most black American texts "have been considered excessively didactic, and when they have been acknowledged for their utilitarian quality, white critics have felt compelled to point out that such *utile* has been purchased 'at the expense of the *dulce.*'"[10] Evidence for this conclusion is abundant. For example, historians and an occasional critic valued slave narratives, not as literature but as documents of the abolitionist crusade. W. E. B. Du Bois in *The Souls of Black Folk* and a shelf full of additional volumes revealed himself to scholars as merely a brilliant "polemicist." Routinely, critics read novels by Richard Wright, Ann Petry, and James Baldwin as sociology and dramas by Lorraine Hansberry and Amiri Baraka as protest or propaganda. Departing from the work of mainly white scholars and critics of an earlier generation, much of the work in African American literary study over the last quarter century has been devoted to defining aesthetic principles and to demonstrating the dual quests for freedom and for beauty in black writing.

The Black Aesthetic movement of the 1970s offers a dramatic case in point. It embraced the definition of black literature as didactic or ideological; indeed, despite its label, it marks one of the most intensely ideological moments in African American literary history. Stephen Henderson charged that "Black poetry in the United States has been widely misunderstood, misinterpreted, and undervalued for a variety of reasons—aesthetic, cultural, and political."[11] Only by devising a critical practice that took all these reasons into account could black poetry be well read. Addison Gayle wrote in the introduction to the movement's signal anthology that "the question for the black critic today is not how beautiful is a melody, a play, a poem, or a novel, but how much more beautiful has the poem, melody, play, or novel made the life of a single black man?"[12] Few critics then or now would venture to evaluate a text in terms of this question; its usefulness was rhetorical and inherent in the asking. It aimed toward an ideal where ethics and aesthetics were one.

Black Aestheticians treated concerns that were more conventionally viewed as aesthetic largely by analogy to the sister arts, most especially music. In *Black Fire,* an anthology edited by Amiri Baraka and Larry Neal, as in *The Black Aesthetic,* extended sections were devoted to music. Moreover, in its most imaginative gestures, like Henderson's theorizing in *Understanding the New Black Poetry,* the Black Aestheticians derived their theories from black speech and black music.[13] Although their efforts might have gained impetus from the work Hurston had done in the 1930s, her work was rarely cited.[14] By contrast, Richard Wright, widely regarded as the most influential black writer of his time, continued to represent an ideal which the next generation strove to emulate. A 1968 article in *Black World,* "Black Writers' Views on Literary Lions and Values," celebrated "a spirit of revolution" abroad in the world of black letters. Wright, who was pictured on the cover, was seen as its guiding light. More than half of thirty-eight writers polled rated him as the most important black writer in history.[15] In the early

1970s, "Blueprint for Negro Literature" was reprinted in two influential anthologies. *Amistad 2,* edited by John A. Williams and Charles F. Harris, was dedicated to Wright; "Blueprint," published for the first time in its original version, was its lead essay. Editor Addison Gayle chose a slightly different version to introduce the section on fiction in *The Black Aesthetic.* In the preface to the volume, Gayle represented the black artist at war with society; Richard Wright was the prototypical warrior/writer.

Gayle reconferred on Wright the mantle of heroic manhood, which he had claimed for himself in "Blueprint." There he referred contemptuously to the black writing of earlier generations in images of humiliation and emasculation. Black writing "had been confined to humble novels, poems, and plays, decorous ambassadors who go a-begging to white America. They entered the Court of American Public Opinion dressed in the knee-pants of servility, curtsying to show that the Negro was not inferior, that he was human, and that he had a life comparable to that of other people" (4–5).

Although it is difficult at first to see how Hurston's texts could be subsumed in Wright's description, since they seem hardly decorous or humble—and curtsying is not a cultural practice they record—Wright's review of her novel, *Their Eyes Were Watching God,* shows clearly that he included her writing in his indictment. The novel, in his view, lacked a theme and any claim at all to seriousness. He located it instead in the tradition of minstrelsy and described its characters as caught "in that safe and narrow orbit in which America likes to see the Negro live: between laughter and tears."[16] He defined it, in other words, as a novel of feeling rather than of ideas. In so doing, he placed its author in the sphere of the feminine.

Wright's bias is apparent throughout this review, in which seriousness and ideas are masculine coded terms.[17] But nowhere is the sexism more telling than in Wright's remarks on the language of Hurston's text. Her prose, he charges, "is cloaked in that facile sensuality that has dogged Negro expression since the days of Phillis Wheatley" (25). Most readers will see, or more aptly, hear, little resemblance between Hurston's blues-inflected prose and Wheatley's neoclassical poetry. The reference to sensuality is egregious. Wright's invocation of Wheatley serves mainly to link Hurston to a politics he deemed reactionary and to a quest for the beautiful which, to him, served no "serious" purpose.

Wright's review of *Their Eyes* and Hurston's review of his *Uncle Tom's Children*—which I will discuss below—exemplify the extent to which the debate over aesthetics and ideology in African American literature is a gendered debate.[18] The beautiful is perceived to be ornamental and superfluous. At best, the beautiful distracts attention from the overriding goal of social and political liberation. At worst, it undermines and trivializes that struggle. What enables both of these conclusions is the unspoken assumption that the beautiful is ascriptively feminine and that the goal of the struggle is the liberation of the black man.

Hurston betrayed a gender bias of her own when she wrote of *Uncle Tom's Children* that it contained, "perhaps," enough killing "to satisfy all black male readers."[19] Or, perhaps, she was just signifying, that is, employing the African American rhetorical device of communicating by indirection; the purpose is often to ridicule.[20] The object of ridicule in the foregoing quotation might be Wright, the fantasies of his black male readers, and/or the images of black men running through the minds of white readers of the *Saturday Review* which published her critique. Surely, signifying is the impulse behind her dismissal of Wright's rendering of black vernacular speech. She pretended to wonder if he was "tone-deaf." Her point was that Wright's dialogue captured none of the drama or the adornment she viewed as characteristic of black expression. She was willing to grant that he was not deaf to beauty elsewhere. "But aside from the broken speech of his characters, the book contains some beautiful writing. One hopes that Mr. Wright will find in Negro life a vehicle for his talents" (32). As is often the case with signifying, this last remark scores a rhetorical point while misstating fact: Wright's stories were obviously representations of African American lives. The remark does contain a certain truth, however. From Hurston's perspective, Wright's misinterpretation of those lives was too profound to be credible.

Critics and readers disagreed; after the success of *Uncle Tom's Children,* Wright went on with the publication of *Native Son* to the greatest success theretofore achieved by a black writer. His contemporaries, even those like James Baldwin and Ralph Ellison, whose aesthetic and ideological assumptions were substantially different from his, responded to Wright's example. Hurston's books went out of print.

Writing just as the movement to recuperate Hurston's works and reputation gained force, June Jordan published an essay, "Notes Toward a Black Balancing of Love and Hatred," in *Black World,* a journal which had been a chief promoter of the Black Aesthetic. Hurston's photograph appeared on the cover of the August 1974 issue. In her essay, Jordan sketched a path toward reconciling the views of Hurston and Wright. She argued that "affirmation of Black values and lifestyle within the American context is, indeed, an act of protest. Therefore, Hurston's affirmative work is profoundly defiant, just as Wright's protest unmistakably asserts our need for an alternative, benign environment."[21]

Here Jordan gestures toward the ideology implicit in Hurston's aesthetic. By rejecting the definitions of themselves the dominant society attempted to impose, and by preserving, adapting, and creating their own cultural practices, African Americans had waged a persistent struggle of political resistance. The failure to acknowledge the political implications of Hurston's art produces the kind of critical blindness Toni Morrison identifies in *Playing in the Dark*: "Criticism as a form of knowledge is capable of robbing literature not only of its own implicit and explicit ideology but of its ideas as well."[22]

In the balancing spirit of Jordan's essay, I would gesture toward Wright's concern with aesthetics. Referring to what he called the autonomy of craft and thereby declaring his own artistic independence—from both his black literary precursors and his white Marxist patrons—Wright asserted that "the limitations of the craft constitute some of its greatest virtues" (18). He cautioned that fiction was not a social mirror and warned the writer against attempting "a too literal translation of experiences into images" (18). While Wright called for a simplicity in presentation (black workers were the literature's implied audience), he disparaged the simplistic. He insisted instead that "all the complexity, the strangeness, the magic wonder of life that plays like a bright sheen over even the most sordid existence, should be there. To borrow a phrase from the Russians, it should have a *complex simplicity*" (12)

One might observe merely that Wright's position is more nuanced than is sometimes acknowledged. But I would argue that those nuances, like Hurston's implicit rhetoric of resistance, establish the categories of aesthetics and ideology in African American literature as mutually constituted. The spare prose and detached descriptions of graphic violence in *Black Boy* deepen the protest against the unrelievedly bleak representation of poor black Southerners' lives. Contrariwise, poetic metaphor in *Their Eyes Were Watching God* seems to decorate a decoration both in the novel's most intensely lyrical passages and in those fierce arguments in which Janie "specifies" against Joe. This adorned language registers affirmation of African American discursive traditions and protests against the oppressive structures imposed directly or indirectly by the dominant society.

▪ ▪ ▪

For most recent black writers, the opposition of aesthetics and ideology seems patently false. Yet, to reconcile the imperatives of these complementary concerns, writers recuperate and revise the positions set forth above. To illustrate how these positions are renegotiated, I turn to Alice Walker's *In Search of Our Mothers' Gardens: Womanist Prose*. This volume collects essays, speeches, and reviews written between 1966 and 1982. Many of the topics are literary, as Walker attempts to chart traditions in which to locate her own work. She writes most famously about Hurston, but also about

Nella Larsen, Jean Toomer, Langston Hughes, Flannery O'Connor, and Virginia Woolf. A substantial number of the topics are social and political: the Civil Rights Movement; the dissolution of community and the concomitant rise of crime and spiritual despair in urban black America; the antinuclear movement; and womanism, a concept which is defined in the prologue and elaborated upon throughout these essays. Carefully crafted, Walker's strongest essays enact the fusion of aesthetics and ideology.

Several pieces in the volume, notably the title essay and "Looking for Zora," are among Walker's best known and most memorable works. Indeed, I would make the case that Walker, despite her reputation as a novelist, short story writer, and poet, has done her best work in the essay—a genre that has at present little critical currency. Consequently, few critics have commented on the lucidity of Walker's prose, the richness of her humor and irony, and the power of her passion in these pieces. The form of the essay which strives to produce the effect of the spontaneous, the tentative, and the open-ended lends itself to exploring the complex and contentious issues which Walker addresses.[23] She invites readers to puzzle the issues out with her and welcomes them to share those epiphanies she achieves. Yet writer and readers have to accept the reality that most of these issues have no easy resolution.

Along with Toni Morrison, Paule Marshall, and Audre Lorde, Alice Walker is in the vanguard of a group of black women writers who have remade the literary landscape of our time. She is by many accounts the most controversial. Perceived in some quarters as the exemplar of political correctness, Walker is often accused of sacrificing art to politics. But if she is deemed politically correct by more conservative white critics, within the African American literary community, not to mention among African Americans generally, her politics are often considered heretical. In the essay "Reading Family Matters," Deborah McDowell analyzes incisively the critical reception of Walker's fiction.[24] McDowell's analysis clarifies the extent to which the debates over aesthetics and ideology remain gendered debates. The charge in Walker's case is not that her work lacks ideas or seriousness; it is rather that Walker in her commitment to feminism has endorsed the wrong ideology. Interestingly, Walker in her essays anticipates repeatedly the attacks that have been levelled at her and her work. She determines early on to "Be nobody's darling; / Be an outcast / Qualified to live / Among your dead."[25]

Richard Wright, as well as Zora Hurston, is among Walker's "dead." She revises both their positions in her endeavor to unify the quest for freedom and beauty.[26] This quest is the theme of *In Search of Our Mother's Gardens,* and Walker's revisions of her precursors' views may be read even in her manipulation of the image the title encodes. The garden is the initial signifier of the beautiful. In the title essay, Walker writes vividly of her mother's garden, "so brilliant with colors, so original in its design, so magnificent with life and creativity" that strangers drive out of their way to view it.[27] Writing is for the daughter what gardening is for the mother: "work her soul must have." The mother in her garden, like the daughter at her desk, is "ordering the universe in the image of her personal conception of Beauty" (241). Both, Walker insists, are artists. But the beauty of the garden does not blind Walker to the poverty and racism that have scarred the family's life. If "memories of poverty are seen through a screen of blooms," they are seen nonetheless. The perspective through which Walker remembers is akin to the perspective Wright called upon black writers to develop.

The essay alludes directly to Virginia Woolf's *A Room of One's Own* in its discussion of Phillis Wheatley, who, Walker observes, did not own herself, let alone the room (with key and lock) Woolf maintained the woman writer required. But Woolf's room contrasts as well with the mother's gardens. Due to the itinerant life the Walkers as sharecroppers lived, the mother planted many gardens. Their beauty nurtured Walker's spirit, but the family's dispossession—and that of the generations of black women artists whose legacies Walker wishes to recuperate—motivates her political commitment. In the tradition of Richard Wright, Walker wants her writing to serve political ends.

She invokes Wright specifically in three of her essays, "The Black Writer and the Southern Experience," "The Unglamorous but Worthwhile Duties of the Black Revolutionary Artist, or of the Black Writer Who Simply Works and Writes," and "Beyond the Peacock: The Reconstruction of Flannery O'Connor." In the first two, she protests the exclusion of Wright and other black writers from the Southern writers course she took at Sarah Lawrence College. Having taught such a course herself by 1971, she determines that Wright's *Black Boy* and "The Ethics of Living Jim Crow" are indispensable. The first duty she has faced as a black writer, who eschews the label revolutionary, is to teach herself black writing; the second is to teach it to others. The ultimate duty is to write.

In "Beyond the Peacock," Walker proclaims her unwillingness ever to settle for a segregated literature. O'Connor had been on the college reading list, of course, and Walker admired deeply "the magic, the wit, and the mystery" of her writing. She wants very much to reclaim O'Connor's work and to place it alongside that of the black authors whose writing she has had subsequently to seek out by herself. To do so however, she has to put their lives (and her own) in perspective.

The essay recounts a pilgrimage Walker makes, accompanied by her mother, first to the abandoned sharecropper cabin the Walkers once rented and then to Andalusia, the O'Connor country house, where the author had moved after being crippled by lupus. To Walker's surprise, the houses stand on either side of the same field; the field she had loved as a girl, she now recognizes was "Flannery's field." This and subsequent revelations threaten to overwhelm Walker's empathy and admiration for O'Connor. Knocking on the door of the O'Connor house, which is unoccupied but in good repair, Walker reflects bitterly on "the fact that in Mississippi no one even remembers where Richard Wright lived, while Faulkner's house is maintained by a black caretaker."[28] The racial identity of the grounds-keeper in Milledgeville, Georgia, can only be inferred; but not only is the house cared for, so are the peacocks. These birds, beloved by O'Connor, become a problematic signifier of beauty and privilege. Walker's mother observes that peacocks "eat up your blooms," and the reader recalls that Mrs. Walker's daffodils bloom still around the long abandoned cabin. As the essay's title implies, before she can reconstruct O'Connor's legacy, Walker has to get beyond the peacocks. That she does is implied by the essay's invitation to interpret her rage in the terms it uses earlier to gloss "The Displaced Person" as a "moment of revelation, when the individual comes face to face with her own limitations and comprehends 'the true frontiers of her own inner country'" (56). The limitations here are both Walker's and O'Connor's; but they are more profoundly those of the society which would segregate two kindred spirits in literature as it had in life.

"Beyond the Peacock" quotes from O'Connor's essays, letters, and short stories; it sketches her biography. Walker interweaves anecdotes from her own life, both as a child growing up in Georgia and as an adult writer. These are often contradicted within the essay by the memories and conclusions of Walker's mother, a woman whose pithy and poetic speech might remind readers of voices they have heard in fiction by both Walker and O'Connor. As much as the essay respects the integrity of Minnie Lou Walker's voice and her experiences, however, it challenges her conclusions too. No speaker has a monopoly on truth.

In his article entitled "The Essay and Discovery," Michael Hall makes the following observations on the essays of Montaigne, who named and defined the genre: "The many quotations from and allusions to classical authors, along with anecdotes from history and Montaigne's personal experience, are not deployed as proofs or as undisputed authority presented to confirm a single thesis but are assembled as conflicting cases and contradictory evidence."[29] Through her references to modern American authors, contemporary history, and her own experiences, Walker employs a similar technique.

"Beyond the Peacock" represents a way of piecing together a new understanding, one that the history of the recently desegregated South makes possible.[30] To comprehend that history, one must survey the (real) estates of the Walkers as well as the O'Connors—not only what they owned, but what they valued, and what in particular they perceived to be beautiful. Daffodils and peacocks signify the contrast in values, of course, but they also represent Walker's quest for historical and political meaning in the apparently tangential. The essay's elegant digressions extend this thematic. As Walker asserts, "I believe the truth about any subject only comes when all the sides of the story are put together, and all their different meanings make one new one. Each writer writes the missing part of the other writer's story. And the whole story is what I'm after" (49). The statement might be read as a gloss on Walker's view of history, literature, and the art of the essay.

Like "Beyond the Peacock," "My Father's Country Is the Poor" is among Walker's most exquisitely crafted pieces. While it does not allude directly to Richard Wright, it offers one of several instances where Walker's writing seems actively in dialogue with his. Racism, poverty, socialist revolution, and violence are central concerns. On one level, the essay presents reportage of a trip Walker makes to Cuba with a group of African American artists. From the vantage point of Cuba, it develops a critique of the treatment of the poor and of people of African descent in the U.S. On a philosophical level, the essay is a meditation on the morality of violence as a means to revolution, a frequent theme in Walker's writing. On a personal level, the essay records Walker's spiritual reconciliation with her recently deceased father, from whom she had long been estranged. Dispossessed by racism and poverty, Walker's father had no country to claim. She speculates on the difference a revolution might have made in his life and in her relationship with him.

Many voices speak through "My Father's Country Is the Poor": Cuban officials (the texts of Castro and Ernesto Cardenal), U.S. revolutionaries (Angela Davis and Huey Newton), individuals whom Walker meets in Cuba, dissenters in the U.S. who speak of and for the silenced dissenters in Cuba (homosexuals, Jehovah's Witnesses, and political prisoners), members of the tour group, and, through her memories and dreams, Alice Walker's father. Walker speaks plainly for herself: "My own bias, when considering a country like Cuba is to think almost entirely of the gains of the formerly dispossessed."[31] Yet the range of voices the essay interpolates allows for readers with different biases to enter into dialogue with the writer on the subject at hand.

The essay's form is digressive. A long epigraph from Angela Davis's autobiography describes the performance the Cuban delegation presented at the 1962 World Youth Peace Festival in Helsinki. The essay proper opens with the statement, "Perhaps I saw Angela Davis at the festival," and contrasts the political sophistication Davis's memories imply with Walker's na-ivete. As a student, Walker did not analyze the political implications of the performance, she was just impressed by the spirit of the multiracial Cuban dance troupe. The contrast produces a second, perhaps unintended, effect: Walker will seem a more credible guide in Cuba because, unlike Davis, she is not a Marxist.

Walker dates her desire to visit Cuba from the performance she viewed in Helsinki. She determines to go, not least to ease the despair she felt "due to my sense of political powerlessness, caused to some extent by a lack of living models. I believed poor people could not win. . . . But here at last was a revolutionary people I could respect, and they made it quite clear they did not intend to lose" (202).

Walker is drawn to Cuba also because she "was eager to see the effect on the people of having used violence to liberate themselves." As "a pacifist and a believer in nonviolent means to effect social change," she "needed to know that the use of violence did not necessarily destroy one's humanity." She finds hope for this view in an unexpected source. "I wanted to confirm the truth of one of my favorite lines from Flannery O'Connor: 'Violence is a force that can be used for good or evil, and among the things taken by it is the Kingdom of Heaven'" (202).

Responding to Americans who say that life in Cuba is hard, Walker states, "And it is." But that judgment lacks a context. Walker provides one in her list of the revolution's accomplishments—the elimination of poverty and racism, the achievement of universal literacy and free medical care, and the promise of decent housing for all. What those Americans invoked above do not say, Walker suspects, is what she feels: "A hard life shared equally by all is preferable to a life of ease and plenty enjoyed by a few" (203).

At several junctures the essay explores the gaps between the ideal of revolution and the actuality. Huey Newton, the exiled Black Panther leader, is represented as a figure of ambiguity. Walker recounts rumors she hears of dissenters whom the revolution has dispossessed. She wonders, too, about the cost of cultural assimilation for darker-skinned Cubans. Walker's doubts and queries are all restated at the essay's conclusion, but they are suspended at its heart where revolutionary Cuba helps Walker make peace with her dead father.

"A week before I flew to Cuba, I began to dream about my father," Walker writes, noting that four years after his death, it was not unusual for her to dream of him. But she could not place the pose he assumed now, "standing by the side of a road in front of a filling station, his hat in his hands, watching me as I moved farther and farther away from him" (212). In a paragraph she sketches her father's physical features and his life: the hard labor, the subsistence wage, and the struggle to support a family of ten. From her adult perspective, she recognizes that his condition was that of "millions of peasants the world over." But, she confesses, "as a child I was not aware of any others. I thought it was my father's own peculiar failing that we were poor" (213).

The essay's most dramatic and riskiest moment comes when Walker, arriving in Cuba, proclaims that her father was waiting for her there. Sustaining the moment of epiphany, she repeats the physical description and announces, "My father's name in Havana was Pablo Diaz" (213). The information that he spoke Spanish, which she did not understand, returns the essay to the realm of the real. Once a peasant like her father, Pablo Diaz is an official historian of the revolution. Lecturing to the group, he speaks proudly and in a steady cadence. Walker watches him and envies his children.

This moment is analogous to that in "Looking for Zora," when Walker stands knee deep in the weeds of the Garden of Heavenly Rest Cemetery, searching for Hurston's unmarked grave. For the third time, she calls out "Zo-ra," and her foot sinks into a hole. Walker orders a stone monument to mark the site of what she identifies as Hurston's grave. Whether it is or is not is both unknowable and unimportant. The essay is Hurston's monument, just as "My Father's Country Is The Poor" is a tribute to Willie Lee Walker.

The spiritual reunions that occur throughout Walker's essays are highly dramatic, yet they do not require the same suspension of disbelief which those in her fiction demand. In the essays these encounters are understood to be psychic rather than physical. They are Walker's way of coming to terms with her dead: black and white, writers and workers, artistic ancestors and close kin.

After her encounter with Pablo Diaz, Walker is able to interpret the dream about her father. The narrative of her interpretation is, she concedes, a simple story. But its themes (economics, politics, and class) are not. The story recalls the incident which inspires her dream. She is on her way to college and is bidding her father farewell. As she boards the bus, he stands, hat in hand, by the side of the road. If education is her route out of poverty, it comes at the expense of her relationship with her father. "This separation," she concludes, "is what poverty engenders. It is what injustice means" (216).

The narrative of Walker's spiritual reconciliation with her father might be read against the narrative of Richard Wright's failed reconciliation with his father in *Black Boy*. Wright breaks the chronology of his autobiography to describe his reunion with his father twenty-five years after their bitter parting in Memphis. He draws a pitiable portrait of a defeated man (one that may be hung alongside that of Wright's paralyzed mother, whose suffering becomes one of the book's key metaphors). Aged beyond his years, white-haired, toothless, body-bent and dressed in ragged overalls, the prodigal father stands alone on the Mississippi plantation where he crops shares. His son, now an author and man of the world, concludes that "we were forever strangers, speaking a different language, living on vastly distant planes of reality."[32]

Having achieved the spiritual reconciliation with her father's memory, Walker draws a different kind of conclusion. Looking back, she remembers not a defeated "peasant," but a "brilliant man"—"great at mathematics" and "unbeatable at storytelling" (216). Recognizing his gifts, she can measure their loss. Walker is not content to let her father or any of the "poor" remain abstractions.

In several respects the public positions Wright and Walker occupy are analogous. As was Wright, Walker is identified with a political movement —in his case Communism, in hers feminism—that is based outside the African American community. Just as the Left provided Wright with his first publishing outlets, feminist publications supported Walker's early work. Many of the essays in *In Search* were first published in *Ms.* magazine. Perhaps in response to their situations as black artists within white progressive organizations which gave them a platform—both in the sense of a place to speak from and in the sense of an orthodoxy to speak—the issue of autonomy looms large. Walker addresses it in her subtitle with the designation of her prose as "womanist." Prominent among the volume's front matter is an extended definition.

The definition, with its deliberate borrowing of dictionary form, announces Walker's intention to invent and define her own terms. She defines the word first by establishing what it is not. Its antonyms include "'girlish,' i.e. frivolous, irresponsible, not serious." A womanist is a black feminist or feminist of color, presumably a new phenomenon in the world. But Walker's definition immediately connects the new and the old. The etymology of her word ["from *womanish*"] establishes its derivation from black vernacular speech, as do the illustrations of usage that follow. Walker refers specifically to "the black folk expression of mothers to female children, 'you acting womanish,' i.e. like a woman." Like any good lexicographer, she notes the occasions on which the word might be used by these women, to wit, in response to "outrageous, audacious, courageous or *willful* behavior." The entry goes on to note that the expression from which womanist is derived is "interchangeable" with another black folk expression, "You trying to be grown." The first entry concludes with synonyms for Walker's neologism "Responsible. In charge. *Serious.*"

Additional meanings for "womanist" denote what one does, including loving other women, sexually and/or nonsexually; appreciating and preferring women's culture; sometimes loving individual men, sexually or and/or nonsexually and being "committed to survival and wholeness of entire people, male *and* female" (xi). Here, too, the definition insists that despite the introduction of political and sexual dimensions not associated with the expression from which "womanist" descends, the concept is traditional in African American history and culture.

This aspect of the definition encapsulates Walker's representation of Zora Neale Hurston as well, particularly the quality that Walker sees as most "characteristic" of her precursor's work: "racial health; a sense of black people as complete, complex *undiminished* human beings."[33] *In Search* is replete with encomiums to Hurston, but a most telling example of Walker's Hurstonian sensibility is reflected in her gloss on her own poem "Revolutionary Petunias." The poem's subject, Sammy Lou, has killed her husband's murderer and become a political heroine in the process. But she does not recognize herself in the picture drawn by movement singers and versifiers. She sees herself instead this way:

> A backwoods woman
> her house was prepared with
> funeral home calendars and
> faces appropriate for a Mississippi
> Sunday School. She raised a George,
> a Martha, a Jackie and a Kennedy. Also
> a John Wesley Junior.

Sammy Lou's last words are "Don't yall forget to *water* / my purple petunias."[34]

Walker explains that her motive in "Revolutionary Petunias" was "to create a person who engaged in a final struggle with her oppressor and won, but who in every other way, was incorrect."[35] Most importantly, Sammy Lou refuses to see killing as heroic; she is amused by other people's attempts to make it so. Despite their clamor, she declines to change her life or herself to suit the expectations of others.

The poem's description of Sammy Lou's house is reminiscent of the room Hurston wrote about in "Characteristics of Negro Expression." According to Walker's gloss, "the walls of her house contain no signs of her blackness—though that in itself reveals it; anyone walking into that empty house would know Sammy Lou is black" (266). Anyone would know from her garden that Sammy Lou adheres to the tenet that there can never be enough of beauty let alone too much. Walker makes explicit the ideology implicit in Hurston's theory. Walker demonstrates moreover the ways in which the preservation of cultural values and practices may be the spring-board for political action.

The Civil Rights Movement is the historical pivot on which Walker's revision of Wright's and Hurston's world views turns. Most of her "models" for behavior are movement activists. She credits one, Mrs. Winsom Hudson, of Harmony, Mississippi, for inspiring her research on black women writers.[36] The movement was, significantly, based in the South; its soldiers were the sons and daughters of the African Americans whose culture Zora Hurston had honored and preserved. Apart from Hurston, Martin Luther King is the book's most haunting and revered presence.

The essay, "Choosing to Stay at Home: Ten Years After the March on Washington," opens with a flashback to that historic event. Walker, then a sophomore at Spelman College in Atlanta, journeys to Washington and takes as a vantage point a tree far from the Lincoln Memorial. Perched on this limb, she can see very little, but in the retelling, she becomes her reader's ear; it hears "everything."

As is typical of the skill with which she handles the form, Walker pauses in the essay's narrative of the March to interpolate another narrative. The year before, her speech and drama instructor in Atlanta had sent his class to hear Martin Luther King lecture. He cautioned them to pay atten-tion *only* to his speech; the instructor was not interested in King's politics. Walker had done as she was told and written a term paper from which she quotes in the essay. "Martin Luther King, Jr., is a surprisingly effective ora-tor, although *terribly* under the influence of the Baptist church so that his utterances sound overdramatic and too weighty to be taken seriously."[37]

At the March, of course, neither Walker nor anyone else is trying to separate form and content, aesthetics and ideology. They are perfectly fused. King's "tone" was as "electrifying as his message." What stirred her most was King's command to the marchers to go back to Mississippi, Ala-bama, and Georgia; his injunction for them to go back home. The effect on Walker was immediate and prolonged. At that moment, she avers, "I saw again what he was always uniquely able to make me see: that I, in fact, had claim to the land of my birth" (160). Two years later, she decides to forego a trip to Senegal to go to Mississippi. Eventually, she would make her home there for seven years, acting out of the belief that she "could never live hap-pily in Africa—or anywhere else—until [she] could live freely in Missis-sippi" (163).

King gives her the inspiration and the courage to make this choice. But he is a model for Walker the writer as well as for Walker the woman. Retro-spectively, in this essay written five years after King's death, she describes her response to his voice on the August day.

Martin Luther King was a man who truly had his tongue wrapped around the roots of Southern black religious consciousness, and when his resounding voice swelled and broke over the heads of the thousands of people assembled at the Lincoln Memorial I felt what a Southern person brought up in the church *always* feels when those cadences—not the words themselves necessarily but the rhythmic spirals of passionate emotion, followed by even more passionate pauses—roll off the tongue of a really first-rate preacher. I felt my soul rising from the sheer force of Martin King's eloquent goodness. (159)

"Eloquent goodness" might also serve as the standard to which Alice Walker, the essayist, aspires. It is one she often meets. Moreover, by embracing that standard, Walker keeps faith with African American literary tradition. For her, as for many black writers, the will to adorn registers the freedom already achieved as it expresses the commitment to struggle for freedom yet denied.

Notes

I thank Marianne DeKoven, Deborah McDowell, Judylyn Ryan, and Rachel Stein for their helpful comments on earlier drafts of this essay.

1. Zora Neale Hurston, "Characteristics of Negro Expression," 1934. Reprinted in *The Gender of Modernism*, ed. Bonnie Kime Scott (Bloomington: Indiana University Press, 1990), 176, 178.

2. Richard Wright, "Blueprint for Negro Literature," 1937. Reprinted in *Amistad 2*, ed. John A. Williams and Charles Harris (New York: Random House, 1971), 7–8.

3. Alice Walker, "In Search of Our Mothers' Gardens." 1974. Reprinted in *In Search of Our Mothers' Gardens* (New York: Harcourt Brace Jovanovich, 1983), 241.

4. Robert Hemenway, Hurston's biographer, estimates that Hurston wrote this essay in 1930, but it was first published in *Negro: An Anthology*, edited by Nancy Cunard, in 1934. My citations in the text are to the essay reprinted in Scott, *Gender of Modernism*, 175–187.

5. Originally published in *New Challenge* in November 1937. Reprinted in Williams and Harris, *Amistad 2*, 3–20. All citations are to this edition and are noted parenthetically.

6. Wright introduced this evocative phrase to refer to "folk utterances, spirituals, blues, work songs, and folklore" in "The Literature of the Negro in the United States," published in *White Man Listen!* (New York: Doubleday, 1957; reprint Anchor Books, 1964), 83.

7. I borrow the term "generative source" from Houston Baker.

8. "No one listening to a Southern white man talk could deny this,"

Hurston wrote. She pointed to specific changes, such as the softening of strongly consonanted words like aren't to ain't, and more generally to the adoption by whites of metaphors invented by blacks.

9. The jook was a combination dance hall, gaming parlor, and bawdy house. Not only was it the birthplace of the blues, which as Hurston pointed out was the foundation of jazz, the jook was the point of origin as well for the dance and theater that had so lately defined popular culture in the United States.

10. Houston Baker, "'Utile Dulci' and the Literature of the Black American," 1972; reprinted in Singers of the Daybreak (Washington, D.C.: Howard University Press, 1974), 3.

11. Stephen Henderson, Understanding the New Black Poetry (New York: William Morrow, 1972), 3.

12. Addison Gayle, The Black Aesthetic (New York: Doubleday, 1972), xxii.

13. Among the notable critiques and assessments of the Black Aesthetic are Henry Louis Gates, "Preface to Blackness: Text and Pretext," in Afro-American Literature: The Reconstruction of Instruction, ed. Dexter Fisher and Robert B. Stepto (New York: Modern Language Association, 1978), 44–69, and chap. 3 of Houston Baker, Blues, Ideology, and Afro-American Literature (Chicago: University of Chicago Press, 1984).

14. An important exception was Larry Neal, who wrote introductions to the reprints of Hurston's first novel, Jonah's Gourd Vine, and autobiography, Dust Tracks on a Road, in 1971.

15. The group of writers, described as "both famous and unknown," was diverse enough to include poets Robert Hayden and Don L. Lee, critics Addison Gayle and Saunders Redding, novelists John A. Williams and Ernest Gaines, and newcomers Alice Walker and John Edgar Wideman. Extended statements from the authors' questionnaires are reprinted in Black World, January 1968, 10–48, 81–89.

16. Richard Wright, "Between Laughter and Tears," New Masses, 5 October 1937, 22, 25. Further citations to this article will be made parenthetically.

17. In his conclusion, for example, Wright compares Hurston to a black male writer, Walter Turpin, whose novel These Low Grounds was also under review: "Turpin's faults as a writer are those of an honest man trying desperately to say something; but Zora Neale Hurston lacks even that excuse" (25).

18. I am, of course, not suggesting that the debate between Hurston and Wright is only about gender. The debates among Wright, Baldwin, and Ellison raise many of the same issues of how to represent African American life and culture. But I would maintain that attention to the gendered inflections in the exchanges between Hurston and Wright clarify some of the unspoken assumptions in all these debates.

19. Zora Neale Hurston, "Stories of Conflict," Saturday Review, 2 April 1938, 32. Further citations will be made parenthetically.

20. Signifying is the generative source of Henry Louis Gates's theory of Afro-American literary criticism; the definition I refer to here is borrowed from

J. L. Dillard and quoted in Gates, *The Signifying Monkey* (New York: Oxford University Press, 1987), 70.

21. June Jordan, "Notes Toward a Black Balancing of Love and Hatred," reprinted in *Civil Wars* (Boston, Beacon Press, 1980), 87. A more recent essay by Hazel Carby reinscribes the oppositionality of Hurston's and Wright's positions. See "The Politics of Fiction, Anthropology, and the Folk: Zora Neale Hurston," in *New Essays on "Their Eyes Were Watching God*," ed. Michael Awkward (New York: Cambridge University Press, 1990), 71–93.

22. Toni Morrison, *Playing in the Dark: Whiteness and the Literary Imagination* (Cambridge: Harvard University Press, 1992), 9.

23. For interesting perspectives on the formal qualities of the essay, see Michael L. Hall, "The Essay and Discovery," in *Essays on the Essay: Redefining the Genre*, ed. Alexander J. Butrym (Athens: University of Georgia Press, 1989), 73–91.

24. Deborah McDowell, "Reading Family Matters," in *Changing Our Own Words: Essays on Criticism, Theory, and Writing by Black Women*, ed. Cheryl A. Wall (New Brunswick, N.J.: Rutgers University Press, 1989), 75–97.

25. Quoted in "A Talk: Convocation 1972," in Walker, *Our Mothers' Gardens*, 40.

26. Writing of Walker's fiction, Gayl Jones reaches conclusions that are suggestive for her essays as well. "In Walker's work the precedents of Wright and Hurston gain a sense of a formed whole. She maintains the intimate focus of Hurston, the perspective that Hurston restored within the African American community, and cultivates Hurston's interest in psychology, motivation, human complexity and possibility; but hers is a more violent and teratologic South than Hurston's, a South of social and economic terrors that still do not cause us to shift our attention from the black people themselves" (*Liberating Voices: Oral Traditions in African American Literature* [Cambridge: Harvard University Press, 1991], 154).

27. "In Search of Our Mothers' Gardens," in Walker, *Our Mothers' Gardens*, 241. Further citations will be noted parenthetically.

28. "Beyond the Peacock," 1975, in ibid., 58. Further citations will be noted parenthetically.

29. Hall, "The Essay," 80.

30. In "Alice Walker: The Black Woman Artist as Wayward," Barbara Christian suggests that quilt making is a model for Walker's art. "For through [quilting], one can create out of seemingly disparate everyday materials patterns of clarity, imagination, and beauty" (*Black Women Writers (1950–1980): A Critical Evaluation*, ed. Mari Evans [New York: Anchor Books, 1983], 461).

31. "My Father's Country Is the Poor," 1977, in Walker, *Our Mothers' Gardens*, 221. Further citations will be made parenthetically.

32. Richard Wright, *Black Boy* (1945; New York: Harper and Row, 1966), 42.

33. "Zora Neale Hurston: A Cautionary Tale and a Partisan View," in Walker, *Our Mothers' Gardens*, 85.

34. Alice Walker, *Her Blue Body Everything We Know: Earthling Poems, 1965–1990 Complete* (New York: Harcourt Brace, 1991), 189–190.

35. "From An Interview," in Walker, *Our Mothers' Gardens*, 266. Further citations will be made parenthetically.

36. See "A Talk: Convocation 1972" and "But Yet and Still the Cotton Gin Kept on Working," in Walker, *Our Mothers' Gardens*. When Walker met her, Mrs. Hudson was writing an autobiography. As an activist, she knew her life was in jeopardy, and she wanted "to leave some kind of record" of that life for her community. She did not seek a wider audience. Walker, who became her typist and editor, gives Mrs. Hudson a wider readership by including an excerpt from her writing in *Our Mothers' Gardens*.

37. "Choosing To Stay At Home: Ten Years After the March on Washington," 1973, in ibid., 159. Further citations will be made parenthetically.

▪ NOTES ON CONTRIBUTORS ▪

DEREK ATTRIDGE teaches English at Rutgers University, New Brunswick. Among his books are *Peculiar Language: Literature as Difference from the Renaissance to James Joyce* (Cornell, 1988) and, as editor, Jacques Derrida's *Acts of Literature* (Routledge, 1992).

PETER BROOKS is Tripp Professor of Humanities, and Chairman of the Department of Comparative Literature, Yale University. His most recent books are *Body Work* (Harvard University Press, 1993) and *Psychoanalysis and Storytelling* (Basil Blackwell, 1994).

MARIA DIBATTISTA, Professor of English and Comparative Literature at Princeton University, is the author of *Virginia Woolf: The Fables of Anon* and *First Love: The Affections of Modern Fiction*. She is currently coediting with Lucy MacDiarmid a collection of essays, *High and Low Moderns: Literature and Culture, 1889–1939,* and completing a book on women and film comedy.

FRANCES FERGUSON is Professor of English and the Humanities at The Johns Hopkins University. She is the author of *Wordsworth: Language as Counter-Spirit* (Yale) and *Solitude and the Sublime: Romanticism and the Aesthetics of Individuation* (Routledge). She is currently at work on a book called *Pornography: The Theory.*

REGENIA GAGNIER is Professor of English and Director of the Program in Modern Thought and Literature at Stanford University. She teaches nineteenth-century British culture and society, social theory, and feminist theory. Her books include *Idylls of the Marketplace: Oscar Wilde and the Victorian Public* (Stanford, 1986), *Critical Essays on Oscar Wilde* (G. K. Hall, 1991), and *Subjectivities: A History of Self-Representation in Britain, 1832–1920* (Oxford, 1991). She has received a number of honors and fellowships, most recently a Guggenheim Fellowship (1991–1992) for a historical study of comparative attitudes toward private property and the Marta Sutton Weeks

Faculty Scholarship in the Humanities for 1992–1995. She is currently writing a book on economics and aesthetics, or the values of market society.

GEOFFREY GALT HARPHAM is the author of several books, including *The Ascetic Imperative in Culture and Criticism* (University of Chicago Press) and *Getting It Right: Language, Literature, and Ethics* (University of Chicago Press). He teaches at Tulane University.

MYRA JEHLEN is Board of Governors Professor of Literature and Culture at Rutgers University. She is the author of *American Incarnation: The Individual, the Nation and the Continent* and forthcoming, *The Literature of Colonization.*

WILLIAM KEACH teaches in the English Department at Brown University and is the author of *Shelley's Style* (1984). He is currently working on an edition of Coleridge's poems for the Penguin English Poets series and on a book about politics and language in British romantic writing.

OSCAR KENSHUR is Professor of Comparative Literature and Adjunct Professor of Philosophy and of English at Indiana University, Bloomington. He is the author of *Open Form and the Shape of Ideas* (1986) and *Dilemmas of Enlightenment: Studies in the Rhetoric and Logic of Ideology* (1993).

GEORGE LEVINE is Director of the Center for the Critical Analysis of Contemporary Culture and Kenneth Burke Professor of English at Rutgers University. Among his books are *The Realistic Imagination* and *Darwin and the Novelists*. Most recently he has edited two Center-related volumes, *Constructions of the Self* (Rutgers University Press) and *Realism and Representation* (University of Wisconsin Press). His current work is on the ideal of objectivity in scientific and literary discourse.

MARY POOVEY is Professor of English at The Johns Hopkins University. Her most recent book is *Uneven Developments: The Ideological Work of Gender in Mid-Victorian England*. She is currently working on a study of the relationship between aesthetics and statistical representation, entitled *Figures of Arithmetic, Figures of Speech.*

ARNOLD RAMPERSAD is Woodrow Wilson Professor of Literature and Director of the Program in American Studies at Princeton University. His books include the two-volume *Life of Langston Hughes* and, with Arthur Ashe, *Days of Grace: A Memoir* (1993).

CHERYL A. WALL teaches American and African American literature at Rutgers University. She is the editor of *Changing Our Own Words: Essays on Criticism, Theory, and Writing by Black Women.*

SUSAN J. WOLFSON is Professor of English at Princeton University and the author of several essays and articles on English Romantic writing, as well as *The Questioning Presence: Wordsworth, Keats, and the Interrogative Mode in Romantic Poetry*. Her essay in this volume is related to her forthcoming book, *Formal Changes*, a study of how the controversies about formalist criticism emerge from and are situated in the volatile and self-conscious formalist poetics of Romanticism.

▪ Index ▪